D1602550

THE GEORGE GUND FOUNDATION
IMPRINT IN AFRICAN AMERICAN STUDIES

The George Gund Foundation has endowed
this imprint to advance understanding of
the history, culture, and current issues
of African Americans.

The publisher gratefully acknowledges the generous contributions to this book provided by the Center for Black Music Research and by the African American Studies Endowment Fund of the University of California Press Foundation, which is supported by a major gift from the George Gund Foundation.

MUSIC OF THE AFRICAN DIASPORA

Samuel A. Floyd, Jr., Editor Emeritus
Guthrie P. Ramsey, Jr., Editor

The Memoirs of
Alton Augustus Adams, Sr.

Alton Augustus Adams, Sr., in 1961. Courtesy Alton Augustus Adams Collection, Center for Black Music Research, and Alton Adams Family Trust.

The Memoirs of
Alton Augustus Adams, Sr.

First Black Bandmaster of the United States Navy

Edited by
MARK CLAGUE

Foreword by Samuel Floyd, Jr.

University of California Press
BERKELEY   LOS ANGELES   LONDON

Center for Black Music Research
COLUMBIA COLLEGE CHICAGO

University of California Press, one of the most distinguished university presses in the United States, enriches lives around the world by advancing scholarship in the humanities, social sciences, and natural sciences. Its activities are supported by the UC Press Foundation and by philanthropic contributions from individuals and institutions. For more information, visit www.ucpress.edu.

Unless otherwise noted, all photographs are courtesy of the Alton Adams Family Trust.

University of California Press
Berkeley and Los Angeles, California

University of California Press, Ltd.
London, England

Center for Black Music Research
Columbia College Chicago

Library of Congress Cataloging-in-Publication Data

Adams, Alton A.
    The memoirs of Alton Augustus Adams, Sr. : first black bandmaster of the United States Navy / edited by Mark Clague ; foreword by Samuel Floyd, Jr.
        p.   cm.—(Music of the African diaspora ; 12)
    Includes bibliographical references (p.) and index.
    ISBN 978-0-520-25131-1 (cloth : alk. paper)
    1. Adams, Alton A.   2. Bandmasters—Virgin Islands of the United States—Biography.   3. Virgin Islands of the United States—Social conditions—20th century.   I. Clague, Mark, [date].   II. Title.
ML422.A245A3   2008
784.092—dc22   2007012025

Manufactured in the United States of America

17   16   15   14   13   12   11   10   09   08
10   9   8   7   6   5   4   3   2   1

This book is printed on Natures Book, which contains 50% post-consumer waste and meets the minimum requirements of ANSI/NISO Z39.48–1992 (R 1997) (Permanence of Paper).

To my wife, Ella; sister, Edna; brother, Julien;
and my fellow bandsmen
and
to the people of the Virgin Islands

Alton Augustus Adams, Sr.

Contents

Foreword

Samuel A. Floyd, Jr.

In the early 1970s I ran across two or three items indicating that in 1917 an Alton Augustus Adams became "the first black bandmaster in the United States Navy." These items surprised and puzzled me, since it was well known that before World War II blacks could serve in the navy only as mess attendants and stewards, and since I personally knew individuals who had been members of what were supposed to have been the first black musical units in the navy—the bands that were trained in 1941 at the Great Lakes Naval Training Station near Chicago. Those bands included such notables as saxophonist and bandleader Hayes Pillars of the Alphonso Trent and Jeter Pillars bands; trumpeters Clark Terry, Jimmie Nottingham, and Ernie Royal; saxophonists Ernie Wilkins and Marshall Royal; trombonists Al Gray and Bootie Wood; bassist Major Holly; arranger and trumpeter Gerald Wilson; arranger and pianist Luther Henderson; violinist Brenton Banks; cellist Donald White; composer Ulysses Kay; and many others.

Curious, in 1976 I called the Enid Baa Library on St. Thomas and requested information about this Alton Augustus Adams, who, if he had been a navy bandmaster in 1917, had surely long since passed away. Surprisingly, however, I was given Mr. Adams's telephone number and was encouraged to call him. Immediately I did so and had a pleasant, stimulating, and provocative conversation with this august former bandmaster and civic leader, during which he invited me to his home for a visit. I eagerly accepted, going for interviews to St. Thomas not just once but twice within a few years. When I arrived at his eighteenth-century Danish home on my first visit, Mr. Adams was standing on his upstairs veranda. When he saw me approaching, he came to attention and gave me a military salute, which I took as a sign of welcome and appreciation for my visit.

Eventually I wrote an article about him, played a role in having him awarded an honorary doctorate at Fisk University, and maintained a friendship with him until his death in 1987. At some point during our relationship, I asked Mr. Adams about the possibility of his donating his personal and professional papers to Fisk and, later, to Columbia College Chicago's Center for Black Music Research. Unfortunately, he had already promised his materials to another institution located in the United States.

Several years later, in 1992, during one of what had become for me annual and sometimes semiannual writing trips to the island of St. John, I went to nearby St. Thomas to shop and decided to stop by and say hello to the former bandmaster's son, Alton Augustus Adams, Jr., whom I had met in 1979 when he accompanied his father to receive the honorary degree. During the course of the conversation he asked, "What are we going to do about my father's papers?" Stunned, I learned that his father had decided before his death that he wanted the collection to remain in the Virgin Islands. We quickly arranged for his papers to be transferred to Columbia College for processing and conservation in a climate-controlled environment. They were to be returned to the Virgin Islands when a facility had been established to receive and properly care for them. A duplicate copy of the reproducible portions of the collection would be held in the archives of the Center for Black Music Research in Chicago.

It seems to be in the nature of things that many of the most profound contributions of black Americans to social and cultural history and to race relations have been subtle, unheralded, and relegated to footnotes and incidental acknowledgment. Even such major movements as the Harlem Renaissance of the 1920s find little or no place in American music history books. The recording of such contributions is left to special studies and to memoirs such as the present volume, a fact that only underscores its importance.

This book is no mere recounting of personal recollections. It stands as a humanistic document, representing a broad range of concerns about, and a historical view of, the United States Virgin Islands from the sympathetic but no less critical perspective of one of their native sons. This memoir was written by a St. Thomian who during his long life was greatly concerned about the future of his culture and society and who saw changing racial attitudes as potentially destructive of the Virgin Islands' most valued cultural possessions. In fact, the racial tensions of the 1960s gave added impetus to the development of this volume.

Naturally, such a document reveals its author's preferences, predispositions, and prejudices. Clearly a product of his time, Adams here reveals, in his desire to "measure up" to external standards for the good of the "race,"

his sensitivity to the perceptions of the Caucasian observers and participants in his native culture. Grateful for his success and achievements and
for the accolades bestowed upon him, Adams pays tribute to his parents
and other relatives and to the other islanders who encouraged, taught, and
assisted him during his formative years. He ascribes the positive traits of
the islands' cultural environment to the musical culture of St. Thomas,
commenting on the native music and, especially, the music continuously
imported from the United States and Europe during the nineteenth and
early twentieth centuries, revealing those influences to be instrumental in
his own artistic development.

As a result of his musical achievements, Adams formed lasting friendships and acquaintances with such well-known personalities as W. E. B.
DuBois; George Schulyer and his pianist-composer daughter, Philippa; the
violinist Joseph Douglass; bibliophile Arthur Schomburg; bandmaster-
composers John Philip Sousa, Edwin Franko Goldman, H. A. Vandercook,
Walter Jacobs, and Frank Seltzer; pianist and author Maude Cuney-Hare;
newspaper columnist Drew Pearson; and the composers William Dawson,
W. C. Handy, and Harry T. Burleigh.

Not until 1976 did musical America officially recognize Adams's talents.
In that year one of his marches, "The Governor's Own," was recorded and
included in a record album entitled *The Pride of America*. The album,
which appeared in the New World Records series celebrating the American
bicentennial, also includes marches by two of Adams's principal musical
supporters on the mainland—Sousa and Goldman. The inclusion of Adams
in a national commemorative series was a significant tribute—a recognition of his substantive contributions to American culture. The honor was
enhanced by the placement of the work as the first cut on the album.

The acclaim and attention that Adams received during his years as a
navy bandmaster were well earned. Reports of those who heard his band
during its peak years (particularly during its 1924 tour of the United
States) reveal its performances to have been remarkably musical; some
observers believed it to be the best in the United States Navy. That Adams,
who had little formal musical training, created a musical organization of
such high caliber from the youthful raw talents of his charges in the
Adams Juvenile Band and developed it—in a relatively isolated location
(notwithstanding the islands' cosmopolitan character)—into such a powerful aggregation was a phenomenal feat. It stands as a milestone not only of
black but also of human achievement.

This memoir makes clear the need for continuing research about music
of all kinds in the Western Hemisphere, about the societies in which it

flourished, and about the cultural influences and interactions that produced it. The relationship between art and society and the tremendous impact that social forces can have on cultural development are only some of the issues raised in this book. If this publication does no more than inspire additional studies, its contribution to the elucidation of American musical and cultural history will have been far-reaching.

Acknowledgments

Mark Clague

This project would have been impossible without the generous assistance and expert support of a number of individuals and institutions. The partnership between Samuel Floyd, founder of the Center for Black Music Research (CBMR), and Alton Augustus Adams, Jr., a business leader in the Virgin Islands and son of the memoirs' author, established its foundation. It was during my work in 1995 as an editorial assistant for the CBMR's *International Dictionary of Black Composers* project that box upon box of archival material arrived in Chicago from the Virgin Islands. Dr. Floyd encouraged me to explore these materials and to write Adams's entry for the dictionary; later he asked if I would edit these memoirs for publication. Dr. Floyd has continued to advise the development of this manuscript and, during his own writing trips to St. John, has served as liaison with Adams's descendants and local scholars. Without his guidance and generosity this volume would not exist.

Alton Augustus Adams, Jr., provided additional commentary as well as vital archival material from his private collection and administered travel support from the Alton Augustus Adams Family Trust. He read and offered detailed suggestions and clarifications at every stage of the book's growth. Band scholars including Raoul Camus and Patrick Warfield have graciously welcomed me to the field and shared their expertise. Professor Kevin Gaines at the University of Michigan's Center for Afro-American and African Studies, along with Professor Ronald Radano at the University of Wisconsin–Madison, provided encouragement and essential comments on the editor's introductory essay, as did participants in the University of Michigan's American Culture Program manuscript workshop. Chief Musician Kevin Dines of the United States Navy Band offered insights into navy life today and in the past, while music educator and Virgin Islands researcher Kirsten Kienberger offered suggestions and provided guidance regarding the archive at Frederick Evangelical Lutheran Church. Myron Jackson, a historical preservation expert on the islands, and UVI Professor Emeritus Aimery Caron offered further insights into Virgin Island life.

The Rackham Graduate School at the University of Michigan funded a summer research assistantship for Katherine Brucher, who scanned and proofed the initial word-processing documents for the main memoirs text; later, as a professor and band scholar herself, Dr. Brucher offered comments on the manuscript. Thanks too go to Dean Karen Wolff at the University of Michigan School of Music, who provided travel funding for archival research, and to Rosita Sands, director of the Center for Black Music Research, who provided use of the CBMR fellow's apartment in St. Thomas for one of my research visits. Music editor Mary Francis at the University of California Press, who has been invariably encouraging through this manuscript's long genesis, shepherded the book over its final hurdles. I am similarly grateful to project editor Laura Harger and copyeditor Steven Baker, both of whom offered insightful comments and corrections.

CBMR archivist Suzanne Flandreau not only traveled to St. Thomas to sort and ship Adams's materials to Chicago for preservation but also proved an invaluable resource and guide to the collection. Since my initial work on these materials began, funding from Columbia College Chicago has facilitated creation of a complete digital archive of the Alton Augustus Adams Collection. This processing has been extraordinarily helpful in gaining a fuller understanding of Adams's correspondence. Shirley Lincoln at the Adams Music Research Institute (AMRI) in St. Thomas has helped with fact checking and located copies of Isidor Paiewonsky's *History Corner* articles; and Patricia Matthew at the University of the Virgin Islands Library went beyond the call of duty in this regard as well. Beverly Smith, who manages the Von Scholten Collection at the Enid Baa Library in Charlotte Amalie, was ever gracious and suggested new veins of research material. The library staff at the University of Michigan, particularly interlibrary loan, provided essential support. Videographer Nicole Franklin generously provided copies of video interviews she conducted with Alton Adams, Jr.

Finally, I want to thank my children, Michaela, Hannah, and Ronan, for their smiles of support, as well as my wife, Laura Jackson, for her confidence and cheers, which kept me going, especially when it seemed as if I could not possibly find the source materials necessary to make this book as rich and comprehensive as it needed to be. I also thank the extended Adams family, both in St. Thomas and the U.S. mainland, for their assistance, patience, and support.

Introduction

The Soul of Alton Adams

Mark Clague

> The people of the Virgin Islands were without a feeling of self and
> had no sense of belonging. Alton Adams and his music inspired us
> to become Virgin Islanders.
>
> Ruth Moolenaar, Virgin Islands author and educator

Alton Augustus Adams and W. E. B. DuBois made for a remarkable pair of
friends. The first was anything but a revolutionary, while the other was
labeled a radical. They were born twenty-one years and seventeen hundred
miles apart—one in a Danish colony in the West Indies, the other in Massachusetts. Yet the goals of Adams and DuBois were the same: "to be both an
American and a Negro"—that is, to participate in a society of equals while
retaining their own seamless identity.[1] They were united by a tireless passion for equality, political strength, and a firm belief in scholarship and education. Both found African American spirituals to be a source of affirmation
and believed in the transformative power of music; both used the pen as a
political tool, and both sought to change the world. Despite their shared
beliefs, methods, and goals, however, their tactics quickly diverged: Adams
embraced, while DuBois challenged. Upon almost any point of strategy,
they disagreed—because their individual experiences in two very different
places had led them to different conclusions about the state of race relations.
DuBois had come of age in an America of broken promises, the hopes of
post–Civil War reconstruction dashed by lynchings and Jim Crow laws—a
life separate and increasingly unequal. Adams had grown up in a Danish
colony during a time of economic disappointments, but with what he felt
was a racially "tolerant" and "benign" administration—a life, in contrast to
DuBois's, of decreasing racial distinction.[2] While DuBois turned to black
nationalism, Pan-Africanism, and eventually communism, Adams's activities focused on the local: the economic base of political power and educational institutions and the vitality of a cosmopolitan Virgin Islands identity.

In Adams's lifetime as today, blacks made up the vast majority of the Virgin Islands' population, while economic status and education tempered skin
pigment as the marker of social difference.[3] For Adams, a strong economy

1

was prerequisite for social and political justice.[4] In the islands, liberty had long depended on financial strength, as slaves had purchased their freedom only after being allowed to own property, sell crops, and work skilled crafts to earn their own future. In contrast to their U.S. counterparts, African slaves in the West Indies had secured limited educational and economic advantages. Beginning in 1773 (three years before the American Revolution), slave children in the Virgin Islands had access to formal education in Lutheran and later Moravian missionary schools.[5] In 1802 Denmark abolished slave trading. By 1834 a royal decree had granted free blacks legal equality with whites,[6] while acute labor shortages contributed to further social openness. Free immigrants—any immigrants—were welcomed as both customers and community members, leading to further ethnic and religious diversity. In 1847 a compromise between abolitionists and slave owners established a process to liberate all slaves in twelve years. However, as the slaves themselves were not consulted, one year later a revolt both forced the situation and gave Governor Peter von Scholten the opportunity to declare all slaves free. Thus, slavery in the Virgin Islands ended some fifteen years before Abraham Lincoln's Emancipation Proclamation. Despite certain political advantages, however, slavery here as elsewhere still meant work by force and being owned by another. To call the Virgin Islands a racial paradise would be egregious.

Racism had long existed in the Virgin Islands, which had been ruled by white slaveholding Europeans since 1672.[7] Even though the Jim Crow laws typical of post-Reconstruction America were relatively unknown in the islands during Adams's childhood, slavery's legacy persisted. Slavery required racism to justify itself and to control the bodies, minds, and hearts of human labor in a plantation economy. Yet by the time of his encounter with DuBois, memories of slavery's past were less pernicious for Adams than the threat of the racist present in the United States. It was not until U.S. tourism increased, for example, that Jim Crow exclusions arrived in the islands. By 1940 the government-owned hotel rented only to whites, and while similar policies at smaller hotels were disabled after public outcry, rooms marked "tourists only" served much the same purpose.[8] Yet the falling economic fortunes of the late-nineteenth-century port of Adams's youth tended to level class and thus reduce racial distinctions. Further, Adams had grown up in the Savan district, a diverse interracial neighborhood on St. Thomas that had been the traditional home of the islands' Catholics, Jews, and free blacks. Adams and DuBois, while sharing a common black philosophical heritage, grew up in worlds apart. Their lived experiences suggested very different trajectories in race relations.

Their first meeting in 1922 left the younger man "disappointed" that the author of *The Souls of Black Folk* could be so "cold and informal . . . bordering the rude." Their second meeting two years later was warmer as DuBois belatedly but vociferously supported the American tour of Adams's ensemble—the United States Navy Band of the Virgin Islands. Yet nearly thirty years had passed when in 1952 the pair's friendship deepened and DuBois visited the Virgin Islands and stayed in Adams's home.[9] Chapter 11 of these memoirs offers Adams's recollections of their conversations:

> The most stimulating moments we spent together during his all-too-short stay took place in the evenings at my home, when the two of us discussed world affairs, particularly as they touched on racial matters. I spoke about my native islands and why I thought that because of our unique background and environment we held a different racial attitude than American Negroes. Indeed, as I explained, race had little meaning for most Virgin Islanders because we judged a person by his deeds and not his color. And we expected the same in return. DuBois tended to see everything and everyone in purely racial terms, but he admitted that he envied me for my indifference to racial considerations. He had a dry sense of humor, and his conversation revealed the deep love he had for his race. However, I found his broad genius and great intelligence somewhat disturbing and self-damaging because of his overriding preoccupation with race. And I often pondered, and still ponder, whether this great man was mentally still a slave—a slave to embittered passion and hatred for the white man. This concern so affected me, that each night upon leaving his room after our discussion, I was possessed by an intensely sympathetic feeling for him. And I felt sorry for mankind because his great mind, which could be so useful to the world at large, had to be dedicated solely to the Negro problem.[10]

Adams had come to know DuBois through the pages of his 1903 book, which proposed the existence of two black souls—a double consciousness informed by the simultaneous view of self from inside the black community and from outside through the veil of white perspective. For DuBois, such a dual identity was forced upon African Americans by the incongruity of their black difference in a land of pervasive whiteness. This double consciousness was both a curse and a way out, a way to understand and to grapple with the dehumanizing experience of being black in America.

In contrast, Adams's understanding of race reflected his Caribbean experience. Whereas in the United States the notion of race has only recently expanded beyond a white/black dialectic, in the Caribbean, life had long suggested that race was both broader (including Latins, Indians, and Asians, among others) and more fluid (in that individuals can often claim several racial affiliations and these can shift within families over the course of just a few generations). At the crowded nucleus of identity in the United States, however, the legacy of slavery, civil war, emancipation, Reconstruction, Jim Crow, the Ku Klux Klan, and the fight for civil rights produced what for Adams was a limited racial polarity—a black and white consciousness. In Adams's experience, race was not the central issue; social class trumped race as an arbiter of identity, while education offered the promise of social transformation. He resisted the influence of what he saw as the divisive race politics of the U.S. mainland, affirming a tradition of tolerance that he credited to the cosmopolitan heritage of the islands.[11] Such contrasting assumptions about the dynamics of race and class help explain the different opinions of Adams and DuBois. Rather than a multiple sense of self, Adams advocated a single self-concept of cosmopolitan embrace. As these memoirs demonstrate, Alton Augustus Adams, Sr., insisted on but one soul, one guiding principle that shaped his life and informed his decisions: an undying passion for the promise of the individual linked to the welfare of his island home.[12]

At times the reader senses Adams's overt act of will to hold this singular soul together. When confronted by acts of discrimination, he strove to deny the power of racism a victory over his own mind. In a 1977 interview for the student-produced magazine *All-Ah-Wee*, Adams articulated his philosophy:

> It's the quality of the individual, not the color. . . . Human nature is all the same and color has nothing to do with it. It is divided not by the question of color, but the quality of reason. That is what you should teach children. Don't allow hatred and bitterness to enter their minds, especially the things that happened centuries ago. You still have people today who are not emancipated, white and black, because the body you see, you can emancipate, but not the mind.[13]

Adams's memoirs contain an implicit argument for his "one soul" social strategy. As explained in his own introduction, he hoped to convince the youth of the Virgin Islands to follow this path—to develop a sense of self and history that would serve as a spiritual and social guide, combining community tolerance with personal ambition. While DuBois used awareness of double consciousness as a source of resistance, Adams did everything within his power to deny such patterns of racialized thinking a place in his Virgin Islands.

Adams is part of a larger social phenomenon within the black diaspora, what Jamaican American historian Ifeoma Kiddoe Nwanko calls Black Cosmopolitanism.[14] Associated with diaspora—in which traditional identity has been forcibly disrupted, even intentionally erased (by the "conditioning" of slaves, for example)—cosmopolitanism allowed elite black intellectuals to rebuild a notion of self and soul that relocated the individual within parameters of community, nation, race, and globe, especially those of the black diaspora. Adams's memoirs are a tool of such identity restoration and reconfiguration. As such, Adams can be seen as among a larger group of black writers and musicians, including DuBois and also Booker T. Washington, Paul Lawrence Dunbar, Marcus Garvey, W. C. Handy, Claude McKay, Duke Ellington, George Schuyler, Langston Hughes, Zora Neale Hurston, William Grant Still, and others, who brought their unique perspectives to bear on the question of their community's relationship to the world around them. The variety of their opinions and tactics strengthened cosmopolitanism as a strategy of resistance.

Adams was intensely proud to represent his race and proud of his black cultural heritage. He drew inspiration from the biographies of accomplished black intellectuals and artists: political and religious leaders such as Edward Blyden, Reverend Daniel E. Wiseman, Frederick Douglass, Booker T. Washington, and DuBois; artists such as violinist Brindis de Salas and soprano Sissieretta Jones; scholars and scientists such as Arthur Schomburg and George Washington Carver; and such local island role models as Adolph "Ding" Sixto, Elphege Sebastien, and D. Hamilton Jackson. Yet Adams also held white role models in high esteem: presidents Abraham Lincoln, James Garfield, and Theodore Roosevelt; United States founding father Alexander Hamilton; explorer Robert Edwin Peary; Chicago capitalist Marshall Field; German navy captain Count Felix von Luckner;[15] inventor Benjamin Franklin; scientist Sir Isaac Newton; author Mark Twain; music educator Thomas Tapper; and musicians Ludwig van Beethoven and John Philip Sousa.[16] Adams was keenly aware of race, of his racial identity and the disease of racism. Yet his strategy to overcome discrimination was to appeal to a heritage of tolerance rooted in the islands' cosmopolitan past, to actively bridge the racial divide.

Adams could be described as essentially an integrationist who saw economic prosperity (through education and opportunity) as the key to lowering class and in turn racial barriers. He had no interest in the revolutionary impulses often associated with the Caribbean: the Back to Africa movement of Marcus Garvey, the Communism that appealed to many British West Indians, and the workers' socialism of some fellow Danish Virgin Islanders held no promise for Adams. For some, Adams remains a controversial, conservative, and paternalistic figure. He opposed the replacement of the naval government with a civilian administration because the departure of the navy would remove a vital prop to the islands' economy. He opposed an increase in the local minimum wage for fear it would injure the nascent tourist industry. He repeatedly argued for putting off increased self-determination for the islands, fearing it might distance and thus reduce the U.S. government's commitment to the islands' welfare. Critics of Adams were impatient with such strategies, which nurtured business interests while delaying economic and social benefits to labor. While any critique of Adams's politics must be tempered by acknowledging his advocacy of D. Hamilton Jackson's field laborers union in 1916, Adams generally placed economic development before political development and social reform. While local activists such as Rothschild Francis and Lionel Roberts won battles for citizenship and political rights, Adams wondered about the benefits of such rights without economic prosperity. At such points, Adams's ideas appeared elitist and conservative to many. Yet all of these Virgin Islands leaders shared the same goals. They differed in the answer they gave to questions of how to accomplish reform: through cooperation or protest, by working within the system to change it or pressuring it from without. In *The Crisis of the Negro Intellectual* (1967), Harold Cruse articulated the post–World War I tensions among black leaders searching for the best path to equality—black nationalism, segregation, revolution, education, cultural change, socialism, Communism, or integration.[17] Such strategic questions would arise again in the 1960s with the struggle for civil rights in the United States. The Virgin Islands participated in these same debates. In fact, Adams's decision to inscribe his life story in memoirs was a response to this confusion. Against the din of ideas that tended to discard past values in favor of future hopes, Adams tells the story of what brought the islands to this point of opportunity and argues that cultural traditions are vital to future success.

In chapter 1 Adams tells of his birth on November 4, 1889, on the island of St. Thomas, in what had been since the late seventeenth century the Danish West Indies. The son of aspiring artisan parents, Adams attended elementary school and later apprenticed to become a carpenter and then a shoemaker. Chapter 2 discusses the values of hard work, skill, and education espoused by the free black artisans of the islands and instilled by the islands' apprenticeship system. However, Adams dreamt of being a professional musician like "march king" John Philip Sousa, even though no precedent for such a career existed in the Virgin Islands. While studying other trades, the young Adams nurtured two passions—music and literature. He learned music in church, from recordings, from visiting shipboard bands, and by imitating more accomplished players in local dance bands.

He devoured books in the family library and explored a world of ideas in conversations with an assortment of local intellectuals. As detailed in chapter 4, Adams learned the piccolo (chosen primarily because the miniature was less expensive than a full-size flute) and joined the Native Brass Band in 1907. He learned the cornet, trombone, and clarinet, and continued mastering flute and piccolo—his primary solo instruments. He soon became assistant director of the native band. Late into the night, he studied music theory and composition through correspondence courses with Dr. Hugh A. Clark at the University of Pennsylvania. In June 1910, Adams formed his own ensemble, the Adams Juvenile Band, with the financial backing of Elphege Sebastien, a local black pharmacist. Adams's band developed rapidly, giving its first concert in February 1911, and soon became part of the social fabric of the islands' capital, the port of Charlotte Amalie, by playing a variety of charitable events as well as regular concerts in the bandstand at Emancipation Garden.[18]

Lacking local music schools or regular teachers, Adams had come to depend on music magazines from the U.S. mainland as a source of ideas and learning. As early as 1910 he contributed his own article about music to a local paper.[19] In 1915 Adams became the music editor for the St. Croix newspaper the *Herald,* and a few months later he became the band columnist for Boston's *Jacobs' Band Monthly.* His grandiloquent prose amplified a philosophy of social idealism about music's role in the community and garnered the attention of leading musicians in the States. When on the eve of its entrance into World War I the United States purchased the Virgin Islands from Denmark, Adams was ideally placed to capitalize on any opportunity to make his dream of a professional music career a reality. He possessed strong administrative, teaching, writing, and compositional skills, a record of community service, and professional credibility on the U.S. mainland and was largely free of problematic political entanglements.

On June 2, 1917, Adams and his entire Juvenile Band were inducted into the United States Navy as a unit, thus becoming the first African Americans to receive naval appointments as musicians since as early as the War of 1812. Adams was made the navy's first black bandmaster.[20] As chapter 5 reveals, it was an exceptional situation inspired by exceptional circumstance: the need to bridge an all-white naval administration and a predominantly black population. Adams and his bandsmen were exempted from a training period of sea duty, and while the white personnel around them rotated in and out, they remained stationed at the Virgin Islands base.[21] For Adams these naval appointments represented an incredible artistic and social opportunity—the chance to make music at a higher artistic level and to participate in the islands' administration. For critics of naval rule, however, that these black native musicians donned the white uniforms of the navy made them little more than gullible collaborators. For them the band was no more than a manipulative stunt to garner positive publicity for naval leaders and distract attention from what they felt was the navy's racist treatment of the islands' populace. Adams vehemently disagreed on both counts, fully appreciating the symbiotic relationship between band and administration and distinguishing racist actions by a few enlisted naval personnel from the genuine commitment to the islands' welfare of local naval leadership, especially its governors. Further, Adams used his position of authority as a source of power, wealth, and influence.[22] Not only did his band's induction help defuse the racial tension that plagued the navy's early presence on the islands, but also the band and Adams in particular helped educate naval administrators about the needs and attitudes of Virgin Islanders.

Adams and his bandsmen leveraged their new position to advantage. Their stable jobs made them relatively wealthy, helping to revitalize the island's flagging middle class. They operated a unique independent local newspaper, the *St. Thomas Times* (1921–23), that focused on cultural and community affairs.[23] Adams himself continued to grow into his role as a social leader, serving as an officer of the local chapter of the Red Cross, helping to found the public library in Charlotte Amalie, and developing the islands' public school music program. He traveled off island for the first time in 1922 to research music education on the U.S. mainland, play informal recitals, and meet his idol, music educator Thomas Tapper. His contacts with black intellectuals and musicians in Washington, D.C., and New York laid the groundwork for the high point of the band's activities: its triumphant 1924 tour of the eastern seaboard, described in chapter 6. Adams with his band in top form won accolades from concert and radio audiences in Hampton Roads, Virginia; Washington, D.C.; Philadelphia; New York; and Boston.[24] Adams even conducted the Goldman Band in Central Park (playing his "Virgin Islands March"), becoming possibly the first black American to conduct a leading white ensemble.[25] Thus the U.S. purchase had given Adams opportunities impossible under Danish rule. Genuinely grateful and patriotic, he enthusiastically embraced the potential of an American future.

Adams's best-known compositions, "Virgin Islands March" (1919), "The Governor's Own" (1921), and "Spirit of the U.S.N." (1924), are composed in the idiom of Adams's inspiration, Sousa, and were performed throughout the United States and Europe by leading ensembles directed by such musicians as Sousa, Goldman, Herbert Clarke, Patrick Conway, and William H. Santelmann. Sources newly discovered for this publication offer the first views into Adams's life in the later 1920s (chapter 7), 1930s (chapter 9), and 1940s (chapter 10). Tragically, a 1932 fire, detailed in chapter 9, destroyed Adams's St. Thomas home, killing his daughter Hazel and burning a cache of manuscripts that contained both scholarly writings and unpublished compositions. Only about a dozen of Adams's musical works are known to have survived this fire. Besides this tragedy, the low point of Adams's career was undoubtedly his unit's transfer to Guantánamo Bay, Cuba, in 1931. This move separated Adams from his children, pregnant wife, family, friends, and source of social influence. It detached the United States Navy Band of the Virgin Islands from its home and thus from its purpose. Adding insult to injury, Adams was stung deeply by the dismissal under a cloud of controversy of the naval governors, men with whom Adams had worked and come to respect and even admire. The musicians of the Virgin Islands band were in turn sent into obscurity. Rather than being disbanded, with individuals transferred to other bands to fill needs, Adams's unit of black musicians was sequestered and effectively segregated in Cuba. In 1933, after fulfilling his service commitment and qualifying for a pension, Adams retired to the Naval Fleet Reserve and returned to St. Thomas, not long thereafter resuming his duties for the public school music program.

As chronicled in chapter 10, a brief return to local newspaper editorship for the *Bulletin* was cut short by the Japanese attack on Pearl Harbor. The rapid naval buildup in response to that catastrophe created an acute shortage of manpower, and Adams was recalled to active duty and sent back to Guantánamo. Despite some objections, he took over an all-white unit and soon received permission to reinstate eight of his former bandsmen, thus creating the first racially integrated band sanctioned by the U.S. Navy.[26] The next year, Adams and the eight other islanders were transferred back to St. Thomas to reconstitute their original unit, again as an all-black ensemble. This second (resegregated) United States Navy Band of the Virgin Islands would be transferred once more in 1944, this time to Puerto Rico. Soon after the end of the war in 1945, Adams retired from the navy permanently.[27]

Back in St. Thomas, Adams fused his interests in business and the community when he accepted an appointment to the governing committee of the St. Thomas Power Authority. Still searching for a new career and renewed purpose, Adams entered the islands' burgeoning tourist industry, as covered in chapter 11. In 1947 he answered a call to increase the number of hotel rooms in St. Thomas by opening his home as the Adams 1799 Guest House. In 1952 Adams became a charter member of the Virgin

Islands Hotel Association and was soon elected president, a position he held until 1971. During this postwar period, Adams served as a reporter, working as a stringer for the Associated Press as well as the Associated Negro Press and contributing regular articles to George Schuyler's influential black newspaper, the *Pittsburgh Courier.* Although Adams never ran for public office, he was closely affiliated with island politics as a gubernatorial adviser and editorial commentator in print and on radio. In 1963 the islands' legislature accepted the rededication of his "Virgin Islands March" to the people of the Virgin Islands, and in 1982 the composition became the official territorial anthem. In about 1972 Adams began these memoirs, working on them in two batches: first chapters 1 through 6, 8, and 11, and in the early 1980s the remaining chapters. Adams closed his guest house around 1983 and, after a gentle decline, died on November 23, 1987, a few weeks past his ninety-eighth birthday.

The life story of Alton Augustus Adams, Sr., and his music for the Virgin Islands speaks to the relationship of the margins to the center, to the ways the periphery critiques the so-called core and thereby brings the very notion of a center itself into question. Adams's name was not to be found in music encyclopedias until the Center for Black Music Research published the *International Dictionary of Black Composers* in 1999.[28] Presumably at the suggestion of bandleader Richard Franko Goldman, Adams's most popular march, "The Governor's Own," appears as the first cut on the bicentennial LP release *The Pride of America: The Golden Age of the American March,* but comprehensive information about Adams was not available until Samuel Floyd's 1977 article "Alton Augustus Adams: The First Black Bandmaster in the United States Navy." As a result, Raoul Camus included "The Governor's Own" in his 1992 collection *American Wind and Percussion Music.*[29] Yet other than in these few publications, Adams is mentioned only rarely and often inaccurately.[30] Such an uneven historical legacy poses the question of neglect or marginality. Does the relative absence of Adams from relevant histories (in studies of American band music, chronicles of the U.S. Navy, writings on the Harlem Renaissance, inquiries into the use of early radio and the press, or analyses of tourism) mark him as simply a marginal figure, or does his absence reveal more about the blind spots in the stories we tell about ourselves—a centripetal distortion in history? The lack of coverage results from multiple factors: his residence in the Virgin Islands, far from the power centers of academic research and historical memory; historical accident such as the destruction of his manuscripts by fire; and the likely racial bias that pushed awareness of his 1924 tour into knowledge's shadows. The story of Alton Adams tempers historical hubris; it reminds us how little we often know outside the central narratives we tell about our past.

Adams well understood the power of history and can legitimately be placed alongside native historians, such as J. Antonio Jarvis, who tell the story of the Virgin Islands in their own words. Adams is a faithful reporter, dedicated to telling a native version of the past through unabashed personal experience. His stories are unusually precise as his memoirs are based not only on distant memories but also on contemporary newspaper clippings he preserved in a series of large, generally chronological scrapbooks.[31] Cut from mainland and island newspapers, many of the articles preserved were written by Adams himself. Thus the events, ideas, and even personal attitudes reported in the memoirs are drawn from contemporary sources. One exception seems to be the dialogue that Adams quotes. The words "spoken" by such figures as Irving Berlin appear at least partially reinvented. Although as a newspaperman Adams was known to have taken notes during his conversations with notable figures, the ideas in the quotations are more reliable than the precise wording.

From the inception of his work on the memoirs, two themes inspired his story: a revisionist critique of totalitarian and racist depictions of the islands' U.S. Navy governors, and the assertion of a unique Virgin Islands identity, one distinct from both its colonial past and U.S. present and characterized by middle-class ambition and racial tolerance. Readers should see Adams's writing not as biased but as acknowledging history's power to invent a new world and as affirming the inevitable and necessary aspects of personal perspective that motivate and shape the historian's story. Adams may be criticized for minimizing certain racial and especially class tensions and for espousing his own political views, but the stories he relates are generally accurate, as false statements of fact would undercut his credibility and thus his goals.

Adams also wrote these memoirs to redress the racial and ethnic silences in available histories. Adams explains:

> I believe such a broad, interpretive, and factual account by a native Virgin Islander is desperately needed at this time. The study of the history and culture of black people in the Virgin Islands—as in the West Indies generally—has suffered from a lack of personalized historical data, such as diaries, memoirs, narratives, etc. There are, for example, no slave narratives, as in the United States, from which we might reconstruct the past from the perspective of the [Virgin Island] Negro. . . . Accordingly, students genuinely interested in learning about the thoughts, feelings,

and lifestyle of their forefathers have been forced to rely upon the writings of white men—some sympathetic, others not—who, at best, had only a surface understanding of the people about whom they were writing. The point I wish to make is that the human dimension of the black experience in the Virgin Islands is conspicuously missing from existing accounts. My memoir will, I hope, help fill a serious gap in our self-knowledge and perhaps encourage others to recount their experiences and observations for our posterity.[32]

Adams's critique of white authors writing on the black experience of the Virgin Islands likely refers to books such as John Knox's *A Historical Account of St. Thomas, W. I.* (1852) and Albert A. Campbell's *St. Thomas Negroes: A Study in Personality and Culture* (1943). Adams criticizes Campbell's conclusions in particular, dismissing him as an outsider prone to exaggerating racial issues. Adams's initial purpose of recovering the black voice in history is not made explicit in the memoirs' final draft. This may be because his overall message of racial tolerance and cultural mixture inspired Adams to drop this argument to avoid reifying the black/white dialectic. Yet the important goal of recovering black experience is clearly demonstrated in the memoir's rich stream of biographical information about the contributions of local black leaders to island life.

Adams was also inspired by the desire to write a history of the Virgin Islands—what he called a "historical memoir." His engagement with other histories, extensive quotations of primary sources, and use of footnotes reflect this scholarly impulse. (To preserve Adams's authorial voice, the comments offered in footnotes in the following chapters present Adams's own original notes. My editorial commentary is presented in notes at the back of the book.) A key personal experience that shaped Adams's historical consciousness was the assistance he provided the islands' government in 1954 in the transfer of old administrative records to the National Archives in Washington, D.C. This work not only nurtured his passion for the past but also offered vital information to fuel his thinking:

> Besides my lifelong personal experience and contacts, I was fortunate to be employed by the island's government as an assistant archivist to Dr. Harold Lawson, . . . to sort and remove particular objects from the archives here to be placed in the archives in Washington, D.C. It was not a difficult task, as the Danes were known to be very meticulous in whatever they undertook to do. This contact opened to me a world of information, and provided such matters that touched on the cultural output of the 19th and into the 20th century in St. Thomas, particularly in respect to these islands. It substantiated and improved the belief I held about the high cultural development of the people of the islands,

resulting from its [*sic*] unique location and favorable environment, as well as the paternalistic attitude of the Danish administration.[33]

Inspired by this experience, Adams stated in a 1979 grant proposal that "the memoirs will not only be a spiritual document, but also an historical one that will recreate the atmosphere, central events, personalities, and attitudes of a largely unrecorded past, as well as indicating what the tremendous transformations in Virgin Islands life during the twentieth century have meant in human terms."[34]

Early drafts of the memoirs contain lengthy passages of historical analysis, particularly concerning the Danish period. While much of this information remains in the final version, it has been softened as Adams retreats somewhat from his idea of writing an objective history and a subjective memoir simultaneously. Rather than a historical memoir, the result might be termed an *analytical memoir.* This label gets at Adams's goal of presenting his personal experience within its historical context in order to examine the larger social forces at work. Not just a literary conceit, this approach suggests how Adams viewed his activities as socially motivated.

The stories Adams tells in his memoirs leave out certain events and details, especially incidents of overt racism. At least part of the motivation for these gaps seems strategic—to depict a life consistent with the author's ideals of tolerance, his practice of letting go of personal anger and frustration in race issues, and the message of hope he wished to send to Virgin Islands youth. One family anecdote not mentioned in the text, for example, concerns the identification cards originally given to Adams and his bandsmen when they were inducted into the navy. Identification photos were taken in St. Thomas, and the undeveloped film was sent to the mainland for processing. When the cards arrived back in the islands, the prints had been drastically underexposed, making the bandsmen and their leader appear white. Apparently, the idea that members of the navy's new band were of African descent was so inconceivable to the technicians in the navy's photo lab that they manipulated the film to make the resulting images meet their expectations.[35] Adams may have simply neglected to include this humorous but bittersweet anecdote in his text. More intriguing is the possibility that he "forgot" this story intentionally, as the attitudes it reveals run counter to his goal of rehabilitating the image of the navy's tenure on the islands.

The notion that Adams had no direct experience with racism is false. In chapter 6, he tells of a confrontation in Philadelphia during the 1924 tour concerning the seating provided for his band. Adams was also present at the dedication of the Lincoln Memorial in Washington, D.C., on Memorial Day in 1922. In chapter 5 he describes the "privilege" of watching the unveiling of "the nineteen-foot statue of one of the greatest men in history," but neglects to mention that he could have observed the event only from a segregated gallery at the back of the crowd.

The most glaring racist incident tempered in the memoirs is the rejection of Adams's 1932 application to join the American Bandmasters Association (ABA). Adams discusses this debacle in chapter 6 but minimizes the racial component. He reports his rejection more fully in eulogistic essays not included in the memoirs that praise the wide racial embrace of Sousa and Edwin Franko Goldman.[36] Documents from the ABA archives offer additional clarity. Apparently, Adams had suggested the formation of an association of American bandleaders in his *Jacobs' Monthly* columns, but when Sousa and Goldman founded such an organization in 1928–29, Adams did not immediately apply for membership. In preparation for leaving active duty in 1932, Adams sought admission but was turned down without explanation. A letter from Goldman five years later admitting that Adams was "black-balled" by "southern members" and inviting reapplication is quoted in both essays as well as chapter 6 and survives among Adams's papers.[37] Adams did submit another application a few days later (dated February 6), but this was also tabled by the ABA, according to another letter from Goldman, dated March 9 of the same year, which explained that no new members were taken on because there was "such a long list of applicants."[38] Adams apparently never received another communication from the association.

Records in the ABA archives reveal that Goldman leavened the story of Adams's rejection. The 1937 minutes show that the ABA accepted members in all categories that year, but tabled the applications of Adams and four others. Adams's nomination appears again on the candidate roster in 1939, but is not listed again. Amazingly, the association's 1932 minutes detailing the original discussion of Adams's candidacy reveal the treacherous arena of 1932 race relations in the United States. In an open meeting with the entire membership, Goldman answers the secretary's introduction of Adams's name supportively, saying that the applicant is "a very fine musician" and "an United States Bandmaster," "has composed marches," and is "a very cultured gentleman." However, Goldman also confesses, "he has one defect, he is colored." The discussion continues idealistically, with ABA president Frank Simon expressing support for Adams's application by stating that "music knows no creeds or colors" and that as "music is God's language, and God made us all," Simon cares nothing about "what color his skin is." Goldman builds on this affirmation by stating that before Sousa had died (earlier that same year on March 6, 1932), the pair had discussed Adams's case and Sousa had said, "We are living in America, and the Declaration of Independence says, 'without regard to race, creed or color.'" This rhetoric is, of course, not precisely correct. The Declaration of Independence says nothing about race, creed, or color. Rather, the passage Sousa may have referred to reads: "We hold these truths to be self-evident, that all men are created equal, that they are endowed by their Creator with certain unalienable Rights, that among these are Life, Liberty and the pursuit of Happiness." Of course, what the founding fathers meant by "men" here was precisely limited in terms of race, gender, and class. Yet Goldman evokes Sousa's well-known racial views in support of Adams, his recent death likely adding gravity and weight to the evocation.

It is at this point that the discussion turns along north-south geographical lines and against Adams's candidacy. Goldman points out that although he is himself a "Southerner," he does "not have their feeling." Another delegate, however, states "I would hate to take pictures back to Texas with Mr. McCracken and myself shaking hands with this gentleman. If we were to have this convention in the South, it would be embarrassing. . . . Everybody in the South realizes the condition as I do . . . it is not tolerated down there. We could not have him come into a hotel or sit at the table with us." As the discussion continues, concerns are expressed about the resignation of southern members if Adams were admitted. One delegate worries that Adams might not behave "properly," since he does not live in an area that would indoctrinate him in the social practices of segregation. The discussion ends when a Mr. Glover, though supportive of Simon's views on racial inclusion, suggests that Adams's acceptance "would place the Negro gentleman in as embarrassing a position by bringing him into our Association as it would be for us." Goldman and Simon voice no further objection, and unlike other candidacies, Adams's application gets no vote. The matter is simply dropped.[39]

That such a discussion was recorded verbatim in the association's minutes suggests its matter-of-fact reality. Inclusion of a "Negro" in an all-white professional association in 1932 could be considered but was obviously unacceptable; thus no vote was needed. The leaders of the ABA did not seize the opportunity to overturn the social norm; the price of further action was too high, and thus a lack of action was rationalized as a beneficent gesture toward avoiding embarrassment for all. One can only wonder, given such a situation, how Adams reacted. Did he, if only momentarily, see himself through the veil of whiteness of which DuBois warned?

Did such an experience reinforce his belief that the U.S. mainland was no place for a Virgin Islander and thus strengthen his resolve to protect his homeland from the malignant influence of U.S. racism? Adams's memoir is silent, maybe profoundly so, on this matter.[40]

Identity continues to be contested in the Virgin Islands today. As cultural critic Stuart Hall has noted, identity is "always . . . a problem to Caribbean people" due to complex interactions among many factors: traumas of conquest, colonization, and slavery; the extinction of indigenous populations; and the mixture of a great variety of peoples, religions, and cultures (almost always from somewhere else). Identity is not an absolute but a representation. It is invented, not discovered. It is created by choices. Identity is unfinished, characteristically open to revision, a changing same. Yet "what constitutes a Caribbean cultural identity is," according to Hall, "of extraordinary importance." His analysis would place Adams's memoirs project at the forefront of the region's concerns in the twenty-first century: as belonging with that "passionate research by Caribbean writers, artists, and political leaders, that quest for identity" that Hall describes as having been "the very form in which much of our artistic endeavor in all the Caribbean languages has been conducted."[41] Adams would have agreed; his memoirs are a guidebook for young Virgin Islanders of the late twentieth century trying to resolve what their author sensed was another "identity crisis." Adams makes this purpose explicit in an early draft of his introduction: "Although I have drawn from my own life and experience, the purpose of these memoirs is not self-aggrandizement, but the presentation of a humanistic message to a generation of my fellow Virgin Islanders, restlessly searching for a more meaningful and purposeful identity during an era of change and self-doubt."[42]

As a genre, memoir responds to the crisis of identity by locating ideas and observations about the Caribbean experience in a rich first-person account. In her collection *Caribbean Autobiography: Cultural Identity and Self-Representation*, Sandra Pouchet Paquet analyzes autobiography as a vital site for understanding the intercultural process that is the Anglo-Caribbean.[43] The notion of West Indian culture comprises such a remarkably diverse region that little can be understood, she argues, without locating individual and community in a specific place and time. Autobiography provides for this specificity, and Virgin Islanders have responded to this impulse with a vibrant tradition of memoirs, contributing more than two-dozen works that describe individual identity solutions in chronicles of personal experience. Ruth Moolenaar, known well for her *Profiles of*

Outstanding Virgin Islanders, has published her own observations in *Legacies of Upstreet: The Transformation of a Virgin Islands Neighborhood* (2005).[44] Christopher Brathwaite, who moved to St. Thomas from Barbados, offers his advice for success in *There Are No Mistakes, Only Lessons: A Modern Caribbean Success Story* (1998). Richard A. Schrader, Sr., was named Virgin Islands Humanist of the Year in 1994 for his poetry and prose that preserve local history in a combination of personal stories, interviews, and archival research. Beginning with *A Sharing of My Thoughts* (1984), *Islands' "Pride"* (1985), and *Home Sweet Home* (1986), Schrader has written a dozen books, including *Notes of a Crucian Son* (1989), *St. Croix in Another Time* (1990), *Kallaloo* (1991), *Fungi* (1993), *Maufe, Quelbe and T'ing* (1994), *Under de Taman Tree* (1996), and *Hurricane Blows All Skin One Color* (1997). The genealogy project of Elton E. Vrede, Jr., combined with family tales, produced *Ancestors and Descendants* (2002). Even two of Adams's St. Croix bandsmen have published memoirs: tuba player Ogese T. McKay wrote *Now It Can Be Told* (1991), and Peter Thurland's story was printed by his daughter in 1994 as *Peter G. Thurland, Sr.: Master Cabinetmaker and Bandleader.*[45] Adams's own writings as a journalist blazed an earlier trail in this tradition, to which these memoirs offer a more comprehensive conclusion.

Like making music, writing for Adams was a social tool, offering the chance to shape the people and events of his islands. Writing had fascinated Adams from childhood. His grandmother's elegant penmanship, the books on his Uncle Dinzey's shelves, and the stimulating discussions of literature with local intellectual Adolph Sixto taught Adams that to read was an essential activity to the cultivated life and that to write was to have power. Writing was transformative in his own life: it was in the pages of music magazines and through correspondence courses that he honed his musical enthusiasms into skills.[46] Thus, what is at stake in Adams's writings is profound—nothing short of the right to life itself.

Adams's identity project spans eight decades, beginning with the purchase of the islands by the United States in 1917. This military real estate transaction included not just land and a prime natural harbor—one the United States feared would be seized for German U-boats—but the people of the islands as well. Thus the sale threatened again to reduce the islands' inhabitants to commodities bought and sold, a status uncomfortably close to the legacy of chattel slavery. While the language of the sales treaty allowed individuals to choose Danish or American citizenship, in fact, the U.S. Constitution did not readily follow the flag. Danish law remained in effect; islanders were left in a legal limbo, not officially becoming U.S.

citizens until 1927.[47] As of 2007, the U.S. Virgin Islands remain an unincorporated and organized United States territory. Virgin Islanders cannot vote in U.S. presidential elections, and their single delegate to Congress cannot participate in floor votes. Despite federal initiatives, such as allowing islanders to elect their own governor since 1970, and failed referenda seeking statehood, the Virgin Islands remain (controversially) on the United Nations list of Non-Self-Governing Territories. The passion of Adams's search for identity is rooted in this ambiguity—the limbo between colony and country. The strategies of asserting a history for the Virgin Islands, validating the experience of the native islander, and celebrating a unique Virgin Islands culture actively resist the collapse of the native soul into a colonial persona; they assert Adams's right and, by extension, the right of all Virgin Islanders to remain, in DuBois's terms, conscious at all. These memoirs thus are the author's labor of love, for his family and for his people—a gift of the past as hope for the future.

The Memoirs of
Alton Augustus Adams, Sr.,
1889–1987

1   A Historical Memoir

Editor's Note: *In this opening chapter, Adams reveals the memoirs to be a response to a Virgin Islands "identity crisis" left in the wake of racial pressures from the U.S. mainland as well as the islands' own continuing economic struggles. With the Virgin Islands facing a "critical crossroad" in their history, Adams's prescription is a return to three local and traditional values he credits in part to the Danish past: discipline, a vibrant cosmopolitan culture, and tolerance. Instilled by the apprenticeship system and by community and family cohesion, and enforced by law, discipline was fostered in the islands by the structures of daily life. According to Adams, cosmopolitanism resulted from trade that nurtured the free exchange of people and ideas as well as goods, producing local thinkers and leaders with a broad perspective. This cosmopolitism produced a tolerance of other ways of living that encouraged racial cooperation. Certainly, racism was present in the islands, but Adams experienced a tolerant, open society without institutionalized racial barriers. More than the seas and glorious flora, Adams credits these values with giving the Virgin Islands their distinctive beauty. As one of the few remaining culture bearers of the nineteenth-century Danish West Indian experience, Adams wishes to instill these fading values in the contemporary youth of the community through his historical reminiscences. Thus, his book is a social tool for shaping the self-concept of Virgin Islanders and preserving the strengths Adams feels are central to his islands' future.*

I have undertaken to write this historical memoir at the insistence of many friends and relatives and because of a deeply rooted sense of responsibility to younger generations of Virgin Islanders seeking knowledge about their past and a more meaningful understanding of their distinct cultural heritage.

This book makes no claim to being a comprehensive history of the Virgin Islands, an endeavor for which I readily admit I lack both the training and time to write. Instead, it seeks to provide glimpses and insights into our history and culture through a recording of my own experiences and reflections.

I believe such a book to be both timely and necessary. Guided by a lifelong dedication to the cultural enrichment of my people, I am convinced that they have reached a critical crossroad in their historical and personal development. People, especially the youth of these islands, seem confused and uncertain about themselves—about their past, their present, and their future. They have begun to ask important, fundamental questions. What is a Virgin Islander? What, if anything, makes us unique? What is the meaning of our history and its relevance to the present? Do we possess a distinctive culture? If so, what part of it is worthy of preservation? And how can our culture help us improve the present and serve as a guide to the future? These are indeed profound and difficult questions that all of us collectively must confront and answer if we want to continue on the pathway of progress.

Through this memoir I want to record and document my personal conviction that the way out of this modern dilemma, this "identity crisis," does not lead through a remote African past, nor through the uncritical emulation of Danish rule, nor the humanistic influence of the Moravian and Catholic Churches, nor the historical position of the Virgin Islands as an entrepôt of world trade. My own experience is that under Danish sovereignty considerable racial mobility existed, racial discrimination and prejudice were held within tolerable limits, and blacks not only had easy access to an international culture but also played a significant role in enriching its content. In 1917 America inherited this tradition of racial democracy on the islands, recognized its value, and took steps to further its development.

Only in the past few years has this pattern of racial harmony and understanding been disrupted under the impact of change and modernization. This new racism is inimical to the character and heritage of Virgin Islanders, as well as to the institutional network of our society. Yet, unfortunately, its influence is spreading. If we are to retain that tolerant and humanistic spirit bequeathed to us by our ancestors and our cultural traditions, then we must take immediate steps to check the further development of this racist cancer by elaborating and instituting a comprehensive program of controlled development and cultural revitalization that will mesh traditional virtues, values, and attitudes with newer demands for material prosperity and greater control over local conditions. To my mind, far too much attention is paid today to purely materialistic demands. There is a corresponding need for spiritual uplift and rejuvenation. I hope to redress the current imbalance toward materialism by reminding my people of the intrinsic worth of older values and customs, by pointing out their relevance for present concerns, and by stressing the urgent need for their future preservation.

Much of what is best about our culture and ourselves derives from the period of Danish rule, 1672 to 1917. Danish rule had its good and bad points. It is not my intention to make a comprehensive assessment of either in this memoir. Suffice it to say, however, that those who condemn the Danes out of hand show a poor appreciation of their positive contributions to the unique cultural heritage and value system of Virgin Islanders. To my mind three attributes are particularly worthy of being singled out as constituting beneficial legacies of Danish rule: a strong sense of discipline, a cosmopolitan culture of high refinement, and a social atmosphere and cast of mind free of invidious racial distinctions and prejudices.

The discipline of which I speak carried no connotations of severity, unreasonable curtailment of freedom, or arbitrary or unjust demands of authority. It meant a voluntary adherence by the individual to a time-tested set of rules judged best suited to govern relations between individual members of the social body so as to protect and promote the interest of the whole. Embedded in this concept of discipline are the old-time virtues of respect, thrift, cleanliness, dependability, honesty, integrity, common decency, and a general respect for the rights and persons of others. These virtues, rigidly upheld by Danish administrators as beacon lights to community aspiration and behavior, were inculcated into the individual by way of the home, the church, the school, and the apprenticeship system.

This type of discipline was the order of the day years ago. The outstanding demeanor and general hospitality of St. Thomians was a source of personal and civic pride. Drunkenness and rowdiness were uncommon, even among the so-called lower orders. Charles Edwin Taylor, a prescient observer of St. Thomas in the last quarter of the nineteenth century, recorded that "the very coal women, whose lives are the most laborious, are as orderly and decent a people for the class to which they belong as you would meet anywhere in the world."[*] Cleanliness, whether in the person or community, was an ingrained characteristic. The daily bath was a rigidly enforced imperative in family life. The homes of even the most indigent,

---

[*]Charles Edwin Taylor, *St. Thomas, as a Naval and Coaling Station* (St. Thomas, D.W.I.: J. N. Lightbourne, 1891). [These footnotes were written by Adams himself; editorial notes are presented at the back of the book.—*Editor*]

though sparsely decorated, were kept immaculately clean inside and out. No litter law existed, for inner pride prevented even the humblest persons from discarding refuse about the street or in their yards.

"The Danes," one local has observed, "taught one to know his place, to respect his superiors, and to behave with good manners."* Indeed, it paid off to be decent and well behaved under Danish rule. The Danes frowned on loafers and beggars and enacted strict vagrancy laws to deal with them. The law stipulated that some kind of work be found for those unwilling to find jobs on their own. The few criminals were quickly apprehended and severely dealt with. Strict measures were adopted to insure respectable and lawful behavior on the part of the youth. A nightly curfew was imposed to keep young people off the streets and out of trouble, while a complaint by a respectable citizen against boisterous behavior might lead to a public whipping by the Danish authorities. The whipping was, in fact, seldom employed. Its mere threat was sufficient deterrent to compel respectful and orderly behavior.

A thorough and effective apprenticeship system helped instill discipline. Boys had to apprentice themselves to a master craftsman in the hours after school, while girls received their training at home, learning such feminine pursuits as sewing, cooking, painting, or how to work in the lace and hardanger industry, which was prominent at that time.[1] The boss, or master craftsman, wielded as much influence over his apprentices as did a child's parents, who themselves kept a close watch over the activities and behavior of their children. Whether apprentices intended to follow the trade in later life was not as important a consideration as the fact that the apprenticeship system kept young people off the streets and out of trouble, teaching them the values of the craft system. This compulsory placement of children in some sort of regularized work situation paid off handsomely. Not only did it provide skills with which to earn a decent living, but it also instilled a sense of personal pride, for in those days skillful work with the hands was not considered menial or degrading, but dignified and useful. In fact, tradespeople were among the leading representatives of that vibrant cultural life of which we boast today.

The noted French writer Romain Rolland said that the political life of a nation is only the most superficial aspect of its being, and that in order to know its interior life, it is necessary to penetrate to its soul through literature, philosophy, and the arts—for in these are reflected the ideas, the pas-

*Quoted in Albert A. Campbell, "St. Thomas Negroes: A Study of Personality and Culture," *Psychological Monographs* 55:5 (1943): 49.

sions, and the dreams of a whole people. *Culture* is the word generally used to describe that interior life of a nation mentioned by Rolland. As the word *culture* conveys several meanings and is thereby subjected to different interpretations, it is necessary to clarify its meaning as used in this memoir.

The *Random House Dictionary of the English Language* defines *culture* as follows:

> The quality in a person or society that arises in an acquaintance with what is generally regarded as excellent in arts, letters, manners, scholarly pursuits . . . that which is excellent in arts, letters, manners . . . a particular form or stage of civilization as that of certain nations or periods; the sum total of living built up by a group of human beings and transmitted from one generation to another . . .

Webster's Encyclopedic Dictionary defines it as:

> Tillage, cultivation, training, or discipline by which man's moral and intellectual nature is elevated, the result of such training, enlightenment, civilization, refinement.

Matthew Arnold, the famous writer, defines the word as "to know the best that has been said and thought."[2] The archbishop of the West Indies, Dr. Alan John Knight, in referring to Premier Forbes Burnham's plan to make obeah a part of Guyana's culture, said:

> The word culture is fashionable now, but it is a silly word to use in this context because no one knows exactly what it signifies. By derivation the word must mean something that grows, and seemingly it could hardly be applied to a moribund relic of a bygone age of illiteracy and ignorance.[3]

The definition of the word *culture*, as used in this work, must not be construed as something static or immobile or that which can be taught or attained merely by pursuing courses in schools. Rather, it is that which must be developed from within and comes most forcibly by contact with and receptiveness to people (the cultured and the refined) whose high intellectual attainments are then absorbed into the spiritual substance and bloodstream, as it were, of one's being. In the Virgin Islands of my youth, the evidence of this civilized stage of development was discernible in the higher-ups as well as those in the ordinary, humble walks of life.

In the early days of our islands' history, when there was no mad rush after political power and bureaucratic sinecures, there lived a number of men and women who could well be regarded as the embodiment of culture and refinement. Without the advantages of higher education, these people industriously worked out their own enlightenment by private reading, study, association with others, and a judicious use of their spare time. In consequence, they attained a very high level of cultural understanding and discourse. Most homes contained bookcases filled with the works of the great writers of Western literature—Charles Dickens, Leo Tolstoy, William Shakespeare, Jean-Jacques Rousseau, Ralph Waldo Emerson, Miguel de Cervantes, and so many others.[4] Not only did the Bible occupy the most respected position on the shelves, but its words were constantly read and understood. The daily conversations of those ancestors proved that they not only read these works but also digested their contents. Equally, in their music, our forebears showed a distinct appreciation of a variety of musical forms and idioms, from Johann Sebastian Bach's masses and Ludwig van Beethoven's symphonies to the lyrical *habañera* rhythms of our Cuban neighbors and social dances like the waltz or schottische, as well as local bamboulas.

The native Virgin Islander encompasses in his person a common blending of many cultures and influences, aptly described by one writer as Spanish upon English upon Dutch upon Danish, like a layer cake with an American icing on top as an embellishment. It is the Virgin Islander's particular genius to absorb the best of other cultures and then adapt these influences to his or her own environment and situation.

The key to understanding the cultural history of St. Thomas can be found in the island's unique position as a commercial center of international significance. Only during the first sixty years of Danish rule was St. Thomas anything like an agricultural colony. Unlike St. Croix, where sugar cultivation prospered into the twentieth century, the rugged terrain and limited land area of St. Thomas made crop production a costly enterprise. After the acquisition of St. Croix in 1733, the Danish gradually allowed St. Thomas to develop into a free port. During the next century and a half, St. Thomas served as a vital trade emporium and communications center. Few ships from Europe or North America sailed Caribbean waters without entering the bustling port of Charlotte Amalie.

Along with the free circulation of goods went the free circulation of ideas. Businessmen of the more progressive European and American nations who flocked to the island to take advantage of opportunities offered by its central geographical location and tax-free port facilities brought with them a culture and refinement that soon permeated the entire community. Not only businessmen but also musicians, artists, scientists, writers, and actors of distinction regularly visited us, graced our concert halls, lived, and married among us. Each group brought to an increasingly receptive community its distinctive aspect of civilization—indeed a priceless treasure and heritage.

It should never be forgotten that St. Thomas, though a tiny spot on the map, once served as a social forge in which many heterogeneous groups were welded into a vibrant, functional entity whose underlying standard was unity in diversity. The central geographical location of the islands, their maritime importance under the benign administration of the Danes, and their cosmopolitan spirit generated a broad humanistic outlook among the inhabitants that had its highest expression in a tolerant approach to the question of race.

Some nonresident writers, most notably Albert Angus Campbell, who spent only a few short months in St. Thomas, have exaggerated the extent of racism and racial prejudice in the Danish West Indies. That some sort of prejudice and discrimination existed cannot be denied. But what was unique about Danish colonial rule was the relative absence of racial disharmony and discriminatory legislation. Social and political considerations, not racism, underlay the few discriminatory laws governing the free people of color during the first century and a half of Danish rule. In the nineteenth century, manumission [the freeing of slaves by their owners] was encouraged, the free colored were granted full rights of citizenship, and career opportunities gradually were opened to men of talent regardless of race.

The Danes set the example by mingling with the Negro upper classes, taking Negro mistresses, and sometimes even marrying Negroes. After 1848, the Danes even appointed qualified Negroes to the Colonial Councils. The absence of prejudice in both law and social behavior never failed to impress discerning foreign visitors. In 1877, for example, the American consul informed the secretary of state that

> no distinction is made by the government on account of race or color. The races intermarry and mingle together in all public places and are associated in business.*

Subsequent visitors have marveled at the prevailing atmosphere of racial harmony. Permit me to quote at length from two such persons of different races, from different countries with different backgrounds, who visited the islands in 1962 for two different purposes.

The late Evalyn Marvel, a veteran Paris correspondent for *Universal Service, Newark Evening News,* and the Paris edition of the *New York Herald Tribune,* as well as the author of a number of books, writes:

---

*U.S. Consular Dispatches, St. Thomas 1804–1906, V. V. Smith to F. W. Seward, Nov. 1, 1877 (Dept. of State microfilm).

Since the capital of St. Thomas was the most important slave market in the whole Caribbean area, and the local merchant and plantation owner naturally had first choice of the auction block, the Virgin Islander can claim with some reason that his forefathers were the most distinguished of the captured—tribal chieftains and those of outstanding intelligence, as well as the best physical specimens.

The Virgin Islander is a quietly proud man, and being in the majority and not subject to the indignities of the continental Negro, he lacks racial bias. Indeed, one charming elderly gentleman confided to me that colored visitors from the states frequently distressed them with talk of racial problems. Here, he said, "we have none."[5] This commendable state of affairs has not been mentioned in anything I have read on the Virgin Islands, but it is quite as significant as their natural beauty and Danish architecture. So important does it seem to me that I believe it is best explained in terms of personal experience.

It happens that I had met only a few Negroes on a social basis, and although I like to think myself devoid of racial prejudice, I found little common ground with those I had encountered. Secretly I had felt self-conscious, as if I must prove my sympathy for them. In the Virgin Islands this subconscious reaction was nonexistent.

Prior to my visit I had been told that the population was "mainly colored." But I was still not prepared for the impact of a society composed of an entirely different race. It had not occurred to me that this referred to all social strata, and that the most cultivated group I would meet would be men and women of color. I went open minded, but knowing no one. By the time I left, I had formed several cherished friendships. I met a number of white residents, but for the highlights of my stay I am indebted to the true Virgin Islander, with his kindness and courtesy. What I most appreciated was that they made no distinction about me, or the shade of my skin. We met on the common ground of mutual interests. They assisted me in the garnering of facts, lent me rare and precious books for historical research—greatest of all, they opened their homes to me and accepted me into their midst.

Theirs is a life completely lacking in racial hostility. . . . It was an atmosphere that I had never before breathed, one which gave me confidence in the brotherhood of man.[*]

At a press conference held at St. Thomas's Government House for Sylvanus Olympio, later president of the African Republic of Togo, during his visit in 1952, which he described as pleasant, profitable, gratifying, and instructive, he said:

[*] Evalyn Marvel, *Guide to Puerto Rico and the Virgin Islands* (New York: Crown Publishers, 1960; rev., 1963), 161–62.

I have been very impressed with the friendliness of the people here. Everyone seems to be very cheerful and, what is more, there is a racial harmony which you don't see very much in this part of the world and that has greatly impressed me, and I have been trying to find out how they have been able to do that, because it should be an example to many other parts of the world.

As you are no doubt aware, the racial problem is a very acute one in some parts of the world, and if in any particular corner this can be solved in such a friendly atmosphere and that every one is so happy about, it is a thing we should all learn from that particular place.[6]

I believe the attributes of discipline, culture, and racial harmony to be among our finest qualities as a people. Yet today these qualities are in danger of eradication by mindless barbarians whose violent actions and alien beliefs threaten the fabric of our community. Although their rhetoric is one of cultural pride, they are in fact betrayers of our most fundamental values and beliefs. I can only hope that this memoir will stimulate Virgin Islanders, particularly the younger people, to undertake a wider study and deeper reflection into their historical and cultural background. It is a background of which they can be justifiably proud and that is worth passing on to their children. Yet only to the extent that they can appreciate and perpetuate the underlying humanistic values of their rich cultural heritage can they truly claim to be worthy upholders of our ancestors' enlightened traditions.

It is my deep conviction that the true charm of these islands lies less in their physical beauty, great as it may be, than in the warmth, hospitality, dignity, generosity, and common decency of their people. If, acting together as one people, we can convince ourselves, as well as the outside world, of that fundamental truth, then we can look to our past with veneration, to our present with pride, and to our future with hopeful anticipation.

2 The St. Thomas Craftsmen of the Nineteenth Century

Editor's Note: Here Adams reviews his childhood and family history to highlight two of the traditional values he holds are essential to the Virgin Islands: discipline and culture. Adams grew up within the artisan community in the port and administrative capital of St. Thomas, Charlotte Amalie, surrounded by people who were highly skilled, ambitious, thrifty, and hardworking. Each of these characteristics is included in the value of discipline that Adams highlights. Historical circumstance allowed this black middle class to thrive, particularly during the economic boom of the midnineteenth century, when the islands were a vital Caribbean trading port. A vibrant intellectual life centered on discussions of current events and literature, while amateur music making filled the leisure time of Adams's family and friends, offering support for his argument that the commercial activity of its thriving port paralleled the cosmopolitan exchange of ideas and provided for the spiritual dimensions of a healthy, tolerant society. Trading vessels stimulated this cultural life as well, often bringing touring musicians to the islands. Adams's efforts as a writer, musician, and civic leader can be seen as a quest to regain the best aspects of this halcyon period. Its example fueled his social thinking, as Adams believed economic strength was the foundation of a harmonious society. Adams further articulates his strategy of identity formation in his portrayal of the islands' craftsmen, who derived a deep sense of self and purpose from their creations "as mirroring themselves." Adams hopes that retelling this story of the Virgin Islands' Danish past will help preserve these same core values as a source from which young Virgin Islanders may draw inspiration and strength.

The backbone of the St. Thomas community in the nineteenth century was the native artisan class. The roots of this class extended back into the days of slavery. Chronic shortages of white settlers forced many early planta-tion owners striving to attain the maximum in self-sufficiency to assign a small number of bondsmen to skilled occupations. As the St. Thomas econ-omy shifted from agriculture to commerce during the eighteenth century, many of these skilled workers made their way (often clandestinely) to the bustling port of Charlotte Amalie, where they found ready employment as tradesmen. The ranks of these urban craftsmen were further augmented by newly imported Africans, selected either because they had been artisans in their native country or because they showed superior intelligence, appearance, and demeanor.

Slave artisans were desirable not only because they were cheaper to hire than their white counterparts but also because they generally proved more dependable than transitory Europeans. Slave artisans either worked directly under their owner or hired themselves out with his permission. In the latter arrangement, they paid their masters a fixed percentage of their wages, keeping the rest for themselves. They usually had to provide for their own maintenance, but in compensation escaped from direct supervision after working hours. In this way, many artisans achieved a degree of freedom and self-reliance, a sense of dignity and self-respect denied plantation field slaves. Independency replaced dependency as they learned the techniques of survival in an open, competitive, capitalist soci-ety. Within time not a few of the most enterprising and resourceful among them managed to purchase their freedom out of their savings, a fact clearly reflected in the growing free colored population of Charlotte Amalie. Some grew so prosperous that they could afford to purchase slaves of their own.

Once they had become freedmen, black craftsmen continued to practice their trades unhindered by local law or prejudice. Indeed, their aspirations were nurtured by the liberal policies of the Danes, who recognized the sig-nificant contribution of the craftsmen to the stability, prosperity, and gen-eral culture of the local community.* As part of their post-1792 reform program of promoting the upward mobility of the free coloreds, the Danish government ensured these craftsmen recognition and pay commensurate with their skills. Laws were enacted regulating the various trades in accor-dance with the interests of the tradesmen and defining the relationship

---

*Compare this to the American South, where racist laws effectively eliminated Negro freemen from skilled occupations during the first half of the nineteenth cen-tury. See Richard C. Wade, *Slavery in the Cities: The South, 1820–1860* (New York: Oxford University Press, 1964).

between masters, journeymen, and apprentices.* Although the Danes did not establish local trade schools, they did make provisions for sending promising apprentices and journeymen to Denmark to complete their education and training.† Other aspiring artisans received instruction at the Moravian missions. But the vast majority of newcomers acquired their skills by apprenticing themselves to master craftsmen in the islands. "Every workman," noted one local historian, "is followed through the day by his juvenile apprentice, whose early years indicate that for some time to come he can only be expected to do his master's bidding, in handing his tools as they may be required and such like services."‡

The quality of workmanship of these native craftsmen was high. Exacting standards were prescribed for those wishing to become master craftsmen or even journeymen. Nissen recorded in the 1830s that the repute and numbers of St. Thomian artisans had grown so high that their services were sought by employers from Puerto Rico to British Guiana.§ Even Pastor John P. Knox, the islands' first historian and a staunch advocate of the myth of Negro laziness, had to concede that "many in all these trades are excellent workmen and can always command employment."** The many ancient buildings that still grace the towns of the Virgin Islands (including the majestic Government House, erected in 1865–67 for the Danish Colonial Council, and the Cathedral of All Saints Church, constructed by the freed slaves in 1848), as well as the fine mahogany furniture found in the homes of natives, stand today as eloquent testimony to the accuracy of his observation.

From the outset the development of the artisan class was closely linked to that of Charlotte Amalie. As that town grew into a commercial center of size and importance, the artisans likewise increased in numbers, wealth, and influence. When emancipation occurred near the peak of St. Thomas's

* See, for example, the Ordinance of September 30, 1902. According to its provisions, only those men who obtained "master briefs" could legally employ journeymen or apprentices. Craftsmen receiving mere "certificates" possessed no such right but could work on their own as journeymen. Journeymen without certificates could not work for themselves but had to find a "boss."

†See St. Thomas Tidende (May 16, 1906, and October 3, 1908).

‡John P. Knox, A Historical Account of St. Thomas, W.I. (New York: C. Scribner, 1852), 128–29.

§Johan Peter Nissen (1767?–1837), Reminiscences of a 46 Years' Residence in the Island of St. Thomas in the West Indies (n.p.: printed by Senseman & Co., 1838), entry for 1837.

**Knox, 126.

commercial prosperity in 1848, a sizeable percentage of natives were already engaged in well-paying skilled occupations. Writing about native workers in 1849, Knox notes:

> Laborers in certain trades abound among the men. Carpenters, masons, tailors, shoemakers, shipwrights, joiners, cigar makers and porters are the most numerous. . . . The wages of all these are comparatively high, averaging from $6 to $25 per month.[*]

The next few decades were the halcyon days of the island's artisan class. Its numbers increased substantially as freemen from the countryside flooded into Charlotte Amalie, and wages rose as St. Thomas enjoyed her final economic boom under Danish rule. It was during this period of prosperity that the craftsmen established themselves as the exemplars and leaders of the native community, commanding respect and admiration from all walks of life.

Encouraged and rewarded by liberal Danish policy and an economic situation that made it possible for a man of skill, intelligence, and industry to elevate himself, the craftsmen set the tone of the native community's attitude toward work. They considered work—hard, disciplined work—a virtue, not something to be shunned or avoided. They gained a deep sense of personal pride and dignity from practicing their professions. I have never forgotten the sense of accomplishment that the average mason, tailor, or shoemaker took in his job. He would lay out his work with care and precision and then step back with satisfaction, knowing that the finished product represented tangible evidence of his own worth and creativity. Money was important, to be sure, but so was the inner satisfaction that came with a job well done.

Believing that talent and intelligence constituted the primary criteria of character, status, and respectability and highly conscious of their own significant contributions to the building and direction of their community, the island's craftsmen viewed with contempt, and sometimes amusement, the pretensions of lesser men, black and white, who professed superiority because of color or nationality. This egalitarian attitude filtered down among members of the lower classes who looked to the artisans with respect and admiration, knowing that someday they or their children might achieve a comparable status through hard work and education.

Although the artisans valued individualism, they also recognized the virtues of mutualism in a society in which social services were limited.

[*] Ibid.

They formed guilds to protect their socioeconomic interests, as well as mutual aid societies—like the St. Joseph Society, the Free Masons, and the Odd Fellows—in order to assist one another in times of emergency and death. These societies, which simultaneously reflected and reinforced the spirit of cooperation within the native community, also provided a much-needed focal point for social interaction and recreational activities.

Among the many outstanding craftsmen of my youth, I can recollect with pride the following: Gifft, Maupé, and Wright—blacksmiths; Adams, Burnet, Esannason, Hall, Joseph, Ottley, Pierre, Simmonds, and Steele—joiners/cabinet makers; Audain, Benjamin, Desplant, Dinzey, Elois, Fleming, Industrious, Lopez, and Rodwell—tailors; Daniel, Maduro, McKetney, Moolenaar, Sprauve, and Steele—masons; Corneiro, Donastorg, Steele, Toledano, and Vialet—jewelers; Barzey, Francis, McLean, Michael, Sasso, and Thraen—shoemakers. As I write, descendants of these men are still among our most prominent business and community leaders.

Unfortunately, the golden era of the artisan class proved short-lived. By the close of the nineteenth century the artisans found themselves engulfed in the general economic depression affecting the island. The resultant drop in trade, shipping, and construction threw many of them out of work. And, like St. Thomas itself, they too became the victims of industrial civilization and technological progress, as cheap, mass-produced goods from Great Britain and the United States flooded the marketplace.

In consequence, many distressed craftsmen emigrated, seeking work on the Panama Canal or in the United States. Others sold their tools, swallowed their pride, and joined the ranks of the chronically underemployed, unskilled masses. The decline of the artisan class around the turn of the century is told dramatically, albeit impersonally, by statistics. The 1880 census listed 7,409 Virgin Islanders as being engaged in "industry," while by 1911 this figure had fallen to 4,571.[*] Using somewhat different criteria, the more comprehensive American census of 1917 found only 2,802 persons engaged in craft occupations.[†] Seventy years later, as I write these words, the craft tradition survives only among a small handful of dedicated artisans, and the important material and spiritual contribution of this creative group to the development of the St. Thomian community is all but forgotten. Different types of leaders have emerged with different sets of values.

[*] Luther K. Zabriskie, *The Virgin Islands of the United States of America: Historical and Descriptive, Commercial, and Industrial Facts, Figures, and Resources* (New York and London: G. P. Putnam's Sons, 1918), 28, 186.
[†] U.S. Bureau of the Census, *Census of the Virgin Islands of the United States, November 1, 1917* (Washington, D.C., 1918), 77.

FAMILY LIFE

It was into this proud, enterprising class of tradesmen that I was born on November 4, 1889.[1] Despite the fact that the Machine Age had already begun to render the artisans and their way of life anachronistic, during my youth they still dominated community life, and their values and attitudes permeated the world of my childhood, infusing it with meaning and purpose.

My father, Jacob Henry Adams, was a carpenter. He was born on the neighboring island of St. John in 1862. At that time the agricultural economy of St. John was in an acute state of stagnation, due largely to the debilitating effect of the iniquitous Labor Law of 1851. This law set pitifully low wages for agricultural workers and regulated their lives in other unjust ways so as to ensure their continued subordination to the plantations after emancipation. Although my father's family owned some property, they, like so many St. Johnians of the period, moved to St. Thomas in quest of greater personal freedom, educational advantage, and economic opportunity.

Within time my father was apprenticed to the trade of carpentry and cabinetmaking. After he acquired the necessary training, he was employed by the Royal Mail Steam Packet Company, the largest such enterprise then operating on the island. The company, located on what is now called Hassel Island, consisted of a floating dock capable of receiving steamers and large vessels over two thousand tons. It also possessed a spacious dockyard for repairing small boats, as well as a large workshop—called the Royal Mail Factory—for repairs and the casting of brass and iron parts for vessels of all sizes. The factory was also used for training purposes, and it was there that hundreds of skilled workers received their training as boilermakers, carpenters, locksmiths, caulkers, and so forth. My father spent thirty-eight years in the employ of the company, advancing to the position of foreman ship carpenter with the generous (for those days) wage of $48 a month. His first job was to design and supervise the construction of the Lazaretto, a building of immense importance to the island's economy for it was there that visitors with contagious diseases were housed, thus protecting the city of Charlotte Amalie from the periodic epidemics that had hitherto devastated her population and reputation.

Jacob Adams took considerable pride in his craft. He left our home in Savan at six o'clock each morning,[2] returned for an hour's lunch (taking this opportunity to dry his damp boots at the heat of a coal pot whenever he worked on the floating dock), and finished his day's labor at six in the evening. He was a dedicated worker who, until the tragic day in 1916 he collapsed on the job from a stroke, boasted of never missing a single day's work.

This stroke, however, permanently paralyzed him, and he never worked again. During the first weeks of his disability, he received one-half pay from the company. But, despite his years of loyal service, even this stipend was discontinued, and he was replaced by another worker. My siblings and I, along with my wife, Ella, took care of him until his death on February 17, 1919, considering it a privilege to do so.[3] When the dockmaster offered to purchase my father's valuable set of tools, I refused to sell them, knowing how much they meant to him even when he could no longer use them.

Although my father's family was a remarkably long-lived one (his two sisters, Henrietta Krigger of Hackensack, New Jersey, and Wilhelmina Martin of Jamaica, Long Island, died in their late nineties, while his cousin Mary Harvey of St. John lived to the age of 104), the strenuous work he performed without respite, I believe, cut his life to fifty-seven years, which, nevertheless, was considered quite old in those days. He died a moderately wealthy man, leaving a bank account of $180.00 and, perhaps more important from his point of view, no debts.

I remember my father in my early youth as stern and inflexible with a gruff exterior. It was in later years that I learned his true character of being kind and loving, with a dry sense of humor. He was a quiet man who enjoyed few affiliations outside of the Old Unity Lodge of St. Thomas, which he helped found.[4] Typical of the fathers of that era, he was a strict disciplinarian, holding a conservative and demanding attitude with regard to the cardinal virtues of discipline, obedience, and respectful behavior. I can recall at no time hearing a cross word pass between him and my mother.

In these days, parents exerted a great influence over their children, especially in the line of discipline. Not only your parents but all older people, if they saw you misbehaving in the streets, would not hesitate to correct you, sometimes physically. And you accepted this correction because you owed respect to an older admonisher and also because if word ever reached your parents that you had been defiant, you would be duly punished. The same was true of your teachers. To complain to your parents about your teacher was to invite trouble. The first thing your parents would say was: "Tell me something, do you think your teacher is crazy? *You* must have been doing something wrong." Parents, indeed the community in general, assumed a guardian-like responsibility for the proper upbringing of the younger generation, and they did not hesitate to resort to strict punishments to achieve this end.

Although strict, my father always treated the members of his family, as well as other people, with consideration, sympathy, and understanding. His authority was not mindless or arbitrary but designed to inculcate moral lessons and qualities that he believed important. Our home, which at times may have lacked in material possessions, was always rich in spiritual values, which he embodied and transmitted to my brother, sister, and myself to help guide us through life's journey. Jacob Henry Adams was a good husband, a good father, a good friend; in sum, he was an authentically good man.

I never met my father's mother, Anne Augusta Adams.[5] Apparently she had received a good education, for while on St. Thomas she was often employed by Danish families as a governess to instruct their children in the English language, which even then was the language of business and commerce throughout the Danish West Indies.[6] She was widowed before moving to St. Thomas, and before my birth she left St. Thomas for Denmark, never to return. It appears that a Danish family, the Brøndsteds, came to St. Thomas to take up residence, but for some reason or other their stay was cut short to six months. This short residency did not permit sufficient time for their children to learn as much English as they had wished. Consequently, they induced my grandmother to accompany them to Copenhagen for nine months. She agreed, and her stay stretched out to thirty-nine years.

My grandmother maintained a regular correspondence with her three children until the time of her death, keeping them up to date with her varied activities. Her letters ended with high praise for the kindness of the Brondsteds, who treated her as a member of their family. Unfortunately, I was too young to appreciate the many things that filled her letters, but I was impressed with her excellent handwriting, which further convinced me that she must somehow have received an outstanding education. Mainly I was interested in those letters that mentioned she had sent us Danish ham, cheese, sausage, and other foodstuffs. I particularly recall my ecstasy when she wrote that along with a guitar for my father she was sending me a flageolet. It was this very instrument that became the pivot of my early musical interest and career. My grandmother died a well-to-do woman, bequeathing a considerable sum in cash and jewels to her three children. The first time I ever saw tears running down my father's cheeks occurred when he received the news of his mother's death. He cried like a child, and it impressed me that despite his impassive exterior, he had a soft spot deep in his heart. Anne Adams must have been an extraordinary woman, and I regret not having known her.

My mother, Petrina Evangeline (Dinzey), was born on St. Thomas in 1860 and died there in 1906.[7] Her parents were from the island of St. Martin and had a strong artisan background. Her father was a gifted tailor, and she herself was a dressmaker—one of the finest in the community. A quiet, soft-spoken woman who was deeply religious, she empathized with less fortunate people and actively participated in charitable work. She had a way with people, a sense of individual human worth, that made a profound impression upon me. Let me try to illustrate this quality by relating an incident that had a great impact upon me in my youth.

I was a pupil at the Moravian Town School, of which Miss Mary Meyers was principal. Classes were arranged by number, and your class standing depended on the quality of your work as shown by your marks. There was always intense competition among students for the honor of being top of the class. For several years I headed my class. In the eleventh grade, however, I met my Waterloo. I was topped by Althea Peterson, a girl pupil (which was especially humiliating to me because my better was female).[8] My friends taunted me: "Man, you let a girl top you? How could you let something like that happen?" I could not withstand my pride, and therefore sought revenge as an outlet. Somehow I managed to create a situation in order to heap upon this girl the bitterness I felt. In an exchange of words during our confrontation, I used one which at that time was considered obscene. The next day I learned in quite a dramatic manner that the young girl had related the incident to her mother. Although there were no telephones, news traveled fast. As I was speaking to a friend at the gate of my home, I suddenly received a sharp slap on my face. It came from my father, angry beyond words. Later that evening, I mulled over the blow (the only one I ever received from him) and the words of reprimand that eventually followed. While I was plotting further revenge on the girl I believed to be the sole cause of my disgrace, my mother, who had just returned from a church meeting, entered my room. She advanced slowly toward me, looked at me sorrowfully, and with a hymnbook in her hand and tears in her eyes she said softly, "I'm surprised by what I heard. I'm disappointed in you and ashamed of your conduct toward a young girl whose only offense lay in showing a superiority over you in her schoolwork. How would you like someone to treat your sister in the manner that you treated that poor girl?" Then abruptly turning her back on me, she left the room. Her simple words and quiet manner had revealed to me my true self as a coward who could not stand defeat and therefore acted ignominiously. The next day, on my own initiative, I sheepishly made my way to the girl's house to offer my apology, which to my amazement was graciously accepted by her and her mother. Thereafter, we became the best of friends. (I later named one of my own daughters after her.) I had learned my lesson, thanks to the gentle humanity of my mother, who throughout her life continued to exercise a wonderful influence over me. She taught me not only to be honest with myself and others but also to love, respect, and treat with charity my fellow man.

I was the eldest child in our family. My sister Edna Augusta Adams was born on January 18, 1894, and my brother Julien Zeitzemar Adams arrived on December 30, 1895.[9] Two other sisters died in childhood, not an unusual occurrence in those days of poor sanitation, inadequate medical facilities, and primitive medical science.[10] We three surviving children were always quite close to one another, playing together as youngsters and sticking together in later life. Julien, who died in 1961, joined the U.S. Navy Band with me.[11] It was he, a fine tailor, who made the band's uniforms. Edna is an excellent dressmaker who to this day lives in my household, a constant friend and companion to me and the members of my family.[12]

Like most artisan families, we lived modestly but well. We rented our two-bedroom home for around eight dollars a month. Few natives owned their own homes in those days. Most of the houses belonged to wealthy people who leased them out. The poorer folk simply could not amass sufficient capital to buy or build their own homes. Many had a hard enough time just paying the rent, which meant a certain insecurity of tenure as their landlord was legally free to evict them at any time. We always had sufficient food, clothing, and other necessities of life, but my father was always careful not to stretch his budget to indulge in what he considered superfluous wants. The artisans as a whole made a sharp distinction between essential and artificial needs. They strove always to live within their means, ever mindful that debt would deprive them of their precious independence. "You must cut your cloth to suit your clothes" was a favorite saying among this thrifty class of people. We did, however, enjoy a few luxuries. One necessity that most artisan households, including mine, felt they could not do without was a maid to cook and help with general housekeeping chores. Usually these household helpers came from Tortola, but they were treated as part of the family.

My father was a staunch member of the Moravian Church and my mother a devoted member of the Dutch Reformed Church (later, the St. Thomas Reformed Church). Significantly, however, their offspring were members of the Evangelical Lutheran Church. To further complicate this seemingly religious disarray, my wife, Ella, and all our children are Roman Catholics.[13] But this multireligious potpourri did not in any way or manner alter or affect the love, respect, and harmony that existed among us, and is in itself characteristic of the islands.

My mother's family, the Dinzeys, formed an integral part of our home life. The Dinzeys were a highly cultured group. One branch of the family resided in Santo Domingo, what is now the Dominican Republic, where they rose to great prominence as politicians, lawyers, and businessmen. Of the local Dinzeys, the person with whom I enjoyed the greatest contact was my uncle, Archibald Dinzey. He was a man of medium height, straight as an arrow, who gracefully carried his two-hundred-pound weight. A stocky, robust man, Uncle Dinzey was a master tailor, one of the most respected and influential artisans on the island. He took pride in the epithet ascribed to him by many that "when Dinzey fits you, it is like a fashion plate." During my early years, Dinzey, his wife, Isabella, three sons, and one daughter lived together with our family.[14] The combination was a happy and harmonious one, which enriched our home life and led to the formation of a loyal and loving family unit dedicated to each other.

Tradesmen in those days took great pride in the quality of their work, which they accepted as mirroring themselves both as people and as craftsmen. They believed themselves to be the salt of the community as well as its real aristocracy—an aristocracy not by birth but of talent and accomplishment. Many of them had risen to an educational level commensurate with their skill and craftsmanship and, as builders, they believed themselves to be of vast importance in community life. The work they left behind is salient proof of their belief.

A literate and highly cultivated man, Uncle Dinzey exercised a profound influence over me. He had traveled widely throughout the Caribbean and South America and spoke often to me of Santo Domingo and Haiti. He possessed an excellent library that contained the works of the leading poets, writers, and historians. His learning was broad and he spoke several languages. He taught me much about life, work, art, and the achievements of great men. I remember one night hearing him declare in his deep, stentorian voice which brooked no contradiction: "There are two Washingtons—George Washington and Booker T. Washington." That was when I first heard of the great Negro statesman.

Dinzey was not unique. Rather he typified the broad cultivation of the artisan class. My father, for example, spoke French, Spanish, and English, along with a smattering of Danish and Dutch Papiamento. My father also owned a fine library from which I read voraciously. He and his friends could frequently be overheard discussing the works of the great writers—Lord Byron, John Ruskin, William Makepeace Thackeray, and so forth. Similarly, most artisans were familiar with world events and personalities beyond our shores. I have always marveled at the breadth of learning displayed by the people of those days and have tried to understand from whence it came. Today I believe that it derived from St. Thomas's unrivaled situation as a cosmopolitan commercial center and as a port of call for ships of all nations plying the Caribbean waterways.

Almost everyone knew how to read and write. They learned to do so partially from the compulsory schooling required by the Danes, partially from everyday experience and contact. People from all over the world milled through the city streets: "Every day St. Thomas shakes hands with the universe," noted one visitor. A number of magazines and newspapers were always available. Lectures by local citizens or visiting professors were frequently given and well attended. And then there was the telegraph. Because of its central location, St. Thomas had one of the first telegraph companies in the West Indies—the West India and Panama Telegraph Company—founded in 1869, but not operating until 1873. The people were always kept up to date on current events, for the Danes posted the telegrams in select public places around the island. People of all walks of life, going to and from their jobs, would invariably stop to read what was happening and would discuss it with their fellow citizens. I recall overhearing animated conversations over the events of the Spanish-American (1898) and Boer (1899–1902) wars. Men and women argued knowledgeably over military tactics, imperialism (American activities in Puerto Rico and Cuba were particularly reprobated), and great-power diplomacy. In other words, the minds of Virgin Islanders were not insular; they were alert and alive to world horizons and universalistic ideas.

Proud of their cultivation, the craftsmen were determined to pass on to their children their knowledge and curiosity. Sundays were dreary days for me as a youth, for following the drills of Sunday school and church, the ruling heads of the allied Adams-Dinzey family assembled all the children in the afternoon to recite poems from the works of the masters that had been given to us during the week to memorize. I could never erase from my mind the conviction that because of my age—just ripe for literary onslaught—I was selected as the special victim of poetic memorization. I can still remember quite vividly Lord Byron's "The Prisoner of Chillon" (1816), for that poem gave me the most trouble. How can I ever forget reciting those memorable lines:

> My hair is gray, but not with years,
> Nor grew it white
> In a single night,
> As men's have grown from sudden fears.

While I was fearful of missing a word or two, my ears rang with the joyful shouts of my neighborhood friends outside—playing at marbles, leap frog, cricket, flying bat, and cashew nuts.* How I envied my friends. And how I hated the poem and its author, who I believed had written it especially to torment me. Before long, however, that great healer and innovator Time came to my rescue by revealing to me at least some of the beauty and hidden meaning, not only of Byron's poem but also of the works by other writers whose contribution to mankind will stand for ages to come as vital forces of civilization. Soon I too began to build my own little library and from it manufactured my own world of dreams.

Along with their keen interest in literature and world affairs, the craftsmen, like all other ranks of island society, had a compelling love of music. Indeed, music was the leading component of our cultural lives. Here again the fact that St. Thomas was a port of call for ships of all nations was of cardinal importance, since the people benefited from the many musical talents and traditions that entered the harbor. Today it has been largely forgotten how much these visiting virtuosos enriched the culture of the Virgin Islands. A random sampling of the local newspapers shows that an astonishing number of prominent musicians from throughout the world performed in St. Thomas during the Danish period.

As far back as 1843 the Italian Opera Company visited St. Thomas, bringing with it the renowned tenor Felipe Galli, one of the greatest Italian singers. The company returned twelve years later, this time featuring the world-famous vocalists Fiorentina and Salvi. Among the accompanying group on this occasion were Bellite, the most celebrated clarinet virtuoso of his time, and Giovanni Bottesini, the greatest contrabass player the world has yet produced. Next came Adelina Patti and Louis Moreau Gottschalk, who gave several concerts together at the Commercial Hotel (later, the Grand Hotel) in June 1857. Gottschalk, a creole from Louisiana, was a highly regarded composer and pianist whose salon compositions were popular among all pianists and whose artistry rivaled that of the great Sigismund Thalberg. Patti, then just in her thirteenth year, rose to be arguably the greatest operatic coloratura soprano of all times.

The *St. Thomas Times* newspaper dated July 1, 1857, carried the program of one of these concerts as follows:

---

* For those who may have forgotten the last two games, flying bat was played with two sticks of unequal length. The shorter was placed in a hole and then struck with the larger in order to lift it into the air. The person hitting the flying bat the most times before it hit the ground won. Cashew nuts was played by "chouking" a handful of cashew nuts toward a hole in the ground about five feet away, the winner being the one who got the most nuts in the hole.

CELEBRATED GRAND CONCERT

Mr. L. M. Gottschalk, the celebrated pianist and composer, accompanied
by Miss Adelina Patti, the juvenile and imminent Prima-Donna will
give a Third Grand Concert on Wednesday, 1 July 1857 at The Commercial Hotel.

PROGRAM

Jerusalem—A Fantasia—David Babura by Gottschalk followed by the
Cavatina from the opera Barber of Seville with the variations introduced in it by the immortal Malibran.[15]

The *Times* of Wednesday, June 24, 1857, offered a review of an earlier
program:

The Concert: Miss Adelina Patti and Mr. Louis Gottschalk need no
Tedesco to trumpet their praises or herald their powers. In themselves,
they rise by illustration superior to either of these. Nor is it necessary
to analyze with operatic perspicuity whether it is in the execution of a
soprano or contralto or whether it is in the bass, tenor, or treble the
most excellence is to be found, for in all of them we may with truth
say, that in the youthful lady and gifted gentleman there is *harmony,
melody, perfection!*

Gentlemen, the sense of gratification and pleasure depicted on every
countenance that composed the audience of last evening is the true
critic that tells largest in favor of the distinguished artists of whom this
article speaks. Never have we before beheld in the salon of The Commercial Hotel, crowded as it was, so much unbounded satisfaction, so
much applauding, and, "possibly not the most pleasing to the performers," so much encoring. Nevertheless, be it said with thanks that Miss
Patti on every occasion after being encored returned to her task with
the evident intention to surpass, if such were possible, her last effort
and to receive with unlimited enthusiasm still greater applause! Where
everything is good, there can be very little to choose, yet we believe
that the birdsong executed on the piano by Mr. Gottschalk may be
taken as one of those master efforts to be classed in the superlative
degree of his attainments.

To Miss Patti, if we may presume to make choice, her rondo in a
finale of *Somnambula* was the bewitching strain that drew down the
house and was vociferously encored. The performance of last evening
cannot fail to enlist in the behalf of these professionals who we believe
will be if not now co-equal with a Thalbert or a Jenny Lind the most
liberal patronage during their stay in this island and we can scarcely
doubt that with such musical perfection in the city it must excite a general desire with everyone to participate in an evening's entertainment

of the kind. It may therefore be reasonably expected that there will be a series of successful concerts given by Miss Adelina Patti and Mr. Louis Gottschalk.

Among other musicians to visit St. Thomas in the 1850s were the eighteen-year-old Italian violin virtuoso Lavinia Bandini, hailed throughout Europe as the female Paganini, and Tibesini, the celebrated French tenor, assisted by the distinguished basso Gasparoni and pianist Nicolai. Both groups gave concerts at the Commercial Hotel. The demise of St. Thomas as a port of call in the latter part of the nineteenth century only slightly diminished this galaxy of stars entering her harbor. In September and November 1866, Lablanche, one of the finest singers of his time, concertized at the Commercial Hotel. In 1890 Daisy Hope and Ernesto del Castillo entertained at the same location. In the following year the fantastic Sissieretta Jones, called the Black Patti, appeared with the Tennessee Jubilee Singers at the newly opened Apollo Theater, while the world-famous piano soloist Señora Luisa Terzi captivated audiences at the Commercial Hotel. Angel Celestino Morales, lead soloist at the Madrid Conservatory of Music, appeared in 1906, followed the next year by the distinguished violinist David Saavedra of the Berlin Conservatory of Music.

The list, of course, could easily be extended. Suffice it to note that this continuous impress of talent and creativity, no matter how fleeting each visit had been, must have left a deep imprint upon local culture. Skeptics might recall the following anecdote. A noted scholar was once questioned as to whether or not a certain successful individual who had lived during the age of Socrates possessed the qualifications of the famous Athenian Academy. The scholar reminded his questioner that although the person in question did not attend the Academy, he might nevertheless have walked and talked with Socrates himself. The fact was that the performances of these artists were received with enthusiasm and the people were quick to appreciate and inculcate the skills and repertoires they had seen and heard. I recollect my father frequently mentioning the vocal artistry of Sissieretta Jones, especially her number "A Ship on Fire," which carried the house. He related, in a tense voice, how angered the audience became when a young man started to whisper during her performance and how quickly they whisked him out into the street.

Besides these touring musicians, there were several artists of quality who took up residence in St. Thomas. Among them were Arturo Giglioli and Santi Hestres.[16] Giglioli of Florence, Italy, composed several famous masses and played the organ in the island's Roman Catholic Church. A superb teacher, he instructed many Virgin Islanders in music.[17] Hestres, a native of France who had graduated as a bass singer from the Conservatory of Paris, came to St. Thomas as the general manager of Barthelomeo Lange's shipping firm. He not only contributed to local music as a singer in the Roman Catholic Church choir but also served for many years as a member of the Colonial Council and actively participated in other civic endeavors with men like Avictoria, Elcotti, and A. H. Riise. Another celebrated musician, a native of St. Thomas, was Alfred Nemours (formerly Levy), who studied music in Germany.* A composer and pianist of note, he created compositions that were published in Europe and played in the Royal Opera House of Berlin. He was a fellow student in the class with the famous conductor Bruno Walter at the Berlin Conservatory. Not only did each of these distinguished musicians make significant contributions to our local musical heritage, but the fact that they choose to live here is an indication that St. Thomas was far from being a cultural backwater.

The extent of the community's appreciation of fine musical talent is well illustrated by the story of Brindis de Salas, the world-famous violinist. One day Auguste Victorio, a leading citizen of Charlotte Amalie, in company with Barthelomeo Lange, overheard someone playing the violin in one of the less reputable saloons. Upon inquiring of the saloonkeeper who was doing the playing, he was told that it was a little black boy from a Cuban sugar vessel in the harbor. Victorio was so impressed that he invited the lad to visit him at the Masonic Lodge to perform for some of his fellow Masons, including Santi Hestres, Fontano, and Desora. The wealthy civic leaders who attended were so pleased with the boy's skills that they immediately raised sufficient money among them to send Brindis to study at the Paris Conservatory. After graduating with honors, Claudio José Domingo Brindis de Salas returned to St. Thomas to give one of his first concerts and later went on to become one of the most acclaimed violinists in the world. It speaks well indeed for the high level of cultural attainment of St. Thomas that its citizens were capable of appreciating, and were willing to subsidize, the budding genius of a Brindis de Salas.

Men of education and wealth were not the only ones to contribute to the Virgin Island's vibrant musical heritage. Most craftsmen played some kind of instrument or sang in local choirs. And they made music an integral part of their home life. My father was an excellent guitar player who possessed a razor-sharp ear for music, although he never studied it formally. Like most

---

* Because of the anti-Semitism he encountered in Germany, he changed his last name from Levy to Nemours. Ironically, he was outspokenly pro-German in sentiment during the heated debates about the Transfer after the turn of the century.

local musicians of his day, he played not by note but by ear—"parrotine," as it was then called because he imitated the music he heard much the way a parrot would. I would sit at my father's feet enjoying every lovely melody, music filling my heart and soul.[18] Together with Joseph Monsanto, our downstairs neighbor who played violin, and several other friends, he formed a musical group of vocalists and instrumentalists that frequently played at our home on Vester Gade on Sundays.[19] Uncle Dinzey, who sang bass in the choir of the Evangelical Lutheran Church, of which he was a staunch member (I suspect his affiliation was the cause of my family's multireligious persuasions), his son Eldred, also a bass in the choir, and his daughter Evelyn, who was the choir's leading soprano, would join in these Sunday musical jamborees.[20] After the music had finished, the men would often engage in discussions of the relative merits of the great composers, as well as the literary classics. These warm family sessions, full of good humor and revolving around the twin pillars of music and literature, were to be the overtures, the beginnings, of what was to be my career as musician and writer.

3 The Value of Education

Editor's Note: *The aspirations of the artisan class fueled an "insatiable hunger for knowledge" that supported a broad system of private religious and public schools in the Virgin Islands. The availability of education for blacks supports Adams's argument of a beneficent Danish government. Adams argues that many black families, even of the lower classes, did all within their power to take advantage of educational opportunities. He describes the system of public and private schools on the islands and gives a sense of the day-to-day lives of the islands' children. His experience shows that dedicated teachers, such as Mary Meyers, built a solid foundation of language and math skills while inspiring a love of knowledge. Learning in the islands continued in the home, with discussions of literature and music, as well as in the artisan apprenticeship system, which instilled discipline while providing skill in a trade. Adams was also a strong advocate of correspondence study by which islanders might expand their education beyond the limits of local expertise. (The College of the Virgin Islands was not founded until 1962.) He profiles Adolph Sixto, a local intellectual and gadfly who served as an inspiration to Adams and others in this regard. Sixto's charisma and confident vision for the islands may well have inspired Adams's deep and sincere dedication to their future. Adams's personal story of success in securing the skills and knowledge needed for a successful music career in an environment with few instructors and no music schools or curriculum propels his advocacy of self-study and hard work as a means of creating opportunity.*

Like almost all of my contemporaries, I began school at the age of six. My siblings and I first attended Mrs. Vialet's school. The Danes were strong believers in public education and were among the earliest Europeans to adopt free compulsory education in the eighteenth century. Their public schools were considered the finest in Europe. Danish educational enthusiasm extended into the West Indies in the 1780s. Mandatory elementary education for all white children in the islands was decreed in 1788.[*] More significantly, official efforts to expand educational benefits to Negroes commenced as early as 1787, when the government authorized the Lutheran Church to establish government schools, staffed by free people of color in the three islands. Suffering from shortages of funds and qualified teachers—two problems that would continuously plague Danish educational efforts—the Lutherans managed to set up only four schools (one in St. Thomas), which catered primarily to upper-class white and free colored children.[†] Meanwhile, Moravian missionaries, who had established themselves in the islands in the 1730s, and Roman Catholic missionaries, who had arrived in the 1750s, were busy setting up church schools for slaves and free coloreds who belonged to their congregations. Thus early educational efforts in the Danish West Indies owed much to the pioneering efforts of dedicated church missionaries, rather than secular authorities.

The Virgin Islands public school movement began on June 4, 1839, when the Danish government, anxious to educate blacks for freedom, decreed that country schools be established. The law stipulated that all estate children between the ages of six and thirteen had to attend school or their parents would be fined for each day they missed.[‡] This time the Moravian missionaries were selected by the Danish authorities to superintend and staff the schools, because they had abundant missionaries on the scene and over a century of experience in educating the slaves. During the 1840s nearly fifteen rural schools were established throughout the islands. Reflecting the general political objectives of the Danish administrators and the general orientation of Moravian missionary practice in the Caribbean, the country schools concentrated more on molding the moral character of the students than on providing them with a basic education that would

---

[*] The Dutch Reformed Church opened the first recorded (church) school in 1747. See K. Fjeldsøe, "The Development of the Educational System in the Danish West Indian Islands," an English translation by Eva Lawaetz of six articles from *Folkeskolen* 33 (1916) held by the St. Thomas Public Library.

[†] The trial and tribulations of the early Lutheran educators are recounted in Jens Larsen, *Virgin Islands Story* (Philadelphia: Fortress Press, 1950), chs. 7–8.

[‡] The law was revised slightly in 1847 and again in 1853. The 1843 "Regulation of Country Schools" can be found in *Collection of the Most Important Laws, Ordinances, Publications etc., Valid in or Referring to the Danish West India Islands* (Copenhagen, Denmark: J. H. Schultz, 1884).

help them to improve their socioeconomic status.* Order and discipline were stressed in the classroom, while religious subjects dominated the curriculum and the Bible served as the basic textbook.

That type of discipline was the order of the day in the long ago. It was one established and observed in the home and, by way of the schools, was carried into the community. Many parents, because of the lack of educational advantages, could not go far into subjects of reading, writing, and arithmetic, but they were able to lay the foundation on which all true education is built, the development of the will, the spirit—in short, the development of the whole man by means of guidance in points of respect, decency, cleanliness, truthfulness, honesty, and due regard for the feelings of others.

There was established a kind of curfew law, one which was strict and exacting and which brooked no excuses whatever. It was a law not laid down by the government, but by parents and those responsible for the young in their charge. A bugle was sounded five minutes before a gun—a canon, to be exact—was to be fired at eight o'clock every night from Fort Christian. It meant that all children below a certain age who happened to be on the streets had to be at home at eight o'clock pronto, for on guard there was certain to be the watchdog of the family, stationed at the door to see that there was no escape. It was a sight for us boys to see one another traveling at jet speed from all directions to make the home-port landing before the gun fired. Invariably we made it—for we had to.[1]

The following account written in 1841 by Reverend J. Gardin, superintendent of schools on St. Croix, provides an excellent description of a typical day in the government schools:†

I was delighted with the beautiful appearance of the schoolhouses; they are sixty feet long and thirty feet deep. . . .

The schools are conducted in the following manner. . . . The children . . . are sent to the schoolhouse under the guidance of a trustworthy female, who receives their hats, turbans, etc. at the door. They are always required to be neat and decent in their apparel. . . . Upon the ringing of the bell, the boys and girls place themselves separately before their respective doors and then march in measured time into the schoolrooms holding their hands on their backs; each division being preceded by its teacher. The children then place themselves in rows before their respective teachers. Upon a given signal they all stretch out

* See Oliver W. Furley, "Moravian Missionaries and Slaves in the West Indies," *Caribbean Studies* 5:1 (April 1965).
†As reprinted in *The Bulletin* (St. Thomas), March 14 and 15, 1941.

their hands to show that they are clean; then each class is individually summoned, and marches to its place.

There are eight classes on each side and each class has its particular seat; the ninth is occupied by the monitors as those children are called who are more advanced and who assist the younger ones to read and spell. Then they are seated, the word is given, "Hands on knees! Hands up! Fold arms!" This is done quickly and simultaneously by everyone. The teachers then commence singing a morning hymn, which the scholars have previously learned by heart. Then they all kneel down, and the teachers offer up a prayer; the children folding their hands and closing their eyes. Then follows the Bible lesson. The teacher stands behind his desk and reads: a verse or longer portion of a chapter; he then steps forward, and converses with the children upon what has been read. . . . He asks them leading questions and then they often arrive at important truths, acquire a habit of thinking, and what they read becomes impressed on their memories. If only one of the children gives a correct answer, as very frequently happens, it must be repeated by all the rest. At the conclusion of every lesson the doctrine and the moral application of the subject under consideration are especially dwelt upon by the teacher. . . .

When the lesson is ended, the children rise, and then the word is given: "Hands behind! Turn monitors out!" The monitors then place themselves at the head of their classes, and they all march to their respective reading posts, where they arrange themselves in a semicircle that is marked on the floor. At the first stroke of the bell the monitors take up their pointers; at the second they point to the first word on the board; and at the third, all the children begin to read and spell. . . . After a quarter of an hour the teacher gives a shrill-toned whistle, and as soon as this is heard every other sound is hushed. The teacher then commences singing a lively tune, in which the children join, and again march in measured time to their seats. The teacher next writes a word upon the blackboard and all the children spell it; they are then required to explain its meaning. . . . Hereupon, they are desired to mention a word composed of the same letters as the word on the slate, and this they continue as long as they can find such words. After this, they read three-quarters of an hour in classes, and close with mental arithmetic, natural history, spelling or vocal music. . . .

The school is . . . closed with a prayer.

It is a fact that a large number of less privileged children did attend both the expensive and the less expensive private schools because many parents were prepared even to go into debt in order to give their children the opportunity of a better education. At the Moravian Town School, for example, a good many of the students came from the lower strata of society. The same was true of other Moravian and Roman Catholic schools.

The public (communal) schools were somewhat secularized by new educational ordinances of November 1875 and February 1876 which transferred their supervision from the Moravians to district school boards and a superintendent appointed by the Danish Crown. School districts were redrawn to allow for the establishment of communal schools in the towns. Catechism and Bible history remained required subjects, but the curriculum was broadened to include reading and writing (in English), mental arithmetic, geography, natural history, and, for the first time, the Danish language.[*] Although initially some Moravians continued to serve as teachers, increasingly the teaching staff in the communal schools was comprised of native islanders who had been trained at the Teachers Training College in Antigua. As a consequence of this trend, the influence of the English educational system was very strong in our public schools, despite the efforts by some Danish superintendents to implement the Danish system.[†]

Considerable controversy surrounds the quality of the public educational system in the Danish West Indies. Some have praised the system, pointing out that the percentage of school-age children actually receiving an elementary education (around 90 percent) was one of the highest in the world at that time. Such writers also note that the efficiency of the system was so widely recognized that educational experts from other West Indian islands visited St. Thomas and St. Croix to study its operation.[‡] On the other side, numerous critics have argued that, despite the impressive attendance figures, the quality of public education was poor under the Danes. They have maintained that the teachers were of inferior quality because of improper training and low salaries, that the curriculum was too narrow, and that there was no opportunity for advanced training because there was no vocational program and no public high school. Citing the miniscule budgetary appropriation for education (6 percent of the annual operating budget), critics have charged, with some justification, that the Danish government was remiss in honoring its 1838 resolve to educate Negroes. As one "Son of Africa" noted in 1907, the Danish educational system was not preparing lower-class natives to rise above their inferior socioeconomic status. Instead of being a vehicle of self-improvement, education tended to

---

[*] The 1876 ordinance which relates to St. Thomas and St. John can be found in *Collection of the Most Important Laws.*

[†] Larsen, 206–34; Aminta C. Nathalia Burnet, *Education in the Virgin Islands under Denmark and the United States* (Master's thesis, City College of New York, 1940).

[‡] See, for example, the letter of J. P. Jorgensen, member of the St. Thomas School Board, in *The Bulletin* (St. Thomas), March 4, 1907; and Larsen, 206–34.

perpetuate a rigidly hierarchical system in which black people as a group had little hope for upward mobility.* Such damning indictments by liberal natives were confirmed by the first American naval governor, James H. Oliver, who reported in 1917 that

> the existing system of public instruction in these islands leaves every-
> thing in the way of an adequate system to be desired. A large propor-
> tion of the children have grown up without the hope of improving their
> lot in life. . . . Where there is no ambition and hope of betterment there
> is bound to be an indifferent attitude toward the family. . . . Improved
> conditions of civilization largely flow from the hope that man generally
> has of giving his children better opportunities than he has himself pos-
> sessed. But in these islands few of the natives can see any better oppor-
> tunities for their children than they themselves have had, . . . in
> general, amounting to barely more than an opportunity to exist.†

Because of the many serious deficiencies in the public schools, those parents who could afford it sent their children to private and parochial schools where they would be exposed to better teachers and a broader aca-demic curriculum. At the end of the nineteenth century, there were many such schools and their enrollment exceeded that of the public schools.‡ Among the private and parochial schools there was a definite hierarchy, ranging from the school run by McConney and Speed, two British teach-ers who charged around eight dollars per month, to the semiprivate Mora-vian Town School, which I attended at a cost of only five cents a week. The Moravian Town School was located in the building on Back Street where *The Daily News* is today. Mr. Burnet, the cabinetmaker, had his shop down-stairs. There was just one entrance off the street to the flight of stairs that led to the schoolroom. Children who attended public schools went either in the morning or afternoon. Students in private schools, like the Moravian Town School, attended all day.[2]

There was no system of racial segregation. Class, not race, determined who attended which school. Whites and blacks alike attended all these pri-vate and parochial schools, their choice depending on their parents' income.

---

*See the letters by the "Son of Africa," "The Committee," and "A Liberal" in *The Bulletin* (St. Thomas) of March 1, 4, and 5, 1907, and Burnet, *Education in the Virgin Islands*.
†Quoted in Valdemar A. Hill, Sr., *Rise to Recognition: An Account of Virgin Islanders from Slavery to Self-Government* (St. Thomas, VI: n.p., 1971), 55.
‡In 1872, according to Larsen (206), the town of Charlotte Amalie alone could boast of twenty-four private and parochial schools. The school report of 1890 listed 655 students in private and parochial schools compared with 556 students in the public schools; see Campbell, 26.

Almost all of the teachers were colored natives. James Chesterfield Roberts, for example, a prominent member of a native family who had attended the Mico Training College of Antigua and Howard University, was head teacher at a private school established and partly supported by Bartholomei Bornn and several other civic-minded citizens. Psychologist Albert Campbell exaggerated when he wrote that as a rule

> the private schools tended to be made up of the white and light-skinned children. The dark-skinned parents were for the most part among the economically underprivileged, and their children necessarily went to the communal school.*

A considerable number of darker children did in fact attend the private schools, because many parents were prepared to go into debt to give their offspring the opportunity of a better education.

There is no doubt that the teachers at the private and parochial schools were of high caliber. Many of them had studied at the Teacher's Training College in Antigua, while a few others had received their education and training in Denmark. Among the former was my teacher, Mary Meyers, a native who had been trained in Antigua.

Miss Meyers was an exceptional teacher as well as an inspiration and spiritual guide.[3] Hers was the day of personal pedagogy. The profession had not yet been mechanized and, if the presumption will be pardoned, not overburdened with rigid schedules, experimental techniques, and standardized teaching procedures. The pupil was treated as an individual with special learning problems and proclivities rather than a mere number to be processed through the system, signed, sealed, and delivered into society with a meaningless, perhaps even unearned, degree. Quality, not quantity, counted in Miss Meyers's school. Moreover, there was more to the educational experience than programmed knowledge. She taught mainly by example, by personal influence, and impressive power. The profession was viewed not only as a science and an art but also as a sacred trust, it being widely recognized, to quote from Cardinal Henry Edward Manning, that

> it is not the Latin and Mathematics we teach the boy that makes him a true and capable man. It is by the life we ourselves live before his eyes. Our own lives and the every movement and gesture and expression which reveal our lives are probably the most potent influences in the education of the young.[4]

* Campbell, 26.

I loved and drew inspiration from Miss Meyers because of her patient dedication, her gentle simplicity, her loving disposition, and her ability to rise above momentary disappointments or misunderstandings and, unshaken in her endeavor, to bring joy and knowledge to those in her charge. Her noble character, committed to a lifetime of service to the youth of the community, has remained to me and countless others as a constant example throughout the rugged road of life. "I am glad," she wrote, "to have the grateful acknowledgment of many young men and women whom it was my duty to teach. I say this more with feeling of pleasure than pride, because I feel that the gift was given me to be used for the benefit of others and I have been thankful to God that he could use me in this way." Miss Mary Meyers, like the other teachers whom she personified, helped to make the teaching profession fine in having sanctified it by a lifetime of devotion to an ideal of unselfish service.[5] And Mary Meyers was not the exception.

There were other such exemplary teachers in our school system in those days who made lasting contributions to the well-being of our community. To cite only a few: At the Convent School, known as the Nun School, head teacher Madame Rose established a wide reputation for her excellent work; Misses Semedair and Victoria Shalders at St. Mary's; Madam Canéz and Julia James and Messrs. Anderson and James Watt at St. Alphonsus Grammar School. Earlier teachers included Miss Elvina Gomez, Miss Ellen Hay, Miss Hope, Miss Stephens, and Mrs. Octavie Vialet. In the public schools were Miss Anna Callwood and Miss Stephens, Mrs. Martha Kearney and Miss Luisa Vival, Miss Howard and Mr. Dunlop. At the Moravian Town School was Miss Mary Meyers, Mr. Benjamin Oliver was at Lincoln School, and Mr. James Chesterfield Roberts taught at the Bethesda School. Other teachers included Lewis Audain, Gertrude Benjamin, Miss Adelaide Dunbavin, Elizabeth Jones, Sebastian Leffe, Mr. McConney, Esther Malone, Lucinda Sewer Millin, Victoria Rene, Mr. Speed, Mrs. Mary Vessup, and Edith Williams. The St. Thomas College was also established around 1877 by Father DeBuggenoms of the Redemptorist Fathers, which on account of financial problems was short-lived, but significantly among its students was Arthur Schomburg, the noted Negro bibliophile.[6]

From the beginning I enjoyed school and eagerly applied myself to the rigorous study of all subjects, although literature and poetry were my particular favorites. We read mostly British writers, but it was the great American transcendentalist Ralph Waldo Emerson who was my personal favorite, and I was deeply influenced by his philosophy of individualism. Among the other writers who particularly inspired my youth were John Ruskin, William Makepeace Thackeray, and Victor Hugo.

Unfortunately we had no musical education in the schools. My early stimulus and training in this field, as in so many others, came from my total sociocultural environment. For my generation, education did not begin and end in the classroom. And while we valued educational degrees, much of our most important knowledge and training derived from daily life experiences in the cosmopolitan atmosphere of our bustling port city. It was in the streets (and for some on the seas) that we learned foreign languages and an understanding of world affairs. Our instruction in the humanities, especially literature and music, came largely from our families and their larger social circle. Philosophy and current affairs were acquired not only from home reading but also from listening to inspired discussions, led by men like Adolph Sixto, on the street corners and in the cafes.

SELF-STUDY

It is not so easy for today's youth to appreciate the obstacles and discouragement the youth of my day had to face in acquiring an education. Knowledge was a privileged commodity. Many who had knowledge and learning guarded it, refusing to share it with those less fortunate. Ambitious individuals had to acquire knowledge wherever and however they could through their own creative endeavors. Like my contemporaries, I possessed an insatiable hunger for knowledge and eagerly devoured every morsel I could find. Even after I left school, I never came to believe that my education was at an end or that the world owed me a living. Today, after a lifetime of learning, I freely acknowledge that I am still more impressed by what I do not know than by what I do.

In my youth we had not the educational opportunities enjoyed by young people today. There was no high school, let alone a college, no public library, no mass media. Yet, perhaps because of these very deficiencies, we were consumed with a desire to improve our knowledge, our skills, ourselves, through the medium of self-help and self-instruction activities. Education in those days was not looked upon as a right, but as a goal to be earned through perseverance and self-discipline. We prized knowledge and sought it wherever and whenever we could. In music, as well as other fields, one could obtain some expertise by studying with local practitioners and, on occasion, attending lectures and lessons given by temporary visitors. But for those of us, and there were more than a handful, who aspired to wider knowledge, the maximum use of limited local resources was not enough. Hence, many people took correspondence courses offered by experts in the United States and abroad. In this way we were able to considerably broaden our horizons as individuals and as a people.

The leading exponent of self-study was Adolph Sixto, affectionately known as "Ding." Sixto was an imposing and influential figure in the community as well as the region at the turn of the century. Born February 17, 1858, in Vieques, but raised by his St. Thomian mother on St. Thomas, Sixto received no formal education. Nevertheless he was blessed with common sense, a splendid imagination, and a rough native wit that enabled him to educate himself. He spoke fluently several languages, including French, Spanish, Italian, German, even Russian, and was an exponent here of Papiamento and Dutch Creole. He read extensively and traveled widely, thus acquiring impressive intellectual qualities which earned him a reputation as an "unforgettable character" throughout the Caribbean. He lived right opposite what is now Crown Motors, an uptown gasoline station; the alley leading from his home to the waterfront was called Ding's Alley, so popular a figure was he.[7]

A charming, fascinating conversationalist and outstanding public speaker, Sixto had a rich, melodious, well-modulated voice, with a power and pitch and range that needed no microphone even in a good-sized hall. He discoursed eloquently on the beauties of Homer, Dante, Milton, and Shakespeare as well as on local happenings and possessed an inexhaustible supply of humor and wit. He stood a little above medium height and walked with a kind of shuffle. He failed in almost every commercial undertaking he attempted,[*] for he was essentially a dreamer, a visionary, a scholar, who believed sincerely in the unlimited potential of St. Thomas and its people. Too often we are prone to estimate a man's value and importance from the standpoint of material possessions, dollars and cents, forgetting entirely his spiritual values.

I knew him well. Taking an interest in me, Sixto often allowed me the privilege of listening in on his discussions at Miss Elsa's Ice Cream Parlor (located at the site of the present Chase Manhattan Bank building on the corner of Kommandant Gade and Dronningens Gade [Main Street]). A gracious elderly lady, Miss Elsa sold ice cream and soft drinks, cigars and cigarettes. The clean polished marble floors with booths on both sides gave the place an aristocratic appearance and an inviting feeling of welcome. The entrance was covered with a huge canvas awning projecting over the sidewalk, under which would sit the island's solons, facing the street, from about 8:00 to 10:00 P.M. every night, gathered to discuss local and international events

---

[*] In the 1890 census, Sixto is listed as a butcher.

gleaned from the island's chief source of information—the British Cable Office. Sixto usually dominated this group, which included Hans Behagen, secretary to the Colonial Council; Justin Burnet, master cabinetmaker; Auguste Vance, merchant; George Ridgway, chief clerk of the British Cable Office; and Leroy Nolte, newspaper editor of the *St. Thomas Tidende* and the *Bulletin*.

I recall one typical evening when Sixto, taking exception to someone's remark that St. Thomas was never going to improve, pontificated for nearly an hour on the vast future possibilities in store for the island, a theme which he more fully developed in his book *Time and I; or, Looking Forward*.[8] He pointed to the Long Bay and Sugar Estate areas, then a wilderness, and prophesized beautiful buildings and stores erected, industries sprouting forth all over the island, enraptured tourists from all over the world, and a political system and economy second to none in the West Indies.[9] The eloquence and logic of Sixto's remarks, however, failed to convince his adversary, who, after a puff on his huge cigar, declared with an air of finality that "St. Thomas *never* got to rise." This pessimistic statement outraged Sixto, who beckoned me to walk down the street with him. I knew he wanted to talk about the fellow, so with a feeling for melee I accompanied him. When we got out of earshot, Sixto stopped, threw his hands over his head, chuckled, and said, "My good God, how do you expect St. Thomas to rise as long as you've got such ignorance anchored on it. It needs a tidal wave to wash fellows like that away if this island is to make any progress."

Everywhere he went, Sixto preached the virtues of self-help, exhorting the youth to study wherever and whenever they could. It was he who introduced the international correspondence schools to our islanders and urged young men like me to take advantage of their offerings. My own experience has taught me the wisdom of his advice, for without self-study I could hardly have hoped to achieve success in my chosen field of endeavor. Sixto was greatly misunderstood and often maligned unjustly by his many critics, who were unable to appreciate and evaluate the contributions of the man to the community.[10] At a time when the youth of the islands hankered for a higher education than was afforded them here, Sixto introduced correspondence schools. He lectured throughout the West Indies, where his name was a household word, exhorting young people to look forward, to study in order to take their just place in a changing world. I was among those during that period in whom he inspired hope and to whom he gave encouragement and urged to carry aloft the banner inscribed EXCELSIOR.

My own thoughts on the value of self-study are best summed up in an editorial I wrote in the *Bulletin* of September 28, 1940, which I feel compelled to reprint here in its entirety since I believe it has relevance for our community.[11]

> There are in this community, many students who, having completed their high school course, find themselves unable to attend institutions of higher learning. Such students often, in consequence, take a gloomy outlook on life. Perhaps students so hampered may find some encouragement in this quotation:
>
>> Our resources and activities of mind and body are developed only when we are in difficulties. All the world over, necessity is the mother of invention. When there is nothing to conquer and all things are done for him, man becomes only weak and useless.
>
> Our seemingly discouraged students may gain a useful perspective by looking into the lives of the world's greatest men. Such students would not fail to find out that they, when compared with such celebrities in the early stages of a career, are blessed with teeming opportunities for self-development. There are no impassable roads to the attainment of an education in a community which offers such opportunities as are found here. Ambitious students have at their disposal such conveniences as: (1) the public library, (2) the radio when judiciously and intelligently utilized, (3) occasionally, an awakening and inspiring lecture, and (4) the opportunity offered through correspondence study. Besides, youngsters nowadays may enjoy the advantage of earning money while plodding their way through the course of study.
>
> To get an idea of the advantages which may be derived from the pursuit of knowledge while engaged in some bread-winning activity, our young people should read the biographies of such men as Abraham Lincoln, Benjamin Franklin, Booker T. Washington, James A. Garfield, Andrew Carnegie, and others. Youngsters would find that the two things which count most in the winning of a place in life are: (1) adaptation for a particular line of endeavor and (2) the desire to engage persistently in that line.
>
> But the most discouraging factor is found not so much in the youngsters themselves as in the cold-water-pourings of many of those who profess to be leaders of the young. This includes a small number of half-baked college graduates and so-called professional experts, who strut about the streets with an offensive air of competence not justified by their achievements. These latter can be seen with smiling mien, patronizingly looking down on those who have industriously worked out their own salvation by private reading, study, association with others, and a wise use of their spare time.
>
> Then there are the local Know-It-Alls—those self-constituted leaders who too often act like "Foxes without Tails" in one of Aesop's Fables.[12] Having themselves attained only mediocrity in their life-

activities, these "sages" do not hesitate to tell a youth that he or she cannot achieve anything savoring of greatness. A youth is beset by such phrases as: "My son, remember you're black"; "You must remember that this is a small field"; "Man, our brains are not the brains of those great men in other places"; "See me, in spite of the chances I had in life, see what I am now." Yet our would-be leaders never admit their own failures and thus fail again—fail to warn the young away from the pitfalls that led to their own disappointments.

The way, then, is not at all barred to those (young or old) who are filled with an ardent desire for something higher in life. As a wise one said, "Genius is one-tenth inspiration plus nine-tenths perspiration."[13] In other words, where there is just an adaptation for a line of activity, persistent application can, with that adaptation, achieve remarkable results.

Again, someone has wisely remarked, "Intelligence, industry, persistence, and determination are a combination which rivals mere genius." Hence, to all seemingly discouraged students, I enjoin: find out the field of activity to which you are best adapted; choose your goal in that field; then cultivate a burning desire for the attainment of proficiency in your field; and finally, applying the combination which rivals mere genius, push your way to the front.

THE APPRENTICESHIP SYSTEM

An informal system of vocational training rounded off the educational curriculum under the Danes. This was the apprenticeship system. Most children, whether they attended private or public school, had to apprentice themselves to a "baas" [boss]—a master craftsman who would teach them a trade and for whom they would work every afternoon immediately after school. Girls generally worked as cooks or seamstresses, while boys took jobs as blacksmiths, tailors, carpenters, shoemakers, and the like. Although the apprenticeship system was not required by law, it was assiduously fostered by the Danish administrators. It evolved as a customary practice in response to local conditions and needs, because, in the first place, parents recognized that only limited opportunities existed for natives with limited means to enter what today we call white-collar occupations. They wanted their children to acquire a practical skill so that, whatever their aspirations, they would have something to sustain them throughout life. In the second place, because most parents worked all day, they needed someone to control their children and to keep them off the streets and out of mischief. The craftsmen willingly cooperated because they were always eager to have additional helpers at little or no cost. As a consequence, the craftsmen became surrogate parents and educators, with the responsibility of inculcating the community through its youth with those virtues of discipline and enterprise that they embodied.

Like most morally and practically beneficial activities, apprenticeship was not easy. Initially, apprentices received no pay, and in many cases, such as those who worked at the Royal Mail Packet, their parents actually paid money for the privilege.[14] Only after you had worked for a certain number of years and had achieved a certain level of skill could you expect to receive a small wage. In the first years you were chiefly required to run errands and perform shop-cleaning chores—tasks of drudgery that made you feel more a servant than a student. Only gradually, after you demonstrated the ability to accept and carry out orders, were you taught the rudiments of the craft. Discipline was strict, and unflinching obedience demanded. In the corner of every workshop hung the dreaded tar rope, constantly reminding you of the whipping you would certainly receive if you misbehaved or failed to do what you were told—quickly and effectively. The tar rope was more a symbol of authority than an instrument of punishment. Usually, the fear of it was sufficient as a behavior modifier.

I had an unusual motive in selecting those men to whom I apprenticed myself during my youth—learning music. My first "baas," Jean Pierre, was a joiner. But I chose him because he knew music and once played the flute, and not because I had any particular desire to pursue my father's trade of carpentry. After Pierre died, I apprenticed myself to my Uncle Dinzey, the master tailor. I stayed with him for several years, mostly doing errands rather than learning much about tailoring. At the age of fifteen I became an apprentice to Albert Francis (the father of Rothschild Francis), an outstanding local shoemaker and flute player of dance music, who counted among his customers the Danish soldiers and many of the most prominent local merchants. From Francis I learned much about the art of shoemaking and even made shoes for myself and my family. Although I eventually devoted myself to a musical rather than an artisan career, I nevertheless look back to my years as an apprentice as being morally and abstractly beneficial to both my chosen profession and my private life.

4 Music in the Virgin Islands and the Founding of the Adams Juvenile Band (1910)

Editor's Note: *The founding of the Adams Juvenile Band retold here illustrates points made in the two previous chapters—that local culture should be valued and that dedicated hard work, especially in both education and self-study, produces opportunity. Adams begins by describing the pervasive importance of musical activities in the artisan environment of his upbringing and argues against a simplistic, essentialized understanding of music and race by claiming that European and Latin musics had a more pervasive influence on the music of the Virgin Islands than purely African sources. Music for Adams is an idealized space of free exchange of ideas without the limits of racial politics. He shares his fascination with the flute and recounts his struggles to learn the instrument without benefit of a regular teacher. In particular, he overcomes two traumatic incidents that only fuel his feisty determination and forge his commitment to educating youth. One result of this service ethic alloyed with musical ambition is the formation of the Juvenile Band. A compelling portrait of the band's unheralded patron, Elphege Sebastien, shows how the island's community support network functioned to provide not only financial assistance but instruction and mentorship as well. Adams's activities as a bandleader, composer, and music journalist opened doors to unlikely opportunities that break through any supposed limitations of an isolated island life. His example offers further clarification, though not made explicit here, of the path that Adams hopes youth in the Virgin Islands will follow today. This chapter also touches on the islands' first carnival and the hurricane of 1916, but Adams's interests here, for reasons of personal taste and chronology, do not include popular music on the islands, such as quelbe or the later influences of jazz, calypso, steel pan, rhythm and blues, reggae, or pop.*

In my youth St. Thomas was alive with the sound of music. Not only was music an integral part of my family life, but it permeated the entire community, constituting the core of our cultural life. Our rich musical heritage derives from many sources. Contrary to those who would trace all our cultural traditions back to Africa, or at least to the slave plantations, our music is more European and Latin American in content than anything else. Our most popular dances, the schottisches, mazurkas, quadrilles, and lancers, were all adaptations from European originals. The same is true of most of our "folk songs," a fact that I discovered during my own extensive researches into their origins.[1] Our favorite and most commonly used instruments, the violin, guitar, flute, and other woodwinds, are also European in origin.

Only the bamboula, with its distinctive polyrhythms and pulsating drumbeats, can legitimately be attributed to Africa. Yet it should be noted that it was not danced by sophisticated people of my era or even before. This fact is clearly recorded by Nissen, who wrote in 1832:

> The dances of the Negroes are of one sort, moving and twisting about. They have no regular dances. The principal instrument is called the Gombee. This is a small barrel, the bottom of which being taken out, a goatskin is drawn over the rim. They must have a beat, and on this purpose are continually knocking this Gombee, which sounds very hard and makes a great deal of noise.
>
> But this music and sort of dancing is more a custom among the lower class of Negroes and slaves, for amongst the well educated persons, they have learned dancing, have very good music, and often give balls like the white inhabitants.[2]

Indeed, so vulgar and barbaric was the bamboula considered in my youth that the Danish authorities outlawed it and would arrest anyone who dared dance it publicly. This policy was enthusiastically endorsed by the Colonial Council and the most refined citizens of the community.

The disappearance of African musical idioms by the early part of the nineteenth century is not surprising considering the open system of slavery that prevailed on St. Thomas. Unlike in South America and other agricultural countries, the open slave system on St. Thomas provided no isolation from the mainstream of general commercial life to encourage the development of an independent folk expression. The black population here was directly and constantly in close contact with European peoples and cultures and was quick to adopt and then adapt the latest musical dances. Even on St. Croix, where agriculture was central to the local economy and plantation slaves were more hermetically sealed off from outside influences, European influences dominated by the nineteenth century. The Latin influence, which came from Puerto Rico, one of our principal trading partners, was particularly strong at the turn of the century and beyond. From this source we learned and inculcated the basic *habañera* rhythm, which was a distinctive blending of African rhythms with Spanish melodies.

THE FLUTE

Of all the many instruments I encountered as a child, the flute exercised the greatest fascination for me. To this day I can vividly recall the many mornings when I was happily awakened at an early hour by the soft, sweet notes which drifted into my bedroom from the flutes of some serenading group of local troubadours. The early-morning serenade, adopted from our Latin neighbors, was quite a feature of the long ago. It commemorated as well as celebrated a happy event, such as a birthday or wedding anniversary, by the playing of appropriate sweet music under the window of its unexpecting audience. I was drawn to the soft, lyrical sounds of the flute and soon developed a great desire to learn how to play the instrument. As I could not afford to buy a flute, and as my parents had much to do to make ends meet already, my only recourse was to make my own instrument. I would cut the protruding stems of the papaya tree to size, cover one open end with fine tissue paper, and make six holes to accommodate the fingers.[3] I would imitate the flute playing I had heard. The difficulty was, however, that the papaya stems dried up quickly, thus necessitating innumerable cuttings.

It was not long after I began these instrument-building attempts that my grandmother who lived in Copenhagen sent a large package to my father which, among other things, contained a guitar for him and a flageolet for me. The flageolet was an instrument made of wood with a mouthpiece and a tube in which finger holes and keys were placed. Types of the flageolet, a member of the flute family, were also called recorders, flute douches, ocarinas, and whistles.[4] My joy on receiving this instrument was unbounded. But as for the music, there was no one to help me. I had to learn to play myself and thus became my own teacher. On squares of cardboard that I obtained from merchants in the community, I sketched a flute on one side and on the other wrote the words, as I recollect, of two hymns—"Nearer My God to Thee" and "Safe in the Arms of Jesus." I then matched, as best I could, the fingerings I knew with the words and their appropriate pitches in the melody. Through this process I created my own sheet music. It might seem a clumsy way of studying, but it was all I had as a guide, and I confess to being proud of my ingenuity and took delight in displaying it to my friends—who considered me a genius.

Among the outstanding artisans of my youthful days was Jean Pierre, a master cabinetmaker of French extract who made beautiful wood carvings on bedsteads, bookcases, tables, chairs, and the like—many of them still in evidence today. His workshop was located on the street in speaking distance from my home. Often I would look from my window, admiring and marveling at the dexterity and skill with which he manipulated his various tools while carving. From mahogany, teak, and lignum vitae, he pulled forms and designs such as rope cable and pineapple wood. No less marvelous to me was the carefree manner in which he removed from his eyes, while still carving, the dust from the shavings made by the lathe. I often wonder how he did it. In those days there was no electricity to set the large revolving wheel in motion. It had to be done by hand. The spinning of the lathe was often accompanied with the singing and often the grunts of this marvelous craftsman.

Up to this day, in my mind's eye I can see Jean Pierre—tall, handsome, somewhat stooped from the many years he lived, well groomed, with gray hair on his head and face, and a little goatee and pointed moustache. I recall his well-shaped mouth minus several front teeth, tender and welcoming bluish-gray eyes, a complexion the shade of the light mahogany on which he so assiduously worked all his life. I can still hear his soft, low-pitched voice—still vibrant despite his age. Like most of the artisans of his day, he was a lover of good music. One day when I was about nine or ten years of age he called to me from his workshop and said, "I heard you playing the flute." "Yes, I play the flute," I replied. "Do you play by music?" he asked. To which I replied in the affirmative. Continuing, he said, "I once played the flute myself but that was so long ago. Bring your music along with the flute to me. I would like to see your music and to hear you play."

I needed no further invitation. Hastily I took my flageolet and my music to his home, located opposite his workshop. As he saw me coming, he opened the door. I entered holding the instrument in my left hand and two bundles of cardboard tied together and tucked neatly under my right arm. He looked on with amazement. "What's that?" he asked, pointing to the bundles. "That's my music," I told him. "The one bundle is 'Safe in the Arms of Jesus' and the other is 'Nearer My God to Thee.'"

Jean Pierre was astonished. "What do you mean?" he asked and started to laugh. Slightly irritated, I said inwardly, "Laugh, I'll show you." Eagerly I spread the one bundle out on his floor and began playing. When I was through, I looked at him with a proud laugh now expressed on my face. He looked at me seriously, but tenderly, and said "That's not music."

To which I replied, "That's *my* music."

"That may be your music, but it is not *music*," he explained. Looking me squarely in the face, he instructed me to ask my father when I got home to buy a couple of sheets of blank music paper and also to buy a piccolo or flute with an instruction book from the United States. But in the meantime, I was to come to him and he would help me.

I got the music paper and went every day after his work hours for lessons. He taught me about the lines and spaces of the musical staff, the names of the notes and how to sing them, as well as the diatonic scale. "You must know your theory; you must learn to sing the notes before you attempt to play an instrument; you must know *solfeggio*," he strongly advised. Unfortunately, the lessons were not to last long, for six months after they began, Jean Pierre died. But what he taught me during that time, including the many conversations we had on music and musicians, did not die but lives with me. His example serves as a beacon light ahead of me and exemplifies the inner life of this great man, devoted to service, dedicated to mankind. His words, "Bring your music and flute to me," still ring in my ears. That wooden piccolo that he inspired my father to buy from Butler Brothers cost only $1.60 (plus fifty cents for the instruction book), but it meant more to me than even the costly genuine sterling silver Boehm system flute later awarded to me by the firm of Cundy-Bettoney Co. in Boston for my many articles on the flute that appeared in my columns for the *Jacobs' Band Monthly*.

The piccolo and instruction book arrived by mail just a few days after Jean Pierre's death. Without a teacher, I again had to become my own tutor. Buoyed up by the injunction (the soundness of which I was too young to question) that where there is a will, there is a way, and brought to a higher level of knowledge by six months of music instruction in the basics, I eagerly accepted the challenge and applied myself diligently to the further study of music. For many nights after the piccolo's arrival, I was unable to sleep. At intervals I got up, lit my kerosene lamp, and opened the black velvet-lined case to view my instrument and admire its shining German silver keys and to inhale the scent of the almond oil used to prevent cracks in the grenadilla wood out of which it was made. Not long afterwards, in conformity with local demands and customs as well as the desire of my parents, I apprenticed myself to a shoemaker's shop owned by Albert Francis. I chose this shop for two reasons: Francis was a master craftsman, but he also played the flute wonderfully. One day my boss heard me struggling with my two hymns and, in jest, clapped his hands to his ears and laughed. "Come in, my lad," he said. "If you really want to play the flute, let me show you how." Under his guidance, I learned the proper way to handle the instrument. I was an avid pupil.

Music was Francis's first love; shoemaking was an economic necessity. Every spare moment, he worked in the back of his shop with his musical ensemble. Known as "Butty" in the community, Francis led a well-known group comprised of flutes, clarinets, violins, guitars, guiro, and in later years a bombardon. He was a good-looking man of dark complexion, medium height, and beardless but sporting a heavy moustache which enhanced his fine appearance. It was a pleasure and a delight to dance to the music of Francis's group, which played remarkably well and was sought after by most everybody for dance purposes. Among the members were Francis himself on the flute or clarinet, Wilford Bazey on the violin, Isaac Lindo on the flute, Freddie Hoheb on guitar, Willy Sinclair with guiro, and Enrique Nathaniel on the bombardon, a military-styled, valved tuba. Nathaniel, a native of Santo Domingo, made his home in St. Thomas and had introduced the instrument to the local dancing public. I watched how Francis coordinated the flute players and the violins, the guitars, drums, and guiros (dried gourds played by scraping a piece of wire along their serrated surfaces.) By observing these rehearsals, I gained valuable insight into the intricacies of band leadership that was to serve me well later.[5]

Music being a powerful factor in community life, it seemed only natural that while working in Francis's shop, we all would sing the popular tunes of the day led by our master and would accompany ourselves with the rhythmic pounding of leather soles on laps. We were indeed a happy group of lads, but we went our separate ways after the death of Francis in his early thirties.[6] Thereafter I apprenticed myself to another master craftsman shoemaker, John McLean, who also served on the local police force. A tall, massively built man, McLean took considerable pride in his two-hundred-pound avoirdupois physique and his tremendous muscles which, when contracted, resembled heavy chunks of iron. The fact that he was invariably kind and courteous did not lessen the dread of incorrigible youth and wrongdoers whenever he was on patrol. Unlike my previous boss, McLean was not a musician. He was, however, extremely well read and showed great interest in me because of our common interest in books and literature. Frankly, I never relished the trade of shoemaking as a means of future livelihood. I went through the apprenticeship because it was mandatory for boys my age, and for no other reason. My real, all-consuming interest was music, and I was more and more inclined to make a career for myself in that field.

Through incessant practice and many new contacts with local musicians, my musical horizons were steadily expanding and my ambitions growing. A key episode in this development occurred the eventful day that McLean brought with him from Puerto Rico a large box which contained an assortment of tools for his shop. Among the paper wrappings was a music magazine, the *Etude*, published in Philadelphia, which McLean gave me. One of the most valuable gifts that I have ever received, this journal became the open sesame to my dreams and aspirations. It made me fully aware, for the first time, of the wondrous world of music outside our small community. I was overjoyed with its valuable suggestions and lessons, not to mention the amount of music contained within its pages—and all at so little cost. I quickly became a subscriber, not only to *The Etude* but also to several other musical publications, such as the *Metronome* of Carl Fischer, the *Musical Observer,* and the *Musical Courier,* in order to further my musical education. In the pages of these journals, I came to understand the higher purpose and mission of music as a civilizing agency, as well as a precise art form requiring many years of study and practice, struggle and sacrifice. And I realized that if I aspired to be a true musician, a man whose life was devoted to music in both its spiritual and practical manifestations, I had to dedicate myself to broadening my musical knowledge and education.[7]

Imbued with this sense of mission, I terminated my apprenticeship with McLean and found employment as a collector for a local bakery so as to acquire money to purchase the books, music, instruments, and other requirements essential to my musical education. Meanwhile, in the advertising pages of the *Etude*, I came across the name of Dr. Hugh A. Clarke, professor of music at the University of Pennsylvania, who offered instruction by mail in the science of harmony, counterpoint, and composition—subjects in which I badly needed instruction.[8] Recalling a fascinating article I had read by this same Dr. Clarke entitled "Enquiry into the Laws of the Beautiful in Music," I decided to enroll as his pupil in 1906. And he, after reviewing some of my compositions, agreed to become my teacher. This was the beginning of my formal musical education. A Canadian, Dr. Clarke was among the first musicians to hold a chair as professor of music in a leading university of the United States. He was a renowned organist, a composer of note, and the author of many influential textbooks on music and literature. Through correspondence courses, I studied with him for over three years, after which I received a diploma along with a special letter of commendation in 1910. In subsequent years I undertook other studies through correspondence from such places as the School of Musical Theory of Carnegie Hall in New York City (certificate in harmony, counterpoint, and composition; studies with Carl M. Vett [trained at the Academy of Fine Arts, Paris], 1914); the Royal Academy of Music in London; and the University Extension Conservatory of Music in Chicago, from which I was awarded the degree of Bachelor of Music in 1931.[9]

Not all of my experiences at the outset of my musical career were pleasurable. As my range of musical acquaintances and experiences expanded, I applied myself even more diligently to practice and study. It was a time of hard work and personal sacrifice. I have always been a taskmaster, striving for the best in myself as well as others. Many were the occasions that my father would awaken me in the morning at my study table, where I had fallen asleep from sheer exhaustion among my music sheets after hours and hours of intense work. It was thus I spent the better part of my adolescence. But it was clear to me then, as it is now, that those seriously aspiring to a musical career must devote themselves entirely to mastering their art, and that means theory as well as voice or instrumental performance. Practice makes perfect, and I have always, like the master craftsmen of old, striven for perfection. Even adversity, discouraging as it may be, teaches valuable lessons and sets one in directions that can alter one's life and outlook for the better. One such incident which particularly affected me about this time in my life had to do with the Donastorg family.

During my early years, the musical life of the Charlotte Amalie community was dominated, nay controlled, by the Donastorg family. This musical family consisted of four brothers who specialized as performers on violin, viola, cello, and flute. One of the brothers made music his profession as an instructor on the violin. The other brothers made their livelihood as a tailor, a goldsmith, and the manager of a grocery store. The goldsmith–flute player was a friend of mine. One day he caught me playing some trivial pieces of music on the guitar and, influenced no doubt by my youthfulness, thought the playing to be wonderful and thereby mistakenly referred me to his brother as a great performer. The fact was that I was merely a tyro on the instrument.

Surprisingly, one day I received an invitation to attend one of the family's usual Sunday afternoon recitals. Needless to say, I was impressed and happy and felt honored to attend what I believed was a sanctuary of musical brotherhood and achievement. I was, however, to receive my first lesson in coxcombery and discouragement. The audience comprised members of the family and a select group from the community. I sat eagerly awaiting the beginning of the recital which soon after began with the playing of a few dance numbers of the *habañera* type, which were greeted with expected applause. At the conclusion of these numbers, the maestro, pointing to a guitar nearby, abruptly told me to accompany him. Seizing his violin, he swiftly ran over several difficult passages taken from a music book which, I learned afterwards, contained studies for the violin by Alard, the great violin instructor. Having barely an elementary knowledge of the guitar, I was unable even to attempt to accompany him in his musical gymnastics. Noting my embarrassment and apparently wanting to display his greatness and importance in front of his invited guests at my expense, he turned to his flutist brother and remarked admonishingly, "You told me this fellow can play the guitar. He doesn't even know how to hold the instrument properly," and with a proud attitude and satisfied feeling that he had erased me completely from his list of worthy aspirants to musical fame, continued the recital.[10]

With an indescribable feeling of humiliation and discouragement I left the room unobserved. Coming out into the market square, I stood dejectedly, tears running down my cheeks, not only because of the insult I had just received but also because of the discouragement I felt. I was thoroughly convinced that music was not for me and I might as well accept the fact. I walked home hopeless, discouraged, and in a haze. My father was seated in a rocking chair on my arrival and after some moments of silence inquired about the result of my visit in a manner that suggested he expected it to go in a minor key, but not as dissonant as it actually turned out. When I told him of the ordeal I went through and my decision to quit as a result, his manner changed completely. Angered beyond words and with eyes seemingly darting fire, he blurted out in a stern voice, "Don't mind that man. He is a damned jackass. It is he who doesn't know how to tune his violin. Go on with your studies, if just to show him what a conceited and stupid ass he is." I always believed in my father. He was my idol whose judgment I trusted and whose advice I always heeded. His tense manner, coupled with his admonition, crude as the words might have been, had the desired effect. I emerged from my haze a new lad—a different person not only with the courage, eagerness, and determination to pursue my musical studies but also with a strong desire to get even with the coxcomb someday.

However, as time wore on and I grew to understand more of human nature with its different motivations and manners of behavior, I learned a valuable lesson that was to guide me through life. Instead of bitterness and the idea of getting even, out of the experience at the Donastorgs there emerged a burning desire and a firm determination never to turn a deaf ear or refuse help to anyone who, like me, lacking the wherewithal to sustain his trek through life, or without a father like mine to set him on the true course with proper guidance and inspiration, might fall along the wayside hopeless, helpless, lost. Throughout my youth and ever after, I have kept in mind the words of a writer, whose name I do not now remember: that the divine creator of energy did not make us all of one mold, but gave us all one power, namely, to aid the other man in his quest to find the power and beauty of his life. The Donastorg incident engendered in me a commitment to do everything in my power to assist and educate the youth in their musical and other studies, which even to this day has been one of the driving forces of my life. With the advice of my father and the encouragement of a growing circle of friends, I managed to overcome the traumatic impact of the Donastorg incident and to apply myself with renewed vigor to my musical studies. Fortunately about this time I came into contact with one of the seminal influences in my early musical and cultural career, Elphege Sebastien.

ELPHEGE SEBASTIEN

Following the death of my mother in her forty-sixth year, my father, brother, and myself moved to a new house in the Savan area of Charlotte Amalie. Our new home stood abreast a large two-story building named Dilly Hall owned by Elphege Sebastien, who lived in part of the building and leased the other part as a dance hall. A close friendship quickly developed between the older man and myself after Sebastien commented favorably on my flute playing. A man of considerable musical and literary ability, Sebastien was then employed as chief pharmacist at the St. Thomas Apothecary Hall, a well-known local establishment owned and operated by A. H. Riise. Sebastien, a true Renaissance man, was knowledgeable in botany, literature, local shells, sports, and medicine as well as music. He was an outstanding clarinet player and performed with several musical groups, including one under the direction of the Danish bandmaster Lars Sorensen and a local orchestra led by the Dominican composer Julio Acosta.

Sebastien, born August 2, 1873, in St, Thomas, received his elementary education under private tutelage. On May 1, 1893, he joined Riise's as a clerk, but his intelligence and interest in the pharmaceutical arts led his employer to sponsor his studies in the field of chemistry, and in September 1902 he passed the required Danish examination in pharmaceutical chemistry under the Danish doctor of medicine Kalmar of St. Croix, assisted by apothecary Paludan Muller and pharmacist Cramer Petersen. Sebastien soon became chief chemist at Riise's and was largely responsible for the fine reputation of that organization in the first half of the twentieth century. In these days of my youth, drugs had to be compounded from local bushes, plants, and herbs, as well as the most recently discovered chemical compounds. It was the age of asafetida, children's powder, and, for external use, mustard plasters, cupping, Spanish fly, and even leeches for bloodletting. Although thoroughly conversant with the most recent drugs, Sebastien also appreciated the medicinal qualities of local folk remedies and was not averse to using them whenever required. It should be mentioned that today physicians do not so easily frown upon those early folk remedies, but now seek to learn as much as possible about their properties and uses. The father of the medical profession, Hippocrates himself, stated that one should not abhor asking the simple folk, even the alleged quacks, whether something is useful as a remedy. Despite his great service to the community as a pharmacist, what particularly drew me to this gentle, highly decent man was his enormous personal library of books and journals and, more important, his musical talent. I loved browsing through his library, listening to his melodious clarinet playing, and participating in many stimulating conversations on music, literature, history, and current affairs.

Sebastien was a deep student not only of his profession but also of science in general. He was a lifelong subscriber to *Scientific American.* He chose botany as an avocation. He was an ardent lover of sports, especially boxing, and sponsored many boxing matches in the community. According to many continentals of his day, if you wanted to know everything about the good old St. Croix rum, you must consult Elphege Sebastien, the man who knew more about rum than any other person in the Virgin Islands. The old St. Croix rum, it will be remembered, has always been manufactured by the firm of A. H. Riise at St. Thomas. Sebastien was honesty personified. He was one of the trustees of the now defunct St. Thomas Savings Bank and for many years filled the offices of secretary and treasurer of that institution. He was also the last remaining link of the "Les Cœurs Sincères" Ancient Free and Accepted Masons (AFAM) Lodge in St. Thomas. He died in 1940 after succumbing to a brief illness of four days on November 19. His life stands out to all our young men and women as an example of intelligence, thrift, persistence, and unflinching determination.[11]

Sebastien not only encouraged me in the pursuit of my musical career but also introduced me to many other fine musicians in the community. Among these new acquaintances were Hubert Lanclos, an accountant at Riise's whose skill on the flute was renowned throughout the community; Daniel de Windt, an excellent pianist; Alberto de Lagarde, a pianist, clarinet player, and composer; and Leonardo Lafranque, a superb guitar and mandolin player whose sparkling conversation and vivacious good humor always enlivened our musical gatherings.[12] Of these excellent musicians, each of them many years my elder, Hubert Lanclos particularly attracted and influenced me. His expertise on the flute stimulated my knowledge and love of the instrument. Many fine evenings and Sunday afternoons were spent at his home, which was graced by his angelic wife and lovely children, playing duets from the works of Tulou, Drouet, and other masters of the flute. These sessions would periodically be graced with voice and piano accompaniment by his two daughters. Hubert Lanclos was a gentleman in the fullest sense of the word, and the time I spent in his home was memorable because of the togetherness, hospitality, and inspiring setting.

Other musicians with whom I came into contact through Sebastien were A. Cherubin, a cornet player who was one of the many Haitian political refugees who sought asylum in St. Thomas; the Jamaican George Reed, who once played clarinet with the famous West India Regiment Band; Enrique Nathaniel from Santo Domingo, who played the baritone or bombardon; and one simply known as George, also a native of Jamaica, who played the tuba. Each of these men introduced me to the musical heritage of his native land, and his presence, like those of so many others, did much to enrich the musical culture of St. Thomas. Then there was old Wilford Bazey, one of the pivotal musical influences in our community. A fine-looking man with a small goatee, Bazey was a superior violinist. He taught violin to many of our musicians, and it was he who introduced the local population to European dances and music.

Sebastien, Cherubin, Bazey, Lafranque, and a few others, including myself, formed a small mixed orchestral group, with clarinet, cornet, guitar, violin, flute, and other instruments, to play at private homes and gatherings. Additionally, people would often invite our cosmopolitan group to their homes in order to have the opportunity to play along with it. In this way I came into even greater contact with many superb musicians whose encouragement and techniques exercised a considerable influence on my own development. One such influence was Enrique "Coco" Delerme, one of the most brilliant flutists of Puerto Rico. Coco and his brother Antoine, a guitarist, lived on Vieques Island and frequently vacationed on St. Thomas, where they stayed at the home of Mrs. Edith Schon. Mrs. Schon, who knew Sebastien, would often request our group to participate in musical concerts at her house, and it was through these experiences that I gained a foundation in Afro-Spanish musical traditions. Coco, for whom my admiration knew no bounds, gave me considerable encouragement and advice on many, many occasions.

As our musical group grew in size and experience, Sebastien decided that it should be formally organized into a band in 1907.[13] This was the origin of the first local "Native Brass Band," later the Municipal Band, which has for so long been associated with the name of Lionel Roberts.[14] Sebastien's association with Riise's precluded his direct involvement with the new band, since Mr. Riise, like so many other merchants and shopkeepers of the period, held that it was beneath the dignity of any of *his* employees to publicly associate with a local band that would play professionally, that is, for money. Thus, although Sebastien helped organize and equip the Brass Band from behind the scenes, he asked Lionel Roberts—a well-known local sports figure—to assume the role of bandmaster.

Roberts was a popular figure, and like most of the other musicians, I welcomed his leadership, less because of his musical abilities than because of his prowess as a sportsman and cricketer.[15] A forceful man, Roberts quickly established his personal imprint on the embryonic band. He brought in several new musicians and became so domineering that he alienated many of the original players, who had seen the new organization as an opportunity to play music. Eventually Sebastien and Roberts quarreled violently over the management of the band's money, and as a consequence Sebastien, joined by most of the original bandsmen who were his friends, left the band. I found myself in a difficult position. On the one hand, I felt bound by ties of friendship and loyalty to Sebastien. On the other hand, I was too young to fully appreciate the nature of the dispute between Roberts and Sebastien, and I desperately wanted to be part of the only native band on the island. Hence, I elected to stay on. At first it seemed a good decision, for although Roberts never fully accepted me, he nevertheless respected my musical abilities and came to rely upon me for assistance in training the band. Eventually, however, I too became disenchanted with Roberts's methods and style of leadership.[16]

My rupture with Roberts came about in the following manner. My studies with Dr. Clarke had led me to try my hand in writing musical compositions, several of which met with Dr. Clarke's enthusiastic approval. Naturally I cherished a keen desire to hear one of my pieces played by the band of which I was a member. So it was that I arrived at one rehearsal with a band composition upon which I had lavished a considerable amount of time and effort. With my heart eagerly thumping, I asked Roberts if he would have the band run over the piece so that I could hear how it sounded. Making no effort to conceal his displeasure with my request, the leader snatched the music from me and tossed it on a nearby seat where it remained unused throughout the rehearsal. As can well be imagined, I was deeply stung by the bandmaster's callous indifference to my musical endeavors, and soon after I quit his band.[17] This discouraging episode, like the Donastorg incident, did not dampen my spirit, but had the reverse effect of stimulating my aspirations and determination; for at once I resolved to organize a band in which I could hear my own compositions played and in which every encouragement would be given to youthful talent and creativity. My break with Roberts thus led directly to the birth of the Adams Juvenile Band, which later became the U.S. Navy Band of the Virgin Islands.[18]

Another important consideration lay behind my decision and had to do with my own evolving notion about what the precise role of the bandmaster should be. For some time I had been thoroughly dissatisfied with the nonprofessional quality of the leadership of the Municipal Band. The leader and I looked at music in general and the band in particular from different angles. I viewed it from a strictly professional angle, while to him it was just one part of his daily activities. The qualifications I held to be necessary for effective band leadership were:

1. an innate musical ability,
2. a long period of broad and intelligent music study,
3. an attractive and forceful personality with a sense of humor,
4. a creative imagination,
5. a magnetic leadership and organizing ability, and
6. an ability to be an understanding taskmaster.

A bandmaster must have confidence in his general ability and in his knowledge of the music he handles. He not only must know, but also must know that he knows. In other words, a leader not only must know music, but must also have confidence in his ear, in his rhythmic precision, in his tastes, in his judgment of tempo, and, most of all, in his musical scholarship. Moreover, the bandmaster needs to be more than a leader; he must be a teacher as well. He has to be personally conversant with each of the band's instruments, so that he can help his players improve as well as train aspiring musicians to become band members. A bandmaster must, in short, be a dedicated, knowledgeable, skillful, professional musician—not a dilettante. These are the qualifications I strove to attain in my years of study and which I carried to the Adams Juvenile Band. What had been done before by others, though commendable, did not aspire to this level of professionalism. There is a German proverb suggesting that when one has climbed the highest mountain peak, heaven is not so much nearer, but one's vision is broader. This notion strengthened my conviction to live beyond my limited horizon.

It was toward this broader vision of musicianship that I elected to carry with me the youth I selected from the schools, churches, and homes of the Virgin Islands community.[19] And although I possessed the will and determination to make this dream a reality, I did not have the money to make it possible. A start, however, was necessary. From my meager earnings, I put aside the sum of ninety dollars, rented a room adjacent to my home at two dollars a month, bought some kerosene lamps, and nailed up some wood for seats. The lads, like myself, were poor and therefore had no money to pay for instruction, and I was too proud to beg. My band would be independent and make its own way. Remembering the lessons of my first teacher, Jean Pierre, I began teaching as he had taught me with singing scales—in short, with *solfeggio*—followed by rhythm instruction.[20] I devised these drills myself, following the Tonic Sol-Fa system of England's John Curwen, but substituting letters with figures. Instead of "tra fa ti fi," we recited "one it is ah."[21] Together with my brother, Julien, whom I had taught for several years and who was to become one of the best euphonium players to be found anywhere, I began to lay the foundations of a disciplined, quality band.

It was at this crucial moment, when all I could contribute was the will to do and the ambition to achieve, that Elphege Sebastien came of his own will to our rescue. I will repeat his words, as they meant much to me: "I cannot see you struggle so earnestly in such commendable work without offering you whatever assistance that lies in my power. If you will allow me, I want to offer you the free use of my house for your rehearsals. I spoke today with a merchant of this city concerning the possibility of supplying you with musical instruments for which I have promised to stand responsible." Looking at me squarely in the face, he continued: "I do this because I know you will succeed, as I have for some time been watching you studying into the wee hours of the morning, unaided, alone, in order to be efficient." And reading my thoughts, he went on, "Do not think of the money. Pay me how you like, when you like, and if you like, but count me as your friend and believe that I will do anything that lies in my power to help you."[22]

Only those of us who have experienced such friendship and such affection of the human heart as depicted above can readily, in these days of hard, cold commercialism in which gold, selfishness, and ingratitude are common ingredients, sympathize with the opening lines in Emerson's essay on friendship, which reads:

> We have a deal more kindness than is ever spoken. Maugre all the selfishness that chills like east winds the world, the whole human family is bathed with an element of love like a fine ether. How many persons we meet in houses, whom we scarcely speak to, whom yet we honor, and who honor us! How many we see in the street, or sit with in the church, whom, though silently, we warmly rejoice to be with! Read the language of these wondering eye-beams. The heart knoweth.[23]

The inspirational advice, acts of sympathy, and kind words of encouragement which I received from Sebastien in many moments of dark discouragement have been of incalculable benefit, and I appreciate them the more when I consider the unselfishness of spirit which characterized them.

Through the local firm of E. Delerme, Sebastien ordered eighteen instruments from the Kessels Musical Instrument Factory in Holland, the cost of which was around $500.00. In those days the price of a cornet or trumpet was about $5.00 and a bass horn about $20.00. The silvering cost more than the instrument itself. To us the instruments were like manna from on high. We started to work with enthusiasm. Sebastien and some members of his band frequently came to hear us practice and gave us professional advice. A doctor off the Danish ship *Ingolf* taught us how to walk and march.[24] After eight months of hard, steady practice, we gave our first concert on February 27, 1911.[25] A local reviewer gave us encouragement:

> Adams Juvenile Band made its first public appearance last evening in All Saints Parish Hall which was crowded with listeners. The band, numbering 18, is comprised mostly of boys and lads with brass instruments, and acquitted itself in a manner that won the admiration and deserving praise of all. Before beginning the program the Bandmaster Mr. Alton Adams asked the audience to overlook the defects and not to expect too much from the boys who had only been training for 8 months. Well, we can only say, from the execution of the pieces that followed—especially the ouverture—that the audience got far more than they expected, and if the result of a few months has been so satisfactory and showed such progress and promise, as time goes on the improvement should develop the youths into very proficient players. We compliment both the director and his pupils on the fine entertainment, and hope they will remain united and continue their leisure hours in a pleasant and profitable study.
>
> Although the bandmaster is well known to all, the public may not be aware of his competency in music for which he received in June a Certificate in Harmony, Counterpoint and Composition from H. A. Clarke, Doctor of Music at the University of Pennsylvania, with which Institute he took lessons by correspondence. Among his compositions is the "Ingolf March," the score of which he submitted to the Professor who returned it with the remarks "Good—no corrections" and complimenting him upon his capacity for arranging band music.[26]

I made it quite clear from the beginning to all my aspiring bandsmen what I expected from them and the band: that the band room was to serve also as a music school in which strict discipline and proper behavior would be upheld and enforced. With discipline, wonders can be accomplished; without it, nothing. Hence the success of the band would be in direct proportion to the discipline maintained. The band room was to be kept clean and the general atmosphere free of foul language. In short, it would be a place in which proper behavior was maintained to such a degree that one might enter at anytime without being embarrassed. Pupils were to be instructed not only in proper playing of their instruments but also in the meaning of the music they performed and, if possible, in knowledge of the lives of the composers. The aim was to stimulate the pupils' interest in the music they performed. Instrumental instruction included correct breathing habits coming from the diaphragm (commonly called belly breathing), correct articulation, and proper body poise. Instruction books on the different instruments were supplied, and the blackboard served as an important tool for lessons. The progress of each pupil, as well as the band itself, was to be appraised at the end of each month from a calculated timetable of eight months, at the end of which the band would be expected, everything else being well, to make its first public appearance.

"A stream rises no higher than its source"; so runs the old principle of physics. Thus, the band can become just as fine as its leader's ideal of what is possible. In his role as taskmaster, the leader from the very beginning should be extremely careful not to destroy by unduly harsh measures and unnecessary criticisms the essential qualities of respect and confidence he seeks to instill in his pupils. On the other hand, experience teaches that pupils will complain little when they are made to toe the mark, but secretly admire the teacher who gets something done when properly inspired. Pupils will take advantage of any teacher who allows them to do as they please. The main objective therefore of the teacher or leader is to inspire in his pupils the feeling that the thing being done is a vital one, a big thing, crucial to the life of the community and done with a real love in their heart for the work. This aim, which includes a proper method toward the desired achievement, was what inspired the young juveniles in the band to reach their initial goal. Their concert proved to be so successful in securing community interest and involvement that lads of different ages sought membership in the group. The rapid musical progress and high deportment of the band during the next few years won it the admiration of the general public, and the band quickly grew to be a factor in the life of the community—not only of St. Thomas but also of our sister island St. Croix. Our influence extended even to the British Virgin Islands.

The Juvenile Band attained that position mainly by virtue of the eager interest it took in the life and general welfare of the community. It gave freely of its services to programs for the children's home and the elders of the community—in fact, to every worthy cause in which it could be of help. Naturally, we encountered the slings and arrows of disappointed ones and peewee political figures. But these complaints were insignificant when compared with the overwhelming support of the community. Gifts of instruments, music, and even offers to pay tuition for any pupil I selected were soon forthcoming. My service was given freely to my young student musicians, and I felt better having it that way. Many men and women came forward voluntarily with offers of assistance. Among them were Christopher Payne, U.S. consul to the Virgin Islands; bank director Axel Holst of the Danish National Bank, who was also a literary man and a splendid player on the violin; the merchants Antonio deLugo, Thomas Graham, Henry Hassell, Mardenborough, Valdemar Miller, Eduardo Moron, J. H. Souffront, Eliot Thomas, and J. P. Thorsen; jewelers Conrad Corneiro, Freddie Steele, and Theodore Vialet; Dr. Knud-Hansen and Adolph Sixto; editors John N. Lightbourn and Leroy Nolte of the newspapers *Mail Notes* and the *Bulletin*; tonsorialists Theodore Estornel and Charles Perkins; composers and organists Hans Behagen, Arturo Giglioli, Auguste I. Leon, and Felix Padilla; Waldemar Riise, owner of Apothecary Hall; and the Reverend Father van den Bemden of the Roman Catholic Church. It was encouraging to receive moral support not only from those of affluence among the leaders and merchants but also from the poorer elements of the community. We seldom played for money. The volunteer services given by the band included performances for schools and churches, holiday parades, and public concerts in the Emancipation Garden and at the hospital. Accompanying silent motion pictures, which were first introduced here by Elphege Sebastien, and for which we played regularly, provided the means of the band's sustenance. Sometimes when we played concerts at the Grand Hotel, we also received money. We needed income to buy and repair instruments and to pay the debt we owed our benefactor.

During this time, Carnival came to life in the Virgin Islands at a meeting held in the Grand Hotel on the night of January 10, 1912. The idea was proposed by local businessman L. P. Aggerholm, a native of Denmark. A committee consisting of Aggerholm, George Levi, Gustave Ffrench, and Valdemar Miller was appointed. The first Carnival queen was Mrs. Cassilda Duurloo and the king was Valdemar Miller. The pages for that Carnival were Louis Barentzen and a future governor of the Virgin Islands, Ralph M. Paiewonsky. After a lapse of many years, Carnival was revived as an annual event in 1952 by Ron de Lugo, then an announcer at radio station WSTA. The revived celebration became more elaborate and colorful and, instead of being an occasion for a particular group of people on a particular day, it became a celebration of the entire community. It extended to practically a week of fun and merriment, with persons also taking part in St. John, St. Croix, and the British West Indies. The spirit of Carnival is today embodied in the Virgin Islands Mocko Jumbie stilt dancers, to which is added the calypso singers and steel bands, originally from the British West Indies.[27]

Several prominent Crucians first heard the band play while visiting St. Thomas, among them Dr. D. C. Canegata, Kenneth Henderson, D. Hamilton Jackson, and Gustave Lange. These men formed a committee for the purpose of inviting the band to St. Croix to play a series of concerts, including performances in its two largest towns, Christiansted and Frederiksted. Previous to the band's visit, I was invited by the Nielsen brothers (Eric, who played violin, and Harry, piano, both of whom had studied abroad) to appear at the St. John School in Frederiksted in a recital given for charity. My reputation as a flute player had preceded me there. When I told Sebastien of the invitation, he was elated and especially so when I told him that I was also to give a brief history on the life of Franz Schubert. There and then, he insisted that I must appear in coattails. I was astounded at the idea and, to get out of it, told him that I did not possess such apparel. Not to be outmaneuvered, he insisted that I use *his* pair. The question of apparel settled, I consented. The recital was at the request of Mrs. Rosa Hageman, formerly Benjamin, who headed the elite social life of Frederiksted. Mrs. Hageman was a strikingly beautiful woman—rich, well educated, and humane, by which I mean that she took leadership in the welfare of the community, especially the poor. The program proved a success, and my talk on the life of Schubert received a stunning ovation. But no one knew the suffering I was undergoing the entire evening in Sebastien's coat: how, despite my calm demeanor, perspiration was running down my entire body. I felt miserable. It was hot and the crowded room did not help matters. During my talk on Schubert, especially on his sufferings, no one suspected my own distress. But for this, it was a delightful evening, capped by a gala reception given at the spacious mansion of the Hagemans. It was one of those evenings of the long ago when people met happily for social enjoyment regardless of race, color, nationality, or religious persuasion.

The appearance later of the band in St. Croix added greatly to the morale of the Juveniles. The band was met at the landing wharf in Christiansted by D. Hamilton Jackson, Kenneth Hendersen, Gustave Lange, and an enthusiastic crowd, which seemed to comprise all the inhabitants of the island. We serenaded His Excellency Governor Lars Christian Helweg-Larsen at the Government House, followed this with another serenade at Dr. D. C. Canegata's residence, and thereafter paraded through streets lined with an immense crowd of onlookers who waved, clapped their hands, and shouted words of welcome as the band marched by. Our audiences were estimated at 1,000 to 1,200 people. The Juveniles had won the hearts of the good people of St. Croix and guaranteed a feeling of good will which lasted throughout the life of the band.

Thereafter I visited St. Croix on several other occasions. I was pleased to learn that Crucians were as appreciative of good music as St. Thomians. I remember, for example, visiting several bands on St. Croix to offer advice and encouragement. Not long after one such engagement with the Christiansted Industrial Brass Band, a "Card of Appreciation" appeared in the Cruzan newspaper, the *St. Croix Avis:*

> In the name of the Christiansted Industrial Brass Band we take this medium of expressing our heartfelt gratitude to Bandmaster Alton A. Adams of St. Thomas for his valuable assistance, instructions, and advice given us during his (unfortunately too short) stay on this island. His words of advice and encouragement, have acted on us like a tonic, putting new life and vigor, and his instructions we are fully assured, have put us further on the right road to success. Whether in the band room or on the streets, this modest and unassuming Bandmaster was always found to be appreciable by all of us, and ever ready with some words of encouragement along with his instructions.
>
> We again tender our thanks, and wish for Bandmaster Adams and the Juvenile Band every success; and can assure him that, his personality, ability, and kindness, have won for him as true and loving friends of those of his own island home.
> Committee
> Christiansted Industrial Brass Band
> 1914

On another occasion, the Juvenile Band gave a concert in Frederiksted, during which I played two flute solos by Fred Lax. Afterwards a well-groomed young man, owner of a visiting yacht in the harbor, approached me to offer his congratulations for what he called my "wonderful rendition" of the two solos by Lax, whom he said he knew quite well. On his return, he planned to inform the composer about the playing of his two compositions in what he referred to as a "faraway Danish West Indian island." Frankly, I had quite forgotten the incident when, after a lapse of several months, I received the following letter:

1903 Edmondson Avenue
Baltimore, Maryland

August 11, 1915

Dear Mr. Adams:

Have mailed under this cover, Flute Solo, "Fantasia," "Satanella" (Opera-Balfe) for Flute Solo. You will find it a very "thankful" solo to play. "Pretty" and "moderately easy" and "brilliant." I have written this piece for you, and hope you will like it.

A scholar of mine, Professor A. Soho of Baltimore City College and Peabody Institute, heard you play "Ben Bolt" and the "Mocking Bird" and gave you splendid encomiums. Write me at once, of acceptance of dedication, and your opinion of Solo, and oblige yours,

Fred Lax

My visit to St. Croix and the visit of Professor Soho at the same time was a happy coincidence. It happened that most of my studies for the instrument were through the popular Flute Method written by Lax, who at that time was one of the leading flute players in the world, flute soloist with the famous Patrick S. Gilmore Band, and one of the soloists with the traveling Boston Symphony Orchestra Ensemble.[28] With the aid of the Juvenile Band and a galaxy of leading musicians on the island, a special concert was arranged at the Grand Hotel on the night of June 7, 1916, particularly to premiere the number dedicated to me. The solo was accompanied on the piano by Teddy Jensen, an outstanding local artist. The audience filled the hall. What added to the occasion was the receipt of a postcard next day from Hubert Lanclos, whose flute playing had enraptured me and inspired my early efforts as a student on the instrument. On the postcard was written these words:

This is to congratulate you on the successful rendering last night at the "Grand" of the charming Flute Merceau, "Satanella" by Lax. On the first hearing I was charmed with his brilliant passages so smoothly and pleasingly executed by you on your system Boehm. Wishing you continued success in your musical career.

Yours sincerely,

H. Lanclos

St. Thomas, June 8, 1916

St. Croix has always been like a second home to me. During the course of my career, I spent many happy moments on this largest of the Virgin

Islands and made many lasting friends. Among these I might mention D. Hamilton Jackson, Dr. D. C. Canegata, and Gustave Lange; the Alexanders, Armstrongs, Beattys, Boughs, Browns, Brows, Chaberts, Christensens, Clendinens, Fabios, Flemings, Forbes, Frorups, Goldens, Greenaways, Higgins, Hills, Leaders, Markoes, Merwins, Mottas, Ovesons, Penthenys, Petersens, Rosses, Schjangs, Schneiders, Skeochs; and Postmaster Rene Larson. St. Croix's most colorful characters included "Bengie," who paused at nearly every corner to speak to no one in particular, paper money bills pinned on his shirt, most of which I understood went to feed the crabs found around his house; also "Mr. Jackass," who stopped every now and then, spinning around before and after each stop he made; and, not to be forgotten, "Lil' Man," the self-appointed bearer and carrier of luggage and parcels on his hand truck. These characters completed the motley crowd of the good happy people of the St. Croix of long ago.

The hurricane of October 6, 1916, proved in great measure disastrous to the band and particularly to Mr. Sebastien. The storm blew his house—which was also our band room—to the ground. Mr. Sebastien lost his all: his home, his excellent library, and many things that he held most dear which could never be replaced. During a lull in the hurricane, a little before the second terrific onslaught came, he and I were among the ruins in the pitch darkness with a hurricane lamp, trying to see what could be saved. Before us lay the ruins. Scattered all around us and under us were the leaves of his priceless volumes; large collections of scattered leaves of plants of the island, the result of his botanical researches; his furniture and pictures; and our band instruments twisted forever out of shape. Unmindful of all these things, he was eagerly searching for something which he considered himself most fortunate to find—a gold ring of his dead mother. The Juvenile Band lost eighteen instruments, its entire music library, and its rehearsal room. Even in his distress this friend showed deep love for the organization as he would not be argued out of his belief that he should contribute half of the house rent which we were now forced to pay. And all this was done unbeknownst to the community at large.[29] Few knew the real extent of the support Sebastien gave to the band.

Despite this traumatic setback, forming the Juvenile Band had had the effect of stimulating my own personal musical endeavors and creativity. With enthusiasm I applied myself to learning how to play each of the various instruments so that I could better instruct my bandsmen. And I devoted long hours to composing musical scores, some of them specifically designed for the band. My first serious composition, "Ingolf March," was written in 1910. Previously I had written a few pieces, but they did not quite satisfy me. The "Ingolf March" was written for Bandmaster Koefford of the Danish training ship the *Ingolf*, which was visiting St. Thomas.[30] Koefford came to hear the Juvenile Band practice at Dilly's Hall and stayed to offer us professional advice and encouragement. In gratitude, I wrote the march, which we played for him on a subsequent visit. Interestingly, Prince Axel of Denmark, who was serving as a cadet on the *Ingolf*, heard about the composition and invited me aboard for lunch. Over our meal we chatted amiably about music and later played several duets together. At the end of this memorable day, the prince gave me his card and asked me to visit him whenever I came to Copenhagen.[31]

Encouraged by this experience and the support of many music-minded individuals in the community, I wrote several other compositions, among them "Sweet Dream of Love," a suite of waltzes for piano. Cyril Daniel commissioned it for his then sweetheart,[32] and the composition was later published in 1912 by the firm of Burt M. Cutler in Columbus, Ohio, under a French title, "Doux rêve d'amour: Valse pour piano." About this time also, I became interested in musical acoustics, especially in respect to the band and band music. One day while sitting with some friends, I came across an advertisement in the well-known musical periodical the *Jacobs' Band Monthly* soliciting theoretical articles on the role of the band as a musical entity. Now, it had been my growing conviction that the band as a musical group had achieved a degree of maturity that enabled it to be considered as distinct from the orchestra. The time had come, I believed, for the military band to be treated by composers and arrangers as such, and not as the step-brother of the orchestra. For example, the clarinet section of the band should not be treated like an orchestral violin section, for the simple and obvious reason that two different instruments are involved. Accordingly, the modern military band required its own musical compositions suited to its unique demands, with arrangements written specifically for its instruments and its purpose. Music should be written specifically for band, rather than limiting it to a repertory of orchestral adaptations.

Inspired by these theories, which were rather novel in their day, I submitted an article to the *Jacobs' Monthly*, although I never seriously expected to hear anything more about it. Imagine my surprise when a few months later, I received a reply from the editor not only informing me that my article had been accepted for publication but also asking me to serve as editor for the magazine's band column.[33] This, indeed, was an honor, for the *Jacobs' Monthly* was the leading journal in its field on this side of the Atlantic. I eagerly accepted the offer, or I should say, the challenge, for I recognized with some trepidation that my monthly contribution not only would afford me an unparalleled opportunity to develop my theories before a highly sophisticated audience but also would most likely bring me into contact with many of the leading musicians of my time. I was not mistaken in either of these assumptions. And although my articles tended sometimes to provoke criticism and controversy, I found to my delight that they were warmly endorsed by many of the greatest bandsmen of the period, including Hale A. Vandercook, Herbert L. Clarke, Frank R. Seltzer, and the inimitable March King himself, John Philip Sousa, all of whom wrote me encouraging letters of praise.[34]

I especially treasured Sousa's endorsement, since he, above all others, was my particular idol and inspiration. This man, who for more than thirty years had dominated the world of band and martial music, appeared to me the epitome of all that was worthwhile in musical endeavor and achievement. The rousing Sousa marches, vibrant with their compelling rhythms, seemed the popular expression and embodiment in musical form of the spirit of America itself. They also reflected the strong rhythmic influence and syncopation of Afro-American musical traditions—a quality that Sousa himself admitted was a characteristic feature of his compositions—and this quality, as much as anything else, drew me personally to Sousa's music.[35]

How well I still recall the many hours which my friend Felix Padilla and I spent in rhapsodic ecstasy listening outside the residence of Mr. Alfred Mewton, a kindred spirit who was playing Sousa marches on his phonograph player.[36] At that time, those sporadic phonograph concerts were not mere musical treats to me. They were like manna from on high, feeding a hungry, searching musical soul. So indelibly stamped are those impressions that even today I can easily bring to mind the journey homeward, my feet on the ground, head in the stars, lifted as it were on wings of ecstasy— the beautiful music, the wonderful impeccable rendition, and the interpretation having so completely filled my mind and soul and body. After each of these musical experiences, stretched on my bed, I would imaginatively conduct Sousa's band in one of my own compositions. I was happily building castles in my little dreamworld. Later, however, these dreams and aspirations left their winged ethereal abode and developed into definite action. Assiduously I would put into full band and orchestral score the immortal "Stars and Stripes Forever," "El Capitán," "King Cotton," "Manhattan Beach," "Right Forward," "Semper Fidelis," and others of Sousa's compositions so well known throughout the musical world. In this way, I would clearly analyze and study their content, harmonic progressions, and instrumental arrangements and those original patterns of bass movements so characteristic of their unique style. That is how my own compositional endeavors began. For many months, each night until the wee hours of the morning, that was my musical menu. This experience was imperatively necessary because of my never having experienced the benefits of musical tutorship and guidance. Had anyone told me at that time that in the years to come I would have been privileged to come directly into contact with this famous man, I would have considered such a forecast extravagant, presumptuous, and highly improbable, if not utterly impossible.

Thus, on the eve of the U.S. entrance into World War I, my fondest dreams and aspirations seemed to have been realized. As far as was humanly possible in the Danish West Indies, I had established myself as a professional musician. I taught music to myself, my bandsmen, and to other pupils. My musical compositions had begun to gain recognition and acceptance not only in our small community but also in the United States and elsewhere. I contributed monthly articles to a highly respected musical magazine, and this in turn had brought me into contact with many of the greatest figures in my field of endeavor. My band was steadily improving and gaining a local as well as a regional reputation. My world, my horizons, had widened enormously. Despite my geographical location on a small rock in the middle of the Caribbean Sea, I felt that I was part of the mainstream of international musical developments. At the same time, I was emerging from my island home and opening my arms and mind to embrace the world. Yet that world, that Western civilization which I loved and revered, was careening toward a dreadful holocaust. World War I would profoundly transform the lives and destinies of everyone on our planet, not least of all those of us who lived in the Danish West Indies.

5   The United States Navy Band of the Virgin Islands (1917–1923)

Editor's Note: *Adams offers a firsthand account of the desperate economic and social situation on the Virgin Islands prior to their transfer from Denmark to the United States, setting the stage for his argument about the navy's positive contributions. Following the disruption of shipping caused by World War I and 1916's devastating category 2 hurricane, the islands' economy was in a shambles. Labor strikes on St. Croix and St. Thomas fanned class tensions as well. So the United States and its naval administrators inherited a territory with few prospects and many problems, including an underdeveloped infrastructure (roads, sanitation), poor health care, and a failing and underfunded educational system. Adams details his friendship with D. Hamilton Jackson, a pioneering union leader in St. Croix who published the islands' first pro-labor newspaper, in which Adams began his journalistic career. The story of the United States Navy Band of the Virgin Islands follows—its inception, expanding activities, and social initiatives. This band served as a bridge between the navy and native Virgin Islanders, between white and black. The band's public concerts, educational outreach, unique local newspaper, and tours contributed to the development of both the islands' community identity and their tourist industry. Adams's own success underscores the values of education and ambition set forth in earlier chapters. He is an exemplar of a self-made man who took full advantage of shifting circumstance to realize what many thought impossible—a vibrant musical career in a location once considered lacking in opportunity. By working with the navy, Adams reached new heights of artistic performance and creativity. He helped found the public library, started the islands' music education program, and traveled to the States, meeting remarkable leaders in a number of fields.*

*The chapter ends with an essay on the importance of music in education
and community life.*

The wobbly economy of the Virgin Islands took a sharp plunge in 1914 with
the advent of World War I. Normal channels of trade and commerce were
permanently disrupted. People were thrown out of work, prices rose, and
there were scarcities of foodstuffs and other essentials. Particularly devastating to St. Thomas was the loss of the German-owned Hamburg-American
steamship line, which had been the economic mainstay of our mercantile
economy. Other shipping companies left as well, never to come back to the
trade within the islands. Denmark, with its West Indian Islands in the viselike grip of acute depression, once again turned to thoughts of divesting herself of these colonial liabilities. Previously—in 1867, 1892, and 1902—efforts
had been made to sell the islands to the United States, but they had
foundered at critical moments. The Treaty of 1867 failed when the U.S. Senate declined to ratify it. The 1902 treaty was aborted when the Danish Land-
sting (the upper house of the Rigsdag) refused its approval.

By 1916, however, both nations were eager to come to terms.[1] The Americans wanted the islands not so much for their own sake, but because their
acquisition would deny Germany a military and commercial base of operations in the region; the Danes could no longer afford the luxury of colonies
that did not pay for themselves. Another consideration behind Denmark's
decision to sell was the problem of preserving public order in the islands. St.
Croix, in particular, seethed with discontent as the native population
demanded long-overdue social and economic reforms. The wage paid to field
laborers at the time was a mere twenty cents a day—a day that comprised
twelve hours of arduous work under the hot tropical sun. Field workers,
many of whom had come from the British West Indies, lived desperate lives
on the razor edge of subsistence. Their living conditions, as I can attest from
personal observation, were deplorable, and their children died like flies from
malnutrition and lack of proper medical care. No welfare or charitable
establishments such as the Red Cross existed to help them with basic needs.
And the planters were generally indifferent to their plight.

In 1915 David Hamilton Jackson and a group of other socially conscious
natives organized the first labor union on St. Croix to fight for the rights of
oppressed workers.[2] With the help of Mistress Hjørt Lorentzen, a liberal-
minded Danish woman in Copenhagen, and local financial assistance, Jackson went to Denmark to plead the cause of the people. His appeal fell on
sympathetic ears among leaders of the then ruling Socialist Party, and he

returned to the islands with the right not only to unionize the field laborers but also to establish a newspaper, thus ending government press censorship. Jackson's *St. Croix Herald* became the first independent newspaper
in the history of the islands. Serving as the mouthpiece of the union, it
soon carried strident attacks on the plantocracy and championed the rights
of the laboring poor. Jackson used the *Herald* not only to advance the interest of the disadvantaged but also to educate his readers.

In January 1916 Jackson and the union called a general strike on St.
Croix. Thousands of workers laid down their tools and refused to work until
they received a wage increase as well as improvements in their working and
living conditions. Jackson and his followers held animated meetings and ral-
lies throughout St. Croix. The planters also organized themselves and, fearing for their lives and properties, prevailed upon the Danish authorities
(who were striving to maintain a neutral position) to send military rein-
forcements from St. Thomas. To the relief of everyone, Jackson maintained
effective control over the workers and there was no violence.

After nearly two months, the determination of the workers forced the
planters to agree to a settlement. Wages for first-class workers were
increased to thirty to thirty-five cents for a nine-hour working day, and
overtime of an additional four cents an hour was to be paid thereafter.[3]
Although a few previous privileges like free medical care (which was virtually nonexistent anyway) were lost; other concessions were also made by
the planters.[4] The strike was a great victory, not only because of the wage
increases but also because the nonviolent collective-bargaining process had
proven effective and the colonial government had not overtly sided with
the plantocracy. The victory of the Crucian workers inspired some 2,700
harbor workers and coal carriers in St. Thomas to unionize. Led by George
A. Moorehead, the union carried out a series of strikes in late 1916 that
culminated in a settlement with the Danish West India Company that
increased wages and improved working conditions.

Before these strikes started, I had formed a close personal friendship with
Jackson, one that was to last until his death on May 30, 1946. I first met him
on St. Croix in early 1914 on my way from Christiansted to Frederiksted
when I stopped by the Peter's Rest School, where he was principal. Jackson,
who was a devotee of fine music, had written to me praising an article I had
published in an American music journal and inviting me to visit him. I was
eager to meet him, for I had already heard he was a fine and honorable man
and a sage teacher. Like many other teachers of the time, Jackson had
received his professional education at the Teacher Training School in
Antigua. He once confided in me that he had really wanted to become a

minister, but was persuaded by his father, who was an educator, to pursue a career in education. Our first meeting went well, and we quickly found that we had much in common. As Jackson escorted me to my buggy following our conversation, he suddenly pointed to the laborers working in a nearby field and told me, in a voice trembling with emotion, that he had decided to resign his position as principal in order to devote his life to the welfare and betterment of his people, especially the deprived sugar plantation laborers. His was a decision that would alter the course of Virgin Islands history.[5]

During the next few months, Jackson and I became better acquainted. During my visits to St. Croix, he introduced me to the members of his literary club, with whom I spent many enjoyable hours discussing the great authors and musicians. To know Jackson is to know the two poems that affected him and which he often recited—Thomas Gray's "Elegy Written in a Country Churchyard" and Thomas Hood's "Song of the Shirt." Later Jackson wrote a very flattering newspaper article describing me as a beacon light to young West Indians and evidence against European claims that native Virgin Islanders were not intelligent or creative. I, in turn, came to admire the breadth of his knowledge, as well as his determination, which I shared, to educate the people and make them aware of the great artistic works of Western Civilization. Although it was music and literature that had initially drawn us together, my social conscience was aroused through our contact. I too became involved in his crusade for the material and spiritual uplift of the disadvantaged. Jackson took me around St. Croix to show me the miserable situation of the field workers. I was genuinely shocked and appalled, for like most St. Thomians, I had little direct experience with conditions on the plantations. Because of my aversion to politics, I did not become directly involved in the labor struggles of the period. But I did invite Jackson to come to St. Thomas for the first time and arranged for him to give a lecture at the Apollo Theater on his crusade and his need for support. I also agreed to become the St. Thomas subscription and distribution agent for the *Herald,* to which I also contributed articles on local conditions and musical culture written in a popular vein. I am proud that my start in the field of journalism came about in association with Jackson and the islands' first genuinely free press.[6]

In my estimation, David Hamilton Jackson was one of our most outstanding native sons. A dark, handsome, self-confident man with piercing eyes and a sonorous, almost musical voice, he was the very embodiment of the charismatic leader. Although endowed with unique intellectual gifts, he did not consider himself superior to the people he led. Nor did he abuse his position of authority and trust, as did many of his successors. He led by wisdom and example, not by patronage and fear.

His task as labor leader in the first decades of this century was not an easy one. It required tact, vision, good sense, discretion, caution, patience, and a finely attuned understanding of social dynamics and human psychology. Few other men could have effectively controlled such a volatile situation and achieved, against incredible odds, such a singular triumph. Jackson had the ability to arouse the ambition, hope, and enthusiasm that slumber in even the most downtrodden. He managed to breathe his own hopeful, heroic spirit into the hearts and minds of his people, instilling in them the conviction that they too possessed the ability to climb the mount of human dignity and achievement. The estate workers regarded him as a savior, a Moses leading them toward a promised land of dignity and plenitude. To them, his every word was sacrosanct and was obeyed to the letter. Such was his power over the common people that under his urging, petty crime virtually disappeared and, for the first time in many years, it became possible to make the journey between Christiansted and Frederiksted without protection.

After the islands passed to American sovereignty in May 1917, a purse of $5,000 was collected from well-wishers, including myself, to help Jackson attend law school at Howard University. Having successfully completed his studies, Jackson returned home to resume fighting for the masses—this time in the courts. His many legal successes convinced the naval administrators to name him judge of the St. Croix Municipal Court, the first member of his race to be so honored. The naval governor who made the appointment told Jackson that he did so reluctantly, because thereafter the people would have no one with foresight to defend them. Jackson's performance as judge was a disappointment to many of his followers. His legal training, coupled with his experience in the labor struggle and his contact with men and women of intellectual attainment in Washington, had impressed forcibly upon his mind the preeminence of the principle of equality before the law. Consequently, he refused to interpret the law to the exclusive benefit of one group and so brought upon himself the unjustified stigma of betraying the people. The St. Croix labor union leaders bitterly attacked Jackson in their newspaper, and he lost much of his prestige among the workers. Despite intense public pressure and ostracism from his former followers, Jackson refused to barter his principles for popularity. Through his determined integrity and honesty, Jackson eventually regained the confidence of his people and earned the respect of the ruling classes as well. He is now accorded recognition as one of the great leaders in our struggle for political autonomy and social justice. In my estimation he stands as the greatest, and I urge the youth to study and follow his example of dedication, rectitude, and compassion.[7]

   Social unrest, economic stagnation, and diplomatic pressure from America led Denmark to sign the treaty whereby the Danish West Indies were sold to the United States for $25 million in 1917. There can be no doubt that the transfer of sovereignty was popular on St. Thomas. The United States was no stranger to us. We knew about the nation and what it stood for from books, newspapers, magazines, and the telegraph. A good many natives had gone to the States to take advantage of the economic and educational opportunities offered there. From these immigrants, those remaining on the islands received not only monthly remittances but also stories about the advantages of life under the American flag. Above all, our contact with America came through her ships and sailors who visited our harbor. Mariners from all nations came to St. Thomas, but during my youth the Americans were far and away the best liked and most imitated. People tried to walk and speak like Americans, and when you moved through the streets of old Charlotte Amalie, it was as if you were in a town on the East Coast. We admired the American character, which was individualistic, easygoing, and freedom loving—not unlike our own. One indication of our strong pro-American sentiment is that when we were boys, the wooden boats we built to play in were always named after American vessels that came to St. Thomas. Even the "bumboats"—the small rowboats used to ferry ship's passengers to land—were conspicuously named after American states and cities. No one would have thought of giving these boats a Scandinavian or French name, or even naming them after British places.

   St. Thomians welcomed American sovereignty not because they had been ill used by the Danes (few people harbored any hostility toward them), but because America offered us a strongly rooted democratic tradition, as well as wealth, power, and social opportunity. Denmark, a comparatively poor country, could do little to improve our economic well being. We appreciated that our longstanding colonial government did what it could, but we knew that it was not enough. Denmark's colonialism was benign, and she had bequeathed to us many gifts—a treasured culture, freedom from a pernicious racial bigotry, the advantage of stern discipline, and many other intangible assets of life for which we will always be grateful. If Denmark could have offered us social and economic advantages equivalent to those of the United States, then we would have probably been content to remain with her forever.

   The only groups to oppose the coming of American rule were the islands' Danes and some merchants who feared that they would lose their businesses to enterprising Yankees. A small clique was also anxious because of America's racial policies, which were considered far harsher than anything we had experienced under the Danes. But even these critics did not object too loudly to the sale, because the alternative was most likely Germany, and few wanted to become German. We had come to know the Germans well through their commercial establishments in St. Thomas, and many did not like them. They appeared a cold, stiff, undemocratic, stand-offish sort of people who did not mix well with other nationalities or races. And they had the reputation of notorious misers. The hurricane of October 1916 silenced any remaining critics of the sale. This devastating storm completed our economic ruin. Businesses and homes were destroyed. The harbor facilities were totally wrecked. There was widespread sickness and near-starvation. And there was no money available from Denmark to help us recover. Local merchants had no resources of their own. Everyone was in despair. We did not know what to do or where to turn. Under these circumstances the prospect of becoming part of the wealthy United States was needed emergency relief.

I should note that many older people were less than enthusiastic about the changeover. People like my father had grown up under the Danes, and, while they were not entirely content with Danish rule, they preferred its continued certainties to the uncertainty of the Americans. They felt that change would deprive them of traditional rights and cultural patterns bestowed by the Danes. To them the changeover represented a loss of valued social and cultural bearings. On the other hand, younger people like myself felt the stirring breath of promise and progress that had come from years of contact with America. In my particular case, music was a major reason why I was attracted to the United States. I admired American band music, especially that of Sousa. It was from American teachers like Hugh A. Clarke and Thomas Tapper that I had received a formal musical education. I wrote articles for American musical journals and was in correspondence with many outstanding American musicians. I knew I had little opportunity to expand my musical career under Danish sovereignty. I had hopes and ambitions, and I recognized that there were unparalleled opportunities with America. I appreciated many of the things that Denmark offered, but I knew that it did not offer me enough. I wanted to grow, to move forward, to realize my dreams and aspirations.

All of the conflicting emotions which the St. Thomas community experienced because of the sale swept over the vast throng which gathered to witness the official transfer ceremonies, held on March 31, 1917, at the parade ground in front of the old military barracks (now the home of the Virgin Islands legislature). Many eyes dimmed with tears when the Danish anthem was played and old Dannebrog slowly descended. The flag seemed now and then to be clutching reluctantly to the pole. I too felt a tinge of regret. But when the Stars and Stripes was swiftly run up in its place, I felt a surge of hope and confidence. Like other young people, I fully appreciated that a new age—an age of opportunity, of education, of prosperity—had finally dawned.[8]

President Woodrow Wilson designated officers of the U.S. Navy Department to administer the new territorial possessions, which were renamed the United States Virgin Islands. Although the selection of the navy for this assignment reflected the defense priorities that had led to the acquisition of the islands in the first place, the purely military side of naval stewardship was never of great consequence. No warships were stationed in St. Thomas harbor, and the military garrison, which included a detachment of marines, was never sizeable—even during wartime. The primary purpose of the so-called "naval administration" was to provide good, effective civil government that was responsive to the needs of the local populace. It must be stressed that the naval administration was not really a military government, but a civil administration run, at the direction of Congress and by presidential appointment, by naval officers.

One of the leading objectives of the new administrators was to seek among the native population the needed skills and talents for community growth and betterment, so that with their eventual departure they would leave behind a sound and healthy Virgin Islands ship of state with an able, well-trained Virgin Islands crew. This was the motivation, the philosophy, and the political creed of the men and women who held the reins of government from the transfer in 1917 to their eventual departure in 1931. Among the first of their undertakings in this direction, and perhaps the most notable, was the establishment of a United States Navy Band composed entirely of native Virgin Islanders.

Prior to 1917, a good number of the youths of the community had taken up music as an educational, recreational, and cultural pastime. They saw in music an expression of themselves. As so often happens (as in the case for me of Sebastien), a person of appreciation, of position, of plain human compulsion arrives upon the scene who recognizes the talent and burning ambition of youth and brings it to the attention of the right person, at the right time, in the right place. The idea of forming a native navy band originated with Mrs. White, the wife of Captain William Russell White, chief aide and chief of staff to Admiral James H. Oliver, the first American governor of the Virgin Islands. While staying at the Grand Hotel in downtown Charlotte Amalie, the newly arrived Mrs. White heard a concert given by my Juvenile Band in nearby Emancipation Garden.[9] The quality of the performance so impressed her that she resolved to propose to the administration to have the Juveniles enlisted into the U.S. Navy. Mrs. White, herself an accomplished pianist who had once studied under Italian opera composer Pietro Mascagni, conveyed her idea to me the next day, explaining that through such a band of youngsters, she believed, a close, cooperative relationship could be mutually established between the people of the Virgin Islands and the new administration. She believed that the band could play a valuable role as a liaison—a bridge of communication—between the new naval officials and the community. As a musician, she was well aware of the beneficial role that music can play in community development as a facilitator of cross-cultural dialogue and understanding, as well as a means of demonstrating the need and value of cooperation, unity, and harmony. I will be eternally grateful to this gracious and kind lady, whose keen interest in the band, as well as the social, cultural, and moral advancement of our community was unflagging during the several years she spent in our islands. She and her noble husband can truly be said to have given their souls to the people of the Virgin Islands. The work of bringing the band to a position of cultural leadership in the islands was accomplished largely through the influence of these two liberal-minded humanitarians.[10]

After obtaining enthusiastic consent from myself and the boys for her plan, Mrs. White brought her idea to bear strongly upon Governor Oliver, a man personally committed to involving capable natives in his administration. After satisfying himself that we were indeed the best-qualified local band,[11] Oliver requested and received permission from Washington, less than three months after the transfer, to establish a Navy Band of the United States Virgin Islands. The signer of this directive, which established the first colored band in the U.S. Navy, was Woodrow Wilson. By the president's order I was awarded the rank of chief petty officer and the title of naval bandmaster, the first of my race to be so honored.[12] I was further authorized to select twenty-one of the best musicians from my Juvenile Band for induction with myself into the navy for a term of four years. The men I chose were Henry Galiber, Conrad Gomez, Paludan O. Nicholson, and Louis Taylor, clarinets; Arthur Ramsey, alto saxophone; Raphael Francis, tenor saxophone; Raphael Bonelli, Herbert Brown, Halvor Delemos, and Earle Williams, cornets; Philip Lopez, Arnold Martin, and Oliverre Sebastien, alto horns; Raphael Chapman and Cyril Michael, trombones; Julien Adams, baritone; Bernardo Heyligar, E-flat bass; Alphonse Domingo and Morris Francis, BB-flat bass; Ronald Hennessey, bass drum; and James Brown, snare drum—all of them capable, enterprising young men.[13] The formation of the navy band not only presented me with a golden opportunity to propel my ambitions forward as a musician and a bandmaster but also was an expression of personal satisfaction for myself and the fine youths who served with me in the Juvenile Band. For many of us it meant the beginning of a purposeful and productive career in the United States Navy.

We were officially inducted into the navy on June 2, 1917, by our commanding officer, Captain William Russell White. Our terms of service were exceptional. We were given standard pay of fifty dollars a month, provided with all our instruments and a band room, permitted to live at home rather than in barracks, awarded a subsistence allowance, and subjected to only a few military regulations, such as night curfew.[14] The bandsmen were thus able to live secure, independent lives in their community, and many of them maintained their own businesses or held part-time jobs. Our sole military responsibility was to practice and play music. All in all, it was an ideal situation which proved a turning point in each of our lives.

The editor of the *Jacobs' Band Monthly*, the renowned musical journal with which I was still associated, introduced and hailed the formation of the navy band as follows:

> There has come to the *Jacobs' Band Monthly* a semi-official account of the birth of a new American Band, a new Boy's Band, a new Naval Boy's Band that is sponsored by *"One of us."* "Pshaw!" says somebody, "bands are born as common as babies. What of it?" This is "what of it." In this grand country, which is old enough to be the great grand paternal progenitor of several generations of bands, this organization not only is a new-born band, but it is the first birth of its kind in this country, and to everyone is accorded the right to "holler," over the first born—particularly if it is a husky boy born under the protecting folds of the American flag.
>
> To come down to "brass boys"—technically and not—generally speaking—the "semi-official" account comes through the columns of *Lightbourn's Mail Notes,* a newspaper published at Charlotte Amalie, St. Thomas, V.I., U.S.A., once the D.W.I., and at this point the interest begins to accumulate. These newly taken over islands are by no means the first territorial acquisitions of the U.S.A. but to the best of our knowledge this is the first time in history that the U.S. Government has almost immediately upon possession organized and fathered a Naval Boys' Band from its newly adopted American citizens.
>
> As the readers of this magazine all know, Mr. Alton A. Adams, of THE BAND, is the enthusiastic band generator at St. Thomas, Virgin Islands, U.S.A.—the *band motif,* to put it musically—and his specialty and musical hobby is to organize, educate and train band-boys to become capable bandsmen. That is why Mr. Adams has been officially commissioned by the government to train the new organization and because he

has been so commissioned is the reason for stating above that the new born youngster is sponsored by "one of us."

According to the *Mail Notes*: "It is seldom that one sees real merit better rewarded than in the case of Mr. Alton Adams and his band. The government, finding that many of our boys possessed musical talent, and being desirous of having a naval band, after being satisfied as to his superior claim, commissioned Mr. Adams to organize a band of twenty-two. Mr. Adams being able to make a selection from those whom he has himself trained, presented them to Captain White, and on Saturday (June 2) they were sworn into the service of the United States Navy for four years."

Uniforms, instruments and general equipments will be speedily provided by the government, and then these boys will soon find themselves to be full-fledged United States Naval musicians playing for Uncle Sam. The band will play daily at the hoisting and lowering of the colors and afterwards will give a short concert at the barracks. On Sunday evenings, at the close of church services, the band will play sacred concerts in the Emancipation Garden.

To Bandmaster Adams, who now holds the rank as a Chief Petty Officer and who has wholeheartedly devoted time, attention and much of private funds to bettering band conditions in St. Thomas, there now comes just accruement of interest on invested capital of earned effort. The American officials in the islands are deeply interested in the man, his educational endeavors and his work in the *Jacobs' Band Monthly*. We are sure that every reader of the magazine will most heartily congratulate Mr. Adams upon the honor of becoming the Government Bandmaster of the first naval band of the Virgin Islands of the United States of America, and also most cordially welcome him as an American citizen, while warmly rejoicing in this new "Band's Birthday."[15]

I, of course, was ecstatic over the turn of events. For nights on end I lay awake contemplating the future that had suddenly opened up to me and dreaming about the kind of band that we would create. I knew that I had been presented with a unique opportunity to fulfill my ambitions as a musician and bandmaster, and I was determined not to let this chance of a lifetime slip from my grasp. I knew that it was not going to be easy. We had to justify the navy's faith in us. We had to prove our worth by doing an exemplary job, because we represented not only the Virgin Islands but also the entire colored race. This sense of obligation guided my entire career in the navy and accounts for my diligent efforts to bring out the very best from my men at all times. From the outset I believed strongly in the capabilities of my boys and was convinced that they had it in them to be one of the best bands in the world. That is what I aimed for. Once we had enlisted,

I demanded that the band practice four to six hours every day and that its appearance be immaculate, its conduct irreproachable. The band was already good, but I strove to develop it to a higher plane. It has always been a cardinal tenet of mine that to enjoy true success, our lives must be of incessant, constructive toil each day—always trying to improve ourselves, for at best we are imperfect creatures. I viewed military service not as the culmination of my career but as a new plateau, which widened my horizons and my ambitions.

At that time, I was considered by some of the bandsmen as well as by many in the community to be tough—a hard and exacting taskmaster.[16] Perhaps in certain cases I was, if being tough meant rigid discipline in punctuality, cleanliness, neat appearance, good music, and strict ethical observance in demanding that the band room and band quarters be so kept as would unblushingly welcome without warning a man's wife, mother, or friends. I was, however, never in doubt as to the high quality, excellent home training, loyalty, and burning ambition of the young men I was privileged to guide and teach and represent. Let me take this opportunity to say this to our youthful would-be leaders of musical outfits. The discipline of the captain of a military company is mild compared to that exacted by the successful band and orchestra leader. The success of the music is in direct proportion to the perfection of the discipline.[17]

I had already worked out my own philosophy about the band, and it guided me as I endeavored to bring my unit to a higher degree of excellence. Some of my beliefs and tenets respecting the band are expressed in these excerpts from my writings of the period in the *Jacobs' Band Monthly:*

> The band is an important factor in the present-day life of our modern civilization. It performs many functions, the least of which is to amuse. This fact has been lost sight of by many. Its principal mission is to civilize, humanize, make good, and help to cement the brotherly feeling that has been the mission of religion and art to promote.
>
> While the military band lacks the *finesse* of the orchestra, that deficiency has been compensated for by its greater usefulness as an outdoor instrument, thereby getting more in contact with those who most need its influence as a humanizing medium.
>
> The usefulness of a band to a community cannot be overestimated. One of our modern writers compares it, and rightly so, with the same relation to a community as the choir is to the church—a highly important factor.
>
> Although up to now the band has made wonderful progress, I think that if we as bandsmen consider two things which we seem entirely to lose sight of, the progress and influence would still be more wonderful.

First, the relation of the band to the community of which it forms a part and, secondly, the requisites of ourselves as men and musicians, and our obligations to the band of which *we* form a part.

It is at times both healthful and delightful to take a retrospective view of our organization—more so ourselves. An institution can be nothing more or less than what its members make it—the leader included. An old adage says *"know thyself."*

The band should first of all contain *decent, moral, and ambitious members* who possess enough intelligence to be disciplined, and who feel and know that they are respected and thought more of by thinking people when they *implicitly obey* their leader and give him their moral help, encouragement, and gratitude; who make *punctuality* a principle, *ambition* a virtue, and *Excelsior!* a necessity; who aim at an *ideal,* and are determined, cost what it may, to fight towards the realization of that *ideal;* who are conscious of the fact that to push upward is to rise, and to remain dormant is to descend in the scale of human intelligence and worth; and who will only taste of the true success when their efforts result not only in making them good musicians, but, what is of more importance and far more exemplary, *intellectually and morally better men.*[18]

What is the difference between a good and a bad band? . . . Let us look at the requisite qualities that make up a good reed or brass band. We must first examine our instrumentation and see if the grouping of instruments gives us that correct balance of tonal color necessary to a perfect rendition. . . . No section should be made to dominate, but rather [each should] assist to enrich the melody and give strength, volume and tonal coloring to the harmony. If any section is to be prominent, by all means let it be the woodwind section, which should comprise about half the number of the band, and with its beauty, uniformity and great pliancy of tonal character, distinguishes the purely brass from the reed band. . . .

In my experience, I have found that most bands suffer from poorness of tone and faulty intonation, due to the disregard of individual and collective practice of sustained tones throughout the entire register of their instruments. The question of long sustained tones is an invaluable necessity to the requisition of pure intonation, and those soft, sweet, voluminous tones so pleasant to intelligent hearers. A good tone and perfect intonation are not gifts, as many believe, but simply a faithful observance and practice of long-sustained tones daily. This fact cannot be too much emphasized.

A few words as to the conductor or leader. The leader should have a perfect knowledge of harmony and composition, should be a good arranger, a good soloist, and have a technical knowledge of all the instruments of the band. He should be a thorough disciplinarian, and should have, if possible, the love, but certainly the respect of the entire

organization. A single player may only spoil his part, but a poor conductor ruins the whole composition. The leader should never be a
figure-head, a mere stick-waver. He is the intermediate agent between
the performers and the audience; he is responsible for perfect time and
the various movements indicated in his scores; his individuality and
personality must stand out in his interpretation, and the question of
precision, attack, and steadiness of movement rest entirely with him.
He is the player on that big instrument—THE BAND.

The individual is not only an important factor in the life of a nation
or community, but also in the life of a band. What a band is to be is
what its members make it. The success of the band depends to a great
extent upon the cooperation of the members in *perfect harmony*. The
blending of the various tones of the individual element influences the
general ensemble or composite whole. The personality of each member
reflects itself into the music and either spoils or enhances the harmonic
effect. As a chain is not stronger than its weakest link, so a band cannot
rise above its weakest member. As a sum-total for a good effect and the
success of the band, we arrive at these requirements: ambitious members who are willing to put forth their very best energy for their
advancement and the general welfare of the band; good instruments as
nearly perfect in tune and tone as can be had; and last, but by no means
least, the band's good appearance, which has quite a great influence
upon any audience.

I did more than make the men learn the music; I taught them to understand it and to appreciate the intention and the methods of the composer, for
only then could they enter into the music that they played. I remember one
time when I had the boys practice for several hours a band arrangement
which I had written of Austrian composer Franz Schubert's *Unfinished Symphony*. At the end, when the exhausted bandsmen were leaving the room,
one of them sighed, "Lucky thing that fellow didn't live to finish that." His
remark gave me an idea. The next time the band met, I dissected the *Unfinished Symphony* section by section with them, and we played each part so
that they understood Schubert's ideas and technique. Then we played my
band arrangement, and they did an excellent job. Shortly thereafter, when we
had to go with the governor to St. Croix, I asked them what we should play
over there. With one voice they shouted: "The Unfinished Symphony."

I had trouble with the bandsmen only on one occasion, when some local
agitators tried to stir up trouble by telling some of them that I was unjus-
tifiably harsh and that they were being discriminated against in terms of
ratings and pay. These charges were patently false. Still, a few of the men
got upset. Upon being satisfied on the matter, they rallied around me and
wrote a public letter in my support, which read in part:

We the members of the U.S. Naval Band beg to say that there was no serious disagreement among us or any spirit of distrust toward our honest and able leader, but simply a misunderstanding which was satisfactorily cleared to us by our Captain and which proved our leader to be perfectly right in all that he demanded of us. We thank no one for endeavoring to espouse our cause, especially in such a malicious manner as that adopted. . . .

"Let envy and malice alone, they will punish themselves."

This unfortunate misunderstanding was soon forgotten as our collective exertions began to bear fruit.

To judge from the capacity crowds that were now filling the Emancipation Garden and its environs, it was evident that our Sunday night concerts were becoming more and more popular with the island inhabitants. One particular Sunday evening, as we had taken our places in the bandstand, word spread among us that Governor Oliver, his wife, staff officers, and their wives had taken over a section of the Grand Hotel terrace to listen to our concert. Their presence may have been an inspiration. Whatever the reason, every phrase of the concert was rendered magnificently. No bandmaster could have expected more of his men. The applause following each rendition was spontaneous and continuous. When the concert ended, Governor Oliver and his group were waiting for us at the foot of the bandstand. The governor reached for my hand: "Mr. Adams, congratulations! In fact, congratulations alone cannot convey my feelings. The concert was superb. If this keeps up, I will no longer miss what used to be my favorite musical group, the Marine Band of Washington, D.C."[19]

From the outset the naval administrators had been more than satisfied with our performance. The band had no sooner started its work when another navy band reported for duty at St. Thomas. When Governor Oliver was informed of it, he ordered that the men be sent aboard ship immediately, and thereupon dispatched a message to the navy department stating that he was fully satisfied with the navy band of musicians under his command, which he believed would soon be molded into one of the finest bands in the world, and adding that he did not miss the world-famous Marine Band in Washington. Captain White was so pleased with the development of the band that he obtained permission to have me sent to St. Croix [in 1918] to organize similar units in Christiansted and Frederiksted, which I accomplished in six months, using some of my former bandsmen in St. Thomas as starters.[20] After these bands were established, I was appointed bandmaster-in-charge of all three local naval bands. Musicians who heard these youngsters play conceded that their efforts were remarkable. I must say here and now that I could never have accomplished what I did without the help and solid support of my brother, Julien. In my absence he conducted the bands in professional style. Because of his genial disposition and ability to get along with people, members of the band accepted his tough rehearsal schedules and gave him their complete loyalty and support.[21]

During the almost fourteen years of its existence (1917–31) the United States Navy Band of the Virgin Islands achieved one of the highest records in the navy for discipline, appearance, behavior, and musical performance. Our music and deportment won high acclaim from military men the like of General "Black Jack" Pershing; Admirals Coontz, Wells, and Eberle; Secretaries of the Navy Denby and Wilbur; and Assistant Secretary Theodore Roosevelt—each of whom reviewed us. General Pershing personally told me that he had never heard a finer band. Encomiums also came from many musical connoisseurs who heard the band play in the islands or during our tour of the eastern United States in 1924. The Congress of the United States even joined in the praise, approving a 1920 report [#734] that declared:

> One of the best pieces of work done by the Navy has been the development of a splendid band—one at St. Thomas and one at St. Croix. These young men in the bands are moral, enterprising, and set a good example to the other young men of the islands. There is a great ambition among them to become members of the bands. Great credit is due to Commander White for his work along these lines.

I have been reliably informed that the excellent record and abilities of our band were extremely influential in having other colored bands and orchestras organized under the Navy Department during World War II.

The Virgin Islands community received us with enthusiasm and pointed to us with pride. Often following our concerts, the band formed up and led a jubilant tramp through town. Applause was showered upon us by local culture buffs, as well as the popular classes. One of our best-known native intellectuals, J. Antonio Jarvis, wrote of us:

> Life would be inexpressively drab and drear in St. Thomas were it not for the inspiring comfort of good music such as the Navy Band gave us last evening; and which we enjoy periodically through its concerts.
>
> This is not the stage where one needs to praise the renditions, for its achievements are records of its high quality: but it is especially worthwhile to offer some appreciation for unexpected treats that they may be repeated.

A special feature, that was most satisfying, was the solo by Bandmaster Adams; words cannot do justice in description; we hope to hear
him frequently:

> "Sure, the larks and mocking birds,
> Wailing out their minor thirds,
> Stop their thrilling,
> Cease their shrilling—
> By its magic sounds struck mute—
> When an Adams plays the flute."

The band's repertoire was wide-ranging. We played marches, classics, local
folk melodies, waltzes, sacred music, popular tunes, songs, overtures, even
jazz.[22] Sometimes, I would give a brief presentation on a musical subject or
some prominent musician.

The band was not confined to St. Thomas. We played often in St. Croix,
since the governors usually took us with them whenever they visited our
sister island. The Crucians thronged to see us, even though they had their
own bands, and our visits often took on the air of a holiday. Word of our
band's ability and performance had spread off-island. Early in July 1921 I
received an invitation for our band to give several concerts in neighboring
Puerto Rico. The invitation came from Luis Miranda, the outstanding
Puerto Rican composer and director of that island's military band, the Fifteenth Infantry Regiment Band. I proceeded to clear the matter with the
governor's office. A change of governors had taken place. On April 26,
1921, our good friend Governor Oman was replaced by Rear Admiral
Sumner E. W. Kittelle.

From the beginning Governor Kittelle (1921–22) was as ardent a backer of
our band as his predecessor. Not only did he give his consent and blessing to
our trip, but he also ordered that naval transportation be made available to
take us to Puerto Rico and back. There must have been widespread publicity
of our coming, because the night of our first concert in San Juan found us in
an open-air stadium looking out on a capacity crowd. It was a beautiful moon-
lit night, clear and cool. I felt proud of my bandsmen in that spacious bandstand. How neat and poised they looked in their spotless white uniforms,
ready to perform. We opened our concert with the "Virgin Islands March,"
which more and more was becoming our opening trademark. We continued
with selections of Cuban *habañera* music as well as several of our own native
bamboulas. These exciting dance rhythms delighted the audience. We received
hearty applause and calls for encores. The classical section of our program featured overtures from the Italian masters with Rossini and Verdi dominating.
Also included were melodious selections from Mexican composer Juventino

Rosas's "Impassioned Dreams" and from "Robin Hood" by American composer Reginald De Koven. We concluded our concert with several beautiful Puerto Rican dances composed by our host, Luis Miranda. The crowd went wild. We gave two more concerts in Puerto Rico to large, enthusiastic, and happy audiences. From the praise we received on all sides, it was evident that our first off-island concerts had been very successful. On August 8, 1921, I received a letter from Miranda expressing his happiness with our visit.

> I hope you are enjoying good health as usual. I am very sorry that I could not see you before you left San Juan. I went to Cataño, but, from there, I was hearing [about] your excellent band. I wish to tell you that the people of San Juan received a very good impression of your fine organization and particularly of you as its Master. I congratulate you for your success in San Juan, and expect that you will continue receiving constantly the reward of your great efforts in having the best Band of the U.S. Navy. With kindest regards and very best wishes for everybody of your Band.[23]

The band became an effective mediator between the ideals of the naval administrators and those of the people. Beginning with the leadership of the first naval administrator, Governor Oliver, music found its rightful place in community life. In the schools, the churches, and the hospitals, as well as in other community activities, the influence of music as an uplifting force was brought to the forefront through the medium of the band and carried far and wide.[24] Governor Oliver, a man of broad culture and fine artistic qualities, spared no pains in using the band as a tool in his endeavors toward public refinement and enlightenment. Oliver insisted that the members of the band live so as to have themselves looked upon as shining examples of the objectives set forth in the plans of the administration, and that, therefore, the home life of the bandsmen in all its aspects—cultural, religious, educational, and social—ought to be so regulated as to serve as a model for community life in general. Accordingly, he urged all of us to get married, settle down, raise families, live model home lives, and be good law-abiding citizens in our community.[25] To meet the governor's expectations, I posted the following set of rules for our organization:

NOTICE TO BANDSMEN
OUR POLICY

With the aim of having the band developed into an organization which fits satisfactorily into the scheme of naval establishments, the following injunctions are issued for the guidance of the bandsmen under my leadership:

1. Due allowances have already been made for those members who, through lack of basic military training, find themselves, as it were, in a strange environment.

2. In keeping with navy regulations, all bandsmen are expected to so carry themselves as to do credit to the service.

3. The fact that others occasionally violate regulations offers no excuse for the violation of those regulations by any individual. Each individual has incumbent on him the bounden duty to make his demeanor stand out as an example of sound discipline and true patriotic common sense.

4. As professionals in the service, all bandsmen have, resting on them, the responsibility for maintaining a high standard of professional skill and dignity. Each one is, in duty, bound to utilize every opportunity offered him for self improvement, thus contributing substantially to the efficiency of the entire organization.

5. Character and ability (professional and general) should be the goal toward which all bandsmen reach out.

6. It must be clearly borne in mind that the band is an institution the purpose of which is to give service to the entire establishment. Each member should therefore show an ever readiness and willingness to cooperate wholeheartedly in any undertaking aiming at the betterment of the whole. Prudent and respectful treatment of every shipmate is expected of all bandsmen.

7. Bandsmen should not close their eyes to the fact that they are, in duty, bound to look on their superior officers with respect, and give to them all considerations indicative of military courtesy.

As leader, naturally I had to make a start, which I willingly did by marrying Ella Eugenia Joseph on October 6, 1917.[26] We brought forth seven daughters and a son and remained happily married until her death February 9, 1978.[27] Most of the bandsmen followed my example, and several of them, such as Cyril Michael, who is now a district court judge, went on to become social pillars of the community.[28] The inspirational impact which the bandsmen had on the tone and tenor of local life can never be overestimated.

The naval administrators encouraged us to influence others not only by example but also by becoming actively and constructively involved in community affairs. Toward this latter goal I joined the newly formed American Red Cross, for which I served as secretary. At the time the local chapter of the Red Cross, which had been set up by the navy, was the primary agency of social welfare in the islands, and I was pleased to become involved in its ministrations to the poor and needy. Within the Red

Cross, I, along with O. S. Kean, was instrumental in establishing the first public library on St. Thomas, in December 1920. There was a great social need for a library because up to that time the public had no place to go where it could be exposed to books or knowledge. The only such organization then existing, the Athenaeum, was run by persons of means and was closed to those who could not afford either the entrance fee or monthly payments. The establishment of the St. Thomas Public Library marked a major advance toward the democratization of knowledge in our community, and I am proud to have been so closely associated with this worthwhile endeavor.

The first practical step toward the realization of a public library for this island was made on June 5, 1920, when a meeting was held in Bethania Hall by a public library commission. Among those present were Mr. Kean, representing the Colonial Council; Mr. Malling-Holm, representing the local chapter of the Red Cross; and director of education Mr. Daniel R. Nase, representing the government. On that evening plans were made for the establishment of a public library. A committee was appointed to get funds from local people, and a request for a donation of books was sent to the American Library Association and the American Red Cross, both of which sent liberal gifts. The Red Cross through Miss Joanna Colcord donated $3,000, while the American Library Association through the lively interest, energy, and progressiveness of Governor Oman, made valuable contributions of books of all sorts. The latter institution also contributed the services of two reliable experts in library work, Misses Adelina Zachart and Eleanor Gleason, who proved their worth in having the library put on a satisfactory working basis.

The formal opening of the St. Thomas Public Library, which marked an epoch in our little island, was held on the evening of December 10, 1920, at the Grand Hotel. As the first chairman of the library commission, Mr. Kean was master of ceremonies. The program opened with an invocation by the Reverend Father Guillo, C.SS.R. This was followed by a welcome by Mr. Kean. The star address of the evening was delivered by the Reverend A. H. Leslie, then of the Dutch Reformed Church. The speaker explained fully the place of the library in the building up of a community, stressing particularly how and what to read. Miss Zachart was then introduced to the audience and gave a succinct account of the work she and Miss Gleason had done. Taken up with her subject, she carried the audience along with her, as phase after phase in the preliminary work of the library was unfolded. At the close of her address, she received a well-deserved ovation. Other items on the program were selections by the U.S. Navy Band, vocal numbers by

Mr. J. Philip Gomez accompanied by Mr. Hugo Bornn on the piano, and the closing address by the Right Reverend Bishop E. C. Greider, president of the American Red Cross and member of the library commission.[29] After the ceremonies at the Grand Hotel were concluded, Governor and Mrs. Oman and members of the Colonial Council, the teachers of the various schools, members of the clergy, and many of the merchants and citizens followed the two tireless workers Misses Zachary and Gleason to the upper story of the building east of the Lutheran Church, the first home of the library.

Everybody including Governor Oman expressed highest appreciation and deep gratitude to the two indefatigable workers, the American Red Cross, and the American Library Association for the precious gift. The total number of books comprising the library was five thousand. During the first six months, from January 1 to June 3, 1921, 17,407 persons visited and 10,800 books were lent to the people for use in their homes; and from the time of its opening until June 30 of the following year, 613 persons were registered as members. The average number of visitors the second year after the opening was 3,000 a month. In September of that year 3,124 persons visited and 1,864 books were drawn. Miss Nellie Richardson was selected as the first librarian.[30]

Another community activity I became involved in was the publication of a weekly newspaper called the *St. Thomas Times*. The newspaper was my idea. It grew out of my interest in spreading culture to my people. At the time, none of the newspapers in St. Thomas concerned themselves with the arts or with educating the citizenry. Few even took cognizance of local community affairs, and when they did, it was usually in the form of gossip. Mostly our papers carried political stories and advertisements. It was my belief that there was a need for a paper that addressed itself to the task of uplifting its readers, rather than titillating them. The *St. Thomas Times* was owned, operated, and printed by the navy band, with the approval and encouragement of Governor Kittelle. We raised $3,000 of our own to purchase a printing press, which we located in the band room. Collectively the band members possessed the requisite technical skills to produce the paper. I served as editor and was ably assisted by Cyril Michael as secretary, H. Kean as treasurer, and Paluden Nicholson as business manager.

From the first, the paper, which appeared once a week, set a high tone, eschewing politics and providing its readers with information about the world of art, literature, music, and drama, as well as local community affairs. The credo of the paper was set forth in my editorial for the first edition, of October 8, 1921:

With this initial issue, *The St. Thomas Times* sounds its greeting to you, and sincerely trusts that it will awaken a responsive tone in the hearts of those who truly stand for the cause of intellectual freedom and moral uplift.

It is not necessary to make an apology for the advent of this publication; its motive justifies its existence. It has no platform, to speak in political parlance; it has a mission founded upon an ideal of service. In the political arena it shall not enter, but it shall, nevertheless, interest you if you are interested in the manhood and womanhood of our island home, in the news of the day, in the cause of music as a human necessity, in the schools, and in what our Government is doing for these islands which so vividly portrays itself all around, as hardly to need being pointed out.

The St. Thomas Times is the advocate of no special class nor creed. Save politics, religious controversies, and abusive personalities, its columns are open to anyone who has something educationally interesting to say that would construct opinion or build character.

There are many speculations with a view to discouragement relative to the success or failure of this venture.

There is no walk in life but has its discouragements; none that is exclusively a path of roses. We are all creatures of our environment and therefore have our limitations to a greater or lesser degree. The words of Goethe that "the tiniest hair throws its shadow" should compensate us somewhat, whatever our limitations, and show us that we exert a wider influence than we at times imagine. Because we cannot reach the Alpine heights, is no valid reason for not making the best use of whatever talent we may be blessed with. If it is not given us to do great things we can at least radiate some personal influence for good which may cause someone to remember that we have lived and to a purpose.

Success is not a final result, but an attendant circumstance; likewise that seed of failure to which we so often yield, though, generally a spur urging us on to greater heights, slumbers in the man and not in the noble themes he has around him for inspiration and guidance; therefore do not appreciate our success or failure from a commercial point of view, but rather by our contribution to the general fund of good.

While maintaining the foregoing, we, however, do not want it to be understood as resenting healthful and constructive criticism. Criticisms of such a nature are necessary for appreciable results in any line of useful endeavor. A little battling with obstacles is good; it is helpful. It brings out many a stern and slumbering force, besides adding to the strength and discipline of mind.

It is with this idea of SERVICE in view that we now enter the field, with the intention of covering that field to the best of our ability. We therefore expect that the motive which prompts us will make some amendment for our many shortcomings.

On that account we appeal to you, fellow citizens and those who are working for our welfare, for help and sympathy so that we may make *The St. Thomas Times* a publication worthy of your good selves, worthy of our purposes and ideals, and worthy of the PRESS.

The *Times* also promoted the ideals of American democracy, good citizenship, and true patriotism, as is reflected in the following editorial, which appeared in the February 4, 1922, edition:

Captain White, whose name is a household word in these islands, beloved and trusted by one and all and whose fatherly care to us bandsmen has helped to implant in us that great yearning for American ideals, believed that we as musicians could help in a great measure to further implant the seed of Americanism in these islands. . . .

The first requisite we found necessary to the success of our task was the reformation of ourselves, a process in which we are still engaged; the implanting of the true seed of Americanism in our own lives, for very often who writes gives all the importance to what is written. The real man must be backed by character.

We found that to be a true American, was to be a patriot and we are ever mindful of that sort of patriotism which Tolstoy claims, and rightly so, is a positive evil. That is, "the reckless braggadocio kind that does not think, that does not care, that makes no difference if a thing be right or wrong, so our side is for it. It becomes a thing of material force, a matter of clubs, fists, knives, and pistols. It is that boastful, brandishing, brutal sort of patriotism whose love of country is a base passion, to be linked with any sort of hurrah, where the old flag may be lugged in. This is a decrepit and wicked patriotism. Patriotism is a life. It is being honest, candid, just, brave. It is founding and conducting a beautiful home. It is being in the community an exponent of the plain and simple truth. It is being loyal to God at all costs, in everything that we do, and there is nothing worth doing that does not concern Him."

Captain White in substance emphasized the foregoing, and impressed on us the fact that we were missionaries in the sense that all men of truth and courage are, whether with pen, hammer, plough, law book, ballot, or Bible.

The year 1922 finds us still aware of the personal responsibility that rests upon us as members and component parts of the glory of American manhood and womanhood; fully aware of the fact that to harm ourselves as individuals is to harm the public as a whole. Turn or twist it how we may, there can be no separation of consequences; the duality we cannot escape. Our duty is plainly to carry upward and onward that spirit of patriotism, as has already been explained, for on that our standard of Americanism will be defined. It is illogical to believe that patriotism can be taught by bulldozing, preaching what we do not practice and by a sort of sham Americanism which borders on the ludicrous if not on the fanatic. But it can be taught by exemplifying our own lives as being truthful, sincere, honest, courageous, and, above all, moral. Patriotism being a plant of slow growth in soil such as ours, must necessarily bloom forth delicately, lovingly and truthfully. . . .

As part of the great American naval machinery, we have fortunately got into closer contact with the officials of these islands than many of our other countrymen, and are living examples of and can bear testimony to the earnestness of the deep founded intention of the officials for the economic, intellectual, and moral betterment of these islands, the further evidences of which are so strikingly manifested all around. We being natives of this island can also authoritatively assert, without the least fear of successful contradiction, that at least 95 percent of the natives are willing to co-operate with the government in the work of reconstruction. . . .

We believe implicitly in the earnestness and honesty of the Administration of these islands.

We believe that the school is an indispensable asset for the absorbing of true American life; that moral and material progress must be parallel with each other, or humanity is debased; that the educated man is he "who absorbs the meaning and spiritual energy of God's expression in the universe, and like an honest man, paying Him back in sincere and dutiful service to humanity;" "that the distinctive idea of an education is not to increase what a man knows, but to augment what a man is;" that the days of slavery will be as long as we are victims to our own negation; and that only those who have shown themselves wise in the humble task of family government and faithful to the trust of family life, should be entrusted with the responsibilities and confidences of municipal housekeeping. We do not believe in the Napoleonic lie that God is on the side of the largest army; the Pilgrim Fathers have disproved that by showing that God is on the side of truth and justice.

We believe that "earnestness, like real grief, is never clamorous."

And we believe in the unlimited possibilities of our people under the parental care of the benign folds of the beautiful *Stars and Stripes.*

Unfortunately the *St. Thomas Times* lasted only two years (1921–23), but during that time it became the best and most popular paper on the island. We all regretted having to give it up, but we had to because of the pressing demands of our other duties.

While my military and community responsibilities kept me well occupied during these years, I did manage to find time to continue my musical writing and composition. Articles of mine on various musical subjects appeared in several stateside musical journals, including the *Army and Navy Musician,* the *Dominant, Jacobs' Band Monthly, Metronome,* the

Music Bulletin, Musical Enterprise, and *Musical Messenger.* Through these writings and the responses they elicited, I came into contact with many excellent American musicians, such as Edwin Franko Goldman and Frank Seltzer.

During this time, too, I wrote several marches, some of which were acclaimed as being among the best of the period. The "Virgin Islands March," which I composed in 1919,[31] was dedicated to Captain William Russell White in appreciation of all he had done on behalf of the band, and was intended for Mrs. White as well. It was my way of expressing deep feeling for two wonderful individuals from whom I had received great help and sincere friendship. On the occasion of the march's publication by the *Jacobs' Band Monthly,*[32] I sent Captain White the following letter:

> Under separate cover I am sending you copies of Jacobs' Band and Orchestra Monthlies of Boston, Massachusetts in which you will find arranged for band and orchestra, a march composition entitled, "Virgin Islands," written by me and respectfully dedicated to you, and which I ask you to accept in the name of the U.S. Navy Bands of the Virgin Islands.
>
>   Sir, this is but a feeble effort of mine to express to you the heartfelt gratitude we owe to you, not only for your untiring efforts—on behalf of our musical advancement, but especially for your kind interest and teachings in the development of our moral and intellectual status. Your kindness and teaching have made us to feel that we have in you more of a father and friend than a Captain; and we trust, with God's help, to carry on the noble work here in these islands, the foundation of which you have so carefully laid and entrusted to us, that is: that our lives should be as shining examples to our fellow natives.
>
>   I cannot help saying that the high esteem in which you and Mrs. White are held by the people of these islands, particularly the very poor and little schoolchildren to whom your home, helpful advice, and charity are always ready, has in a great measure stimulated me to put forth this effort, which if lacking in intrinsic worth, nevertheless is steeped with the sincere love and gratitude of the bandmaster and by the men of the Bands of the Virgin Islands.

The "Virgin Islands March" received instant acclaim by musicians throughout the world. It was widely played by the world's best bands and brought me recognition as a composer of note, particularly in performances by the Goldman Band in New York.[33] On March 13, 1963, the Legislature of the Virgin Islands officially accepted my rededication of the march to the People of the Virgin Islands; it was adopted as the official anthem of the Virgin Islands by virtue of a legislative act in June 1982.[34]

My other best-known marches of this period were "The Governor's Own" (1921) and the "The Spirit of the U.S.N." (1924). I composed the latter march while staying at the Long Island, New York, residence of my good friend Romeo Dougherty, just prior to the band's tour of the Eastern Seaboard. It was dedicated to President Calvin Coolidge as an expression of the loyalty and patriotism of the people of the Virgin Islands to the United States. The origin of "The Governor's Own" is interesting. On one occasion the governor of Puerto Rico paid an official visit to St. Thomas, during which the band struck up the "Virgin Islands March" for him. The visiting governor effusively congratulated Captain White on having such an outstanding composition dedicated to him. All this took place in the hearing of our own governor, Admiral Joseph Wallace Oman.

Oman was a peach of a man, liked by all who met him. He overpowered you with friendliness and good will. Now, Oman had recently done me a singular service by persuading the Navy Department to waive my sea duty requirement and grant me permanent appointment as bandmaster. I left Government House with a wonderful feeling of gratitude, and as I walked down the hill, fragments of a march came to my mind and persisted. The ideas remained with me all afternoon, taking on shape and melody.[35] Oman was a short, jaunty, snappy sort of fellow, and that provided me with my motif. So, out of a combination of gratitude, respect, and sympathy, I went home and that night wrote him a march. Naturally, Oman was jubilant. The official presentation was made during a special concert given by the navy band at Emancipation Garden in honor of the governor and his wife, and it became through custom the march of all the islands' governors.[36] The march was soon accepted by the firm of Carl Fisher and was published in 1921. It won considerable praise in the United States from bandsmen like Herbert Clarke and John Philip Sousa, and for several years it was used as the official march for commencement exercises at Howard University.

For me personally, the most rewarding of my community activities was setting up the music program in the Virgin Islands public schools. At my request the navy appointed me supervisor of music in the public schools, a volunteer position I first held between 1918 and 1931.[37] Having music in the schools had been a dream of mine for many years. Realizing that musical education should begin in early childhood, I had approached the Danish administrators with a project to this effect. Lack of funds precluded the Danes from acting on the matter. The naval administrators, however, possessed both the inclination and the funds to follow through with the plan. Through the Red Cross, I arranged for musical instruments and books for the schools. Between 1918 and 1922 I spent a considerable amount of time working with both teachers and students. Often I would give a talk which I illustrated with music played by the band, stationed just outside of the classroom. I was frequently assisted in my classroom work by Mrs. White and also by Mary Kittelle, the daughter of the governor.

In 1922 Governor Kittelle arranged my first trip to the mainland in order to study methods of musical instruction there as models for the Virgin Islands. I had already written a course of study for grades 1 through 6, which needed to be augmented with courses for the newly established junior and senior high schools.[38] I left St. Thomas the evening of March 5 on the USS *Kittery* and, after a most pleasant voyage, arrived at the Naval Station at Hampton Roads on the 11th. My first destination in the States was Washington, D.C., where, on the recommendation of Kittelle, I stayed at the home of Mrs. Estelle Coffee Carr, a young widow, and her younger sister, a sophomore at Howard University. On arriving there, I believed I had come to the wrong address, for on the porch were apparently two white women. One of them signaled and holloed, "Bandmaster Adams, this is the right place, come right in." Mrs. Carr read to me the letter she had received from the governor in which he referred to me as a special person and requested that everything possible be done to make my stay pleasant and worthwhile. At that time the race question was quite acute, even in the District of Columbia. But on her mantelpiece were photos of black musicians Harry T. Burleigh, Clarence Cameron White, Joseph H. Douglass— grandson of the former slave and abolitionist Frederick Douglass—and R. Nathaniel Dett, among others. Mrs. Carr proved to be a most charming, intellectual, and human person. She was also a good musician and a one-time member of the Treble Clef Club, which was instrumental in getting the famous Afro-British composer Samuel Coleridge-Taylor to visit Washington, D.C., to conduct several of his works in conjunction with the orchestra of the U.S. Marine Band.

Having settled myself at Mrs. Carr's residence, my first visit the next day was the marine barracks to meet the legendary leader of the Marine Band (also known as the President's Band), Captain William H. Santelmann, to whom I had a letter of introduction from Governor Kittelle. Captain Santelmann greeted me with a tight grasp of the hand and a pleasant smile. Perusing Kittelle's letter, he seemed somewhat confused and queried me about the location of the Virgin Islands. It was the first indication I had about how little known my homeland was beyond its horizon. "Where are the Virgin Islands?" he repeated several times to himself, as if trying to connect something. Finally he blurted out: "I know of the 'Virgin Islands March,' which I believe the band is playing this morning at Guard Mount."

The words were hardly out of his mouth when its strains greeted my ears, played with such precision and masterly interpretation as to make even me, its composer, delighted.

Afterwards, Santelmann and I discussed music at great length and became fast friends. He told me that he was amazed to discover that I had no formal musical training. Later, he introduced me to the men of the Marine Band, many of whom praised the "Virgin Islands March" and asked me about the islands. Next day, the *Leatherneck*, the official news organ of the United States Marine Corps, gave a flattering account of my visit.[39] This meeting proved to be an open sesame for me, because through Santelmann I came to meet several fine military musicians and officers who went out of their way to make my trip enjoyable. Taking note of the recognition given me by the white establishment, one colored newspaper wrote: "That he is a musician goes without saying, for the leading white musicians here forgot his color and made his stay one of the most pleasant ever experienced by a man of color."

The following day I called at the home of Reverend Francis J. Grimké, pastor of the Fifteenth Street Presbyterian Church, for whom I had a letter of introduction from a former classmate of his at Princeton, Judge T. McCants Stewart, who had established law offices in St. Thomas. Reverend Grimké was the uncle of the well-known poet Angelina Weld Grimké and brother of the distinguished lawyer Archibald Grimké, who at one time was the United States ambassador to the Dominican Republic.[40] To give a true evaluation of the reverend, I refer to the account of him and his famous church by Dr. William Ferris in his book *The African Abroad:*

> Reverend Grimké is a clergyman whose profound scholarship, reasoning, common sense, dignity and manliness of character, purity of life and kindness of heart, have given him such prestige and standing in the country that it is respected by the leaders of all denominations. . . . The Fifteenth Street Presbyterian Church represents the wealth, culture and social prestige of the community. The old and wealthy families, professors in Howard University, principals of the public schools, government clerks, lawyers, doctors and businessmen, and men living comfortably, attend it.

This outstanding gentleman greeted me warmly. He spoke highly of our mutual friend T. McCants Stewart, recounting his brilliant career as a lawyer and his years in Liberia and London. Grimké was glad to know of the fine friendship between McCants and me in the Virgin Islands. He was also quite interested in my career and the purpose of my visit. His stately, quiet demeanor and his clear intellect deeply impressed me.

True to the genteel manner of the cultivated men and women of the period, Reverend Grimké returned my visit the following day and also invited me to speak at his church the coming Sunday. I, of course, gladly accepted. During my talk I explained the location of the Virgin Islands, its international culture, and the keen interest among our people in the racial question of the United States and elsewhere in the world. My presentation was apparently successful for after the service a large percentage of the congregation surrounded me asking questions about the islands and my mission. Many invited me to their homes, which offers, because of the short duration of my visit, I had to decline. I did, however, have the pleasure of visiting Reverend Grimké several times at his home, where I met many other outstanding men and women of color. Our friendship proved to be a lasting one. We corresponded for many years thereafter, and he presented me with an autographed photo of himself and quite a number of his valuable printed sermons.

Lest I forget, let me mention that my visit to Washington also gave me the unique privilege to attend the ceremonies at the unveiling of the Lincoln Memorial and to look at the nineteen-foot statue of one of the greatest men in history sitting in an armchair meditating.[41] The primary purpose of my visit to Washington, however, was to learn about the techniques of musical education in the public schools. To this end I spoke to several people involved in the field, including Mrs. Lulu Vere Childers, head of the Music Department at Howard University, and the teachers at Dunbar High School. I was not, however, greatly impressed with their methods, which seemed too formalized, too academic. I believed the course of study I had already developed for the elementary schools in the Virgin Islands to be far superior.

While my visit to Washington did not give me much of what I expected to find with respect to music in the schools, it did give me a rare opportunity to meet and talk with many prominent men and women of my race. I was mystified and extremely delighted with the high degree of cultivation and education I found among them. It was indeed a privilege to meet men and women of the caliber of Dr. Kelly Miller, dean of the College of Arts and Sciences at Howard University; Dr. Emmett J. Scott, secretary-treasurer of Howard University; Dr. Garnet Wilkerson, head of the colored public schools in the city; James Weldon Johnson, noted poet and author; Dr. Carter Godwin Woodson, founder of the *Journal of Negro History,* who asked me to write an article on Negro folk music for him;[42] and Mr. and Mrs. Joseph H. Douglass (Fannie was outstanding as a musician in her own right). Most of these illustrious people I met through my distinguished fellow Virgin Islander Reverend Daniel E. Wiseman, who should be more widely known and given due credit in the islands' history books.

Born on January 11, 1858, in St. Thomas, Daniel Wiseman, like another famous native son, Edward Wilmot Blyden, left with his family for the United States while a teenager. In 1881 he entered Howard University and graduated May 9, 1884, from the Theological Department. He joined the Maryland Synod in 1884 and was licensed to preach in the Memorial Lutheran Church of Washington. He simultaneously served as chaplain of Freedman's Hospital and the National Orphan Hospital for several years, and was pastor of the Church of the Redeemer beginning in 1885. He is on record as the organizer of the Theological Alumni of Howard University and was one of the founders of the Association for the Prevention of Tuberculosis. Howard University conferred on him the degree of master of arts in 1895 and the degree of doctor of divinity in 1898. He had the pleasure of laying the cornerstone of Howard's present Theology Department building on August 12, 1893.

A pillar of the Washington colored community, Wiseman was also appreciated and respected by the white establishment. He was one of the few Negroes of his era to serve as a member on federal boards and committees, including the Liberty Board Organization Commission during World War I,[43] the U.S. Employment Bureau Board, the special committee to welcome President Wilson home from abroad in 1919, the committee for the presentation of Medals of Honor to soldiers returning from World War I, and the Inauguration Committee for President Harding. Added to these contributions, he was one of the founders of the Alpha Life Insurance Company and Alpha Bank, organized around 1892 to promote black business. A photograph of the company I obtained shows Wiseman literally at the right hand of Frederick Douglass.[44]

For West Indians, Reverend Wiseman was an institution. The West Indian arriving at Washington, D.C., or even New York City was usually queried, "Have you met Reverend Wiseman?" He and his wife, Almira (affectionately called "Ma" by all of us), offered guidance, assistance, and inspiration to the steady stream of West Indians who came to study or work in the nation's capital in the first part of the twentieth century. Known as "God's Good Man," Daniel Wiseman was accorded reverence, admiration, and respect by all who had the privilege to know him. Before his death I persuaded him to return to his native island, where he often stayed at my home. He delivered an unforgettable sermon at the Lutheran church where he was baptized.

After Washington my search for sound musical pedagogy led me to Philadelphia, where another Virgin Islander of local prominence, the

Reverend Richard Bright, put me in touch with several educators. Again, I was dissatisfied with what I found, and so went on to New York City with the specific intention of discussing the problem with one of my musical mentors—Thomas Tapper. Throughout my early musical career the books written by this gifted educator on music appreciation and the role of music in community life had inspired and guided me. My particular bible was his *The Music Life and How to Succeed in It* (1891), but I devoured each and every one of his works as though my life depended on it. My initial contact with Tapper came through an article I wrote about him in the *Jacobs' Band Monthly* in 1916.[45] In response to my piece, he wrote me a letter and sent me an autographed copy of his most recent book, *Youth and Opportunity* (1912).[46] It was classic Tapper: brimful of vitality, inspiration, moral uplift, and positive thinking. In his letter Tapper asked if Virgin Islanders were "interested in music as community activity?" It was this question that had led me to approach the Danish government about establishing music in the schools, and his writings later guided me in the development of a music course for the elementary schools under the navy. So I looked to him to provide me with the insight and advice I needed to make my trip a success.

Tapper's response to my request for an interview was quick and to the point. He welcomed me enthusiastically and we scheduled an appointment. I went to see him with my friend Harry Watt, who commented on my mental abstraction during our ride. I felt ashamed to tell him the reason. Being fully aware of the fact that the color question exists, and being also sensitive, a little too much so, I had certain fears, for up to that time Dr. Tapper did not know that I was a man of color. On the other hand, I felt in a great measure assured from his writings, for they possessed such a true ring of optimism, high thinking, and broad humanity that it was impossible, I argued within myself, for their author to be obsessed with such a vile, silly, and cowardly thing as race hatred.

The few moments' wait in his office seemed like hours. Various contrary emotions and thoughts swirled like fugal counterpoint through my brain. Suddenly, before me appeared a man slightly below the ordinary height, broad of stature, with a noble, inspiring forehead, well-shaped, strong-looking jaws, a large head covered with fine auburn hair, and eyes flashing with sincere tenderness, intellectuality, and inspiration. By my uniform, he sized me up as the one. I looked for that surprise which, to be frank, I expected. But I was agreeably disappointed. The welcome was genuine. With a strong grasp of the hand and eyes piercing into mine, he seemed in a flash to have read every emotion that was playing through me at the moment. I felt relieved, at home, happy. "At last I have the pleasure of meeting you my dear, young friend. Your career has been very interesting to me and I have followed it through with much satisfaction." So he greeted me.

In the hours that followed, we discussed music and the community. For the first thirty minutes he questioned me not only on the music situation in the Virgin Islands schools but also on my own career and personal life. After all his questions had been answered, he said, "I congratulate you. You have fully forty years of useful activity before you, which I hope you will continue to use for the betterment of the human race." Then, turning to Mr. Watt, he said, "The most appreciative and glowing tribute I have had in my career as a musician came from Mr. Adams several years ago when he wrote me saying that I was instrumental in putting a life on its true course. Now, knowing of his activities in the interest of his countrymen, I feel that I have contributed something miles away from my own home toward the advancement of my fellow men." Following this he advised me about what sort of musical program would be best for the Virgin Islands. I got in a few minutes all that I was looking for in the public schools in Washington and Philadelphia. Tapper was indeed the fountainhead from which I drank freely. As he spoke, I remembered clearly several conversations at the conference of music teachers at Washington's Dunbar High School that Garnet Wilkerson had so kindly arranged for me. The teachers there had referred to Tapper's work as the final authority.[47]

I came away from our interview refreshed and brimming with ideas and energy. Tapper had concluded our interview by giving me a present of fourteen volumes of his piano works, extending an open invitation to call upon him freely for assistance, and asking me to consider him a friend and admirer. On getting to the streets after that interview, the great hustle and bustle of the world's greatest city could not drown these words of Thomas Carlyle kindled by that magnetic life I had just left: "Cast forth thy act, thy word, into the ever-living, ever-working universe; unnoticed today, it will be found flourishing as a banyan grove, perhaps, alas! as a hemlock forest—cast forth thy act, thy word, into the ever-living."[48]

Armed with Tapper's words of wisdom, I returned to the islands. I considered my trip to the States an enormous success. Not only had I accomplished my mission with respect to the musical curriculum, but also I had made many new and lasting acquaintances among the American colored community. One pleasant but totally unexpected result of my trip was the impression I seemed to have made on some of the leading members of that community, who took pride in my achievements and regaled me at every opportunity. Their sentiments were summed up by Henry L. Grant, president of the National Association of Negro Musicians, who wrote to me: "We Negroes in America are proud of you and feel that your work will later pave the way for recognition and higher placement of other men of color in the United States Navy."

My friend and fellow Virgin Islander, Romeo L. Dougherty, sports and drama editor for the *New York Amsterdam News*, summarized my trip as follows:

> Some months ago came to our land a stranger. Not only did he come to inhale a breath of the inspiring wind which has made America what she is today, but to bring a message to our colored musicians, who received him in a manner worthy of those men of the old school in distant lands whose contributions to the world of music will for ages to come inspire ambitious youth and be the light on the distant horizon of artistic endeavor to which youth will ever turn a hopeful eye.
>
> In his little home he had surmounted obstacles that would have tested the grit of even some of our own men who have risen to prominence from obscure surroundings, and to add to his struggles he had to face a narrow environment and patiently bide the time when the Stars and Stripes would open wide the doors even to men of color in this distant land of which we speak.
>
> Assiduously he studied. [There were] [n]o universities to confer degrees upon him but he was unto himself a teacher, a genius recognized by the governors sent to rule his people by America, and soon he wore the chevrons of the only Negro bandmaster in the United States Navy. In the whirlpool of American politics representatives from the House of Congress and the United States Senate went to his island home and they too, joined in the praise which was his. His band under his leadership brought tears of joy to Miranda and the entire Puerto Rican people, and when on his trip here to broaden his mind and study our methods in his chosen field, Santelmann, leader of the United States Marine Band, went out of his way to pay tribute to his genius. And not only this. The universities, both white and colored, welcomed him, and here he found scores of men, white and colored, who had read with much appreciation his contributions to American musical publications, the columns of which were never before graced by the writings of those of us here of color.

Dougherty went on to chastise W. E. B. DuBois for failing to acknowledge my visit and accomplishments:

> Met and welcomed by the leading musicians, legislators and people in every walk of life, the warm reception tendered [Adams] sent him back to his island home with a heart bounding with gratitude and deeper love for his brothers in black here in the United States and one would imagine that for a minute American's so-called cultured leader of the near whites would at least make mention in his *Crisis Magazine* of the visit of Alton A. Adams, Bandmaster, United States Navy Virgin

Islands, U.S.A., even though pictures and other matter bearing on the stranger's visit were placed into his hands by one as cultured and learned even as he, the Honorable Dr. W. E. B. DuBois, but vain and futile has been our search for even one line of welcome to one more deserving than HALF THE NUMBER of those we see monthly spoken of in words to lead us to accept and believe them great when they are but skimming the surface over ground where Adams, superior from every standpoint, long ago covered with glory. Where does he [DuBois] really lend encouragement? Not sitting in his office on Fifth Avenue, unlike the late lamented Booker T. Washington, refusing to enter that section where we are "casting down our buckets."

Once back in the islands I completed the music program and threw myself into its implementation. My first task was to identify some local musicians and train them in my method, so that they could teach it in the schools. Among those whom I selected were Mrs. Galiber, Mrs. Aimee Estornel, and Mrs. Lockhart in St. Thomas and Ms. Markoe in St. Croix. We concentrated on teaching choral music because we had insufficient instruments and because through singing students could learn about the values and techniques of music. We wanted to teach them not to be musicians but to love music and to appreciate its cultural role. For those students who wanted to pursue their study in depth, we formed glee clubs and choruses at the elementary schools and an orchestra at the high school.[49]

Following Tapper, I endeavored to create a course of study that emphasized music appreciation, because to my mind a knowledge of music, its history, its great personalities, and its inner structure, had a vital role to play in both individual and community development. To give some idea of the value I attached to music, let me quote some excerpts from an article I wrote on music appreciation:

MUSIC—AN APPRECIATION

"They who think music ranks among the trifles of existence are in gross error, because from the beginning of the world down to the recent time it has been one of the most forcible instruments for governing the spirit of man."

There are many who believe a musical composition is the mere throwing together of a series of notes or tones, conglomerated as it were into something tuneful. Truly, there are many such so-called compositions, but fortunately they are not classed as music.

Music is independent thought of the highest order, and just as it required thought to master the knowledge contained in the theory of atoms, so the construction of a composition demands the exercise of the musician's deepest brain energy.

Music is a great moral and intellectual stimulus. It quickens the imagination and develops the creative faculty of thought. Under its soothing influence the mind is lifted from the ordinary furrow of its thoughts and only then realizes that it possesses wings to bear it up and soar into mysterious and ethereal realms of beauty otherwise inaccessible. Music portrays certain phases of the emotions that baffle word description more than any other arts can. It addresses the imagination and awakens the feeling for the beautiful and sublime, lifting us above the ordinary environment of everyday life, and by its refining qualities removes the dress of commonplace things and even of vice from our natures, replacing them with higher ideals, loftier aims, and grander and nobler conceptions of what life should be. Architecture takes the means of doing this by its magnificent proportions, noble lines and beautiful groupings; sculpture by its finely imagined forms; poetry by its beautiful characters and philosophical ideas; and music, the art which we are now considering, by beautiful tonal relations and noble or lively rhythms.

Music is the philosophy of love. Love—that grandest and loftiest of motives which has inspired a Raphael's brush or a Shakespeare's pen. Love—the ruling power of the world.

The fact that music can describe and is descriptive has been answered long ago by those melodies which are the product of the inspiration of the great masters who gave voice to the joys, sorrows, and aspirations of the vast people from whose loins they sprang. Listen to the sentiments woven like a thread through its story, telling us something of the pathos of life, of the experiences common to all, and awakening within ourselves an echo of the beautiful and noble feeling it contains. The real mission of music is not to describe scenes in nature (which can better be described by the painter) or to afford mere sensual enjoyment. To claim for music the above alone is to try to deprive or rob it of the highest reason for its existence.

Music is a medium, a language, a complex voice whose highest and real mission is to say something to the human soul, that something which we feel when under the influence of the effect wrought by its mystical tones and which the great philosophers and thinkers have tried hard to define, but lamentably failed. It is not so much a question of hearing what the composer meant to say, but what the composition seems to say to us. For in its indefiniteness and versatility lies its greatest charm. Colonel Parker says: "Without emotion man is nothing. The history of music is the history of the development of the emotion of the human race from the beginning. Music has then for its function the cultivation of the spirit or the higher development of the soul of man. The faculty of the mind which has the dominant influence in deciding the motive and directing the will is the emotion.

Music, then, being the language of the emotions, covers a wider range of usefulness and aesthetic enjoyment than the other arts, and it is also the most versatile and universally loved; loved not only for its sweet tones or the more sensual gratification it gives some, but loved for itself. Loved because it forms a deep influence in the formation of character, because it is a factor for influencing the motives and actions of life, because it breathes all that is attractive in nature—all that is grand and noble in life; loved because it is an ideal echo of all human hearts and events, because it goes deep in the heart and awakens there the desire for a higher moral and ethical plane of existence, and because it is a medium of preparing the soul of man to commune with his God.

"Let me write the songs of a nation and I care not who make its laws." By this is meant that the bard has more influence over the minds of the people and is more powerful in directing their actions than the legislator.

King Edward VII of England in an address at the opening of the Royal School of Music of London said: "The time has come when class can no longer stand aloof from class and that man does his duty best who works most earnestly in bridging over the gulf between different classes, which it is the tendency of increased wealth and increased civilization to widen. I claim for music the merit that it has a voice which speaks in different tones perhaps, but with equal force, to the cultivated and to the ignorant, to the peer and to the peasant. I claim for music a variety of expression which belongs to no other art, and therefore adapts itself more than any other art to produce the union of feeling in which I much desire to promote. Lastly I claim for music the distinction which is awarded to it by Addison: 'That it is the only pleasure in which excess cannot be injurious.' What more, gentlemen, can I say on behalf of the art for the promotion of which we are today opening this institution which I trust will give to music a new impulse, a glorious future and a national life."

Consider how wide a range of usefulness music covers! See the savage and the semi-savages around their wigwams and rude huts, chanting their wild songs in their half chaotic system of tones, though incoherent to civilized ears yet stimulating courage, ardor, and enthusiasm among them; to the mother singing her sweet lullabies so full of tender longing, aspiration, hope, and enthusiastic yearnings of maternal love to her young child—to the national and folk songs feeding us with the fire of patriotism, and inspiring our soul with love for home and country—to the grand solemn deep-toned minor strains of the organ reverberating in the stillness of the church, and arousing the religious emotions of those under its mystical spell by super-inducing a holy state of mind, and inspiring sentiments of praise to the great I AM.

The technicalities or mechanical manipulations of the player, though indispensable to the rendition and interpretation of a composition, are but a means to an end. Showing us how fast and how well he can play, or how high she can sing, simply excites our curiosity; his real mission is to make us forget he is playing, to go deep down in our hearts and awaken there a response to the message of divine inspiration he should deliver—to make us think by transporting us into that wonderful Elysium of Love where the mysteries of the soul will be revealed.

Considering its usefulness from a commercial point of view, we find it one of great magnitude. We need but think of the large sums spent in opera houses, symphony orchestras, military bands, in musical education, in the manufacture of musical instruments, the fabulous amount paid to great singers and artists, of the many whose lives are conditioned upon musical work, to note its commercial value, which more strikingly proves the fact of its indispensability and its claim to uplift morally and intellectually all people. In conclusion, I hope the time will soon come when all will cultivate the love of the beautiful in music to the greatest extent of their ability, recognize its great influence in the home, the school, the church, and in all social, political and other functions; and last, but by no means least, when the musician will be more respected and be considered not only as a dreamer, but as one who pours fourth his whole soul in melting pathos and by its outpouring stirs up in us a continual stream of happiness and pleasure—and he will be thought of as the important bearer of the divine message of Peace and Good Will Towards Men.[50]

6 The Navy Band's 1924 United States Tour

Editor's Note: *That Adams devotes an entire chapter to the 1924 U.S. tour of his U.S. Navy Band of the Virgin Islands suggests its deep personal significance for him. The tour represents not just the "apogee of the navy band's success" but also the triumph of his social project. By serving with the navy (rather than protesting its presence), Adams as a community leader gained access to opportunities that he felt were essential to the future of the islands. Paramount in his mind was the islands' economic foundation, on which, he believed, any social progress would be based. Disrupted by war, trade regulations, and technological changes in seagoing vessels, the Virgin Islands' role as an entrepôt of Caribbean trade was uncertain at best. Instead the islands' future seemed to lie in tourism. The navy band's tour thus offered a huge marketing opportunity, placing Adams and his band in the role of cultural ambassadors introducing American mainlanders to the islands and inviting these future visitors to the winter oasis. That the idea for the tour was first voiced by the black commissioners sent to investigate the naval administration illustrates Adams's argument that the navy genuinely supported the band's efforts, using them for positive publicity certainly, but not exploiting them solely as propaganda. The tour's success is also testament to the tireless efforts of expatriate Virgin Islanders living in the States who helped secure additional publicity and concerts for the band. Adams also sees the tour as a significant event in race relations. It offered a positive example of black accomplishment and racial cooperation at a time when lynchings remained all too common, the insult of Jim Crowism was pervasive even in government, and the racist, KKK-inspired movie* The Birth of a Nation *was still showing nine years after its release. The band's tour also helped further understanding within the black community itself—notably between West Indians and*

African Americans, bringing these groups into conversation and inspiring a shared pride.

The apogee of the navy band's success came in 1924 with its celebrated tour of the eastern United States.[1] Through this tour the band and the Virgin Islands were brought to the attention of millions of Americans who attended our concerts, heard us on the radio, or read about us in newspapers. Everywhere we went, we received honors and acclaim, a fact that redounded to the credit of not only the Virgin Islands but also the colored race generally, for it was widely publicized that we were the only colored unit in the American Navy and that I was the first and only colored bandmaster. These facts were not lost upon the American colored community, which not only hailed our accomplishments but also drew upon them to intensify its claims for increased racial equality. The tour, then, not only was a personal triumph for the bandsmen and me and a major propaganda victory for the navy but also can be looked upon as a minor, albeit significant event in the history of American race relations.

The idea of sending the band to tour the United States was first raised by the members of a federal commission composed of prominent American colored leaders that had been sent by the U.S. Congress to the Virgin Islands in January 1924 to investigate conditions there.[2] While the commission members were in St. Thomas, the band rendered a concert in their honor in Emancipation Garden. The next day, the commission, through its secretary, Charles E. Mitchell, sent me the following letter:

January 28, 1924

Dear Mr. Adams:

I am directed to extend to you, to the members of your excellent band, and to all parties concerned, our most hearty thanks for the supreme pleasure afforded each and every member of the Virgin Islands Commission as we listened (last night, Sunday, January 27th) to the splendid program rendered at the Grand Promenade Concert—given in welcome to the Commission. . . .

We sat spellbound throughout the entire program, richly enjoying every number—from the stirring march composed by yourself, entitled "Virgin Islands," down to the exceptionally fine and impressive rendition of our Nation's song—"THE STAR SPANGLED BANNER."

It would be gratifying beyond measure if some way could be found that would permit your band to make a tour of the United States and thus enable thousands of music lovers there, and citizens generally, to have visible and audible demonstration of what the Virgin Islands have produced. . . .

We desire not only to congratulate you and your men upon your unquestioned ability, but likewise we heartily congratulate the United States Navy upon its splendid policy of thus encouraging and employing musical talent among that group of patriotic Americans to which we proudly belong.[3]

Naval officials responded promptly and enthusiastically to the commission's recommendation, for some of them, particularly Lieutenant Commander Ellis Stone, who was directly in charge of the band, had been thinking along similar lines. Recognizing that a tour would be an excellent method of bringing the Virgin Islands and their people to the attention of the American public, and thus to potential tourists, the U.S. Navy Department gave the project its fullest cooperation and support.

Within a remarkably short time I was sent to Washington, D.C., in order to make the necessary arrangements for the tour. In carrying out this assignment, I worked not only with naval officials but also with committees of leading colored citizens. The Washington Committee was headed by my old friends Reverend Wiseman and Professor Miller, while the New York Committee was led by the redoubtable Romeo Dougherty and Fred R. Moore, who was the editor of the *New York Age*.[4] One of the problems we encountered during this organizational period was a federal law forbidding the competition of service bands with like civilian organizations. Our friend and founding sponsor, Captain White, got us around this seeming impasse when he succeeded in having the band placed under the Keith's Circuit, so that any money generated by our appearances would benefit hospitals in the Virgin Islands.

During this hectic time, I experienced one of the proudest occasions in my life when Dr. Edwin Franko Goldman, the world famous bandmaster, invited me to conduct his band before an audience of thousands in New York's Central Park. My initial contact with Goldman, one of my musical idols, had come a few years earlier when he had sent me a highly flattering letter commending the series of articles that I had written for the *Jacobs' Band Monthly*.[5] I eagerly responded, and thereafter we maintained a regular correspondence on musical subjects. When Dr. Goldman heard that I was coming to New York to make arrangements for the tour, he sent me an invitation to attend one of his concerts on the Mall in Central Park. As it turned out, he invited me to the podium to be guest conductor—the first time a member of my race had been so honored.[6] The following account from a New York newspaper gives some idea of what happened that splendid evening under the stars:

> On last Wednesday night Bandmaster Alton Adams was the guest conductor of Edwin Goldman, leader of the Goldman's Band, which is giving a series of concerts on the Mall in Central Park, and he conducted his own composition entitled the *Virgin Islands March* before a gathering of people estimated at over 20,000.
>
> Before presenting the colored bandmaster to the audience, Mr. Goldman said: "We are always glad to have among us distinguished musicians, especially as guest conductors. This evening I am presenting to you a distinguished musician in the person of Mr. Alton Adams, Bandmaster, United States Navy, born, educated, and trained in the Virgin Islands of the United States, our possession. Mr. Adams and myself have been in correspondence for several years, and this is the first time I have had the privilege of meeting him personally, as it is his first visit here. His work among bands in the islands has won for him the highest praise of all the Governor Generals there. He is indeed a wonderful musician, and I am asking him to conduct one of his own compositions entitled the 'Virgin Islands March.' I take pleasure in presenting to you Bandmaster Alton Adams of the Virgin Islands."
>
> The applause was long and intense before and after the appearance of the bandmaster on the bandstand. He was forced to give several encores. Even the bandsmen at the conclusion laid down their instruments and applauded vociferously the young musician. Mr. Goldman introduced him to every member of the band, which numbers about 75 musicians. The military salutes from Adams in response to the applause were unique to the gathering and seemed to please the vast audience.[7]

One of the things that had brought Goldman and me together was our common concern that a bandmaster's organization should be formed in the United States. In my series of articles on the band, I had strongly advocated the establishment of a bandmaster's guild, having in mind the excellent work done at Kneller Hall in England, which was instrumental in making the military bands in England second to none in the world. In that institution, bandsmen had to undergo four years of intensive training and bandmasters seven years, completion of which not only gave the men the qualification needed but also raised the dignity and status of the profession in that country.

Eventually, under the leadership of Goldman, Sousa, and others, the American Bandmasters Association was duly organized in 1928, and I was invited to become a charter member for the first meeting in 1929. However, I did not see fit at the time to join. Later, on being transferred to the Fleet Naval Reserve after World War I, I realized the advantages to be gained by aligning myself with the body, and so sent in my application. I received no reply and, in time, forgot the whole affair until several years later, in 1937, when Goldman sent me the following letter:

> You will probably be surprised to hear from me, but the fact that you were black-balled by the A.B.A. at its annual meeting some years ago is still in my mind. President Frank Simon and I have just discussed this matter again and we feel that you should be a member of this organization.
>
> I would suggest that you make formal application for membership again at once, because we are having our next convention on the 5th, 6th and 7th of March. . . .
>
> Mr. Sousa and I were both for you the last time, but it seems there were a few southern members who caused the black-balling. The vote was by secret ballot. Mr. Simon and I would like the thing out in the open this year, and if you care to make application we will fight for you, and I feel that we can bring about better results this time.
>
> If I were you I would just write a letter saying that you would like to make application again. You can say that I know you and will vouch for you. If you care to do this, I would do it at once.[8]

To please Goldman, I did reapply for membership. I received a notification that I was eligible for membership, but I did not elect to follow up on the matter any further.[9] Goldman and I remained good friends and kept up our correspondence and personal contacts until his death in 1956. I will always cherish his friendship, for not only was he an admirable musician and composer but he was also a true and staunch believer in the brotherhood of man.

The navy band's tour began on July 1, 1924, when the bandsmen arrived at Hampton Roads, Virginia. Rather than start our schedule immediately, we spent fifteen days on the naval station there, developing and improving our skills. This practice period was necessary because the musical skills of the St. Croix contingent had deteriorated rather drastically during its years away from St. Thomas. My brother, Julien, and I worked hard to bring them up to the required standard, and the men responded nicely to the long, monotonous hours of practice. We played several times for the personnel of the station and won the commendation of both officers and men for our music and discipline. Our first official appearance before the public came on July 6 at the bandstand in the beautiful Norfolk city park. The bandstand there was so enormous that our group of thirty-nine men looked like a mere handful.[10] But the acoustics were excellent and the surroundings inspirational. As was to be the pattern throughout the tour, before beginning the program, we told the audience the reasons for our visit and gave them as much background information as possible about the islands, stressing their attractiveness for winter holidays.

Several other concerts followed, each of which brought us high accolades and increasing recognition among the local citizenry. We discovered, however, that because of discriminatory racial practices, the colored population of Norfolk could not attend our concerts in the public parks. Several colored organizations wrote to the commanding officer of the Norfolk station requesting an opportunity for their people to hear the band. It was arranged for us to play for a gathering of about five hundred of the leading colored people at a lawn party held at the home of Mr. and Mrs. Clarence Russell. We were warmly received and lavishly entertained as champions of the race. That affair was a real eye-opener for us, since it provided our first experiences with the professional caliber, the cultivation, the achievements, and the dignified character of the colored middle class in the United States. Like many islanders, I had a highly stereotyped view of the American Negro as a downtrodden, indolent menial unable to rise above his former slave status. As we mingled and conversed with the urbane, intelligent attendees and learned of their appreciation of fine music, my men and I were compelled to revise our unwarranted feelings of superiority. This lesson was repeatedly reinforced by similar contacts made throughout our tour, so that for us as well, the tour helped break down unfortunate prejudices.

On July 15 I left for Washington, D.C., in advance of the band in order to rearrange our schedule in that city. We hoped to play a special concert for President Calvin Coolidge at which we were to premiere a march that I had written especially for him—"The Spirit of the U.S.N." Unfortunately, due to the recent death of the president's son, it was decided that the situation was too delicate for such a performance.[11] Disappointed but not daunted, I worked with assistant secretary of the navy Colonel Theodore Roosevelt and a committee of colored citizens (consisting of Reverend Wiseman, Dr. Miller, Dr. Emmett J. Scott, Professor William H. Davis of the Federal Commission to the Virgin Islands, and Mr. Richard Grant) to schedule a series of appearances that placed us in the most conspicuous parts of the nation's capital.

Our first program was rendered on July 17 at the Washington Navy Yard. On the following morning, we serenaded Secretary of Labor James J. Davis at his office. Secretary Davis was warm in his praises of the band and posed for a picture with me while directing. Here, as in most other places, the cameramen had us covered from every angle, and our music brought forth good-sized audiences. From the Labor Department, we went to serenade the district commissioners—the three men who administered the city at that time—in front of City Hall. The commissioners shook hands with the entire band, while expressing their appreciation and welcome. Previous to this event we had visited the State Department, where we met Assistant Secretary Lane, who also shook our hands and welcomed us to Washington.

That evening we played at Meridian Hill Park, which was situated in the wealthiest and most aristocratic section of the city. Our audience, estimated at nearly ten thousand, contained the best that Washington could produce of both races, white and colored. On this occasion, as on many others, we opened our concert with Claudio S. Grafulla's "Washington Grays March," one of the best and most difficult marches ever written. This was followed by selections from Giuseppe Verdi's opera *Aïda;* the Virgin Island composer Alfred Nemours's bewitching grand waltz "Soiree de Berlin"; Ernest Seitz and Eugene Lockhart's beautiful song "The World Is Waiting for the Sunrise," a popular number which gained us steady encores everywhere; the overture to Gioacchino Rossini's opera *Semiramide;* the Fred Lax–Alton Adams "Mocking-Bird" piccolo solo; Frédéric Chopin's "Polonaise Militaire"; Luis Miranda's danza "Ugolina"; and the popular native Virgin Islands dance "Sam Polo."

We were told by many in the audience that several of our wealthy listeners were under the impression that we came to amuse them with jazz music, but this impression, to their hearty delight, was soon dispelled by the rendition of the program outlined above. The numerous expressions of appreciation that followed our performance were most gratifying to us, particularly since so many people inquired about the location of the Virgin Islands and expressed their desire to visit. Later that night we made our debut before the microphone at radio station WCAP. To play live for the radio or phonograph is always a challenge, for the performance must be as faultless as possible. Our session went off well and the radio critics were clearly pleased with the results. In the weeks that followed, hundreds of letters and applause cards conveying the delight of the unseen audience were forwarded to us by radio staff. It was an exhilarating but exhausting day, with five performances from sunrise to well after sunset.

The days that followed were less strenuous but no less rewarding. We played throughout the city, and our reception proved so great that we extended our stay from three to seven days. Of the many exhilarating events, one that stands out most clearly in my mind was an impromptu concert for Secretary of the Navy Curtis D. Wilbur, who, upon encountering two of my bandsmen in the Navy Yard, had requested a performance. We serenaded him and other dignitaries at the Navy Department, and although the event had gone unadvertised, it drew an audience of several thousand people.

Secretary Wilbur was a man of striking personality, towering over six feet in height and displaying to full advantage a well-set athletic figure. His handshake, though tender, was viselike in grip. He addressed the band, thanking us for the opportunity given him to hear, as he called it, "our famous music," complimenting us on our performance and appearance, and emphasizing the fact that we gave credit not only to the Virgin Islands but to the navy as well. He conveyed satisfaction that our race had been given the opportunity to express itself so well in the navy. He asked us to convey his greetings to the people of the islands, to assure them that the federal government was interested in their well being and would do everything in its power for them. He reminded us that a policy of patience is necessary in all human endeavors and that every nation, big or small, had its difficulties to contend with. He concluded by saying that he regretted that the band was not touring the entire country, especially the West Coast, and hoped that such a tour could be arranged in the future. Assistant Secretary of the Navy Theodore Roosevelt was also present. He too gave me a tight grasp of the hand, remarking that he had yet to hear a better band. Another friend, former islands governor Henry Hughes Hough (1922–23), then addressed us, expressing his satisfaction with our music and asking us to convey kind remembrances to the people of the Virgin Islands.

Our success among the colored community of the city was as great as that with official Washington. I will always recall with satisfaction the glowing tribute paid to us by Dr. Scott after our concert at Howard University on July 21. This eminent gentleman not only praised our musical performance but also exhorted his fellow colored Americans to take example from our work and achievements. To show their appreciation, the colored people of Washington held a grand reception for the band that same evening at the colonnade of the newly constructed Lincoln Theatre. The reception committee included the leading colored residents of the city, among them Dr. Miller, Dr. Scott, Mr. and Mrs. Gabriel Pelham, Professor Dorcy Thodes of Howard University, Mr. Holland (one of the leading businessmen and bankers of Washington), Mr. and Mrs. Joseph Douglass, Henry Lincoln Johnson, and Dr. W. H. Davis of the federal commission that had visited the islands. The evening at the Lincoln Theater was memorable not only for the tributes we received but also for the vocal performance of my good friend tenor Philip Gomez, who delighted the gathering with selections from *Tosca* and other operas. From Washington we went to Philadelphia.

Through the Reverend Richard Bright, another illustrious Virgin Islander who had achieved considerable prominence in Philadelphia, several engagements were scheduled for us in that city. However, because we had overextended our time in Washington, the Philadelphia schedule was disrupted. To be candid, I must say that with the exception of our concert at the Wanamaker Store, the time spent in Philadelphia was wasted. In the other cities, the hearty cooperation of naval officers with prominent civilians was largely responsible for the considerable interest accorded the band. In Philadelphia, however, such cooperation was not in evidence, and we were not given the opportunity to play in the best or most visible locations.

Because of these problems, charges of discrimination arose from some. It is important to observe that no serious racial incidents permanently marred the band's tour, a fact that underscores my conviction that music is a universalizing human experience. Everywhere we went, we were treated with respect and regard by both colored people and white people. Our audiences, black, white, and mixed, were united in their appreciation of our performance and demeanor. The Navy Department, which many have accused of being racist, certainly showed us no overt discrimination. All the officials and officers with whom we came into contact took great pains to make our tour both pleasant and rewarding and to provide us with maximum public exposure.

One unpleasant incident did occur during our first trip to Philadelphia, but it was satisfactorily resolved. Prior to one of our park concerts, I left the band for a few hours to take care of some personal business. Upon rejoining it immediately before the concert was to begin, I found it unready to play. When I asked my brother, Julien, who served as assistant bandmaster, about the trouble, he pointed to some old boxes scattered about and informed me that the park people wanted us to play seated upon them. Just as I was asking who was responsible, the fellow in charge of the park approached me and said, "What do you want us to do, furnish you with morris chairs?" I replied: "Now listen to me. We don't expect you to furnish us with special chairs. But we do want you to provide us with the same seating arrangements that you would give to John Philip Sousa. Otherwise you won't get any music from us here today. I want you to understand that." He stared at me hard, so I added: "I will give you just half an hour to straighten things out, or I will complain to the navy, and there will be no music." So he sent someone to get the appropriate chairs.[12]

Meanwhile, the concert had been delayed, and one colored man in the audience shouted: "I wonder if while you're waiting you'd play us a piece?" Reverend Bright immediately turned on him, admonishing: "What's the matter with you? This man is fighting for principle, and you can only shout for music. That's why you are in your present condition." Once the band was finally seated, we had only twenty minutes left of the hour we were scheduled to play, and that is all that I allowed the band to play. As we left, the park superintendent came up to me, saying: "Bandmaster, I hope that you won't make a fuss about this thing. You know, I served in the Virgin Islands as a marine." I answered, "Then you should have known better," and walked away.

Our concert at the Wanamaker Store was partial compensation for our other disappointments in Philadelphia. One of the largest department stores in the world at that time, Wanamaker's had under its roof many activities and organizations, one of which was its own broadcasting station, WOO, on which only the finest bands and orchestras played. The store, which at that time employed more colored hands proportionately than any other store in the world, also had two fine military bands, one of which was composed of colored personnel. The colored band was under the able directorship of Bandmaster Grinell, a white man, who was very fraternal to us. After our concert, which was broadcast over WOO to millions of listeners in addition to the very large audience inside, the manager of the store prolifically complimented the playing of the band. His whole demeanor bespoke an agreeable surprise, which he openly admitted. His request that I send him a large picture of myself to be placed in the store alongside those of Sousa, Goldman, Santelmann, and others not only filled me with a good deal of pride but also sent Reverend Bright home in raptures of bliss and satisfaction that "Country," as he termed us, had acquitted itself with such a high degree of success.

From Philadelphia the band went to New York City, where we spent two glorious weeks concertizing, arriving July 20 and departing on August 18. Space does not permit a full account of our many wonderful concerts in the Big Apple. Suffice it to say that we played at the major parks throughout Manhattan, the Bronx, Brooklyn, Staten Island, Jamaica, and even Hackensack, New Jersey. The audiences were always large, enthusiastic, and appreciative. Some events still stand out vividly in my memory, such as our first concert at Harlem's St. Nicholas Park on 137th Street on August 1. Prior to this concert the band was entertained by Imperial Lodge 127 of the Elks at their magnificent auditorium on 129th Street. After a light lunch, we formed up to march to the park through the streets of Harlem, with a sizeable delegation from the lodge serving as our escorts. From the day we landed in Virginia, the people of Harlem, in particular the large Virgin Islands community there, had awaited our appearance with an interest that cannot be described. So, when we started our march up Seventh Avenue to St. Nicholas Park, we found a massive audience lining the sidewalks for blocks, awaiting us with bated breath and smiling faces. We were cheered and applauded wildly as we marched proudly by. After we passed, members of the crowd joined the happy procession to the bandstand. If delirious, spontaneous joy was ever evidenced in any people, it was in those who filled to overflowing St. Nicholas Park on the day of our concert. The Virgin Islanders who did not attend were very few. The aged, the decrepit, the invalid were there, cheering along with everyone else every number on the program.[13]

After the concert it was our intention to march back to the lodge, where a supper had been prepared for us, but that proved impossible. The band was engulfed—consumed—by a crowd so mad with joy and excitement as to cause grave uneasiness at the nearby 16th Police Precinct. Not knowing what had provoked the crowd and not being able to divine why the flow of traffic in that section of the city had been brought to a standstill, several squads of bluecoats were sent out to ease the situation. There was not enough of the force to be of any practical help, so the good captain simply waited until the crowd had spent its ecstasy. As the *Amsterdam News* observed of this "happening": "The band has won its way into the hearts of colored Americans, and nothing is being left undone to show the high appreciation of the people for their ability." The concert, and those that followed, meant much to the people of Harlem, for, besides the music and the relationship, they realized that what we were doing was just vindication of their true status in the cultured part of the human family. I will always remember one man screaming during the explosion of joy that erupted after the concert: "Yes. Yes. Let them find out from this that we are not monkey chasers."[14]

In addition to the fervid response it gave to our music, the colored community of New York outdid itself to entertain us in order to demonstrate its appreciation. Every night we were hosted at one or more affairs attended by the cream of the colored community, who toasted us in eloquent speeches. Among the prominent musicians, artists, writers, and journalists attending these functions were Dr. Harry T. Burleigh, Deacon Johnson, Frank Williams, E. H. Margetson, Romeo Dougherty, Casper Holstein, Bob Slater, Henry Creamer, Lucien H. White, Henry M. Cornelius, Sr., Tim Brymn, Dr. Melville W. Charlton, W. N. Spiller, and Leonard LaBeet. On these convivial occasions, I was able to renew old friendships and establish many lasting new ones. Some idea of what transpired during these receptions and banquets is conveyed by the following newspaper clippings:

BENEVOLENT SOCIETY ENTERTAINS V.I. BAND

After its concert in Staten Island Sunday evening . . . the United States Naval Band of the Virgin Islands was entertained by the American West Indian Benevolent Society, Inc., at a banquet given at the organization's home [at] 149 West 136th Street.

The bandsmen were welcomed by Hugo Jackson, Chairman of the reception committee. The culinary artists, under the direction of Sisters Alberta Thomas and Ada Bastian, seemed not to have omitted anything on their menu which would have added to the perfection of the entertainment. George James greeted the musicians and acquainted them with the purpose of the organization and outlined its progress for the 25 years of its existence. . . . Miss Blanche Prince . . . sang and presented the bandmaster with a costly basket of choice roses. G. J. Fleming greeted the bandsmen on behalf of the juvenile branch of the society and emphasized the good impression the achievement of the band would have on the youths.

CARLTON AVENUE YMCA ENTERTAINS NAVY BAND

The United States Navy Band of the Virgin Islands, led by Bandmaster Alton A. Adams, the only Negro bandmaster in the Navy, filled its engagement to play at Fort Greene Park Saturday evening. . . . On account of the rain, however, the concert was cut short. The entire band made its way to the Carlton Avenue Branch Y.M.C.A., where a reception had been prepared. A very fine collation was prepared by a committee of ladies, . . . speeches of welcome were made by Mr. Louis Yeppa, representing the fraternal organizations of Brooklyn; Reverend P. Dewitt Perryman, who is visiting the city; and the Branch Secretary, A. L. Comither.

Mr. Yeppa, a native of the Virgin Islands, reviewed many points of interest relative to the life and needs of the people of the Virgin Islands and the wholesome impression that this band is making upon both colored and white people of America. Reverend Perryman paid a glowing tribute to the men for their ability in playing the classics. . . . Following these . . . speeches, Bandmaster Adams responded with [a] brief historical outline of the . . . Virgin Islands and their hope under the American flag.[15]

For the enormous success of the New York portion of the tour, great credit was due to Lieutenant J. Sinnott, USN, aide to Admiral Plunkett and friend of Captain White. Lieutenant Sinnott managed to secure the assistance of not only Admiral Plunkett but also the city chamberlain—the Honorable Philip Berolzheimer. Mr. Berolzheimer's interest in the band extended to providing us with two tourist buses for our local transportation and, by paying out of his own pocket, our roundtrip steamboat passages between New York and Boston.

As for Admiral Plunkett, who gave orders that nothing must be left undone that would contribute to our comfort and happiness, many people who knew this gray-haired veteran remarked that they had never seen him in such a happy frame of mind as when interesting himself in the band's work and activities. The name *Virgin Islands* seemed to have been imprinted on his brow, and I recall how pleased he felt when the band gave its concert for the officers at the Brooklyn Navy Yard. The admiral was especially interested in the piccolo solos played by me and in the "tangos," as he termed the Spanish dances and our local bamboulas. (I might note here that the *habañera* type of music, which includes our native bamboulas, everywhere caught the ear of the public and elicited the greatest applause and demand for encores.)

From New York we went to Boston for an all-too-brief visit. We arrived on August 13 and played two concerts, one at the Navy Yard and another aboard the historic ship USS *Constitution*. The next day at noon we performed at the famous Boston Commons, where before an audience of thousands of rapt listeners we played our best concert of the entire tour. Every number, which was a select gem from the masters, was received with wild applause. After we finished, a steady stream of people flowed to the bandstand to express their enjoyment of the concert, some going so far as to say that it was among the best heard there during the past fifteen years. Among those offering their congratulations were members of the Boston Symphony Orchestra and also several members of the New England Conservatory of Music. Our friend, Hans Bishop of St. Croix, was also there, and he happily informed me that this was a red-letter day in the calendar of his Boston life.

I had that same day, August 14, the pleasure of meeting the eminent scholar, author, and editor of the *Boston Guardian* Mr. William Monroe Trotter, who came to offer his services in any way that could be of assistance to us. But to my thinking, the crowning achievement of my whole Boston trip was the privilege, the honor, of meeting one of the world's most charming women, a brilliant musician, lecturer, and author, one of my own race, and a credit to any race—Mrs. Maud Cuney-Hare. Mrs. Hare not only came to the bandstand to express her admiration of our efforts but later sent me a warm personal letter, which contained the following excerpt:

> It is remarkable what you have accomplished in spite of the fact that you have lived far from the large music-centers, and in fact it would have been praiseworthy and notable even in the most musical surroundings. Your achievement causes those who have done so little here,

and those of *us all*, who ought to have accomplished much more, to think seriously and to make new resolves for the future.

On the evening of the next day, we gave a concert in East Weymouth, Massachusetts, that was heard by some fifteen to twenty thousand people. We received a grand ovation, as well as a signal honor paid us by the celebrated woman cornetist Mrs. Fannie Young. Mrs. Young told me that at the request of her husband (a celebrated symphony orchestra leader who had heard the band at Boston Commons), she had journeyed over forty miles to hear us play. This lady was so enraptured over our efforts that she could not resist coming to the bandstand to tell the "boys" how highly she regarded their performance. Attention to nuances, attack, and an even technique, she felt, were the strong points of the band. That evening we were entertained by Boston's best, who listened with attention to what I had to tell them concerning the true conditions existing in the Virgin Islands.

One of the most memorable experiences of the entire tour was a ceremony that took place August 13 on the Boston docks in front of the receiving ship MSS *Southery* when the ladies belonging to the Grand Army of the Republic, which was holding its convention in Boston at the time, presented the band with two American flags: a small silk one on a staff and a very large one made of bunting (which I still have in my home). The presentation was made by their president, Mary L. Rollins, a beautiful woman with a silver voice. Her inspiring oration on this occasion concluded with the following remarks, which will forever ring in my ears:

> Fellowmen of my race from the Virgin Islands, it is my honor on behalf of this delegation to greet you and to bid you welcome to dear old Boston and not far from the spot where Crispus Attucks, one of our people, was one of the first to shed his blood on behalf of the liberty of this great nation. We feel proud to see for the first time in our nation's glorious history, men of our race wearing the chevrons of musicians in our proud and gallant navy. We feel confident that as a result of your beautiful music and exemplary conduct, similar placements will soon be made for other members of our race. On behalf of this delegation and of the city of Boston, we ask that you accept these flags symbolic of the greatest nation on earth. Even though our nation does not as yet give you all for which this emblem stands, we urge you, we beseech you, we entrust you, one and all, to cherish it, love it, fight for it, and if necessary die for it. It represents to us here the epitome of all that is grand, good, and glorious in our nation's history.

To this day I can see the tears slowly trickling down the cheeks of that grand lady, tears that spoke more eloquently than even her beautiful words. I can still feel the grip of that brief silence which preceded the outburst of applause and bravos from the officers and men who lined the ship to witness the touching ceremony.[16]

Leaving Boston, we returned to New York, where we gave two concerts: one at the city park in Brooklyn, the other a farewell one at the Renaissance Casino. The latter gathering, which was reported to be one of the largest assemblages of its kind held in Harlem, was arranged by that dedicated Virgin Islander Casper Holstein, under the auspices of the Virgin Islands Congressional Council. I had met Holstein several years earlier through our mutual friend D. Hamilton Jackson, who was married to Holstein's sister. Since that time, we had always been quite friendly with one another, although we differed fundamentally over politics. We both desired the same good things for the Virgin Islands, but our methods of dealing with local problems were not the same, and we held diametrically opposed views regarding conditions there. It has always been my belief that Holstein was not truthfully informed about conditions in the islands under the naval administration, and that he was taken advantage of by demagogues and idlers who refused to acknowledge the worthwhile achievements of the naval governors.

Because I have never become too involved in politics and never believed it of sufficient truth and sincerity to select or lose friends over, I never allowed political differences to cloud my friendship and respect for Holstein the man. This attitude I believe Holstein reciprocated, because he recognized that what the band had accomplished went beyond politics, or rather, moved politics to a higher level wherein the best interests of the Virgin Islands had been significantly advanced. Certainly, he reflected such sentiments in his energetic organization of the farewell get-together at the Renaissance Casino. All of our friends in Harlem were there, and they entertained us royally. Glowing speeches were given by Armer Alderman, George W. Harris, and Louis Yeppa. Our old friend Charles E. Mitchell of the federal commission also attended and complimented us on our achievements. After the gala affair, Holstein had a reception for the bandsmen at his home and spoke warmly of our efforts to bring the Virgin Islands to the attention of America.

From New York we made an unexpected detour to Philadelphia. There had been much consternation among the colored community of that fine city because the band had been provided with no real opportunity to play for them, and because they, in turn, had not been able to entertain us. They dispatched numerous telegrams to Assistant Secretary of the Navy Theodore Roosevelt, who was a great favorite among Afro-Americans, requesting a special appearance of the band for charitable purposes. Roosevelt gave his authorization for the band to appear at the Dunbar Theater, with the proceeds going to the Frederick Douglass Hospital. The resulting benefit on the evening of August 18 was enjoyed by one and all, and we at last had a chance to meet the leading colored people in the City of Brotherly Love.

We ended our tour with two concerts at the famous Hampton Institute in Virginia. The time spent there was a most enjoyable and fitting termination of our peregrinations. The pleasure was ours to play several times before the summer students and faculty, and the pleasure was mine of addressing that fine body, telling them as best I could about the islands. Six students from the Virgin Islands were beside themselves with joy to have us among them, and took no little pains to show us so and to take us around the grounds of the lovely campus.[17]

The next morning, with our musical tour at an end, the USS *Kittery* was at the dock waiting for us. She was a familiar sight. Prior to and during World War I, this vessel, as the SS *Praesident*, had been a frequent visitor to St. Thomas. She was owned by a German company, the Hamburg-American line, and had plied the Caribbean carrying passengers and cargo. With American entry into the war, the *Praesident* had been seized as a prize of war and converted into the USS *Kittery*.[18] Now a supply transport, the *Kittery* visited St. Thomas once a month, carrying supplies and personnel to the small naval base located there. We were given comfortable accommodations aboard and received first-class treatment all the way. There was plenty of time in transit to reminisce on the wonderful times we had experienced on tour and the warm and friendly people we met.

In the final stages of our tour, however, notes of sadness tempered our enthusiasm. En route to Philadelphia, we received news from St. Thomas of the death of Mrs. P. O. Nicholson, wife of our popular clarinet and saxophone player. "Paluden," as we called him, had left her in the island hale, hearty, and pregnant. Complications had set in. She had been rushed to the local hospital and given every possible aid, but she died in childbirth. The baby girl also died. Paluden was beside himself with grief. Shortly before that, word had come to us of the death in St. Thomas of the father of George Seeley, another of our first-class musicians. As could be expected, George was most anxious to get back home to his family.

Saddest of all, we were leaving behind in a Brooklyn hospital one of our excellent musicians, a fantastic drummer and a perfect gentleman, Ronald Hennessey. He had come down with a terminal illness for which the doctors gave us little optimism. Few of us had hopes of seeing him again. I remember my farewell visit with him. There were tears in his eyes and an expression too deep for utterance. When we said goodbye, he knew and I knew that his time was limited and that his end would come away from family and friends and his beloved island home. Eventually, and with some regret, we boarded the *Kittery* for the return journey home.

Originally, the band was scheduled to stop and play concerts in Cuba, Haiti, Santo Domingo, and Puerto Rico on its way back, but these engagements were canceled, primarily because we had extended our tour in the States. Naturally, we were thrilled to return to the shores of our native land and to the proud embraces of our loved ones.

There can be no doubt that the band's triumphant tour more than accomplished the objectives of advertising the Virgin Islands, its people, and the beneficent rule of the naval administration. This was clearly evidenced not only by the many glowing tributes and speeches made in our honor but also by thousands of congratulatory communications we received from those who had heard us play in concert or over the radio. For example, one Henry C. Larcombe of Latham, Maryland, sent me the following letter on July 19, 1924:

Dear Mr. Adams:

Your program, given through station WCAP last night, did more to put the Virgin Islands on the map than anything since they passed under the government of the United States. . . . There were not many, I dare say, who knew the Islands could appreciate an organization as good as the band has developed into under your leadership, much less furnish the materials from which to make it. You have therefore raised our estimate of the people there, by showing us their taste in music.[19]

Newspaper editorials and articles also bore witness to the success of our mission. A typical example is this editorial, which appeared in the *Boston Chronicle:*

The Navy Band of the Virgin Islands is on a tour of this country. Those who have been privileged to hear them render their inimitable music gain a new appreciation of the aims and aspirations of this little group of peoples who are following the lure of the American ideal. It is to be hoped that the ministry of this band as it carries the benediction of its music to different parts of the country shall not have been in vain. In the final adjustment of their political and civil relations to the parent country may justice be done tempered with mercy. The United States has not yet learned how to deal with darker and weaker peoples either at home or abroad. We have just bought the Virgin Islands and paid for them with a price. It was essentially a real estate transaction for reasons of military strategy. The people were merely attachment to the land. And yet where the American flag floats we expect to see liberty prevail. It was a pathetic [moving] spectacle to see this little island band rising to play "The Star Spangled Banner." Here indeed was a union of patriotism and pathos. May these islanders indeed be made to feel the spirit and thrill of "the land of the free and the home of the brave"![20]

Above all, the tour had a profound and lasting impact upon the minds and attitudes of Afro-Americans, who saw our accomplishments not only as a vindication of the race but also as an opportunity to press for better treatment and greater equality. These points were repeatedly stressed by the prominent American colored leaders who addressed the band in every city we played, and also by the leading Negro newspapers. The *Washington Sentinel* expressed these sentiments well in its editorial of July 26, 1924:

> The triumphant tour of the Virgin Islands Naval Band is emphasizing two very important facts, namely that in the domain of the art and science of the rhythmic combinations of tones, their apprehension, composition, rendition and interpretation and [in] the organization of persons and the selection of instruments to that end, the Colored race is entitled and receives recognition upon absolute equality with other racial groups; and that, whenever the United States Government is just, fair, logical or condescending enough to offer opportunities and adequate encouragements and facilities to members of the Colored race which they unstintingly and insistently offer, or enforce upon, other groups of Americans[,] it matters not in what field of honorable or useful activity, the former group never fails to score honorably[,] fully and satisfactorily. With respect to the Virgin Islands Naval Band, we are grateful to say that it bears the title and significance of a full-fledged naval unit and in point of recognition is classed and treated upon equal terms with all other naval bands. The leader, Prof. A. A. Adams stands high as a gentleman, musical scholar, composer and disciplinarian and is highly respected by the leading bandmasters of this and other countries; and his band is justly esteemed one of the finest in the American navy. Thanks to the naval establishment for the meed [sic] of this opportunity, and acknowledgements and myrtles for the distinguished Virgin Islands bandmaster and his efficient musicians.[21]

The words of an old refrain came to me as I left Hampton Roads and headed south: "'Mid pleasures and palaces / Though we may roam / Be it ever so humble / There's no place like home."[22]

FIGURE 1. Portrait of Bandmaster Alton A. Adams, Chief Musician (E7), likely in New York City, 1922. On the right is a portrait of Adams's inspiration—John Philip Sousa—that is autographed "To Alton Adams Esq from John Philip Sousa 1920." Note that this cherished photo seems to have influenced Adams's own navy publicity shot in terms of the pose, full uniform with hat, expression, and carved high-backed chair. The finely crafted chair in Adams's photo also connects him to the artisan tradition of the Virgin Islands' black middle class, which served as the foundation for his values and accomplishments. In particular, it recalls Adams's first music teacher, Jean Pierre, who was a master wood turner, as well as Adams's own father, Jacob Adams, who was a carpenter.

FIGURE 2 *(above)*. Adams Juvenile Band, photographed near the height of its success, ca. 1915. Among the thirty-five musicians, Adams stands in the center of the photo holding a piccolo, while his brother, Julien, stands in the back right with a euphonium. The variety of uniform styles offers some indication of the band's need to stretch its budget; the players do have music holders (lyres), indicating that they performed from notated sheet music.

FIGURE 3 *(top right)*. An early photo of the United States Navy Band of the Virgin Islands, Charlotte Amalie, St. Thomas, circa 1917. Adams stands in front. The unit's precision is evident, as is its inexperience, in that although the arrangement of bandsmen is disciplined, not all musicians can be seen.

FIGURE 4 *(bottom right)*. Charlotte Amalie Harbor during the Danish period, with several commercial sailing vessels at anchor. *Inset:* The same view early in the U.S. Navy period, circa 1918; note the new radio communication towers but the lack of commercial ships, which signals the economic distress caused by the interruption of trade during World War I. The near slope on the left is Bluebeard's Hill, with the pirate's tower atop—just visible at the edge of each image.

FIGURE 5 *(above)*. Navy band activities included the Navy Day Parade, shown here circa 1918 during World War I and featuring a large number of troops. Adams marches in the parade ahead of his players with his baton at his side. The African American men in the foreground may be local police. The inset shows one of the band's regular weekly concerts at the Emancipation Garden bandstand.

FIGURE 6 *(right)*. Fair copy of Adams's composition "The Governor's Own," 1921, sketched here for piano. Courtesy Alton Augustus Adams Collection, Center for Black Music Research, and Alton Adams Family Trust.

The Governor's Own
— March

By Alton A. Adams
Bandmaster U.S.N.

FIGURE 7 *(above)*. Official tour photo, United States Navy Band of the Virgin Islands, taken at Howard University in Washington, D.C., July 17, 1924. Among the thirty-eight musicians pictured, Adams is seated in the first row center holding a baton and piccolo. Julien is above him in the back row with his by-now-signature double-bell euphonium. Percussionist Ronald Hennessey is seated on the right (he would not survive the tour); James Brown sits on the ground at left; his brother, cornet soloist Herbert Brown, is in the middle row at the left. Courtesy Alton Augustus Adams Collection, Center for Black Music Research, and Alton Adams Family Trust.

FIGURE 8 *(top left and right). Left:* The family of Alton Adams, circa 1930, including *(from left)* Enid, Edna (his sister), Alton, Jr., Gwendolyn, Olyve, Alton, Sr., Althea, Merle, and his wife, Ella. *Right:* Julien Zeitzemar Adams (1895–1961), First Class Petty Officer (E6), circa 1930, brother of Alton A. Adams, who served as the navy band's tailor and one of its assistant conductors. The instrument he holds is a double-bell euphonium. He wears ribbons for national defense (World War I) and good conduct.

FIGURE 9 *(middle and bottom right).* Adams's World War II bands. *Top:* The navy's first sanctioned racially integrated band, Guantánamo Bay, Cuba, 1942. Adams is on the far right with cornet soloist Herbert Brown two persons to the left. The drums and uniforms in this picture are standard navy issue; prior to this date all navy band uniforms and equipment were obtained locally and thus not standardized across the service. *Bottom:* The second United States Navy Band of the Virgin Islands, circa 1944, an all-black unit of twenty-three musicians assigned to the St. Thomas Submarine Base. Adams stands to the far right with Herbert Brown immediately left. J. O. Breedy is the percussionist on the left foreground, while Conrad Gomez holds the clarinet; the percussionist on the right is Arnold "Scrippy" Bolling, a musician from the Great Lakes Training Station who led a small jazz unit from the band to play for navy dances.

FIGURE 10 *(above)*. Adams at age seventy-three conducting his "Virgin Islands March" with the Goldman Band in New York's Central Park, July 5, 1963, and *(inset)* directing the U.S. Army Field Band at age eighty on January 25, 1970, at Lionel Roberts Stadium on St. Thomas.

FIGURE 11 *(right)*. Edwin Franko Goldman portrait signed "To Alton A. Adams—from Edwin Franko Goldman Feb. 1938." *Inset:* Adams (dark jacket) shaking hands with Richard Franko Goldman, Central Park Band Shell, 1963. Adams was a friend of the elder Goldman, who was his strong supporter and advocate. Both father and son invited Adams to conduct their prestigious professional band when he was in New York.

To Alton A. Adams — from
Feb. 1938. Edwin Franko Goldman

FIGURE 12 *(above)*. Portraits sent to Adams by fellow black musicians and composers, including *(from left)* Philippa Schuyler (autographed), Eva Jessye, W. C. Handy (autographed), and Clarence Cameron White (autographed).

FIGURE 13 *(top right)*. Adams (with shovel) at ground-breaking ceremony for the St. Thomas Power Authority Water Treatment Facility, circa 1951. The others pictured are *(from left)* Omar Brown, legislative assembly president; Fred Vailet, executive director; Daniel Ambrose, government secretary; Raymond Plaskett, chauffeur; Walter John, associate contractor, and Virgin Islands governor Morris Fidanque de Castro (1949–54).

FIGURE 14 *(middle right)*. Adams was an informal consultant to many Virgin Islands governors. He is pictured here with Governor John D. Merwin (1958–61, *left*) and Governor Walter A. Gordon (1955–58, *right*) presenting donations from the Virgin Islands Hotel Association for the benefit of the Knud-Hansen Memorial Hospital medicines fund. In the center, he appears with Governor Ralph M. Paiewonsky (1961–69) and the governor's second wife, Bert. Governor Paiewonsky signed into law the bill accepting the rededications of Adams's "Virgin Islands March" and "The Governor's Own" to the people of the Virgin Islands and calling for them to be played on official occasions.

FIGURE 15 *(bottom right)*. Adams (at eighty-nine years old) at a graduation ceremony to receive an Honorary Doctorate of Humane Letters from Fisk University, alongside mezzo-soprano Marian Anderson, Nashville, Tennessee, May 7, 1979.

7 The Close of the Naval Years (1925–1931)

Editor's Note: *Returning to the islands from their triumphant 1924 tour of the East Coast, Adams and his band reinvigorated their concert schedule for admiring audiences. In this chapter, Adams recounts a few remarkable moments in the islands' history to offer views on daily life, including the appearance of a German daredevil with his one-man oceangoing canoe and the early development of air travel to the islands, first in the visit of the Zeppelin airship* Los Angeles *and three years later with the building of an airstrip and the arrival of the first plane. This test flight was preparation for a 1928 visit by Colonel Charles A. Lindbergh, flying his record-setting* Spirit of St. Louis. *Adams profiles two island composers, organist Arturo Giglioli and pianist Alfred Nemours, and tells of the visit of pianist and scholar Maud Cuney-Hare, who along with baritone William H. Richardson presented several recitals in St. Thomas and St. Croix under the auspices of Virgin Islands governor Martin E. Trench. Adams was an ally of Trench and worked to secure support for the governor's work among former islanders and officials on the mainland. A discussion of Trench's progressive initiatives, cut short by his untimely death, offers a prelude to Adams's discussion of island politics. In his view, tumult and treachery often hit the islands without warning. Seemingly small federal decisions made in Washington, D.C., could have profound effects on the lives of Virgin Islanders. The arrival of Herbert D. Brown, chief of the U.S. Bureau of Efficiency, to investigate the islands' budget deficit, for example, would devastate Adams's musical career and his band by promoting the removal of the naval administration. Adams depicts the sad farewell of he United States Navy Band of the Virgin Islands, which was ordered off the islands in 1931 and sent to Guantánamo Bay, Cuba.*

The USS *Kittery*, with our returning bandsmen and luggage on deck, pulled alongside the navy yard dock on Hassel Island at 8:00 P.M. September 13, 1924. Our men disembarked quickly and were transferred to a launch waiting to take them across the harbor to King's Wharf. Waiting there was a crowd of family, friends, and well-wishers. It was a hearty and tearful welcome. The next day, I was bombarded with requests for a homecoming concert. After I talked with my bandsmen, a decision was made to hold this performance the following night, September 15. It was a beautiful evening, and Emancipation Garden and all areas adjacent to it were jammed. From the opening number, "The Spirit of the U.S.N.," to the final piece, "The Star-Spangled Banner," the response and enthusiasm of the crowd were tremendous. Instead of abating, excitement continued to grow, and in response to requests from all sections of the community, we agreed to hold a weekly Sunday evening concert in Emancipation Garden following church services. These performances and the happy street promenades that followed continued throughout the year. I was delighted with the ever increasing appreciation for good music being shown by the people of our island.

Early the following year, I was approached by a group of youngsters with an unusual request—in listing the navy band's concert programs in local newspapers, would I give some background information on the selections? In other words, they were seeking musical education and they were asking me to be their teacher. I said that I would try. Here is one example from the local press about a number to be performed March 5, 1925.

> "Bandanna Sketches" by Clarence Cameron White: This composer
> enjoys the distinction of being the leading black violinist in the world.
> The "Sketches" are his developments of well known Negro spirituals.
> In the hands of a creative composer like Clarence Cameron White,
> these numbers are skillfully and powerfully developed into larger
> musical forms, rhythms, melodies, and cadences deeply expressing the
> inner feelings of slaves and descendants of slaves.[1]

Early in April 1925, I was asked by Governor Philip Williams to organize programs in the islands' communities for the observance of Music Week from May 3 to 9.[2] At 3:00 P.M. on Sunday, May 3, the bells of all the churches would peal forth to herald the event. The various ministers would deliver instructive sermons on music and community life and during the week were to host organ recitals and sacred concerts. Military bands would give open-air concerts and parades in which thousands were to join. Community sings would be given, and over seven thousand school children would parade and hold outdoor musical exercises addressed by the governor. Musical essay contests and exercises would be held in each school, and the press would support the venture by reprinting speeches and running announcements. Well-balanced programs had already gone out to be printed. The week's highlight was to be the maypole dance celebration performed by all the schoolchildren at what is today known as the Lionel Roberts Stadium. The children gleefully danced around several maypoles accompanied by the naval band, and thousands of people turned out to witness the festivities. I might note that this was the first time that the maypole dance was performed in St. Thomas, so that it can hardly be considered one of our "traditional" dances. The celebration was not only a week of gaiety and enjoyment for the general public but also a means of bringing the Virgin Islands to the attention of mainland audiences via the news media.[3] Another musical festivity I helped organize was the annual concert given by the navy in market square on Christmas Eve. Thousands of people attended this event to listen to Christmas music and sing along with carols played by the naval band.

The governor was pleased with my plans. Rising from his desk, he asked me to come with him to his inner office. The governor closed the door. "Adams," he said, "I have some exciting news for you. If all goes well, on Wednesday, May 6, we will have a historic visitor." Reaching for a drawer in his desk, he opened it and handed me a picture—"Isn't she a beauty?" I saw before me a great airship. The caption read: "ZR3, Zeppelin Airship Company, Friedrichshafen, Germany." "Ignore the caption," the governor said, "she has been rechristened the *Los Angeles*. She is ours, built for us as part of Germany's reparation payments to the United States. The point is, the airship is now on her way south and will be in the Caribbean in a few days. I have used all the pull that I have with my friends in the Navy Department to get her to fly over us. They have promised me that after Puerto Rico, we can expect her." Reaching into his desk drawer again, the governor handed me a batch of printed materials. "Here," he said, "take these home and familiarize yourself." Familiarize myself I did. I learned that the great airship was 658 feet long, 92 feet wide, and 100 feet high. When inflated, she carried 2,470,000 cubic feet of helium gas. Her cruising speed was sixty miles per hour. Her cruising radius, without stopping, was over six thousand miles. The ZR3 left Friedrichshafen on October 12, 1924, in the charge of a German crew. She arrived at Lakehurst, New Jersey, Naval Air Station three days later and was turned over to the Americans.[4]

At three o'clock Wednesday afternoon, May 6, 1925, the signal station on Hassel Island announced the sighting of the navy dirigible by hoisting a ball to its signal mast with an American flag below it. Every eye turned westward, eagerly awaiting the approach of the great airship. From the vantage point where I stood with friends and family, we watched with wonder as the huge aircraft approached. She sailed over Frenchtown and Villa Olga. She moved across the harbor, flew over Bluebeard Castle, and continued as far east as Tutu, where she turned and headed back west. The dirigible seemed to move without effort. We could barely hear the sound of her engines. She was a glorious sight glistening in the sun, beautiful to behold, and resembled a graceful whale. When the airship passed almost directly over us, her name, *Los Angeles*, and the words *U.S. Navy* were plainly visible. Over the center of the town, the airship slowed her speed, circled, and dropped several packages addressed to Governor Williams.

The town was bedecked with flags of all nations. A holiday spirit prevailed. Ships in the harbor flew flags and bunting. All craft, big and small, blew their stacks and sirens in welcome. Schools were closed for the occasion and children and teachers were out en masse. Here, from my scrapbook are two articles from local newspapers describing the excitement, especially of the children:

> The afternoon sun was hot and the anxiety of the waiting children was rising. They fixed their eyes on the western sky and watched. Suddenly, someone cried out: "The airship is coming! The airship is coming! There she is!" Majestically the dirigible came until she was in full view of the many and eager young people. The children cheered and cheered. "It looks like a great big fish," one youngster said. A school principal raised her voice over the noise of the children. "Hip, hip, hurrah," she said, "Hip, hip, hurrah!" And the children waved their flags and raised their voices in excited chorus.[5]

> It is more than one month since the giant dirigible Los Angeles of the U.S. Navy flew over our island, but the excitement created by her visit is still with us. For one thing, the popularity of our governor, Philip Williams, has never been higher. Letters to our newspapers and editorial comments have all struck a similar note: heartfelt community thanks for the Governor's good offices in getting the airship to come here thereby affording one and all a rare opportunity to witness this marvel of aeronautical science.

The prominent Main Street firm of A. H. Lockhard & Co. wrote a letter to a local newspaper that is of particular interest to me, dealing as it does with music on airships. I kept a copy of the letter from which I now quote:

> A question appeared in your newspaper, June 6, 1925, in which the questioner asked: "What kind of Graphophone does the dirigible Los Angeles carry?" Our firm is happy to give you the answer. First, let us point out that the name Graphophone is a trademark for a phonograph

that uses wax records. This trademark is held by the Victor Talking Machine Co. of Camden, N.J.

When the dirigible Los Angeles slipped from her mooring at Lakehurst, N.J., and headed south, she took with her a specially engineered Victrola, presented to officers and crew of the airship by the Victor Talking Machine Co. It is the first music-producing instrument to be designed for use in dirigibles. Since each and every item taken aboard this ship is carefully regarded as to design and weight, it is a tribute to the Victor Co. that the instrument was accepted readily and gratefully by the commander and staff of the dirigible. This particular Victrola is ingeniously made of aircraft cloth, plywood, and durolium, fabric reinforced exactly as the fabric in the hull of a dirigible.

As this great airship sails among the stars and through the immensity of space, the music of Victor artists will awaken the silent spaces thousands of feet above the earth. The gallant men who command and operate this giant of the air will have the comfort of great music by great artists in a way hitherto inaccessible to them. One more triumph for the Victor Talking Machine Co.[6]

On May 24, 1925, a longtime local friend and a fine musician, Signor Arturo Giglioli, passed away quietly at his home on St. Thomas. He was eighty-six years old. Because of my long association with him, the local press asked me to contribute a statement telling something about his life and background.

Signor Arturo Giglioli was born in Leghorn, Italy. He was brought up in Florence where he acquired the typical amiability and graceful manners of the Florentine. He studied chemistry and music, but music was his passion. He applied himself steadfastly in this field and later became director of an orchestra in Milan. Several years later, he left Italy and came to St. Thomas via New York. He was a resident of St. Thomas for a long time, probably forty-five years, during which time he dedicated himself to music and the business of photography.

I knew Signor Giglioli for more than thirty years. I recall with pleasure the agreeable and profitable times spent with him at his home at the foot of Government Hill and in the nearby Apollo Theatre, where he tried out some of his musical compositions and invited my criticism. Giglioli was an ardent admirer of the Italian composer Gaetano Donizetti. Probably, that accounted for Donizetti's influence so clearly noticeable in Giglioli's beautiful Masses and Litanies. Giglioli was best known in St. Thomas as organist and choir director for the local Roman Catholic Church, Sts. Peter and Paul. He served in this capacity for more than thirty years. His efficient and dedicated training of the church choir won him the admiration of clergy, congregation, and, in fact, all lovers of good music here.

I was a frequent visitor to Signor Giglioli, up to a short time before his death. A favorite place for our musical discussions was under the heavily laden grape arbor in his garden. The good Signor had imported from Tuscany special vines that bore white grapes. Often there would be a large silver bowl on a nearby table filled with these delicious grapes immersed in ice water. "The soil here is excellent for this variety of grape," Signor Giglioli said. "It is a shame that no one cultivates them commercially." It was in these quiet surroundings that we spent many an afternoon working together to arrange some of his beautiful compositions for use in our band concerts.[7]

Here is a communication about another local musical colleague, which I directed to the St. Thomas *Bulletin* for August 27, 1925:

It was with pleasure that I read the article of Mr. Alfred Nemours in your newspaper of August 25, 1925, complimenting me and my bandsmen for our rendition of his bewitching composition *Comtesse et Marquis*. This was the centerpiece of our recent concert at the Emancipation Garden.

As we all know, Mr. Nemours is a native-born St. Thomian who is presently living here. He received his musical education in Berlin. He is a worthy product of the teachings in harmony and counterpoint by one of the world's greatest theorists, Ludwig Bussler. In piano playing, he was directed by the renowned Felix Dryschock.[8]

No greater acknowledgment and appreciation of Nemours's musicianship can be given than the fact that several of his beautiful compositions have been played at the Berlin Opera House before large and approving audiences. His delightful *Comtesse et Marquis*, in particular, has been a favorite of musical circles in the German capital where music is an important part of daily living. The French name *Comtesse et Marquis* is somewhat misleading in that the music from a technical and aesthetic point of view is essentially and thoroughly German. It shows clearly that strong instinct for organization so typical of the Germanic race.

Nemours makes no bones of the fact that he is thoroughly indoctrinated in things Germanic. Little wonder that this patriotism shows so clearly in his compositions. Simple, dignified, and well organized rhythms and striking harmonic effects appear throughout his work.

Simple as the *Comtesse et Marquis* may look, it is difficult to render and requires intense concentration, practice, and more practice. To hear from Nemours, a musician of high standards, that he was pleased with our rendering of his work is a compliment indeed. Nemours was particularly complimentary about our surprising skill in handling the dance and pantomime sections. This is a crucial test in the proper presentation of the composition. In speaking with me after the concert, Nemours declared: "You and your bandsmen passed that test with flying colors."

It always gives me great pleasure to present the work of a native composer, especially one so technically accomplished as Nemours. His melodious *Soirée de Berlin,* a piece full of memories of happy times in that German city, is often featured by us. Because of its delightful harmony and nostalgic flavor, it is a favorite of music lovers here.[9]

With Governor Williams's term expiring in 1925, President Calvin Coolidge appointed Martin Edward Trench, Captain, U.S. Navy, to succeed him. Trench was sworn in on September 11, 1925. From the beginning, it was apparent that the new governor was no run-of-the-mill official. His career in the U.S. Navy (1889–1927), had been a remarkable one. Born in Dennison, Minnesota, in November 1869, he was admitted twenty years later to the Naval Academy in Annapolis. On account of his great strength and athletic ability, he captained the football team. Two years after graduating, Trench was appointed in 1895 to the engineering division, New York Navy Yard, where he established an excellent record. From there, he was assigned to the USS *Maine.* His sea duty completed, he left that warship shortly before it was blown up in Havana Harbor, February 15, 1898, an act that precipitated the Spanish American War. During that conflict, Trench served with distinction on the USS *Resolute.*

As detail officer in the Bureau of Navigation in 1912, Trench became known as a man who listened attentively to all suggestions, information, and complaints. He carefully weighed all points of view and invariably based his decisions on what he believed to be just and right. Once made, these decisions stood. He developed a reputation for fairness. Later, Trench served as commanding officer of the USS *Denver, Colorado* and USS *St. Louis* before going to the Washington Navy Yard as assistant superintendent of the naval gun factory. Throughout World War I, he commanded the Naval Torpedo Station, where his services won him a Naval Cross "for exceptional meritorious service in a duty of great responsibility." There followed a series of top assignments at naval installations in Washington, Philadelphia, and Charleston. It was while serving as commander of the Charleston Navy Yard that Trench was ordered to the Virgin Islands.[10]

During our band's visit to Boston in August 1924, it was my privilege to meet Mrs. Maud Cuney-Hare (1874–1936). While conversing with her, she mentioned the possibility of her coming to the West Indies in the latter part of 1925 to perform a series of concerts. I assured her that if she did come to the Virgin Islands, I would do everything possible to help with scheduling, details, accommodations, and sponsorship by the top authority, the governor of the Virgin Islands. About a year and three months later—November 1925—I received word from Mrs. Hare that she was definitely coming and that she planned concerts in Puerto Rico, St. Thomas, and St. Croix. She would be accompanied by William H. Richardson, one of America's foremost baritone singers. I invited the two artists to stay as guests in my home and then proceeded to Government House to try to secure gubernatorial sponsorship. Governor Trench was most gracious and helpful. "Bandmaster Adams," he said, "if you recommend them, I will sponsor them. I would appreciate, however, if you would give me some background information for our files."

Months before, at the request of the managing editor of a Grenada newspaper, the *West Indian,* I had written a series of articles dealing with outstanding Negro musicians in America. Richardson and Mrs. Hare were among them. It was a simple matter to take excerpts and submit them to Governor Trench:

> Mrs. Maude C. Hare is renowned pianist, author, and recitalist. She received her musical education at the New England Conservatory of Music, Boston, Massachusetts. Her excellence as a pianist combined with her ability as a lecturer has won prominence and success. Mrs. Hare is a collector of Negro folk melodies. Like Samuel Coleridge-Taylor, she has taken on the worthy task of preserving for posterity the rich musical utterances of her race.
>
> William H. Richardson is one of America's foremost Negro baritones. He was born in Liverpool, Nova Scotia. He studied in Boston under T. Schroeder, noted Boston voice instructor. Robinson was a soloist at St. Peter's Episcopal Church, Cambridge, Massachusetts for years. In recent times, he has been active in concert work and has won considerable critical acclaim.[11]

Cuney-Hare and Richardson gave their first concert on February 10, 1926, at the Apollo Theatre in St. Thomas under the auspices of Governor and Mrs. Trench. The theater was packed. Representatives from the local press were there, and I will let them tell the story of it all in reviews, saved in my scrapbook:

> On the arrival and seating of Governor and Mrs. Trench and party, the concert opened with the playing of a lively number by the U.S. Navy Band. Bandmaster Adams, U.S.N., then introduced the artists whose colorful costumes elicited rounds of applause.
>
> There followed a program ranging from folk songs of the Orient, the deep South, and West Indies to classical and modern music. The richness and depth of Richardson's voice, velvety in finish and clear in diction with a breath control that is remarkable, held the audience enthralled.
>
> Hare's attractive personality, her delightful, fluent speaking voice, the brilliant and scholarly manner in which she interpreted the songs,

pleased the audience. Hare was most effective when she played a series of Creole folk songs from her collection recently published by the Carl Fisher music house of New York.

Two numbers which . . . elicited heavy applause were the Danish song "Gylland" and "Sweet Virgin Isles" composed by bandmaster Adams with words by Herbert Grigg of St. Croix. The composer was called on stage to acknowledge the appreciation of the audience.

The entire program was a delight with the two artists coordinating perfectly. Richardson's beautiful singing in German, Italian, French, and English, with the sympathetic and masterful accompaniment of Hare, with her interpretive talks, created a recital that was out of the ordinary.

The audience was comprised of nearly the entire American and Danish colonists here, plus a splendid representative gathering of local people. At the close of the program, the audience rose to its feet in an expression of admiration for the artists. A young lady went on stage carrying a beautiful bouquet of roses which she presented to Hare, who received them in a most gracious manner.[12]

My scrapbook also contains clippings covering Cuney-Hare and Richardson's second concert. This event took place as scheduled at the Apollo Theatre on Thursday night, February 12, 1926. To quote from the clipping in the St. Thomas *Bulletin* from the next day:

> Just as the first musical recital of the Hare-Richardson team was a great success, so was the second. This time the program was mostly classical with choice selections from well-known operas. Mr. Richardson was in top form. In rendering several numbers from *I Pagliacci*, he sang even better than on the night of Feb. 10. His Italian was flawless. Each word had roundness and tonal finish, sparkling clear.
>
> And so it was all evening as the artists moved from one opera to another, from one melodious theme to another. Again, Mrs. Hare delighted the audience with her skill as a superb accompanist.
>
> During a brief intermission, Bandmaster Adams appeared on stage and thanked Governor and Mrs. Martin E. Trench, who were present, and all those who had contributed toward the success of the tour. According to schedule, said Adams, he had made arrangements for the artists to leave for St. Croix Tuesday, Feb. 17, 1926, so that our friends across the channel may also have an opportunity to enjoy their fine musical renderings.
>
> At the close of the beautiful concert, Mrs. Hare, in appropriate words and speaking on behalf of Mr. Richardson as well, expressed highest appreciation and gratitude for the distinguished patronage of Governor and Mrs. Martin E. Trench and for the reception and dinner given in the artists' honor at Government House, Feb. 11, 1926. This, said Mrs. Hare, was a high point in the warm and wonderful welcome accorded to them since their arrival in St. Thomas.

To the delight of the packed house, Governor Trench went on stage, shook hands with the artists, then turned and addressed the audience. The governor was a man of fine bearing with a clear friendly voice and a very relaxed manner.

He knew that he spoke for many of those before him when he expressed Mrs. Trench's and his delight in meeting and listening to these fine artists who were also highly educated and cultured people with very impressive backgrounds.

The governor thanked the artists for coming to the islands, wished them a safe journey home and hoped that they would return soon. There was thunderous applause. The curtain fell on a wonderful evening of culture and entertainment.[13]

During the second week of September 1926, I received two letters from abroad that gave me a big lift. The first was from C. J. Russell, librarian at the John Philip Sousa Archives, Willow Grove, Pennsylvania. It read:

> J. Philip Sousa has asked me to . . . tell you that he played your march, "Spirit of the U.S. Navy," as an encore at one of his concerts last week and that the audience received it with enthusiasm. Also, Mr. Sousa sends to you his hearty congratulations. While going through the latest music catalog of publisher Carl Fisher, New York, he noticed that your march, "The Governor's Own," has won a prominent place as one of the standard marches of the day.

I was thrilled to receive these compliments from this most popular musical figure, the King of Marches himself.

The second letter was from Los Angeles, California, and it was from Herr Meier, bandmaster of the German cruiser *Hamburg*, which had visited St. Thomas five months earlier—in March and April 1926—for a two-week stay. In his letter, Bandmaster Meier said:

> Greetings from the city of Los Angeles where we arrived recently via the Panama Canal route. We still think and talk of the fine time spent in St. Thomas and the good friends that we made there.
>
> Yesterday, with a few members of my band, we attended an opening for a motion picture featuring Douglas Fairbanks, the great movie star. Imagine my delight during an interlude when the band struck up your march, "The Governor's Own." They played it stirringly and well. I could hardly wait to get back to my ship to write to you about it.[14]

Naturally, I was thrilled by this letter also. While in St. Thomas, the *Hamburg*'s band, conducted by Herr Meier, gave two concerts in Emancipation Garden, March 31 and April 4. Herr Meier and I became good friends and exchanged musical information. He was familiar with my march "The Governor's Own" and asked me for copies, which his band practiced and rendered enthusiastically on the night of the second concert. Herr Meier also knew of Alfred Nemours's music, specifically two numbers, *Soirée de Berlin* and *Air de Ballet*. When told that Nemours lived in St. Thomas, he was eager to meet him. I arranged a luncheon at the Grand Hotel's terrace overlooking Emancipation Garden. The two men had a wonderful time speaking in German about music and reminiscing about the good old Berlin days.[15]

Of all the naval governors I had served under, none won the confidence, respect, and hearts of Virgin Islanders as quickly as Martin Trench. From the day he took office in 1925, the new governor showed a deep interest in the problems of the people and their needs. Governor Trench's commanding figure, his tact, fairness, and innate wisdom, characteristics for which he had been known on the mainland, made themselves felt in the islands from the beginning. The governor made it known early that the door of his office was open to all, rich and poor, and the island people responded. They came away from his office full of admiration and hope. Here was a governor they could talk to and one who really listened and cared. Governor Trench met island problems head-on. His appointment had come at a time when islands politics, fanned by agitators in Harlem, had caused and was continuing to cause, unfavorable and inflammatory articles in the U.S. Negro press against continuing the naval administration of the islands.

One morning I was called to the governor's office. When I got there, he greeted me in his usual gracious manner: "Bandmaster Adams, I sent for you because I need your advice and help." He handed me a batch of newspaper clippings: "I received these from the Navy Department yesterday. As you will note, they are taken from the mainland Negro press, and they are very bitter about the continuing naval administration of these islands. One of the articles, the mildest one, holds more than a degree of truth. The rest are outright falsehoods." The mildest article to which the governor referred was from the *New York Amsterdam News*. It was extremely critical of the short tenure in office of naval governors—at most two years. Since 1917, no governor had been in the islands long enough to develop or carry out a constructive program. This was a real obstacle to the proper development of the islands. "I couldn't agree with that more," said Governor Trench. "When I accepted this office, I made my acceptance contingent on a waiver of the two-year rule. If I start a project, and I have several in mind, I wish to remain here long enough to see it completed. Needless to say, the navy agreed, or I would not be here now. As for the other clippings," said the governor, "look at those headlines: 'Naval Tyranny in the Islands,' 'Battleship Rule Destroying Civilian Rights.' We who are here, on the spot, know that none of this is true. How do we stop this misinformation from spreading?"[16]

I promised the governor that I would do everything in my power to try to set the record straight. I had influential friends in key positions in the U.S. Negro press and in the black communities there. I made a list of these friends and I wrote to them. The list included Caspar Holstein, Romeo Dougherty, Reverend Richard Bright, Dr. Emmett Scott, and other persons who knew me and respected me. In my letters to them, I made it clear that I was very pro-navy and with good reason. The band which I led, made up entirely of black musicians, was pure and simple a creation of the U.S. Navy, maintained by the U.S. Navy. Much that I, a black man, had become, I could attribute directly or indirectly to naval help, friendship, and good will. I had been witness to Virgin Island happenings from the time of naval takeover in 1917 until the present. During that period of nine years, I had witnessed but one set of events that could have justified an unfavorable word in the U.S. Negro press.

In the hectic war years of 1917–18, our islands, particularly St. Thomas, had been overcrowded with military personnel, including some units from the Deep South. Possibly officials at the time were too overburdened to think of the social consequences of such overcrowding or the mental attitudes of some soldiers, but as a result, there had been unfortunate incidents, drunken rioting by military personnel, and harassment of the native population. The situation had been brought under control quickly by the rapid reduction of military personnel and firm action by the authorities. With the war over, relations between the naval administration and the people of the islands had been good and continued to be good. Never had they been better than now under Trench, one of the finest naval governors ever sent to these islands.[17] Governor Trench began an in-depth study of the islands and their needs. He met with a cross section of islanders and heard their views. An attentive listener, he carefully weighed what he heard. He based decisions on what he believed to be the best interests of all. He strove to maintain good relations with the Colonial Councils, setting an example for his officers and staff. In a short time he won the confidence and respect of most islanders.

Meanwhile, harsh criticism in the U.S. Negro press regarding naval rule in the islands quieted. Whether my letters to influential friends on the mainland had any effect I cannot say. What may have turned the tide was the visit to the islands by U.S. Senator Hiram Bingham III (1875–1956) and the widely publicized report that he sent to Congress and the press regarding the state of affairs as he found them in the U.S. Virgin Islands. Bingham and his staff had been in Puerto Rico doing investigative work.

While there, he decided to visit the nearby Virgin Islands to see for himself if charges regarding naval oppression were true or groundless. The senator arrived in the latter part of 1926 and immediately set up a series of hearings for any and all citizens who wished to testify.

His reputation had preceded him. Before entering U.S. politics (he had served as lieutenant governor, governor, and was now U.S. senator for the state of Connecticut), Hiram Bingham was widely known and acclaimed as a distinguished archeologist, historian, and statesman. In the years 1911, 1912, and 1914–15, he headed expeditions sent by Yale University to South America to study ruins of the ancient Inca civilizations. Bingham rediscovered the Inca cities of Vitcos (1911) and Machu Picchu (1912) in Peru. His writings on these explorations and discoveries attracted international attention. Senator Bingham found no evidence of naval oppression in the islands. On the contrary, he found a remarkably good relationship between the navy and the people. Witness after witness declared that no governor before Trench had handled matters with such tact, patience, and good will.[18] In his report, Bingham summed up with this statement: "I was present when Governor Trench departed from the islands on a short vacation. The departure was a signal for an unprecedented demonstration of confidence and goodwill for him on the part of the civilian population of the islands." Before leaving, Governor Trench had sent for me:

Bandmaster Adams, I called you because I consider you one of my trusted friends. As you know, I will be gone for three or possibly four weeks. Should any matter arise that you consider important, contact me. Here is my address on the mainland. My wife and I will be staying at the home of friends, Captain and Mrs. Ralph Earle in Worcester, Massachusetts. He is president of the Polytechnic Institute there. While listed as a vacation, my trip will be anything but that. I am scheduled to appear before several Congressional committees on behalf of the islands. I expect these appearances to result in important benefits for the islands. Bandmaster, the navy will not be here forever. In fact, a change to civilian administration could come overnight and we must be prepared for it. We must upgrade our educational system and we must intensify the training of Virgin Islanders to take over when that time comes. It has been a policy of some of my predecessors to fit intelligent young islanders into the administrative framework here. But, in my opinion, that policy has been sketchy and not enough. I plan to implement that policy to the fullest extent, and I hope that by the time I leave office, a trained cadre of Virgin Islanders will be ready to take over at short notice. We must develop and diversify the economy. At the moment, naval spending is the main prop. The navy maintains the schools, hospitals, and public works. Hospitals are staffed by naval doctors and nurses;

public works, by engineers all paid for out of naval funds. If the navy pulled out tomorrow, the system would collapse. I intend to stress these economic realities before the appropriate committees of Congress, and I will be asking for considerable sums of money to implement sound economic development in the territory.

January 6, 1927, opened bright and sunny, a holiday—Three Kings Day—and masqueraders in colorful costumes were frolicking along the streets when the terrible news came like a bolt out of the blue. Governor Trench had contracted pneumonia and died at the home of Captain Earle in Worcester, Massachusetts. The news put an immediate damper on the merrymaking. I was in a state of shock.[19] With wildfire rapidity, the news of Trench's death spread throughout the islands that evening. There was consternation at the unexpected passing of a man of seemingly robust constitution. People who had seen the governor leave the islands a short time before, hale and hearty, had difficulty believing the report. One and all sensed that they had lost a good friend, talented and dedicated to helping the people of the Virgin Islands.

A solemn memorial service for Governor Trench was held at the Emancipation Garden on Saturday, January 8. High and low, rich and poor, men and women of all walks of life gathered there to pay tribute. As one reporter said, there were no spectators; all were mourners. Promptly at noon, the prelude to the ceremony began with the firing of seventeen guns from the marine battery, with a one-minute interval between each shot. It was an imposing sight to see the ministers of the various religious denominations as well as top islands officials assembled on the bandstand, standing at attention while the cannon boomed the salute. Speaker after speaker extolled the noble traits of the late governor, his great and lovable personality, his important contacts in Washington that were being used on behalf of the islands, the promise of more years of vigorous and creative leadership. Each speaker emphasized the immensity of the loss for the Virgin Islands. After the eulogies, our band rendered Chopin's "Funeral March," the sad strains seeming to transport the assemblage in spirit to Arlington Cemetery in Virginia, where the mortal remains of Governor Trench were being laid to rest. G. J. Anderson, a member of the sixth elected Colonial Council of St. Thomas–St. John, sent a letter addressed to the people of the Virgin Islands dated that day, January 8, 1927:

> I have just returned to my hotel from the funeral of Governor Trench. It was a most impressive ceremony. Military bands, sailors, soldiers, the Secretary of the Navy, his chief of staff, admirals, colonels, captains, and a large gathering of persons who had known and worked with Gover- ·

nor Trench and who held him in great esteem, all were there to pay a final tribute. Beautiful floral wreaths conveying the affection and sincere esteem of Virgin Islanders for Governor Trench were prominently displayed.[20]

On January 25, 1927, word was received over the radio that President Coolidge had appointed retired navy captain Waldo Evans to fill the vacant governorship of the Virgin Islands. Evans was a longtime career man in the U.S. Navy and had filled many executive positions on naval ships and bases. Also, for a time, he had served as naval governor of American Samoa. On the morning of March 3, 1927, Emancipation Garden was packed and overflowing with people. Captain Evans, escorted by acting governor Van Patten came to the bandstand. From my vantage point I had a good look at him, and my first impression was a favorable one. Fifty-eight years old, about six feet tall, and robust, Captain Evans looked the part of a naval commander. He wore a white suit, Panama hat, white shoes, and a black bow tie. At ten o'clock precisely, the ceremony started. The Honorable George Washington Williams, a district court judge clothed in the robes of office, stepped onto the rostrum, called upon Captain Evans to raise his right hand, and proceeded to swear him in as the seventh naval governor of the U.S. Virgin Islands. As Judge Williams concluded, the battery fired a salute of seventeen guns.

Governor Evans, facing the crowd, delivered his inaugural address, which was well stated and very well received. At its conclusion, our band played "The Star-Spangled Banner." Here are some excerpts from the governor's address, which I saved in my scrapbook:

This is a solemn and significant moment of my life. In doing what I have just done (taking the oath of office), I have dedicated myself, my time, my energies and ability to you, the people of the U.S. Virgin Islands. This act of mine has welded together a man and a people, who but a short time ago were strangers to each other. From this moment on, your interests and mine are one.

You must be genuinely happy that recently the U.S. Congress passed legislation to provide you with U.S. citizenship. You will be even happier when I tell you that yesterday, March 2, 1927, President Coolidge signed that legislation (Bill 2270), officially conferring that citizenship upon you. Let me, as the President's representative and your new governor, be the first to congratulate you and welcome you into the family as an integral part of a great nation.[21]

Through the request of the late governor, Martin E. Trench, Senator Hiram Bingham of Connecticut introduced a bill in Congress asking for an initial grant of $100,000 to begin improvements on the roads and highways of the Virgin Islands. I am happy to tell you that Bill HR No.

4933 has passed the U.S. Congress and has been signed by the President. If these islands, so blessed with climate, beaches, crystal-clear waters, and scenic beauty, are to draw a sizeable share of the tourist trade, then a good road system is very important.

You are concerned, too, I am told, with a prompt decision by the U.S. Congress on some form of permanent government for the Virgin Islands. I can tell you that before his sudden and untimely death, Governor Trench appeared before the Committee on Insular Affairs of the House of Representatives and, through his efforts and contacts, was successful in having Bill HR 10865 introduced to provide a permanent government for the U.S. Virgin Islands. I have just come from Washington and I can tell you that Bill HR 10865 is getting the attention of both bodies of Congress. I had hoped that it might be satisfactorily settled in time for my arrival here, but other matters of international importance took priority and have delayed action.

My predecessor, acting through Senator Bingham, was preparing to introduce a bill in Congress to improve the educational system of the islands and to establish here, at federal expense, vocational schools to permit the youth of the islands to acquire technical skills in addition to a good general education. Whatever I can do during my stay here to assist in providing the youth of the islands with the best educational equipment and opportunity, I will do. You can count on me.

I wish to congratulate you on the beauty of your islands. That beauty is God given. Make every effort to preserve it. And you know the saying: Cleanliness is next to Godliness. Cleanliness is an outward manifestation of culture and your culture will be judged by your willingness to keep your surroundings clean. If the American people are to come here to your shores for short or long stays, it is important that you impress them not only with your God-given beauty, but with the clean and orderly appearance of your communities.[22]

The untimely death of Governor Trench left me sad and depressed. Personally, I had lost a wonderful friend. In a broader sense, the islands had lost much more. No other governor in recent times had so quickly won the confidence, love, and respect of the people. No other governor had so quickly gotten to the heart of local problems and moved so fast in Washington to come up with solutions. With the advent of Governor Trench, it seemed that the problem of short tenure by naval governors had been overcome. The incumbent had expressed his willingness to remain here for an indefinite period; Washington had agreed. Little wonder that islanders looked forward with confidence and hope to years of Governor Trench's vigorous and creative leadership—then, it was all over.

With Governor Trench in place, I had paid little or no heed to Bill HR 10865, introduced into the U.S. Congress to provide a permanent form of government for the U.S. Virgin Islands. Local opinion, as well as my own, took it for granted that no matter what came out of the U.S. Congress, Governor Trench would play a central role. The governor's death changed all that. Suddenly, I felt a strong sense of anxiety. What if naval government was removed overnight? What would happen to my bandsmen—thirty-nine local musicians and their families? Naval friends assured me that, without a doubt, the band would be transferred to some other naval station.

As for myself, I had excellent job offers in the civilian musical world. During our mainland tour of 1924 and after a very successful appearance and concert in Ogden Hall, Hampton Institute, there was a standing invitation for me to come and take over the college band and the music department. In 1926 I turned down an invitation to take over the leadership of James Reese Europe's band after the latter's death.[23] In 1927 a group of friends headed by John Philip Sousa recommended that I take charge of the Wanamaker Store's band program in Philadelphia. The great department store had, as part of its widespread cultural activities, two excellent bands, one of which was composed entirely of black musicians. This band had as its bandmaster a Mr. Grinell, whose retirement was imminent pending a suitable replacement. Because of Sousa's strong recommendation, I received about a dozen letters from Wanamaker officials eager to secure my services.[24]

Early in 1928, I was invited to Philadelphia at the company's expense to discuss my taking over their excellent Negro band. When I got to Philadelphia, I found myself among friends. Members of the store's management remembered the concert the navy band had given there during our 1924 tour. We had broadcast over Wanamaker's radio station, WOO, to millions of people. Listener reaction at that time had been so favorable that the store's top manager requested that I send him a picture to be placed in the store. In a friendly and jocular manner, he scolded me for not having kept my promise to do so.

The Wanamaker offer was a tempting one. Not only was the salary excellent, but also the store offered to provide suitable housing and schooling privileges for my family as part of the job offer. There was one drawback to my accepting the offer—an emotional one. My roots, my family's roots, were in the islands. Regardless of financial or other gains, it was not easy to pull up those roots and move elsewhere. Our home, our hearts were in the islands. There it was that I wanted to make a meaningful contribution to the musical culture of my people. Meanwhile, events in Washington made it easier for me to turn down the Wanamaker offer. Bill HR 10865, to provide a permanent government for the islands, had been put on hold. Indications were that it would stay that way for some time.

Governor Trench had been the driving force behind HR 10865. His friend Senator Bingham had been its sponsor. With Trench gone, the bill languished. Governor Trench had drawn up plans for a careful and gradual transition from naval to civilian government. It was taken for granted that he would play a key role in guiding the transition. There would be emphasis on educational training, economic development, replacements of naval personnel by civilians, and expansion of the suffrage. With Trench gone, Senator Bingham made it known that he would leave matters at a standstill until some group or individual assumed responsibility for carrying out provisions for a smooth transition.[25]

At two o'clock the afternoon of January 10, 1928, I received an urgent call from Government House to report to Governor Evans. When I got there, I was directed not to the governor's office but to the reception room upstairs. Several well-known citizens had gotten there before me and more were coming. There were about thirty people present when Governor Evans entered the room. After warm greetings to the gathering, he called for everyone to be seated. The governor then addressed us:

> Gentlemen, as you know, on May 20 and 21 of last year, Charles A. Lindbergh distinguished himself as an aviator by his epoch-making solo flight from New York to Paris in his monoplane, *Spirit of St. Louis.* The courage, ability, and quiet determination of this intrepid flyer won him the admiration of the world and the adulation of all Americans. All eyes are upon him now as he makes a goodwill flight through Central and northern South America. Several days ago on January 6, I sent the following radiogram through the Commandant of the 15th Naval District, Balboa, Canal Zone: "Colonel Lindbergh, the governor and people of the Virgin Islands extend to you a cordial invitation to visit St. Thomas on your way north. We would be honored to have you as our guest." Yesterday, I received the following radiogram from Colonel Lindbergh from San José, Costa Rica: "I accept with pleasure your kind invitation to visit the Virgin Islands. Because my time is so limited, I will be able to remain in St. Thomas two days only, the day of my arrival and the next day, departing on the third day. Will inform you of my date of arrival more accurately later."
>
> Gentleman, I have asked you to come here this afternoon, not only to help me prepare a rousing welcome for this heroic figure, but also to give me your thoughts and advice on some of the major problems that we face. As you know, we do not have an airfield here or anything resembling a landing strip. To date, no plane has landed here. I have asked my engineers to come up with suggestions for a landing strip bearing in mind that safety is the major factor. If safety is not assured, I

would not hesitate to contact Colonel Lindbergh and call the whole thing off. My engineers have come up with two suggestions:

1. A closely cropped pasture between the Sugar Estate road on the north and Long Bay Road on the south. This land has been made available to us for this special occasion through the courtesy of Mr. A. H. Lockhart. Already we have men working, night and day, to extend this area to the maximum.

2. The No. 2 landing strip suggested is on the golf course to the west.[26]

This morning, I received a radiogram from officials of the Aviation Company of San Juan, Puerto Rico. They requested permission to fly a tri-motor biplane to St. Thomas on January 14 to test the landing strips that we are preparing for Colonel Lindbergh. If all goes well and the landing strips prove safe and usable, they request permission to take up passengers on January 15. Also mentioned in the telegram is that the Aviation Company plans, if my permission is given, to send two planes to escort Colonel Lindbergh to San Juan. I replied to the Aviation Company that I welcomed its testing of the airstrips; that the Sugar Estate strip would be ready by noon January 14 and the golf course strip a few days later. Gentlemen, as matters develop, I will keep you posted.

On January 16, 1928, the office of Governor Waldo Evans issued the following press release:

Saturday afternoon, January 14, 1928, a tri-motored biplane, the SANTA MARIA, owned and operated by the Aviation Company of San Juan, Puerto Rico, arrived here, circled both landing strips, but did not land. The pilot dropped a note saying the strips are inadequate. Immediately after the departure of the SANTA MARIA and upon receipt of the dropped note, I sent the following radiogram to Lt. Baker, U.S. Navy, San Juan, P.R.: "Please interview without delay manager and pilot of tri-motored bi-plane, SANTA MARIA, and have them advise me why, in their opinion, the landing strips are inadequate."

I received the following dispatch from the pilot: "I have had 10 years experience in flying aeroplanes. Your Sugar Estate strip, designated No. 1, is almost impossible to use owing to high hills surrounding same on three sides. Prevailing winds are very rough owing to northeast currents tumbling over the hills and down in the valley necessitating excessive speed for control of machine. With a small, easily maneuvered airplane the field could be used, but it is very dangerous. Your No. 2 field (golf course to the west), though smaller, is better as south side is clear, but it will be necessary to land and take off in the same direction. Landing could be made here, but the strip would have to be made smoother as there are some ditches and obstructions in the field."[27]

Governor Waldo Evans accepted the pilot's recommendation and is rushing the improvement of strip No. 2 to prepare an adequate and safe landing for Colonel Charles A. Lindbergh.

On January 20, Governor Evans announced: "I have been advised that the Aerial Express Company of San Juan, P.R., is sending a small monoplane to St. Thomas on January 22, 1928. This plane will land at strip No. 2 (the golf course), and will be the first official test of that strip." On January 23, the *St. Thomas Mail Notes* recounted the event of the first landing on the island:

> Yesterday, amid happy shouts and gestures of applause, the LA NINA, a monoplane of the Aerial Express Company of San Juan, P.R., guided by W. S. Wade, pilot, and carrying four passengers, circled over landing strip No. 2, descended, and landed easily in the middle of the golf course. This was the first airplane and air passengers to land on the soil of St. Thomas. The passengers were: Austin Brewer, manager, San Juan office, Aerial Express Co.; William S. Smallwood, partner of Smallwood Brothers, Ford Agency, San Juan; John C. Nash, chief engineer, San Juan Ice Company; and Roscoe Dunten, general manager, Aerial Express Company.
>
> On alighting, pilot and passengers were greeted by Governor Waldo Evans: "Gentlemen, this is a most historic occasion. You will be remembered in our history as the first plane, pilot, and passengers to land on our soil." After some formalities and introductions to Government Secretary Van Patten and other high officials, pilot and passengers were taken to Government House, where a reception and dinner awaited them. During dinner, Governor Waldo Evans announced that earlier that day he had received a radiogram from Colonel Charles A. Lindbergh giving his itinerary which was as follows:
>
> The colonel planned to leave Colon, Panama, January 27, 1928. He expected to arrive in Bogota, Colombia, that same day. His next stop will be Caracas, Venezuela, on January 29, 1928, then on to St. Thomas, where he is expected to arrive January 31, 1928.[28]

On January 30, 1928, the island was in a state of excitement. The unbelievable was about to happen. Within twenty-four hours, Colonel Charles Lindbergh and his *Spirit of St. Louis* were due to arrive in St. Thomas. The populace was prepared to give Lindbergh a hero's welcome. Various committees had done their work well. Public places were decorated with plants and flowers. Painters were putting finishing touches on storefronts. Streets were spotlessly clean. Flags and bunting were everywhere. A holiday spirit prevailed, encouraged by the proclamation from Government House declaring the day after Lindbergh landed, February 1, 1928, an official island holiday. One and all, young and old, were encouraged to turn out to participate in a great welcome. The passenger-carrying monoplane *Santa Maria*, exploiting the public's excitement, had arrived in St. Thomas as early as January 27 and had been allotted an off-area at the golf course landing strip. Full-page advertisements appeared in the local press: "Here is your chance to fly. Get the feel of it. Witness the magnificent scenery from the sky. Bargain price!" Adventurous islanders lined up for a chance to fly and came back from the short flights flushed with excitement.

At 1:30 P.M., news was flashed by radio and telegraph that Colonel Lindbergh had left Caracas, Venezuela, and was on his way to St. Thomas. The road to the landing strip became crowded with automobiles, carriages, and conveyances of all kinds as well as crowds of pedestrians, all heading west. At about 4:00 P.M., the *Santa Maria* gracefully lifted into the air and winged its way toward St. Croix to act as an escort. It had been officially announced that at the first sighting of Lindbergh's plane, signal guns would be fired. At approximately 4:20 P.M., the guns were heard. This brought loud cheers from the waiting crowd. The *Spirit of St. Louis* was first sighted approaching from an easterly direction.[29] Evidently, Lindbergh had followed a course over and parallel to the chain of West Indian islands on his way from Venezuela. The would-be escort plane did not meet him, as it had headed south, in the direction of St. Croix. Colonel Lindbergh flew in at a low height, circled the airstrip, went out seaward and southward, then turned and made for the golf course, where he landed easily and gracefully. Many enthusiastic spectators rushed for the plane. It was with difficulty that the contingents of police, marine, and navy guards held them back.

There were moments of silence, then the plane door opened and Lindbergh stepped out. He stood there in the sunlight—tall, trim, and boyish looking. The crowd cheered and he waved his hand in acknowledgment. The colonel was escorted to a temporary reception stand where a beautiful wreath of flowers was placed around his shoulders by a lovely young lady, Miss D. Lamb. Lindbergh bent over and kissed her on the cheek while the crowd cheered. The colonel was then formally received by Governor Evans, who presented him to members of his staff as well as to citizen members of the reception committee. When the brief ceremony was over, Lindbergh, with the governor at his side, was driven to Government House, where he was interviewed by newspaper correspondents.

I was a member of the group of questioners, not as Bandmaster Alton A. Adams, but in my capacity as part-time correspondent for the *New York*

Amsterdam News. When my time came, I asked the following question: "Colonel Lindbergh, needless to say we are highly honored by your historic visit. Would it be possible for you to spend another day with us and have our sister island of St. Croix share this honor with us?" The colonel replied: "As I flew over the chain of islands yesterday on my way here, I wished that I could have arranged to spend as many weeks with you as I can spend days. I have never made a more interesting and beautiful flight than that of yesterday, and I regret that it is necessary for me to leave your city tomorrow morning in order to keep my schedule, which requires arrival at Havana on February 8. Tell your friends in St. Croix that when I leave here en route to Puerto Rico, I will fly over Christiansted and Frederiksted, and that they should wave up to me as I will be waving down to them."[30]

At 10:00 A.M. February 1, 1928, Colonel Charles Lindbergh, accompanied by Governor Evans and Government Secretary Van Patten, with an escort of marines and our naval band, headed for Emancipation Garden for a public reception. As the party arrived, there were photographers waiting. Members of the reception committee, the local legislature, and representatives of the press also waited to greet the colonel. A cannon salute was fired from the nearby battery while enthusiastic people cheered.

Bishop Weiss of the Moravian Church delivered the invocation. The hymn, "O God, Our Help in Ages Past," was sung. Then came addresses of welcome by the governor and chairman of the Colonial Council. Next came the presentation of an illumined address and a beautiful mahogany table inlaid with sandalwood, a masterwork of one of our local craftsmen. Colonel Lindbergh then stepped on the speaker's platform and, in a calm and clear voice, thanked all concerned for the fine welcome that he had received. After a hymn, "Prayer for Colonel Lindbergh," specially prepared for the occasion by Bishop Weiss, the crowd stood at attention while our band played "The Star-Spangled Banner." At the conclusion of the anthem, Colonel Lindbergh came over to me, shook my hand, and said: "Bandmaster, I want to thank you for your fine music. I wish to compliment you also on your well-disciplined band. They show the result of excellent training."

Colonel Lindbergh was driven to the two hospitals, then to the Harmonic Lodge. Here he was received with full ritual and presented with a silver trowel suitably inscribed. Next, he attended a special session of the Colonial Council, where he was received with acclamation and presented with the freedom of the city. Horse races and other sport events were held in his honor. Everywhere Lindbergh appeared he was met with cheers and smiling faces. The day's program culminated in a torchlight procession.[31] Colonel Lindbergh took off from the St. Thomas golf course strip at 11:50 A.M. February 2, 1928, and headed for Puerto Rico, an image of the Virgin Islands flag painted on the side of his plane to memorialize his visit. The takeoff was accomplished as easily and as gracefully as his landing had been two days earlier. En route to Puerto Rico, and in keeping with his promise, Colonel Lindbergh flew low over the towns of Christiansted and Frederiksted, St. Croix, signaling his greetings with gyrations of his plane.[32]

A few months later, on July 31, 1928, while I was visiting a friend, George Levi, in his Main Street office, word came that a strange craft had entered St. Thomas Harbor and had tied up at the harbor master's dock. Levi, who represented the local Chamber of Commerce, was asked to come right away. He asked me to accompany him. The dock was but a short distance away. When we got there, a small crowd already had gathered, including photographers and news reporters. The object of their attention was a diminutive rubber canoe with a strange-looking man tightly fitted into it. He looked like someone from another world. His face was like that of Robinson Crusoe—bearded with unkempt hair caked in salt.

With some difficulty, he was helped out of the tiny craft. In a low and tired voice, he told his story, which appeared in the local press the next day, almost verbatim:

> My name is Captain Franz Romer. I am 29 years old and a German by birth. From the time I left Germany in this tiny boat, I have sailed 2,944 nautical miles. On March 3, 1928, I left the port of Lisbon, Portugal, with New York as my destination. I carried with me 600 tins of provisions of which 50 contained water, each tin holding one and a half gallons. After four months and 25 days, I arrived here, St. Thomas.
>
> About 100 miles from the coast of Portugal, I met high winds and very rough seas. I was compelled to take down my sails and just steer the boat. At times, it seemed that I would be overwhelmed. By God's mercy, I reached the port of Las Palmas, Canary Islands. I stayed there for one month, regaining my strength and confidence and then took off again. While sleeping and steering one day, a mountainous wave dashed over the deck and carried away my head gear and garments of clothing that had already been torn by the wind and sea.
>
> While on this perilous journey, constantly gambling with death, I met a Yugoslavian steamer which offered me help. I declined. They left me with an old chart which showed the route to the Virgin Islands. I met other ships. All offered help which I refused. I was determined to reach port on my own. I did ask for specific information on how to get to St. Thomas, which they gave me. I reached the coast of St. Thomas about midnight and dropped anchor. I slept until dawn, awoke, pulled anchor, and started for the harbor. Once inside, I was towed to the harbor master's dock by a rowboat and here I am.[33]

Shortly after he landed on St. Thomas, Romer came under the care of Louis Mendez Monsanto of Krum Bay. Monsanto, who spoke German fluently, took the captain to his home, got him into a tub, gave him a hot meal, and refitted him in a white suit. According to Monsanto, the cleanup process was a painful one. Long days and nights of constant exposure to sun, rain, and salt spray had taken their toll on the captain's body. It was covered with scars and blisters, sore to the touch. The next time Captain Romer faced the press, he was clean-shaven, well dressed, and rested. He took up his story where he had left off. He spoke in good English.

I was born near Lake Constance in Southern Germany. I grew up to be a seaman. The last ship on which I served as Third Officer was the SS Rhodopic. I am also an experienced aviator. Shortly after Colonel Lindbergh made his flight from New York to Paris, I tried to persuade a German aviation company to give me a plane to cross the Atlantic from Hamburg to New York, but the deal did not go through, so I decided to attempt the crossing in a canoe."

My rubber craft, the Deutscher Sport, is 21 feet long and 3 feet wide. Its depth is 1 & 1/2 feet. It is made of a special heavy rubber compound. It has two paddles of eschen wood, a durable timber grown in Germany. The short light mast I constructed of the same wood, and the sails are of specially treated canvas. The deck is made of the same rubber compound overlaid with canvas. It is constructed so that it closes tightly at my waist when I am sitting so that no water can enter.

The canoe was built in Bavaria, Germany, by the Klepper Company, which sells a considerable number for use in European rivers and lakes. It is valued at $2,000. The New York representative of the Klepper Company, as a publicity stunt, has come up with an offer of $25,000 for the first person to cross the Atlantic in the tiny craft—from Germany to New York. I decided to try it. Evidently, I have no competition. I expect to remain in St. Thomas for about a month, during which time I will await two motors which I ordered by cable from Germany. When I leave here, I will hug the shores of the various islands, using motor and sail until I come to the American mainland. Then I will go up the coast to Battery No. 3 Manhattan, N.Y. When I get there, I will walk in and collect my $25,000 prize.[34]

At 2:00 P.M. Friday, August 24, 1928, our band arrived at the Chamber of Commerce headquarters to participate in a grand reception in honor of Captain Romer. The parade started at 3:00 P.M. Hundreds of people followed the open touring cars containing Chamber of Commerce officials and the guest of honor. By the time we got to Emancipation Garden, the crowd had grown to several thousand people. With all dignitaries seated in the bandstand, our band opened the program with a well-known German melody, "Old Comrades." Then the principal speaker took over. Emile Berne, president of the St. Thomas Chamber of Commerce:

> Captain Romer, we are here today to honor you for the marvelous feat of navigation that you have accomplished. You have sailed 2,944 miles from Germany to St. Thomas in a tiny rubber canoe, . . . probably the most diminutive craft ever to attempt such a long and hazardous journey. In recognition of the extraordinary skill, courage, and endurance which you have shown, our organization, in the name of the people of St. Thomas, V.I., hereby presents you with a gold medal symbolic of your brilliant achievement.
>
> This gold medal was crafted by the local firm of F. M. Corneiro, the same gifted artisans who made the gold and silver trowel which was presented to Colonel Charles Lindbergh by the Harmonic Lodge a few months ago. On the face of the medal is a very miniature reproduction of your very miniature craft, the Deutscher Sport. You will note your initials F. R. Within the space of two circles are raised the words: "Germany-Lisbon-St. Thomas." On the back of the medal is engraved the words: "From the people of St. Thomas, V.I., to Capt. Franz Romer for his miraculous crossing of the Atlantic in a canoe, Deutscher Sport, 1928."

Governor Evans was called upon to pin the medal on the recipient. Captain Romer, in response, expressed his thanks. The ceremony came to a close with our band rendering the German national anthem, followed by "The Star-Spangled Banner." Captain Romer stayed in St. Thomas until September 8, 1928, the height of the hurricane season. Then he took his canoe, which was on display at the Chamber of Commerce, and stocked it with water and provisions. Against the advice of experienced weathermen, who did not like the looks of the weather, he decided to make the sixty-mile run to Puerto Rico. He did not make it. Evidently, he ran into a bad storm. He was not heard from again.[35]

The years 1929 and 1930 were quiet ones in the islands despite the economic upheavals in the United States brought on by the stock market crash of October 1929. These upheavals did not affect us directly. Congressional appropriations to run the islands continued as before. Naval money and personnel ran our hospitals, public works, and services. Naval payrolls gave jobs and a degree of stability to our small economy. For me this was a period of personal satisfaction and musical growth. Our band had achieved maturity. Each and every bandsman played and coordinated with the others magnificently. Our band had become very serviceable to the public, available at all community functions on short notice. Sunday night concerts in Emancipation Garden had become regular events, keenly anticipated and enjoyed by large crowds.

This was a period, too, in which we had frequent visits from foreign warships. Many of these ships carried excellent bands which, once asked, were happy to give concerts. Of all these visiting musicians, the German bands excelled. Here, taken from my scrapbook, is an item from the St. Thomas *Bulletin*, February 15, 1930:

> The public was treated to two excellent concerts in Emancipation Garden this week. The first was by our Navy band, Alton A. Adams, conducting. The second was by the band of the German cruiser, Emden, music master Paul Zimmer. These concerts were attended by large audiences whose applause testified to the appreciation of the merits of both bands. A significant feature of last night's program was the honor paid Bandmaster Adams by the splendid playing of his composition, "The Governor's Own," by the Emden's band. We understand that this popular March is one of the favorites of all the regiments and naval bands in Germany, a fact of which we are justly proud.

On March 11, 1930, Governor Evans took the sixteen-member St. Thomas band with him on a down-island cruise aboard the SS *Nerissa*. We went ashore and played at St. Kitts, Antigua, St. Lucia, Barbados, and Trinidad, where we were delighted to discover that our reputation had preceded us. Large crowds turned out to hear us play, and responded with demonstrations of joy and approval. One local newspaper reported that

> there was music . . . as perhaps never heard before anywhere in the British West Indies, with the possible exception of Jamaica, with its experience of the West India Regiment Band.

To be mentioned alongside the incomparable West India Regiment Band was the highest possible praise. The *Antigua Magnet* further declared:

> Whatever be the motive that prompted Governor Evans to offer the island state of Antigua a musical treat, there is no doubt that the concert was enjoyed by all classes. Bandmaster Alton Adams has the confidence and respect of his men. Folks here had a chance to see how alert and responsive the bandsmen were to their duties. Their conduct to the bandstand was the subject of much favourable comment. The news that there was to be a musical recital seems to have been widely circulated judging from the thousands that turned out to listen. . . . Harmony, modulation, rhythm blended in every piece played. The audience went into ecstasies when Conductor Adams played a piccolo solo with a full band accompaniment. With lightning-like rapidity Mr. Adams' fingers manipulated the keys of the instrument and as the notes imitated the song of a bird one was lost in admiration at the skill displayed by the performer. Thunderous applause greeted the finish and in response to a determined encore the Bandmaster rendered another item. The visit

must act as an inspiration to the musically inclined and the non-musically inclined. No particular race or people have the monopoly or prerogative of brains or talent. Were that not true the natives of St. Thomas and St. Croix would not have been able to entertain us as they did Wednesday night. Moral: You who have the ability persist in developing it and assist others to make use of the latent talent they possess.[36]

Yet all was not light and music during this period. For two months of 1929 and for a longer period in 1930, we had a visitor from Washington, a fellow Quaker and a personal friend of President Herbert Hoover. The local press carried a small item: "Mr. Herbert D. Brown, chief of the U.S. Bureau of Efficiency, is here to look over our economy and make recommendations to the President." Later, rumor had it that in 1929, Brown and his wife had planned a vacation. Hawaii was a first choice, the U.S. Virgin Islands a second. Discovering that the U.S. Virgin Islands had a budget problem, a $300,000 shortfall, Brown decided on the Virgin Islands, where a two-month vacation could be written off as a government expense. Whether because of fate or economics, the fact is that Brown and his recommendations were to have a drastic effect on our islands' economy and culture and on my own personal life.[37]

Evidently, Brown and his wife enjoyed their two-month vacation, because he was back again in 1930 for a longer stay. This time, he was on assignment from Washington to make an in-depth study of economic conditions in the territory and report back to the president. Under orders from Governor Evans, local officials cooperated with him. Comfortable office space was set up for him on St. Thomas and St. Croix. A steady stream of people were called in for interviews. Islanders found Brown to be domineering and all-knowing, the kind of man who stuck to his own ideas regardless. During the talks, Brown made frequent reference to his intimate relationship with President Hoover, who would pay close heed to any recommendations that he made.

One day, I received a call to go to Brown's office. When I entered, Brown got up from his chair and came over with outstretched hand: "Bandmaster Adams, I have been waiting for this opportunity to greet you. You have been recommended to me as a man of integrity and long experience in these islands. I have been looking forward to exchanging ideas with you. Please be seated." My quick impression of Brown was that he was a man in his late sixties, tall, with gray hair, thin face, and piercing eyes—forceful and determined, the kind of man one would rather have as a friend than an enemy. He came to the point quickly: "Bandmaster Adams, I head the Bureau of Efficiency in Washington. My job is to cut waste in government and to make things balance, income and expenditure. The president asked me to come down here to look things over. For one thing, there is a shortfall in the local budget of $300,000. Compared to budgetary deficits elsewhere, that is minor. Still, it is a shortfall that has to be balanced. How would you handle that problem, Mr. Adams?"

"You are asking a quick question," I replied, "and I suppose you are expecting a quick reply. You must remember, Mr. Brown, that I am a musician, not an economist. Still, from my observation, I am aware that naval spending here is the main prop of our economy. With a little beefing up of personnel and activity, I believe that sufficient revenues would result to balance the shortfall."[38]

"Bandmaster Adams, as you know," said Brown, "the United States took over the Virgin Islands from Denmark, March 31, 1917, and placed them under the administration of the U.S. Navy. This was a unique situation— naval officers governing a civilian population. A few months later, you and your bandsmen entered the navy as a unit. What is equally unique in your situation is that there was a waiver of sea duty requirements for you and your men. In other words, regardless of the rapid turnover of naval personnel, you and your band remained here as a permanent fixture. Would you agree that, considering naval rules and regulations, this situation is unusual?"

"Yes, Mr. Brown, I agree that the situation is unusual. For me and my men, it has been a Godsend. We are able to live here with family and friends and to perform our functions in the most stimulating environment. Over more than a dozen years, people tell us we have become a showpiece for the naval administration and a cultural entity for our islands. We bless the U.S. Navy every day. What other department of government could have created us and maintained us?"

"What would happen, Bandmaster Adams, if the naval administration of these islands was replaced tomorrow and the islands turned over to another department of government, the U.S. Department of the Interior, for instance?"

"Well, Mr. Brown, I can only hope that such a change will not occur. It would be a crushing blow to me and my men, personally, and a devastating blow to the economy and infrastructure of the island. It is my understanding that the navy spends a minimum of $1.5 million annually, just for salaries and services. If the navy leaves, that same money would be spent elsewhere. What would take its place?"

"Perhaps you are jumping the gun, Bandmaster," said Brown. "The naval base at Culebra was in full swing while there was civilian government in Puerto Rico. I am sure that some similar arrangements can be worked out here. The problem as I see it, Bandmaster Adams, is that the short tenure of naval governors here does not permit them to cope with island problems. Look at what is happening in St. Croix. From March to September last year [1930], a terrible drought devastated the sugarcane crop there. This has resulted in the shutting down of the last three sugar factories. There are severe unemployment and bad times there. While navy spending stabilizes the economy of St. Thomas, it is doing little or nothing for St. Croix. Furthermore, a naval governor on short tenure does not sense an obligation to do something about the problem."[39]

I came away from the interview with a strong feeling of apprehension. Beyond a doubt, Brown was a stubborn man ready to overturn the status quo if necessary in order to have his own way. Evidently he had developed a master plan of his own to rehabilitate the islands based on diversification of agriculture and homesteading. The first phase called for an arrangement whereby the government would buy land, subdivide it into plots, and sell it to natives on an installment plan to encourage them to go back to farming. Seed money to initiate the project was to come from naval funds on hand and earmarked for other purposes. Brown assured the governor that with his land project once started, he would use his influence with the Appropriations Committee of the Congress to have additional money added to the annual funds for the islands to be used to expand his land plan. Governor Evans disagreed with Brown's plans. While they looked good on paper, the governor considered them unworkable due to the droughts that continued to plague the islands. He refused to turn over funds earmarked for other purposes. The men locked horns. Brown threatened to take the matter to his friend Herbert Hoover. As if to make good on his threat, Brown left the islands for Washington.

Things were quiet for a while, then word leaked from the nation's capital that Brown had succeeded in getting through his friend Horton French, of the House Subcommittee on Naval Appropriations, a special grant of $141,000 to be used for projects in the islands, and that expenditures from this appropriation were subject to the approval of Herbert D. Brown and Brown alone. The circumstances under which Congress made the appropriation left no alternative but to go with a dual responsibility in the running of island affairs. Governor Evans refused to be responsible as governor of the Virgin Islands so long as he was circumscribed by his inability to make expenditures from the new fund without Brown's approval. Governor Evans contended that, as the fund was charged to the navy's Virgin Islands appropriations, he should control them. Vehemently opposed to there being two governors of the islands, he submitted his resignation.[40]

Word that Governor Evans had resigned spread rapidly through the islands. There were expressions of dismay on all sides. The St. Thomas Chamber of Commerce met in an emergency session and petitioned the governor to reconsider. The local press was unanimous in voicing similar sentiments. Waldo Evans, a captain in the U.S. Navy, had been a popular and highly respected governor. Unlike other naval governors, who had been limited to two years in office, Evans was just completing a four-year term (March 1927–March 1931). With the good will of island inhabitants and the navy's blessings, there was every indication that he would continue to serve for a longer period.

As one of the islanders expressed it: "Governor Evans is one of the best governors we ever had. He is a level-headed man who has been guiding us well. Herbert D. Brown is a joke. He came here as a so-called efficiency expert to improve our economic conditions and from the looks of things, he is going to mess us up." Friction between Evans and Brown descended to a personal level and spread to their wives. At a dinner in Government House, the two women exchanged sharp words over seating arrangements. Mrs. Brown had written a book, *Grandmother Brown's One Hundred Years.*[41] The book had won literary honors. Mrs. Brown thought very highly of herself and expected to be given the seat of honor at the table. Mrs. Evans thought otherwise. The sharp verbal exchange between the women put a damper on the evening's affair. Next day Brown and Evans met in the governor's office. There was a heated exchange. The men could be heard shouting at each other. Evidently, that did it! Leaving the governor's office in an agitated state, Brown headed for the nearest telegraph office and sent a message to his friend President Hoover, urgently requesting the transfer of the administration of the U.S. Virgin Islands from the Navy Department to the Interior Department.

The clippings in my scrapbook help tell the story. From the local press of February 3, 1931:

> Governor Waldo Evans has been informed by radiogram from the Navy Department that the Secretary of Navy yesterday issued the following order: "It is proposed to transfer in the near future, the administration of the U.S. Virgin Islands from the Navy Department to the Interior Department. As a result, the policy of the Navy Department with regard to the Naval establishment in the U.S. Virgin Islands will be to reduce all naval activities to a minimum, retaining in an active state only the radio station and personnel necessary to care for Navy property."[42]
>
> As fast as naval personnel can be dispensed with, they will be withdrawn, and in no case will they remain in the Virgin Islands longer

than six months from this date. This advance information is given in order to avoid unnecessary expenditures of naval funds and to avoid transportation to the Virgin Islands of reliefs for naval and marine personnel now there. Beginning with the trip of the U.S.S. Kittery, leaving the United States on February 11, 1931, such personnel will be withdrawn as the present governor deems best.

Announcement by President Herbert Hoover, January 31, 1931:

I am proposing to forward to Congress the name of Paul M. Pearson of Pennsylvania for governor. Other civilian officials will be appointed in replacement of naval officers. Mr. Herbert D. Brown, chief of Bureau of Efficiency, and Colonel Roop, director of the budget, have drafted plans for the new civilian administration which are being carried into action.

Dispatch from the *New York Herald Tribune*, January 31, 1931:

Cabled reports that President Hoover had signed a bill creating a civilian government for the Virgin Islands were unfavorably received by a majority of the inhabitants of St. Thomas.

From a Washington dispatch, February 9, 1931:

The naval withdrawal according to high officers was not of its [the navy's] initiative but followed a dispute over dividing administrative responsibility with Herbert D. Brown, chief of the Bureau of Efficiency. Before the post of civilian governor was offered to Dr. Paul M. Pearson of Swarthmore, Pennsylvania, it was refused by Rear Admiral S. S. Robinson, superintendent of the Naval Academy, with the observation that no self-respecting person would take the governorship under the conditions imposed.

From the St. Thomas *Bulletin*, February 2, 1931:

The change of government is the all absorbing topic of the day. One thing stands out prominently, that is, the people to be affected by the change have neither been consulted nor considered. We cannot forget the good the Navy has done here, and the more we think of it, the more we regret the way in which naval relations with us are ending. When Herbert D. Brown came here to investigate economic conditions, we welcomed him. We did not expect his recommendations would cause such undesirable upheaval.[43]

Cablegram sent to President Hoover from the business community of St. Thomas, February 3, 1931:

The Chamber of Commerce has learned, with great regret, that the administration of the Virgin Islands is to be transferred from the Navy Department to the Interior Department. In view of the serious worldwide economic depression, the present time is most inopportune for this change. We urgently request, Mr. President, that despite the change to civilian rule, that naval activities, so beneficial to our economy, be continued.

From *St. Thomas Mail Notes*, February 14, 1931:

Formation of a citizens committee to request the Navy to continue activities here was started Tuesday evening, Feb. 10, 1931. The meeting held at the home of Herbert E. Lockhart was attended by more than 50 of St. Thomas's leading businessmen.

From *St. Thomas Mail Notes*, February 1931:

Navy Secretary Adams has been notified by residents of St. Thomas that they are forwarding to Congress, through him, a memorial requesting that naval activities be continued in this area. The memorial carries the signature of thousands of people in St. Thomas and St. John. Among these are people in every walk of life in the islands—bankers, legislators, merchants, manufacturers, mechanics, artisans, professional men, house and land owners, clerks, laborers, etc.

From the local press, February 1931:

Despite all the hectic activity locally, word from Washington does not offer much hope for retention of naval activities here. We understand that all navy men will be replaced by civilians until some 300 navy men have been withdrawn. Naval physicians will be replaced by doctors from the U.S. Public Health Services. Even the mine-sweeping tug, U.S.S. Grebe, stationed here will be sent elsewhere.

From the local press, February 16, 1931:

A Washington dispatch tells us that the new civilian governor for the Virgin Islands, Paul M. Pearson, is due to arrive here in about two weeks. The Navy has agreed to let the U.S.S. Grebe minesweeper stay for not later than July 1931 for the use of the new governor.

From the local press, February 18, 1931:

The Greek steamer, Captain Rokos, 3,437 tons register, bound for Brazil with general cargo, went ashore on Horse Shoe Reef, Anegada, last night and radioed for help. The U.S.S. Grebe left our port this morning about 9 o'clock to render assistance. How necessary it is to have the U.S.S. Grebe here.[44]

On February 12, 1931, the blow that we were expecting fell! Official word was received from the Navy Department that my bandsmen and I were to prepare to leave St. Thomas on February 17, 1931, for the naval sta-

tion in Guantánamo Bay, Cuba. Arrangements had also been made to transport families of any members of the band who wanted to go. I called my
men together, thirty-two total, and told them that they had approximately
four days to get ready to leave. The men were visibly unhappy. They felt
that they were victims, caught in a squeeze between powerful factions. As
one bandsman expressed it: "So we are being sent into exile." The men were
against any movement of family, considering such action premature.

We gave our farewell concert three days later as described in the local
press:

> Last evening the Navy Band gave its farewell concert at the Emancipa-
> tion Garden. It was a wonderful concert. Each item was heartily
> applauded by the record crowd of several thousand people. The concert
> opened with the popular "Virgin Islands March" composed by Band-
> master Adams. This was followed by a cornet solo, Schaefer's "Die Post
> im Walde," played by First Musician H. Brown. After the "Inter-
> mezzo," "Bridal Song," and various interpretations of southern
> melodies, came the big treat of the night, a piccolo solo played by Band-
> master Adams which was encored.
>
> Heads bowed in sadness and many persons in the crowd began to
> sob as the band sounded the parting note, "Farewell to Thee." Silence
> prevailed for a short time after this composition was rendered.
>
> The Navy band is near and dear to us. Its departure . . . will be
> keenly felt. For nearly 14 years, since its induction as a unit in the U.S.
> Navy, June 2, 1917, and through the courtesy of the various comman-
> dants, the band has rendered efficient public service. It has assisted all
> local efforts where the public was concerned. Diversified in its activities,
> hospitals, churches, schools, institutions, and organizations, both here
> and on St. Croix, have received the benefits of its high training and
> ability, fruits of perseverance and study under the competent direction
> of Bandmaster Adams.
>
> A large and tearful crowd is expected to see the men off to Guan-
> tanamo, Cuba. We hope that as a unit they will continue to distinguish
> themselves through musical ability and discipline and that this hasty
> transfer will be no more than an opportunity to add fresh laurels to the
> U.S. Navy Band of the Virgin Islands.[45]

Our departure two days later was covered in the local papers:

> Several hundred people gathered last night at Kings Wharf to bid a
> sorrowful farewell to the Navy band, departing on short notice for
> Guantanamo, Cuba. As the musicians arrived on the wharf, singly or
> in groups, eager crowds pressed forward to shake hands with friends
> or to embrace relatives. Wives, children, mothers, and grandmothers
> mingled with the crowd, some openly sobbing. With a launch waiting

in readiness to take them to the naval transport anchored in midharbor, the bandsmen tried to be cheerful. Taking out their instruments, they played a few last-minute selections, including "Auld Lang Syne" and the ever popular composition of Bandmaster Adams, the "Virgin Islands March," but there was no clapping of hands or cheering. A heavy cloud of sorrow hung overhead, enveloping every thought, every consideration. The music seemed like an anesthetic that stifled the emotions of the crowd.

The bandsmen put away their instruments, said their final tearful good-byes, and stepped one by one into the waiting launch. As the rope lines were cast off and as the launch with its cargo of musicians faded from sight, the following lines from the verse, "The Burial of John Moore," crossed our minds, with a few changes in the third line to suit our present circumstance:

> "Few and short were the prayers we said
> And we spoke not a word of sorrow
> But we steadfastly gazed at the bandsmen
> That were leaving and bitterly thought
> Of tomorrow . . ."

Yes, we gazed at the bandsmen that were leaving, these young men abruptly taken away from their homes and their families to be landed on a foreign shore, innocent victims on the altar of political revenge. How different this departure was from another we had witnessed. How well we remember the large crowd that had gathered on the same spot when the band had departed for a tour of the eastern states of the United States of America. How well we remember the even greater and exuberant crowd that waited to greet the band on its return from that triumphant tour laden with high praise from musicians of international repute and from top officials of many of the cities visited.[46]

8 The Naval Administration (1917–1931)

An Evaluation

Editor's Note: *A key section in achieving the author's goals for the memoirs, this chapter directly challenges criticisms of the naval administration and its governors and further asserts their positive accomplishments. Confronting totalizing arguments that represent the navy as an "army of occupation," Adams writes of both the personal devotion and practical achievements of the naval governors with whom he worked. These achievements include extending and repairing roads, vastly improving health care, and comprehensively rebuilding the educational system, including opening the islands' first high school. He critiques the analysis of historians Gordon K. Lewis and Lewis Harris Evans as one-sided, while endorsing Virgin Island historian J. Antonio Jarvis, who although critical of the navy offers a balanced assessment based on firsthand knowledge. Adams denies that naval governors were racist and finds naval personnel as a whole, despite isolated early racist incidents, to be dedicated to the welfare of the islands and their people. While Adams does not explicitly criticize the Danish government's long period of colonial neglect, he quotes historian Luther Evans and reports by Governor James Oliver to point out the dire situation that confronted U.S. naval administrators upon arrival in 1917. Adams also counters claims that the removal of the navy in 1931 was due to incompetence; rather, he blames political intrigue (described in chapter 7) for the loss of confidence evidenced by President Hoover. Certainly Adams benefited, both professionally and personally, from the navy's presence and was deeply affected by its dismissal. In an attempt to be more objective here, he avoids personal anecdotes, arguing instead from close readings of published histories.*

A work of history is one that seeks by means of appraisal, assessment, characterization, or evaluation, to chronicle and interpret events, happenings, and, especially, the people of long ago. The method used for presentation therefore should necessarily be rational and scientific and not political, ideological, sentimental, or prejudicial. History is a task that requires seasoned thought, reflection, and reason, particularly when we consider the words of admonition of the young African writer Camara Laye in his book *A Dream of Africa* that "one never knows another person completely, and a race even less. And none of us knows himself completely."[1]

I have selected two books from among the recent works published on the history of the Virgin Islands. The first is Dr. Gordon K. Lewis's *The Virgin Islands—A Caribbean Lilliput,* published in 1972 by the Northwestern University Press of Evanston, Illinois. The other is Lewis Harris Evans's *The Virgin Islands from Naval Base to New Deal,* published three years later by Greenwood Press Publishers of Westport, Connecticut.[2] I selected Dr. Lewis's book because of the author's outstanding reputation as a scholarly writer and because he has been a frequent visitor, off and on, for many years to the Virgin Islands. He also mentions me in his book with respect and understanding, though I never had the pleasure of meeting him personally. The book by Dr. Evans has been selected for the reason that, in my opinion, the author presents an objective, factual account based on research in nonpolitical files and records of both the Department of the Navy and the Congress of the United States. My hope is to present a factual account—using these books as points of departure—based upon my personal involvement and experience of the role and contribution of the naval officers who governed the Virgin Islands during the years 1917 to 1931.

It seems to me that Dr. Lewis has made a number of factual and interpretative errors, based on his misuse or distortion of the source material upon which he relies so heavily. Factually, he has ignored or disregarded the very evidence that comes from this material. Although such biased writing occurs throughout the book, I have chosen to comment upon the author's treatment of the period of "Naval Rule," because I was intimately involved with the major personalities and events at that time and therefore feel qualified to comment on Dr. Lewis's sweeping characterizations.

In his interpretation of the "Naval Administration," Dr. Lewis relied heavily on the writings of J. Antonio Jarvis. There can be no objection to the use of this author of the *Brief History of the Virgin Islands.*[3] Jarvis is a recognized local authority on Virgin Islands history and culture who possesses firsthand knowledge of the quality of this naval rule. What disturbs me, however, is that Dr. Lewis has presented just one side of Jarvis's evaluation of the administration—thereby doing a disservice not only to the navy but to Jarvis himself.

Chapter 2, "The American Beginnings," contains Dr. Lewis's assessment of the role of the naval administration. Let us consider the main points of his rather damning indictment:

1. "That the period was characterized by an undeclared war between the Naval Administration and the popular interests"

2. "That the United States Navy was the wrong agency with which to entrust the government of a dependent civilian population"

3. "That, by training and disposition, the Annapolis mentality was not suited to the demands of popular government"

4. "That administratively, the navy possessed no training program to fit its candidates for what is in effect a colonial civil service"

5. "That appointment to the office of Governor in the new dependent territories—this was to be haphazard"

6. "That the navy was a completely segregated service, having adopted this policy of total racial exclusion in 1920"

7. "That the navy's system of government in short consisted of the private rule of navy governors holding themselves aloof from local society and generally delegating their authority to subordinates"

Since he uses Jarvis as an authority, let us see how the assessment of Dr. Lewis squares with Jarvis's *Brief History of the Virgin Islands:*

When the United States took possession of the Virgin Islands, the officials sent to govern had no idea what sort of a task lay before them. The abrupt transition from Danish to American ownership was likewise difficult for the people, and it speaks well for both sides that no serious incidents marred the first contacts. The few transgressions of good taste that occurred may be put down to the difficulty of getting acquainted in a large way . . . bearded, dignified and retiring, Governor Oliver was still a pleasant, democratic person who loved to ramble through the countryside whenever the cares of office would permit. He carried the huge responsibility of wartime precautions and inducting the islands into the American system with the highest sense of duty that officers of his rank generally feel in positions of that sort. But, there was more punctilio [formality] in him. Governor Oliver's staff set a high standard for administrative and professional ability, and the members took every new job with an enthusiasm which, not even war, could beat.

The problem of health was one of the first tackled, and the doctors were looked upon as saviors because they gave heroic treatment wherever possible. Doctors Mortensen, Knud-Hansen, and Christiansen had done very well before but the new program called for additional hospital facilities and extended medical service. These Danes gave splendid cooperation and did much to effect the changes needed.

With the country engaged in war, there was little time to think of civilian wants, yet the United States began to improve the schools, the roads, and the harbor. The old quarantine station was taken over and made into East Point Marine Station; West Point was at Lindbergh Bay, where the airbase is now located. St. Croix was not neglected because with St. Thomas that island received a new governmental set-up. The big houses of the spacious countryside were always thrown open to welcome American officers and their families and the money they spent improved economic situations there.

Jarvis, evaluating the social situation of Governor Oman, writes:

Governor Oman, another Rear Admiral, was a social, well-meaning person who made the mistake of having the general public to a levy and ruined the dignity of the whole affair by accepting as guests along with pompous burgers, barefooted beggars, Cha-chas and people without any status in local society.[4]

Governor Oman's smiles and bows belied his true ability. He was active and had rare diplomatic skill which is proved by the prodigious amount of work done by the colonial councils during his administration. The new code of laws was finished and approved on March 17, 1921, shortly after Governor Oman left. Judge C. G. Thiele and the late John DeJongh were among the chief exponents of legal position and social fitness of this important code. Normally the laws had been based on Danish statutes, English Common Law, Precedents and Rulings Unique, and liberal interpretations of conditions. The legal aides to the governor as well as the court personnel rendered valuable assistance, but it was the tactfulness of Governor Oman that held all together for the common good. Junior High School was reached, prohibition felt, and the labor problem became acute with manipulation from corrupt police officials.

The following sums up Jarvis's assessment:

Fourteen years of Naval government left the Virgin Islands with much improved health conditions, paved streets, better schools, and the economic situation a little better than the islands had reason to expect. For example, when the United States Naval doctors tried to improve health conditions by proper sanitation, they met very stubborn resistance but a physical examination of school children raised a hornet's nest. Hundreds of parents protested, some even through the press, that the doctors were just fondling and searching girls for pleasure. It was a test of the perseverance and tactfulness of the medical men but they broke down the inhibitions of the people until considerable improvement was made. Captain Waldo Evans, the best-loved of the Naval Governors, able and just, served a double term, had highly cultural assistance, recognized native ability, improved the schools and decided that the Virgin Islands could not be run by two governors simultaneously.

It is obvious, therefore, that Jarvis saw the period of "Naval Administration" in a much more positive, more objective light than Dr. Lewis. Yet Lewis chose to ignore completely Jarvis's balanced assessment. Historical scholarship deserves better from someone trained in the techniques of historical research and evaluation. Moreover, in those instances in which Lewis does accurately follow Jarvis, he, like Jarvis, often distorts the historical record. Take, for example, his harsh condemnation of the personalities of the naval governors. Here he relies upon unsubstantiated character assassinations to support his general argument that naval officers were ill equipped for their administrative roles.

Jarvis's evaluation of Governor Kittelle as "a martinet as small as Oman, . . . made up of hair-triggers and Paul Revere patriotism," is, in fact, the reverse of the man himself. Knowing Jarvis as I did—to be a decent, intelligent, fair-minded, and highly talented citizen—I will ascribe his evaluation to being misinformed. Jarvis did not know Kittelle the man and in his characterization unfortunately trusted to the loudmouth rantings and irresponsible writings of some corrupt politicians of the period. From my experience and perspective, Kittelle's administration made a substantial contribution to the educational, cultural, and economic phases of community life. Kittelle's personal endeavors centered, to the point of dedication, on the educational system. He was at heart and by training an educator and, unlike most military men, an impressive speaker. He was a great lover of nature, especially of trees, and established an annual Arbor Day observance in the islands.

It is not true that Governor Kittelle designed and forced the flag of the Virgin Islands on the people. He believed that the islands, the same as elsewhere, should have a flag of their own and therefore organized a committee of Virgin Islanders for the purpose of designing one. A recent visit from a retired officer who at the time was in the supply corps and had much to do with the committee reminded me that I was the one who recommended the name of Alphonse Wilhelmsen, then a clerk in the store of I. Levin, to design it, which he did. It was Governor Kittelle who made possible my first visit to the United States in 1922, not as a spectacle as Dr. Lewis would have his readers believe, but to observe the methods and workings used in the public schools of the United States to inform the course of music I was preparing for the Department of Education.

Another grave mistake of Jarvis was his reference to Governor Philip Williams as "deaf, amiable, ruled by his executive secretary, passing with nothing startling except for an extra gift from Congress which took a long time to reach [the islands] and was later on spent on reservoirs." The tour of the navy band to the United States in 1924 was made possible by Governor Williams, who was a mathematician and a businessman of high administrative ability, and not one who would pass his duties on to subordinates.

In his broad generalized statements, Dr. Lewis has provided no firm evidence to prove that there is such a thing as a strongly rooted Annapolis mentality; or that, if it did exist, it underlay the attitudes and policies of the naval officials here. The same can be said of a racism that sprang from a southern background introduced into the islands. Dr. Lewis assumed that the navy personnel stationed here were wholly comprised of southerners; this is totally erroneous. They were comprised of men and women from all the states of the union, and the dentists, supply corps officers, chaplains, and legal advisers who helped to administer these islands were not military men per se. Therefore, in the absence of firm quantitative evidence to support these generalizations, Dr. Lewis is wrong to make a blanket condemnation of the temper of naval rule as authoritarian, racist, and insensitive. In the first place, many of the officers were not from the South, and many of them had excellent administrative and technical backgrounds. Many, regardless of their place of origin or training, were generally committed to the needs of the people, and no efforts were made to undermine the society that was the legacy of the Danish period.[5]

Strict authoritarian rule, which Dr. Lewis emphasizes in his criticism as the basis of the naval regime, is not always a reprehensible method of procedure. Many Third World leaders and spokesmen today recognize that a strong executive acting through a well-defined chain of command and fostering the need for discipline and duty is often essential to development and modernization, for only thus can the encrusted power structures and popular indifference inherited from the past be effectively overcome.

My personal recollection of the naval officials is not one of indifferent, insensitive, reclusive, petty tyrants, but as warm, sensitive, active, and humane individuals genuinely concerned with the people of the Virgin Islands and their future development. The contributions of the navy administrators were substantial, as even Jarvis—surely no friend of the navy—was forced to admit. It must be remembered that pioneer work was extremely difficult, especially for the first two governors, Rear Admiral James H. Oliver and Rear Admiral Joseph W. Oman. They could not get the attention of the federal government as they wished, overburdened as it was with weightier problems just after the world war. This situation was aggravated by the loss of the "free port" that had existed under Danish law, thereby reducing trade on the island considerably.[6] Then came Prohibition, which destroyed the beverage market for sugar products. Despite these handicaps, the exemplary spirit of the navy was strikingly manifested. Following are a few irrefutable facts about what was accomplished in these islands during the naval administration.

The school system was extended and the first high school opened. A code of laws more in conformity with American aims was established. Roads were built. Attempts were made to conserve the water supply. Market gardening and tree planting were encouraged. The bay rum industry was saved, and an effort was made to extend the market for St. Croix cattle. The judiciary was placed on a firmer basis. Unrest among the alien labor element in St. Croix was quieted and law and order enforced; the leper colony was saved with a large supply of Chalmugra oil.[7] The care of the sick was improved and native nurses were trained. Sanitation was improved and the death rate reduced. Careful attention was given to mothers in the care of infants. A branch of the American Red Cross was organized, and the first public library was opened. A music program was introduced to the public schools. A branch of the Boy Scouts was organized. Patriotism was encouraged by precept and example, and, of course, the United States Navy Band of the Virgin Islands was organized under native leadership. This represented one of the finest contributions made to our people—particularly because of the confidence shown in the ability of natives in both output and leadership in a delicate and difficult task.

When the navy governors were relieved of the administration of the Virgin Islands, they left behind an enviable record of achievement and fair play. It was, in short, an honest and well-run administration. The names of Rear Admirals James H. Oliver, Joseph W. Oman, and Sumner E. W. Kittelle; Captains Henry H. Hough, Phillip Williams, Martin E. Trench, and Waldo Evans and their assistants; Major Jessie Deyer of the marine corps; Captains William Russell White and Ellis Stone; Commandants C. C. Timmons, J. R. Gaffney, W. Zane; and others too numerous to mention represent the highest type of territorial administrative ability to be found anywhere. Their unselfish service to the Virgin Islands should ever be remembered.

GOVERNORS OF THE VIRGIN ISLANDS DURING
THE NAVY PERIOD (1917–1931)

James Harrison Oliver, Rear Admiral, U.S.N.	April 9, 1917–April 8, 1919
Joseph Wallace Oman, Rear Admiral, U.S.N.	April 8, 1919–April 26, 1921

Summer Ely Wetmore Kittelle, Rear Admiral, U.S.N.	April 26, 1921–Sept. 16, 1922
Henry Hughes Hough, Captain, U.S.N.	Sept. 16, 1922–Dec. 3, 1923
Phillip Williams, Captain, U.S.N.	Dec. 3, 1923–Sept. 11, 1925
Martin Edward Trench, Captain, U.S.N.	Sept. 11, 1925–Jan. 6, 1927
Waldo Evans, Captain, U.S.N.	March 1, 1927–March 18, 1931

A far more accurate appraisal of the legacy of the naval administration to these islands than that of Lewis, or even that of Jarvis, is the study by Luther Evans—*From Naval Base to New Deal*. Evans correctly points out that the navy inherited many serious social and economic problems when it assumed responsibility for the Virgin Islands in 1917. As the following quote from Governor Oliver's letter of August 1, 1917, to the secretary of the navy makes evident, the naval governors clearly perceived the extent of the problems confronting them:

> The death rate is very high, infant mortality being particularly disgraceful to a civilized community. . . . Three hospitals have been run with varying degrees of efficiency—none of them really efficient. There is a lack of proper buildings, proper equipment, trained personnel. . . . Sanitation is in imperative need of improvement. . . . Adequate water supply and a proper system of sewerage is a health necessity. The roads in St. Croix are very fair but repairs have not been properly maintained. There are only about 4 miles of roads in St. Thomas. Fire protection is inadequate. . . . Improved harbor facilities are not an immediate necessity. . . . There are practically no food crops except a small quantity of yams and sweet potatoes. These islands are incapable of self-support and must continue to be aided by Federal appropriations. The existing system of public instruction in these islands leaves about everything in the way of an adequate system to be desired. The natives should be given instruction, above all else, in the use of their hands. Social conditions are extremely bad; there is no proper family life. . . . Infantile mortality reaches shocking proportions . . . the cost of the maintenance of the islands, and of the recommended improvements (totaling $1,952,000) is great, but the need is real and vital, and aside from all other considerations, the situation is one that must be faced and corrected. This unfortunate situation is the natural inevitable result of centuries of neglect.

And as Evans clearly documents, naval administrators took quick and decisive steps to deal with the pressing needs of the local community. After surveying the many accomplishments of the naval administrators between 1917 and 1930, Evans concedes:

> It is impossible to close this chapter without attempting to answer the question whether the Navy should have been withdrawn from the government of the Virgin Islands. There can be no doubt in the minds of anyone who clearly examines the data upon which this chapter is based that the Navy need not be ashamed of what it did for the people of the Virgin Islands. Its record was a good one. A certain lack of regard for some of the best traditions of civil administration serve to place the Naval regime in a much worse light than it deserved. The stereotype of prejudice against a military system worked to the disadvantage of men who were really able administrators of a government clearly civil in character. Neither the record of their accomplishments nor the basic philosophies to which they were attached made them unfit to carry on with the new rehabilitation program. Governor Evans was personally hostile to certain of its features, but fairness demands that he be regarded as a special case, largely because of his personal animosity toward Herbert D. Brown.

Evans further clarifies the circumstances surrounding the transition from naval to civilian rule in 1930. He writes:

> The Navy probably would not have been relieved of its responsibilities in the Virgin Islands had there not been a strong desire in high places to prevent a public airing of certain personal frictions which developed between the summer of 1929 and the autumn of 1930. If the allegations of poker-playing and drinking in Government House, brought to Washington by a judge whom the governor had refused to reappoint, had not been taken seriously, there would have been much less cause for the President to show such a lack of confidence in the Navy. The White House statement of January 30, 1931, informed an inquisitive world that the transfer to the Interior Department was occasioned by the necessity for providing for the execution of the rehabilitation program; a queer statement, when as long as eight months previously Congress had authorized the undertaking of the rehabilitation program under Navy auspices and the President had upheld the position that the Navy Department should have administrative control over the expenditure of the funds involved!
>
> It is clear, therefore, that the Navy was withdrawn without reference to its general record of administrative competence or to either its willingness or its capacity to handle the rehabilitation program. It was withdrawn to prevent the airing of an unwholesome situation which really had little relation to the welfare of the people of the Virgin Islands. The aspersions cast upon the Navy's stewardship by its successors are not deserved. The Navy governors tried diligently to provide

American standards for the Virgin Islands within the limits of the money which they could wheedle from Congress and the councils. Anyone who examines the record with care and impartiality can have no reluctance in stating that they did a surprisingly good job.

Apparently the judge did not give the real reason to his congressman father-in-law as to why the governor decided not to reappoint him. The reason was believed to be a racial one which involved the judge and a committeeman from Tuskegee Institute. The first offense was given by the judge on the arrival of the committee that checked in as guests of the Grand Hotel. As was reported, he immediately checked out and moved to another hotel. This ill will, it is said, was further aggravated by a personal insult that took place in the public street when a black committeeman from Tuskegee was introduced to the same white judge and the latter, it is said, refused to accept the extended hand of the educator. This matter was brought to the attention of Governor Waldo Evans, who immediately summoned the judge to his office, with the result that he was told by the governor that he would not be reappointed at the end of his term. The matter became a public issue. But it took the inimitable Adolph Sixto to sum up the event humorously; with his usual chuckle he said: "That's nothing, ladies and gentlemen, to wail about. For it is said that this man hates black people so much that he refused to eat an egg laid by a black fowl." This, according to the foregoing statement made by the author Evans, was the reason for the transfer of the administration and not what many people were led to believe.

The United States Navy, it should be realized, is a branch of the United States military establishment made up of men and women from all the states, territories, and possessions of the Union. It is, in fact, a microcosm of the entire nation. Its purpose is to protect as well as to defend the country in times of war or any disaster which requires its presence. Unfortunately, only in times of national emergency is its usefulness appreciated. If in times of peace, it is considered to be an evil influence, it represents a necessary evil, since mankind after centuries of so-called civilization has unfortunately not up to the present time arrived at a stage when brotherly love is a reality. As the writer J. B. Priestley put it graphically in the early 1920s, "After years of saying Mass we have arrived at poisoned gas."[8] It is astonishing that so many people, including writers on the islands' history, do not understand one critical aspect about the government of the Virgin Islands as provided by law: that there has been no change in the law as far as the Organic Act is concerned; that the government of the islands has always been a civilian government; and that the fact that previous governors were naval officers by profession did not create a naval government any more than Washington, Jackson, and Grant being soldiers thereby made the government of the United States a military one.

The talk about a military government has always been nonsense and was brought about and furthered by agitators in the islands and elsewhere. Admiral James H. Oliver [the first U.S. governor, 1917–19] was as much a civilian governor as Governor Paul M. Pearson [the first governor after the navy's departure, 1931–35]. The governor was supreme in the islands under the law and had no superior except the president, who being too busy to handle the correspondence, directed that it be handled through and not by the Department of the Navy. All that happened in the case of President Wilson was that he directed that this administrative work be turned over to the Department of the Navy and it was thereby subjected to navy rules. But the government of the Virgin Islands and the people were never placed in this situation. Read Public Law No. 389 of the 64th United States Congress (HR 20755), which created the government for the Virgin Islands in 1917:

> An Act to Provide a Temporary Government for the West Indian Islands acquired by the United States from Denmark by the convention entered into between said countries on the fourth day of August nineteen hundred and sixteen and ratified by the Senate of the United States on the seventh day of September, nineteen hundred and sixteen and for other purposes.
>
> Be it enacted by the Senate and House of Representatives of the United States of America in Congress assembled, That, except as hereinafter provided, all military, civil and judicial powers necessary to govern the West Indian Islands acquired from Denmark shall be vested in a governor and in such person or persons as the President may appoint, and shall be exercised in such manner as the President shall direct until Congress shall provide for the government of said islands: Provided, that the President may assign an officer of the Army or Navy to serve as such governor and perform the duties appertaining to said office.

The Danish flag, the Dannenbrog, which waved over these islands for over 200 years, was officially lowered from the flagpole at the marine barracks in St. Thomas on Saturday, March 31, 1917, at 4:00 P.M., to give swift ascent immediately after to the Stars and Stripes, the emblem of the United States of America. For almost two full decades after that moment in our history, the United States of America through a governor supported by the Navy Department administered these islands. To those of us who shared its beginning or who, in the years that followed, lived part of their mature years in these islands, the significance and contribution of the naval administration is one of the greatest examples of the enlightened manner in which America has dealt with its territorial and insular possessions.

It shall be to the everlasting credit of the naval administration that from the very outset, the task of handling the affairs of the people of the Virgin Islands was undertaken with the sincere conviction of and faith in the ability of our people to do for themselves the things that living in a democratic society demands. And thus, from the enlightened perspective of today, we can truly appraise what the United States Navy achieved, not only in upholding America's tradition but also in laying a solid foundation while pointing at the same time toward the firm direction of our political, economic, and spiritual growth and the intelligent know-how of good and sound government.

The navy's period of service here taught us all that good government and efficient management are the natural products of a wholesome, vigorous, and continued citizen interest and participation in public affairs. Also, it offered the moral lesson that looking down on others deprives the eye of true focus. The lesson has shown also that handling other people successfully must be done on the basis of helping them, and to really help them, one must understand them and their needs; and that the forcible direction, which they of necessity must receive, should be tempered with sympathy.

We often hear the naval administration of these islands referred to as "an army of occupation." Perhaps a just reflection on the work of those early administrators would justify use of the term "an army of transition" instead. By this latter term I refer to the early administrators as the ones who did much to establish a bridge between the cultured and paternal regime of the Danes and the cultured but more self-dependent system of the Americans. From the administration of Governor James H. Oliver to that of Governor Waldo Evans, we find a series of cultured, refined, and self-respecting Americans (women as well as men) who labored unstintingly to develop in the Virgin Islands all the good things which come within the range of the American ideal. Their activities and results have already become history.[9]

9   Civilian Government and Politics (the 1930s)

Editor's Note: *Three tragedies assailed Adams in the early 1930s: the trans-fer of his band to Cuba, the death of his daughter Merle, and a house fire that not only destroyed his library of books, publications, and music manu-scripts but also killed another daughter, Hazel. As soon as he could, Adams left Cuba, retiring (along with several of his bandsmen) and thereby signal-ing the end of the U.S. Navy Band of the Virgin Islands. Adams moved back to St. Thomas, taking up residence in a historic home a few blocks from Government House, and tried to pick up the pieces of a life disrupted and lives lost. Economic stagnation gripped the islands in the wake of the navy's departure, proving one positive contribution of the naval administration. While an ardent navy supporter, Adams worked effectively with the islands' new civilian governor, Paul M. Pearson, and came to admire Pear-son's leadership and economic initiatives. Adams writes extensively about two Pearson projects: Bluebeard Castle Hotel (opened in December 1934) and the draining of "Mosquito Bay." Pearson appointed Adams head of the St. Thomas Cultural Committee and recruited him to head the high school music program and again serve as music supervisor for the public schools. After helping to prepare for the visit of Eleanor Roosevelt and composing a song of welcome, Adams regularly coordinated the governor's reception committee to host visiting dignitaries. Adams would welcome notable fig-ures including President Roosevelt, the poet Edna St. Vincent Millay, playwright Thornton Wilder, and film star Douglas Fairbanks. Pearson's administration, however, was plagued by power struggles that often drew congressional and presidential concern. Conflicts with Paul C. Yates, the appointed assistant to the governor, resulted in a series of investigations that produced no evidence of wrongdoing but did considerable political damage to Pearson. Interior Secretary Harold Ickes remained loyal to the governor and helped foster his courageous vision. When the islands' legis-lature proclaimed the Virgin Islands a refuge for those, especially Jews, fleeing deteriorating conditions in Europe as World War II approached, Ickes championed the humanitarian idea in Washington. Here the tradi-tion of tolerance and openness that Adams claims for the Virgin Islands seems at work, leading the United States as a whole in a more compas-sionate and humanitarian direction.*

Our band arrived in Guantánamo, Cuba, the latter part of February 1931, and in a short time the bandsmen were settled in barracks. The naval reser-vation of which we were now part was a large one located on the southeast coast. Adjustment to our new surroundings was difficult. To a man, we had a feeling that the navy had needed to find a place for us in a hurry and this was it. Our workload was light, and I sensed that boredom and homesick-ness would be forces to contend with if I hoped to keep my men in good musical shape. Our bandsmen had brought to Cuba a feeling of intense anger and bitterness against the man who had caused this upheaval in their lives, Herbert D. Brown, so-called Chief of the Efficiency. Prevailing opin-ion was that Brown had acted from stubbornness and spite, not from good judgment. "What kind of economic efficiency was it," one bandsman asked, "to move naval spending from American possessions to foreign areas? If economy of administration was one of Brown's purposes, under civil regime the administration of the islands will certainly cost more because of the cost of duplication and the need to employ doctors, nurses, technicians, to say nothing of officials to replace naval personnel."

For my part, I had plenty of time to meditate on the workings of fate. More and more, I realized how untimely was the death four years earlier of one of our finest of naval governors, Martin E. Trench. Had Governor Trench lived, none of this upheaval would have come to pass. High on that governor's list was a plan to train islanders to take over government man-agement from naval officials. When that time came, a trusted and respected naval governor, like Trench, would recommend this move. Trench's plan called for the naval station to remain under civil government as one of the economic mainstays of the islands. There is no question in my mind that under Trench the transition would have been smooth and effected with the knowledge and support of the Navy Department. Without a doubt Brown's stubborn and domineering tactics had caused the navy to react angrily and to shut down the station.[1]

One bright spot for us in Guantánamo was the receipt of mail and news-papers from St. Thomas. How starved we were for news of home! I had made arrangements for local newspapers to be mailed to me, and I had urged family and friends to write often and to send news of local happenings. I read these letters and newspapers again and again and saved every important clipping. I shared this information with my men. They did likewise with information they received. In this way we kept up to date with happenings in the islands.

For example, a letter from Ella Gift, a native of St. Thomas, was published in the *Bulletin* on March 13, 1931:

> I want to thank the naval administration for all the good work it has done for the island of St. Thomas. First, I want to thank the naval doctors. Now we have an improved hospital. We have a good ambulance. Cots have been replaced by spring beds. The wards have been renovated to please the eye. The yards are concreted and there are beds planted with flowers The doctors in charge were kind. So were the nurses, all concerned and devoted to the welfare of their patients. Navy employees contributed to the island's economy. They rented houses, hired domestics, and put considerable money in circulation as they spent their salaries here. All this money placed St. Thomas above the bread line as compared with neighboring islands. In Antigua, for instance, they have to attach kitchens to schools to feed needy children. Here as a result of the navy, we have a movie line instead of a bread line. Our theatres are so packed, one of them had to be enlarged recently. We should never bite the hand that fed us and helped us, and we should always be grateful to the naval administration for all that it did for us.
>
> The navy did good work in our educational department. The classrooms were kept clean and well ventilated. Fresh coats of paint were applied regularly. At the start of each school year, text books were available in quantity. School nurses were always on the job watching after the health and happiness of the children. I have seen the U.S.S. Grebe, on her regular visits to St. Croix, taking our children over on vacation and bringing those from St. Croix over here, all for free, to participate in games and contests.
>
> The navy was very strict about sanitation. They had an efficient staff of inspectors visiting and oiling swamps and checking for stagnant water in private yards regularly in a constant war on mosquitoes. We never heard about cases of malaria in navy time, and dengue fever was rare as compared with such fever in neighboring islands. The navy was very strict about litter and the regular collection of garbage. Trucks made the rounds regularly and St. Thomas was a clean island as a result. Our roads were well maintained and more of them were paved as naval money came through for the purpose.

In closing, I can only say to Governor Evans, his staff, and navy personnel:

> We thank you for your kindness
> We thank you for your love
> And may you all be rewarded
> By our great Lord above . . .

Signed, Ella Gift[2]

In the press for March 18 and 19, 1931, we read of the arrival of the new governor:

> On Tuesday afternoon, March 17, Governor Paul M. Pearson arrived in St. Thomas aboard the U.S.S. Grebe. He was accompanied by his staff; his niece, Dorothy Pearson; the Honorable Herbert Brown, chief of the Bureau of Efficiency, Washington, D.C.; and Mrs. Herbert Brown. Also in the group were the Honorable Judge Edwards, Assistant Secretary of Interior; Boyd J. Brown, Lieutenant Governor for St. Thomas; and Dr. Lawrence Cramer, Lieutenant Governor for St. Croix.
>
> Governor Pearson and his entourage were accorded a warm welcome by Governor and Mrs. Waldo Evans and the reception committee which awaited them on King's Wharf. Following a welcoming address by the Honorable Conrad Corneiro, bouquets were presented to Dorothy Pearson by Eldra Monsanto and to Mrs. Herbert D. Brown by Enid Baa. After being introduced to many of the leading citizens and after greeting the colorful array of people who lined both sides of the thoroughfare, the new governor and party entered automobiles and were driven through the city before being taken to Government House. Governor and Mrs. Waldo Evans had moved from the executive mansion several weeks before and for the time being had take up residence on Synagogue Hill.
>
> The inauguration of Dr. Paul M. Pearson, first civilian governor of the U.S. Virgin Islands, took place on March 18, 1931. It drew the greatest crowd that had assembled since the Transfer. The oath of office was administered by Judge Edrington of the District Court.[3]

Not long after Governor Pearson's arrival, President Herbert Hoover himself visited Puerto Rico and the Virgin Islands as part of a vacation, but also to look at the economic conditions there. A letter from a friend described the President's arrival:

> From an early hour on Wednesday morning, March 25 [1931], a large crowd gathered on King's Wharf to witness the landing of President Hoover and his staff. This was a very historic occasion, the first visit to our shores of a U.S. President and I did not want to miss any part of it. I

had a spot very close to the landing and I can tell you, I was taken aback by what I saw. The President of the United States, stepping ashore, wore dirty white shoes and his clothes looked crumpled as if he had slept in them the night before. I could hear people around me commenting unfavorably on his appearance. It was quite a let down from our expectations.

The President, accompanied by Secretary of the Interior Wilbur and Secretary of War Hurley were greeted by Governor Pearson and other local officials and taken to Emancipation Garden to review a parade in their honor. The Community Band was in attendance. The young musicians did their best, but I can tell you, Alton, the pomp and sparkle, the spotless white uniforms, the discipline, the flawless music of you and your band were badly missed.

As you know, our island people form impressions fast. The feeling spread that President Hoover was "a cold fish" and that he did not like us. It didn't take us long to realize that we didn't like him either. After the welcoming ceremony in Emancipation Garden, noticeable for its lack of warmth, the visiting dignitaries, accompanied by local officials, got into waiting cars and headed for the West Side Tennis Club where a tree planting ceremony was to take place.

The President and his party were received with true St. Thomian dignity by Dr. Rudy Lanclos, club president. Holes had been dug and two silk oak trees were on hand to be planted. After the ceremony was over, President Hoover was presented with a beautiful paper knife made of native turtle shell, the handle of which represented a tennis racquet. Next, D. Victor Bornn, chairman of the reception committee, gave him a beautiful mahogany table made of native wood. Secretary of Interior Wilbur and Secretary of War Hurley each was presented with a beautiful box made of the same wood.

Comments and responses were brief and after some handshaking, the President and his party went into town. At 3 PM the President went aboard the U.S.S. Arizona amid the booming of a cannon from old Fort Christian.

Back on ship, the president invited national newsmen into his suite and issued the following statement, here quoted from the *New York Herald Tribune* of March 28, 1931:

When we paid $25 million for the Virgin Islands, we acquired an effective poorhouse comprising ninety percent of the population. The purpose of the transfer of administration from Navy to Interior is to see if we can develop some form of industry or agriculture which will relieve us of the present costs and liabilities in support of the population. Viewed from every point, except remote naval contingencies, it was unfortunate that we ever acquired the islands.

Virgin Islanders were stung to the quick by the president's remarks. Editor George E. Audain wrote for many in his editorial for the *St. Thomas Mail Notes* on April 7:

> Regardless of how much our feelings have been hurt by the unkind and undignified remarks of President Hoover, . . . we must not forget our dignity or our loyalty to the United States. America wanted these islands for more than half a century and when she obtained her desire she did not find them a "poorhouse," but actually proceeded to make them so by application of stupid laws unsuited to our well-being.
>
> An American alluding to the Virgin Islands today as a "poorhouse" can only appear to be devoid of decency, even though that individual may be the President of the United States. St. Thomians were not awed by this big dignitary who appeared before us. In our historic past we have been accustomed to receiving bigger men than President Hoover. We have chatted and dined with these men who constituted the cream of European royalty. These dignitaries not only did not respond to our hospitality with abuse but they landed at King's Wharf nicely dressed and not in a garb as though prepared for a buck dance in the slums as Mr. Hoover did.
>
> As the head of the greatest nation on God's earth, the President of the United States should have known better than to wound the sensibilities of a loyal people who warmly welcomed him to our shores. Instead of causing people to bitterly resent him, he should have made us revere his name.[4]

Not long after, I received another letter from my friend describing the terrible damage done to the islands' economy by the loss of the navy:

> One good feature of you and your bandsmen being in Guantanamo, Cuba, is that you are not here to see your hometown falling apart. The economic situation here is terrible. Daily it is going from bad to worse. With the abrupt withdrawal of the navy, the flow of money has virtually stopped. You just cannot pull out 238 navy personnel, many of them with families, and not expect economic trouble. Merchants complain that their daily sales have dropped more than sixty percent and they are being forced to lay off employees thereby making a bad situation worse. Everyone seems to be complaining right down to the washers, who earned a good living laundering for navy and marine personnel.
>
> You cannot blame this sudden economic downtrend on Governor Pearson. He is a victim caught in the middle of an economic mess. Everyone who has had contact with him says he is a kind, humane, and well-intentioned person. However, he does not seem to have any kind of business background. He spent several years in the Chautauqua Circuit. This is an adult education set-up, that presents summer programs

in religion, education, music, art, and drama. Pearson spent most of his time there as a lecturer. Recently, he joined the staff of Herbert Brown, as a researcher. Rumor has it that Brown wanted the V.I. governorship himself but it would have looked bad after his fight with the navy, so he handpicked Pearson, who he figured he could control.

Last week, under orders from Washington, Governor Pearson was forced to lay off a considerable number of government employees. Cut, cut, cut seems to be the order of the day. When a community suddenly finds itself in the throes of economic depression, dismissing longtime employees from their jobs creates an atmosphere verging on panic. Word has it that some of these employees are from the municipal hospital. As you know, Alton, if there is one good thing that the navy created for us, it was the hospital. One cannot but wonder if this institution, a source of pride in this community, is going back to that former state when people preferred to die or go abroad (if they could afford it) than to walk through its doors.[5]

Yet another of his letters described the well-intentioned, but controversial, cultural program that filled the gap left by the navy band's departure:

The town is broke but Music Week was celebrated with a vengeance. On Saturday night [May 30], Ralph Dunbar, Governor Pearson's community director, and his assistants put on a most successful and artistic production of "H.M.S. Pinafore." Instead of your being stuck in that drab place, Guantanamo, Cuba, you should have been here participating in this real musical treat. The evening was beautiful. The moon rose early, shining down on the harbor from over Bluebeard's Castle. The navy barge, moored at King's Wharf, decorated and converted into a British man-of-war, made a spectacular stage setting. Under the spell of the evening, nobody was thinking of the cost of the barge's conversion or where the money was coming from to pay for this expensive production.

Crowds of spectators came right down to the water's edge, fascinated by this unique presentation of Gilbert and Sullivan. At the end of every act, the crowd roared its approval. All the participants in the operetta, with the exception of Mrs. Dunbar, were natives. They gave ample proof of real musical and acting ability, brought to a maximum by the skillful and efficient management of Dunbar.

Even those who have been questioning the timeliness of the show in a bankrupt community admit that it was a great success. The voices, the orchestra, and not to forget Mr. Cyril Creque at the piano, were great. It is not right to mention a single performer when all were so excellent. Phil Gomez's tenor voice was at its best. As Captain Corcoran he looked the part and played it well. Luther Robles, uniformed and burdened with brass, strutted the stage like the gamecock, Admiral Sir Joseph Porter himself. Lionel Roberts, well cast as Dick Deadeye, leered and

scowled and pranced around trying to scare the wits out of Little But-
tercup who, undaunted, was skillfully portrayed by Alice Vance Car-
ruth. The antics of the Boatswain, played by Bingley Richardson,
brought much laughter from the audience.

A special compliment should be paid to Mr. Ralph Dunbar for his
part, which stamps him as an A-1 stage manager. All along I kept thinking how you, Alton, would have enjoyed working with Dunbar and
what a great team these islands would have had with Martin E. Trench
as governor and Paul M. Pearson as tourism director.[6]

Governor Pearson knew the social value of music, especially the music
festival. He realized that it was the means of gathering people from all
parts of the island and from all walks and conditions of life. Considered also
were its commercial advantages in bringing added business, particularly
during concerts. Taxi drivers, restaurant owners, and many others would
profit thereby. The audience would have its enjoyment, and the island
would profit from the splendid publicity the enterprise would give. The
public performance of Gilbert and Sullivan's popular operetta proved an
instantaneous success from the standpoint of community enrichment and
spiritualization. It was a sane and worthwhile effort to awaken, enliven,
and vitalize. But hard-boiled businessmen without vision, practical politicians interested in votes, and others attempted to weigh culture in a scale
and pronounced the enterprise as nonutilitarian, uneconomic, and unwise.
The show was a waste of public money, they contended. The large returns
in terms of cultural and human value was beyond their limited compre-
hension. Governor Pearson had a keener vision and a sounder idea of community rehabilitation than many realized. His soul was lofty, his mind
broad in spirit and conception.[7]

The first years of the 1930s continued to be unfortunate ones for me.
On May 11, 1932, I received the sad news of the death of one of my children, Merle.[8] Several months afterward, a dreadful hurricane visited the
island of Cuba, leaving in its wake the death of 3,500 persons mostly
through a tidal wave in Santa Cruz del Sur. This hurricane was headed
directly for Guantánamo Bay, but luckily changed course.[9] Taking warning, I packed all of my important personal possessions (scores and the
research on folklore that I had just finished) and sent them to St. Thomas—
the place I believed to be safe.

I had delved into the mysteries of African folk music at the encouragement of Mrs. Ellis Stone.[10] I understood the task, knowing well what it
entailed, that is, a scientific method of approach, not only to the music's origin but also to its intervallic and rhythmic content—the ingredients of its

creation. You must be able to answer the question "How do you know?" if the credibility of your research is questioned. The task is one that entails deep study of this music's ethnological and anthropological background. Helped by a great number of books written on the subject, particularly the excellent study *Afro-American Folksongs* by Henry Krehbiel,[11] and by personal contact with leading musicians and writers, I spent nine years working on twenty-five melodies which I believed at that time to be indigenous creations of the people of the Virgin Islands. Frankly, I was pleased with my work, which just needed a few touches here and there before it was ready for publication.

On the 27th of December of the same year, a cablegram brought the news of the total destruction by fire of my home—a large fifteen-room stone building—with everything in it lost, most tragically including the life of my twelve-year-old child, Hazel, a sufferer for many years from an attack of spinal meningitis. She was caught by the blaze in the upper story of the building before rescue was possible.[12] About three o'clock that afternoon, my brother and fellow bandsman, Julien, had approached me with a paper in his hand and a solemn look in his face. "Alton," he said, "prepare yourself for bad news," and he handed me the cablegram. The navy authorized a leave of absence for us both. Arrangements had been made for us to rejoin our families in St. Thomas at first available opportunity. We left on January 4, 1933, exactly one week later.

Thanks to a St. Thomian friend and amateur ham-radio operator, Richard Spencely, with whom we had daily contact, we received the agonizing details. The fire was caused by an exploding oil stove in the upper story of our residence, No. 9 Kommandant Gade, King's Quarter (at the foot of Bunker Hill). Mrs. Julien Adams, who lived in the upper part of the two-story dwelling, had directed a maid to light the stove and bake a pudding while she went into the kitchen to supervise the midday meals. Mrs. Julien Adams heard nothing amiss until, answering the maid's frantic call for help, she saw a wall of flames cutting off her entrance to the room where the stove was. Panic-stricken, she rushed to the lower floor and gave the alarm to her sister-in-law, Mrs. Alton Adams. The latter made frantic efforts to reach Hazel, her twelve-year-old daughter, who was confined to a bed in a room upstairs. The raging fire drove Mrs. Alton Adams back. In her desperate effort she was aided by a team of volunteers, but to no avail. All members of the house except little Hazel were brought out safely. By the time the firefighters got under way, the Adamses' residence and all of its contents were burnt out. By careful handling of the only hose, which was coupled to a nearby hydrant, the adjacent tiled-roof buildings—those of the Anduze family, Mrs. Thraen, and I. Levin—were saved. Other hose and water sources were finally employed in the later stages of the fire, and the blaze was finally gotten under control. Dying cinders and charred walls were all that marked the place where the substantial two-story building once stood.[13]

Julien and I arrived in St. Thomas the night of January 9 on our hurried trip from Cuba via Puerto Rico. The reunion with our families was a tearful, emotional one. Everyone was still in a state of shock. Members of the family, in the house when the fire occurred, wanted us to know full details of their individual experiences with the tragedy and poured their hearts out to us. Edith, the house servant with whom the calamity originated, took me aside and tearfully confessed to an overwhelming sense of guilt. When ordered to light the stove, she found that there was little or no fuel in it. Securing a bottle of kerosene, she attempted to pour the contents into the stove. In the semidarkness of the corner where the stove was, she missed the tank's opening and some of the kerosene spilled on the floor. Getting a rag, she quickly wiped up the fuel on the floor. Evidently, unknown to her, some of the fuel had spilled on the stove. When she applied a match, the stove caught fire and exploded.

Next day, Julien and I visited the burnt-out house. Nothing was left there but four badly burnt walls open to the sky, blackened wood, twisted sheets of galvanize, and mounds of ash. My precious library was gone: eight hundred to a thousand volumes of choice literary and other books, representing years of sacrificial savings, careful selection, and acquisition. Many of the books were autographed first editions sent by friends in the musical and literary worlds, books that could not easily be replaced. Hundreds of autographed photos and paintings were lost, along with bound volumes of my work for *Jacobs' Band Monthly.* Gone too were hundreds of my own musical manuscripts, unpublished compositions and arrangements, products of years of creative effort. Marches, waltzes, spirituals, calypsos—compositions that had been worked and reworked to get them ready. Then there had been a prized collection of what I believed then to be the indigenous folksongs of the Virgin Islands. I considered this to be one of my finest efforts. Inspired melodies had matched the stories, and I felt that when this was marketed, it would meet with widespread regional approval. This collection was ready for the printer. Publication had been delayed because of the band's sudden shift from St. Thomas to Guantánamo. However, these were material possessions and life could go on without them. Loss of these possessions did not tear the heart and wound the mind like the loss of a beloved child.[14]

Immediately after the disastrous fire and in my absence, friends had helped my family to find temporary residence in an old house on a corner of upper Main Street, directly across from the Moravian parsonage. When I saw the place, I found it to be totally inadequate. I radioed the U.S. Navy and asked for an extension of my leave to permit me to settle my family properly. My request was granted. After a considerable search, I found a house that seemed to answer our needs. It was a solidly built nineteenth-century place, facing west, on the leeward side of Bluebeard's Hill. Over the years, its sheltered location had protected it from hurricanes. Typical of good nineteenth-century construction, the first floor was solid, massive stone masonry. Inviting brick stairways led to the upper floor, which was built of strong timber. Rooms were spacious and cool. Large windows and doors permitted a steady flow of air. A full-length wrought-iron balcony offered an impressive view of town and harbor, east to west. There was a cistern of good size and adequate plumbing, essential for a growing family. Also a large yard with coconut, mango, and genip trees, offering safe play areas for children. I liked what I saw of No. 1B Kongens Gade, King's Quarter, and decided to try to acquire it.

The property was owned by an acquaintance of ours, a lady from a good local family, Maria Charlotte Brewer. From the records, I discovered that she had bought the property at public auction, September 8, 1899, for the sum of $1,475.08. Those were the days of very tight money and depressed values. I offered Mrs. Brewer what was considered at that time a good price: $4,060. Also I agreed to pay the 1932 taxes against the property as well as all other incidental costs connected with the transfer. Mrs. Brewer accepted my offer, agreed to the sale, and on February 15, 1932, the deed of property was turned over to me. I found out from the records, also, that in 1827, its first private owner, Peter von Scholten, had sold the property to Mr. David Padro. Prior to his becoming governor, Peter von Scholten had been a skilled, successful architect with many fine residences in Charlotte Amalie to his credit. He was noted for the layout of his courtyards, his fine brick stairways, and his high-ceilinged, spacious rooms. Evidently, No. 1B Kongens Gade was one of his creations.[15]

I had to start life anew, which I did. But try as I may, I could not erase from my mind a vision of the cruel death of my daughter Hazel. Before she was afflicted, Hazel was a good-looking, intelligent, sprightly, capricious chunk of a kid. I often would recall the occasion which brought about one of my compositions—"Childhood Merriment: Valse Caprice." One day while she was alone at play, I heard her humming to herself the strains of a melody—a phrase so to speak—accompanied with a lithe swinging, capricious, graceful movement of her body which so fascinated me that, there and then, I jotted down both melody and rhythm. I used these contrapuntally as the structural motif for the composition. The piece is dedicated to all my children, but written specifically for her.[16]

With my family comfortably settled, I returned to Guantánamo with the intent to retire from active duty in the U.S. Navy and rejoin my family in St. Thomas as soon as possible. I went through the necessary formalities without difficulty, retired after sixteen years of service in due order, and became a full-fledged member of the U.S. Navy Fleet Reserve on July 23, 1933. Three of my bandsmen, James Brown, Arnold Martin, and Bernardo Heyligar, followed my example. My brother, Julien, also expressed his intention to follow us into retirement. This was the beginning of the breakup of an organization which over the years had received widespread recognition and critical acclaim. Guantánamo regretted our leaving and before our departure honored us with a touching farewell ceremony. We were scheduled to leave for St. Thomas on a naval transport, the USS *Woodcock,* but because of a delay in arrival of that ship, I secured permission to take passage on a French cargo and passenger vessel, the SS *Carimare,* leaving Guantánamo with St. Thomas as one of its ports of call. I arrived in St. Thomas, Monday, July 31, 1933.

Shortly after my return, I received a call from Government House requesting my presence. Governor Pearson had heard of my retirement and wished to discuss certain matters with me. A date was made. The governor was waiting for me in his office. He rose to his feet and greeted me warmly. He was a man of medium height, evidently in his late sixties; his white hair topped a pleasant face:

> Bandmaster Adams, first let me express to you my sincerest sympathy and that of my family over your recent tragic loss. You would have heard more from me but, as you might have heard, I was undergoing major surgery on the mainland. Anyway, I am back at my desk now, trying to catch up with things. Bandmaster, I have asked you to come here for several reasons. I am about to form a St. Thomas Music Committee to stimulate and develop music as an integral part of island culture. I am asking you to accept an appointment to this committee and to serve as its chairman. A similar committee was formed in St. Croix several months ago, and it is already proving effective. That is not all. Once we get going, I have hopes that you will head the new music department in our high school and accept the job to supervise all musical activities in the public schools.[17]

In my dealings with Governor Pearson, I found him to be a kind, soft-spoken, and cultured man. His years of association with the Chautauqua Circuit on the mainland, a popular movement to bring culture to the masses of people, had given him a considerable background with music and musicians. We found common ground for many an interesting discussion. Because of my close work with the governor, I was privileged to meet and know several members of his talented family. Leon Pearson and his wife, on a visit to see his parents, gave an impromptu performance at Government House to which a small group of friends were invited. I was pleased to be one of them. Mrs. Leon Pearson possessed a well-trained, magnificent soprano voice. She accompanied herself on the piano. Her selection of songs covered a wide range and was professionally executed. Alternately, Leon Pearson, a frail and sensitive person, gave poetry readings. Both performers delighted the small audience, and the couple agreed to perform in public with proceeds going to a local charity. I was asked to make the necessary arrangements. Word had gotten around, and the performance at Parish Hall was a sellout and many persons were turned away. This led to another appearance at the Apollo Theatre to a packed house.

Next to appear was Barbara, Leon's sister, fresh from a success as leading lady in an off-Broadway show. A handsome and friendly young lady, she was also hell-bent on making it as an actress. Another of the governor's sons, Drew Pearson, was different. As frail and sensitive as Leon, Drew gave one the impression of toughness. When the governor called me into his office to introduce me, Drew said, "Bandmaster Adams is no stranger to me. When his band toured the mainland, I attended several of his concerts. In fact, one of my earliest stories as a cub reporter dealt with his band." We became good friends. Drew had traveled around the world as a young reporter before joining the *Baltimore Sun* in 1926. In 1932 he started his syndicated column "Washington Merry-Go-Round," which featured sensational exposés of government figures. "I have them squirming on their seats," he said to me, "and they hate me!"[18]

Word was widespread on the islands that Paul Pearson would not be reappointed to the governorship. The news saddened me. Despite the fact that I had always been a strong navy man hoping for the navy's return, my close working relationship with the governor caused me to develop a high regard and respect for him. His persistence in looking after the interests of the islands and his calm tolerance in the face of unjust criticism impressed me. One day he said to me, "Bandmaster Adams, I do not seem to be able to gain the confidence of the people. What am I doing wrong?" "It is not you," I replied; "it is simply a matter of economics. The people miss the security, the jobs, the many benefits they got from the navy. They feel that the navy is better suited to their needs. That is why they are clamoring for its return. That should not be interpreted as a rejection of you personally. They frankly do not feel that you or the Interior Department have the means for their economic survival or stability."

It was shocking to me to learn that Herbert D. Brown could be spoken of as our next governor. I understood that Brown was approached in Washington by a small but influential delegation from St. Croix offering him its unqualified support. Brown is alleged to have said that he would be willing to come to the islands and take the job if the people wanted him—but only at their request. Evidently this report was more than rumor because shortly afterward I received a letter from Drew Pearson. He trusted me, he said, to give him honest answers. Was there real substantial support in St. Croix for Brown? Or was it merely support from a small group of landowners? Could I give him my frank appraisal?

I was blunt in my reply. I told Drew that I was not a political person, but that if I saw any support growing for Herbert D. Brown in the islands, I would do everything in my limited power to counteract it. Yes, Brown's support in St. Croix was limited to a small group of landowners. I offered Drew my fullest support and whatever influence I had in the islands to help block Brown's appointment. Drew hardly needed my support. He had gained national prominence and power with his syndicated column, and he knew how to use that power. On January 16, 1933, the islands' press received a cable from Senator William King, ranking Democrat of Utah, which stated: "I understand that Herbert D. Brown is seeking appointment as governor of the Virgin Islands. In my opinion, he is not the proper person for the position. If appointed, I can assure you that there will be vigorous Senate opposition to his confirmation."[19]

In 1933 the latest word from Washington was that the new secretary of the navy, Claude A. Swanson, was reacting favorably to the idea of the navy once again taking over the administration of the Virgin Islands. Washington friends told us that now was the time for navy supporters in the islands to express themselves strongly. On February 10, 1933, a resolution attached to a petition was introduced in the Virgin Islands Colonial Council asking the president and the U.S. Congress for the return of naval administration. This resolution was sponsored by Councilman Valdemar Miller, a prominent merchant and a strong pro-navy advocate. Councilman Miller stated:

I have the honor to present this petition signed by over 2,000 citizens, residents, and taxpayers of this community, soliciting the Colonial Council of St. Thomas and St. John to forward said petition to the President and Congress of the United States, praying and beseeching that this Municipality be returned to the Navy Department to be administered by that department. I want to make it clear that this petition and resolution is in no manner or form to be construed as unkind criticism or lack of appreciation on the part of the signers of the petition or resolution towards the Department of Interior or to the unceasing and untiring efforts of Governor Paul M. Pearson in our behalf. However, we are convinced that the way to improve our terrible economic condition lies in our being returned to the navy. We seek a return to that department that took good care of us from the time of the transfer, March 31, 1917, to about two years ago, when overnight through the unsought connivance of one individual, Herbert D. Brown, we were transferred without rhyme or reason or without being consulted.

During the naval administration of these islands, there were on the payroll of the navy, hundreds of local employees consisting of clerical workers, artisans, laborers, skilled and unskilled, receiving substantial amounts of money on a regular basis. To this add the officers and enlisted men stationed here whose wages were spent here. Income taxes collected from them went into our local treasury. Every available house was tenanted by naval families bringing substantial rentals to the owners. Domestics, maids, cooks, gardeners were hired. All of this money circulated in the community. What other department of government could provide overnight excellent hospital care, top-notch doctors and nurses who gave freely of their skills to the people of this community? Naval engineers helped us with our roads, our public works, our sanitation.[20]

The Valdemar Miller resolution passed the council by an overwhelming majority. The lone dissenting vote was cast by Councilman Lionel Roberts. In voting no, Councilman Roberts declared: "I am against a naval administration coming here to govern civilians. If on the other hand, the petition and resolution were courteously seeking the establishment of a naval station to bolster our economy, that request would receive my heartiest support and approval." Meanwhile, Drew Pearson left no stone unturned in Washington in trying to promote his father's continuation in office. Drew was a ruthless fighter.

On September 19, 1933, Secretary of the Interior Harold Ickes let it be known that Governor Pearson would continue in office as governor of the Virgin Islands. Critics of the Pearson administration and pro-navy activists charged that a deal had been made between Drew and the secretary. In exchange for keeping his father in office, Harold Ickes would receive nothing but favorable mention in "Washington Merry-Go-Round."[21]

On March 2, 1934, I was called to Government House; Governor Pearson was waiting. "Bandmaster Adams," he said, "Mrs. Eleanor Roosevelt, wife of the president, is due here on Wednesday afternoon, March 7, by special Pan American seaplane. I need your help with the reception arrangements. Also, I would like you to be one of the official greeters. Schools will be closed for the occasion and school children will be out en masse to greet Mrs. Roosevelt. Do you think that in the short time you could compose a song of welcome?" I told the governor that I would try.

The Pan American plane carrying the First Lady and her party motored up to the seaplane ramp at exactly 3:10 on Wednesday afternoon, March 7. Waiting at the float was a welcoming group which escorted Mrs. Roosevelt and her party to the King's Wharf. On landing there to the cheers of a big crowd, Mrs. Roosevelt and party were greeted by the governor and Mrs. Pearson. The visitors were ushered to the porch of the district court building. Rain showers had drenched the schoolchildren. Undaunted, they stood there on the wet concrete and sang the song of welcome I had composed for Mrs. Roosevelt.

> With voices strong, this welcome song, to thee this day we sing,
> And may its notes from loyal throats, o'er hills and valleys ring.
> Welcome, welcome, benefactor of the poor,
> Welcome, welcome to our islands' humble shore,
> Welcome, welcome to our land where nature smiles,
> Welcome, welcome to our sunlit Virgin Isle.[22]

I was delighted with the way they sang it, with feeling and expression, remarkable considering the lack of rehearsal. With thousands of people around King's Wharf waving and shouting, the Community Band played my composition "The Governor's Own." Immediately after, the ceremony began. One of the speakers apologized to Mrs. Roosevelt for the rain showers. In gracious reply she said, "The rain does not mean as much to me as it does to you. I am accustomed not only to rain but to a great deal of snow and ice. I want you to know that rain or shine, I am happy to be here on your beautiful island and I bring you the warm greetings of the president." Mrs. Roosevelt waved to the crowd, which responded with great enthusiasm.

The official party then moved from the district court building to the Municipal Hospital, where chief physician Dr. Knud-Hansen was waiting. Earlier he had called me: "Bandmaster Adams, I understand that you have a lot to do with the reception arrangements. Please use your influence to have Mrs. Roosevelt come here early. We want to name the children's ward after her." The ceremony started right after we got there. Dr. Knud-Hansen said, "Will you, Mrs. Roosevelt, allow us to name this children's ward after you? We would like to do so in memory of your visit and as a token of our gratitude for what you are doing for the welfare of children throughout the United States." "I would be delighted," answered Mrs. Roosevelt.[23]

The largest gathering ever assembled at Government House since the American arrival was present at the reception for Mrs. Roosevelt. After the usual preliminaries, the first lady was formally introduced by Governor Pearson to the packed audience:

> It gives me great pleasure to introduce Mrs. Anna Eleanor Roosevelt, wife of our illustrious President, Franklin Delano Roosevelt, and mother of his five children. Mrs. Roosevelt is no stranger to the realms of power in Washington. She is a niece of a former great President, Teddy Roosevelt. She walked in the halls of Congress as a child, and it is safe to say that she grew up in the shadow of the White House. Mrs. Roosevelt, as we all know, is dedicated to the cause of human welfare. Wherever there is a battle to advance the well being of our citizens, you will find Mrs. Roosevelt at the forefront. She travels all over the country lecturing and observing first hand conditions of the people, especially the plight of the underprivileged. Mrs. Roosevelt has relentlessly worked for the civil rights of minorities in the face of barriers erected by prejudiced and unyielding people. In more than one instance, she has required police protection from surly and threatening crowds. She has never been afraid to face up to them and to state her case. Mrs. Roosevelt has worked hard to combat poverty and its side effects; wretched housing, undernourishment, unemployment, and crime. Mrs. Roosevelt writes a syndicated column, "My Day," and through this medium tells a more affluent citizenry what is going on in the depressed and seamy sections of our country and what should be done about it. In concluding, I wish to express to Mrs. Roosevelt the great honor and pleasure that she has given us by her visit. I know that I speak for everyone here when I ask her to convey to the President, our warmest good wishes and our appreciation for his warm good wishes to us.

Mrs. Roosevelt, tall and stately, in a voice that rang through the room, expressed appreciation for the wonderful welcome. Later, she moved among the large crowd, conversing with people. Her poise and easy grace distinguished her. She left the islands the next day.[24]

So pleased was Governor Pearson with the smooth and efficient handling of the Eleanor Roosevelt visit that he asked his reception team for a repeat performance. Word had been received that the president himself, aboard the

USS *Houston*, planned a short visit to the islands on July 7, 1934. Amid the booming of guns and the shouting of hurrahs from the large crowd ashore, Franklin Delano Roosevelt, president of the United States of America, came down the gangway of the cruiser *Houston* and landed at the West Indian Company dock at 4:20 P.M. on Saturday, July 7, 1934. Using a walking stick and assisted by White House physician Commander Ross T. McIntire and the president's son Franklin, Jr., Mr. Roosevelt managed the descent without difficulty. He was met at the foot of the gangway by Governor Pearson; Dr. Viggo Christensen, chairman of the Colonial Council; and a select group of island dignitaries. After an exchange of greeting, the party proceeded past a large group of children waving flags and singing the song of welcome which I had composed for the earlier visit of the president's wife. The party entered several large open touring cars and drove through an arch of welcome at the entrance of the road leading from the West Indian Company.

The motorcade proceeded directly to Government House. The president was asked to sign his name in the guest book. Seating himself, he took out his glasses, put them on, lighted a cigarette, and then wrote his name. While refreshments were being served, acting commissioner of finance Morris de Castro presented the president with a collection of Danish West Indian banknotes and coins. Mr. de Castro said that he had heard that the president was an avid collector. The president said that he was happy to get these rare items to add to his collection. Taking the gift, which was encased in a specially prepared leather case, the president turned the package over to his son Franklin, Jr., for safekeeping. "You may not know it, Mr. de Castro," the president said, "but fifty years ago, shortly after I graduated from Harvard, I visited St. Thomas and I remember using the Danish West Indian currency." On his way to Government House, President Roosevelt had expressed the desire to visit Bluebeard Castle, where, he had been told, the federal government was building a tourist hotel as part of a comprehensive plan to help the islands' economy. At the request of Governor Pearson, I had Donald Boreham and some of the Public Works staff standing by at Bluebeard. From Government House we proceeded directly to the construction site.[25]

Why was Paul M. Pearson, our first civilian governor, so abruptly removed from his post in July 1935? By the time Pearson got his economic and social program going, battle lines were closely drawn between pro-navy groups on one side and Pearson backers on the other. This situation might have stayed so for awhile, or it might have quieted. Actually it was showing signs of quieting. Slowly it was dawning on some of the most ardent of pro-navy advocates that there was little or no chance for a return to naval administration. On the other hand, Interior Secretary Ickes let no opportunity pass but to give his solid endorsement and backing to Pearson. Ickes took the position that dissension in the islands was mere political claptrap of the "outs" against the "ins."

Suddenly out of a clear blue sky came a Washington announcement that, with powerful congressional backing, a Texas democrat and former editor of the *Houston Post*, Paul C. Yates, had been named administrative assistant to the governor of the Virgin Islands. There was little or no need for the position. It was strictly political. Paul C. Yates arrived in the Virgin Islands on June 8, 1934, on the SS *Catherine* and started work. Brought into close contact by the very nature of the job, the personalities of the two men clashed from the beginning. Here was Pearson, the academic, the man of culture and refinement, soft-spoken, disciplined. In contrast, Yates was a chain-smoking, egotistical swashbuckler with an offensive southern drawl and abrasive manner, wanting from the beginning to be part of decision making. Pearson could not work with Yates. He recoiled from him. He avoided him. Yet he underestimated the man's potential for making trouble. He also underestimated Yates's strong and varied Washington connections.[26]

In September 1933 two other Washington appointees arrived in the islands who, like Yates, were to play an important part in the drama surrounding the ousting of Governor Pearson. One of these appointees, T. Webber Wilson, a former Democratic congressman and prominent lawyer from Laurel, Mississippi, came to fill the position of federal judge. The vacancy had been created by the retirement of Judge Edrington (a Republican) from the islands' district court. The other appointee, attorney Eli Baer, of Baltimore (also a Democrat) came to fill the vacancy created by the removal of government attorney Charles H. Gibson (a Republican). Both of these men, Wilson and Baer, met in New York City and with Wilson's wife, Lucy, boarded the SS *Silvia* and landed in St. Thomas on September 22. Baer was unmarried.

Wilson had strong political backing. The Honorable Homer Cummings, U.S. attorney general and an old friend, had appointed him. Solidly supporting him too was the senior senator from Mississippi, Pat Harrison, who had recommended Wilson for the job. Wilson, a handsome and distinguished man, six feet tall and soft-spoken, made an impressive figure. During his years as district attorney in Mississippi and later as a congressman from the state, Wilson had worked among black people who had learned to love him and respect him. Wilson had shown kind and sympathetic understanding of the problems of the unfortunate and the underprivileged, black and white alike. With his record of sympathy toward the Negro and his problems, Wilson appeared to be an ideal choice for the V.I. judgeship.

Wilson had earned a reputation for courage, fairness, and integrity. It did not take long for these qualities to manifest themselves in the V.I. District Court. In my scrapbook, I saved an article from the *New York Times* with a St. Thomas dateline, January 29, 1934:

> Federal Judge T. Webber Wilson, former congressman from Mississippi, created a sensation at St. Croix during a manslaughter case when he ordered the arrest of Dr. James Knott (white), chief municipal physician and Interior Department appointee, who had ignored a subpoena. Dr. Knott, brought into court for questioning, defied the Judge and was fined. Judge Wilson declared that the country's laws applied to all, white and black alike, and from Governor Pearson down, whereupon the spectators cheered. When the government later questioned the court's action, Judge Wilson said: "I am answerable only to Homer Cummings (U.S. attorney general) and God almighty, and I refuse to be intimidated by any government head."[27]

Paul C. Yates proved an angry and vengeful man. He did not relish being shunted aside and ignored by Pearson and his staff. Yates vowed to undermine them. A veteran of the rough-and-tumble world of Texas politics, Yates was skilled in the art of political sabotage. After careful appraisal of the opposition to Pearson that had quieted down, Yates began to stir the pot. Carefully planted rumors spread of irregularities in the administration, of federal funds involving public works projects in the islands, of fraud and corruption on a large scale. Gossip fanned the rumors. Shrewdly and secretly, Yates enlisted the aid of a Crucian labor agitator, Morris Davis, who professed to be a leader of the masses but was more accurately a professional agitator looking for a cause. Yates gave him one.

Street demonstrations, led by Davis, broke out in St. Croix. Davis pounded on one theme—that after years of misgovernment and mismanagement under Pearson, fraud and corruption on a large scale were coming to the surface; that federal money being sent to the islands to help the people was being stolen. Next Yates went to work on the newly appointed government attorney, Eli Baer, a protégé of Millard Tydings, the powerful Democratic senator from Maryland. An affable young man and an able young lawyer with little or no political experience, Baer was convinced by Yates that the time was right for the "Roosevelt Democrats" to take over the administration of the islands from "that gang of Hoover appointees, Pearson and Co." Yates suggested to Baer that it would be a feather in his cap for a young and ambitious Democrat to uncover corruption in an administration run by decrepit leftover Hoover Republicans. Baer swallowed the bait!

On July 13, 1934, Governor Pearson issued a statement:

On about July 3, 1934, the government attorney, Eli Baer, advised me
that he was proceeding to take depositions in connection with reported
irregularities in the Public Works Department. I advised the government attorney that my administration would cooperate with him in
every way. . . . I requested the Secretary of Interior to send to St.
Thomas immediately an investigator from the Department of Interior
to assist in the investigation. The secretary replied that he was sending
two expert investigators down. He requested that Government Attorney Baer forward to his office in Washington complete information
regarding the entire matter; and that Government Attorney Baer sus-
pend all investigation until further notice.[28]

On August 2, 1934, Secretary Ickes announced that he had dispatched
two investigators, Lee Barton and Leslie Huntt of Interior's Special Investigating Unit, to the Virgin Islands to look into alleged irregularities. Barton and Huntt arrived in the islands and went right to work. Suspense
during the period that followed released a flood of rumor, much of it based
on malice, hearsay, and ignorance. Demonstrations broke out in St. Croix
and St. Thomas, led by Davis with behind-the-scenes prodding by Yates.
This continuous agitation had one theme—undermining and discrediting
the Pearson administration.

Their work finished, Barton and Huntt returned to Washington, taking
their findings with them. Suspense heightened when government attorney
Eli Baer was called to Washington to meet with the two investigators and
Ickes. On September 22, 1934, Ickes released the following statement:

Today I have removed from service Eli Baer of Baltimore, government
attorney for the Virgin Islands. I took this dismissal action after giving
a hearing to Mr. Baer and receiving an unsatisfactory answer to formal
charges made against him. Complaints against Government Attorney
Baer involved his one-man inquisition into public works projects in the
Virgin Islands during which time he took possession of all records and
files and effectively held up a public-works program involving $774,000
including work relief on roads, schools, and hospitals. It developed that
out of about 100 allegations made by government attorney Baer in his
capacity as a one-man grand jury, only one showed a criminal violation.
Mr. Baer's behavior reflected on the good name of the officers of government. Most of Mr. Baer's investigations were founded on frenzied
rumor and gossip. Mr. Baer failed to consult with the governor or the
secretary of interior before initiating the probe.

The investigation by Messrs. Barton and Huntt showed no reason
why all of the records of the Public Works administration in the islands

should have been subpoenaed. Mr. Baer admitted that he was not competent to examine them and no one else in the islands was so qualified. Baer admitted that he was guilty of official misconduct in discussing pending cases with the district judge prior to trial.[29]

There was widespread rumor in the islands that during the questioning of Baer, and under severe pressure, Baer named Yates as the man who urged him to open the investigation. There must have been truth to the rumor, for shortly after the questioning of Baer, Ickes turned his official wrath on Yates. A news clipping from the Associated Press dated October 6, 1934, which I saved in my scrapbook tells the story: "Interior Secretary Harold L. Ickes announced today that he had suspended Paul C. Yates, administrative assistant to Virgin Islands Governor Paul M. Pearson, and has ordered Yates to come to Washington to answer charges of gross disloyalty, insubordination, and inefficiency." Ickes added: "I could no longer ignore grave charges against Mr. Yates that came to me from reliable sources in the islands. When Yates first entered into the Virgin Islands picture as a political appointee, Governor Pearson had asked that he be designated his administrative assistant. In return, Yates has been spending a good deal of his time running around the islands stirring up trouble for the governor."

In a cable to the Associated Press from St. Thomas, Yates declared: "Earlier in the day, I had advised Secretary Ickes that his radiogram seeking to summon me before his drumheaded court-martial arrived too late. My letter, with resignation enclosed, was on its way." Yates said he had notified Ickes on August 15, 1934, that unless prompt action were taken to remedy "the intolerable misgovernment prevailing under Governor Pearson, a leftover Hoover-appointed reactionary Republican, that I would under no circumstances continue as an official under the Interior Department." Yates continued:

> I pointed out to Ickes that Governor Pearson and his crowd of Pennsylvania reactionaries were playing fast and loose with the millions in public works funds that Ickes had allocated to the Virgin Islands; that Messrs. Pearson and cronies have been using these funds to perpetuate themselves in office. Investigators sent down from Interior, ostensibly to assist the then–government attorney Eli Baer in uncovering fraud and corruption in the Pearson administration, enjoyed magnificent hospitality as the governor's guests and returned to Washington with a report that Secretary Ickes apparently interpreted as a complete whitewash. On the basis of this report, Ickes discharged Baer with prejudice. I have a feeling that the U.S. Congress will want to investigate thoroughly this entire disgraceful situation.[30]

Despite these distractions, Governor Pearson persevered.

On November 1, 1934, bids were opened to lease the government-financed Bluebeard Castle Hotel to private operators. The highest bidders and winners of the lease were Mr. and Mrs. Peffer from the U.S. mainland, a managerial team with years of experience in hotel operation. Shortly after the lease agreement was signed, Mr. and Mrs. Peffer arrived in St. Thomas and reported to Government House. Governor Pearson had requested an early appearance so that the new management could work closely with his team in developing a special décor for the hotel. Governor Pearson felt that, wherever possible, Virgin Islands handicraft, products from the fledgling local industries started during his administration, should be used. He indicated a desire for specially designed rugs from the hook rug division of the Virgin Islands Cooperatives, linen towels with local designs, straw work, furniture, pictures, ash trays, pottery—in fact, any suitable product of local manufacture that could fit into the furnishing of the hotel. The governor asked me to head a committee to work closely with the Peffers in this area. The Peffers were cordial and friendly people. They were eager to cooperate. Mrs. Peffer had excellent taste and a flair for design. She promised that within one week she would come up with a series of sketches for me to take to the governor. The governor was pleased with what he saw. "Bandmaster Adams, this is exactly what I want." For the hook rugs and wall hangings he selected colorful designs of pirate ships with Bluebeard Castle in the background. For other products, from linen towels to ashtrays, he choose designs highlighting the castle and its surroundings. The governor gave the order for production to start as soon as possible.

Governor Pearson had set the opening date of the hotel at December 25, 1934, and on that Christmas day, doors were opened to the public. Eighty persons, skilled and unskilled, working under the direction of project architect H. Tallman, had done a fine job. Landscaping around the hotel was beautifully done, a tribute to Mr. Nichols of the Agricultural Extension Service and Mr. Alphonse Nelthropp, a local expert on tropical plants and flowers. On that Christmas morning, the Dutch cruise liner *Statendam* was in port with more than six hundred tourists. Bluebeard Castle was the key exhibit on sightseeing tours. Scores of automobiles loaded with tourists and their cameras headed for the hotel. Once there, everyone was enthusiastic over the place and its fabulous views and layouts.[31]

More than a thousand persons, tourists as well as Virgin Islands residents, visited the new Bluebeard Castle Hotel on opening day. One and all were highly pleased with what they saw. In the evening a capacity crowd overflowed the beautifully decorated dining room, where a sumptuous banquet was served. The menu as well as the service drew favorable comment from the brilliant assembly of officials and citizens. The opening speech of the evening was given by Governor Pearson. He summarized the various stages and obstacles overcome in the creation of the hotel. He paid grateful tribute to the president of the United States, Franklin Delano Roosevelt, Secretary of the Interior Harold L. Ickes, and the U.S. Congress, without whose support the Bluebeard Castle Hotel dream could never have materialized. Governor Pearson then introduced Mr. and Mrs. Peffer and their two daughters. The governor commented on his favorable reaction and the favorable reaction of everyone who had met and worked with the Peffers. Not only were they efficient hotel operators, but they were also charming and talented individuals who were a real asset to their new community.

In response, the Peffers thanked one and all for their many acts of kindness and cooperation. They pledged a total effort to make the hotel a real success and the kind of landmark for which the islands could be proud. Miss Joanna Colcord of Washington, D.C., a member of President Roosevelt's Advisory Council for the Virgin Islands and a close friend of President and Mrs. Roosevelt, was the next speaker. She expressed her happiness at being present. The president had called her at home and asked her to be his personal representative at the opening. He wanted her to convey to the people of the Virgin Islands his best wishes and his congratulations for the opening of the hotel. Governor Pearson then introduced Mr. Tallman, architect for the Bluebeard project, and asked him to say a few words. Mr. Tallman said that he considered himself fortunate to have been chosen to do the job. The first stage of the hotel called for twenty-six self-contained units which were scheduled to be completed on February 15, 1935.[32]

Bluebeard's Tower was then and remains today a landmark of beauty and legend. In 1666 Erik Smidt, a Danish sea captain, took possession of the island of St. Thomas in the name of the kingdom of Denmark. From the beginning he was struck by an ideal location on the eastern hill overlooking the harbor [see figure 4]. He considered creating a fort there. Smidt's plans were cut short by his death but eventually were carried out by a successor, Governor Christopher Heins (1688–90). The tower on Smidt's Hill was completed in 1689 and used as a lookout post with a small garrison quartered nearby. For more than a century and a half this tower, known as Frederik's Fort, stood guard over the harbor and the approaches to it. By 1852 the tower, practically abandoned and in a bad state of repair, was sold to an Italian from French Corsica, Victor Piccioni, who restored it and built a dwelling house nearby. From Mr. Piccioni the ownership passed to his nephew, Mr. Sosthènes Luchetti, French Consul, officer of St. Thomas Bank, and Colonial Council member, who resided in the main building.

The tower, the dwelling house, and grounds rose to prominence when they were acquired in the 1880s by Eduardo H. Moron. Besides occupying a very important position as head of the ship supply firm of Brønsted & Company, Mr. Moron also represented the Italian and Brazilian governments in St. Thomas. In his commercial and consular capacities, Moron entertained many notable personages at his family residence. Among those may be mentioned the Grand Duke Alexis of Russia, who arrived here in St. Thomas on the cruiser *Dimitri Donskay*, under command of Vice Admiral Rasnakof, and Luigi de Savoia, duke of Abruzzi, during his tour on the Italian cruiser *Liguria*. After the death of Mr. Moron in 1909 and the departure of his family from St. Thomas came a lull of several years when the property was acquired by the Reverend A. Nies, who renovated the dwelling house as a residence for his invalid brother, who lived there until his death. In the economic rehabilitation plan for St. Thomas, a modern hotel was urged and Bluebeard Castle selected as the site.[33]

The magnificent dinner given at the opening of Bluebeard Castle Hotel was followed by a stage play representing an episode in the romantic life of the pirate Bluebeard and one of his wives. The play, *Bluebeard's Casket*, was taken from a book of local stories by Dr. Charles Edwin Taylor entitled *An Island of the Sea*.[34] The production was arranged by Alfred Baruch, a playwright on Governor Pearson's staff, and was delightfully carried out by local talent. The direction was under Thursdaon Childs, a teacher at the high school; the costumes were designed by Doris Robinson, the scenery was done by Norris B. Nichols, and the music was written by myself.[35] The action swirled around romance, jealousy, intrigue, witchcraft, and murder. The play concluded with a scene depicting the rescue of Bluebeard's wife from the stake by the daring Bluebeard himself. This was considered by a local critic as symbolic of the rescue of the island from the stake of economic depression by the daring project—Bluebeard Castle Hotel.

As for the story itself: A beautiful young woman, Mercedita, a Creole, lived in St. Thomas. Bluebeard fell madly in love with her at first sight. He pursued her, married her, and installed her in a house adjacent to Bluebeard's tower. After a short honeymoon, he left her to go on a seafaring expedition, promising to return soon. Before leaving, Bluebeard placed in Mercedita's safekeeping a locked casket along with the key and the injunction not to open it unless he was present. For two months Mercedita kept her promise. Finally curiosity got the better of her. Inserting the key into the casket, she gave it a turn. The casket flew open, revealing nothing but a bundle of letters tied with a ribbon. Mercedita read the seven letters addressed to her husband one by one. The passionate love letters were from seven different ladies whom Mercedita had always looked upon as friends. Furious with jealousy, she determined to revenge herself on the whole lot of them. She sought out the services of Madame LaFourche, a notorious Obeah woman from Martinique. From the witch, she obtained a concoction which, the Obeah woman assured her, when given to the seven lady friends, would cure them once and for all of their passion for Bluebeard. Mercedita invited her seven lady friends to take tea with her the following afternoon. The ladies came and had several cups of tea in which Mercedita had put some of the potion. On returning to their homes, each of the seven ladies went to bed and died. There was a public outcry. All fingers pointed to Mercedita.

When the news reached Mercedita that her seven guests had all died, she was stupefied with grief. In desperation, Mercedita hurried to the police master and unburdened herself of the details. She was arrested and put into prison. A police search was made for Madame LaFourche, but nowhere could the Obeah woman be found. Either she had gone into hiding or she had left the island in a hurry. Mercedita was brought to trial before the town court on the charge of killing seven of her townswomen by sundry arts and practices of Obeah. She was found guilty, and the sentence passed by the judge was as follows: that she be conducted to the sands of the sea near a place known as King's Wharf and there, with a pile of sticks around her, be burned to death as an example to those who dared dabble in witchcraft.

On the morning slated for the execution, Mercedita, as she did daily, moved a stool close to the grating of the prison window and stepped up on it to look out on the harbor. There, coming into port, was Bluebeard's schooner. Never had the vessel's lines seemed so beautiful, with the sharp prow and the sails set. If her eyes did not deceive her, there on the poop deck was the gallant form of Bluebeard. "Thank God, I have seen him!" she said. "The man I love best on earth. Now I am ready to die." At the appointed time, the fort bell began to toll. A dozen soldiers with muskets headed the procession followed by the judge, police master, and officers of the law. Mercedita, clad in a gown of white, carried a lighted candle in her hand, her hair falling disheveled around her. The procession stopped before the stake. Mercedita was turned over to the executioner, who without further ado tied her to the stake. The woodpile was about to be lit when a blow from one of Bluebeard's men knocked the executioner senseless. Bluebeard and twenty-five of his men burst into the crowd, scattered people right and left, untied Mercedita from the stake, rushed her to a waiting boat, and made for the schooner in the harbor, ready with all sails set.[36]

My friend Drew Pearson, Washington columnist and son of Governor Pearson, was jubilant about the hotel's opening. In one of his letters to me, he wrote:

Bandmaster Adams, I can't tell you how happy I am to hear of the successful opening of Bluebeard Castle Hotel. I believe it will be one of the major accomplishments of my father's administration and one for which he will be remembered. A few days ago, I visited Secretary Ickes in his Washington office and would you believe it, Bandmaster, the old codger was in high spirits. Some of the island newspapers were spread out on his desk telling of the gala opening of the hotel. Holding up one with a center spread, he beamed and told me: "Drew, my department and I have backed your father solidly on this one. It is a breakthrough for the islands and I am excited about it. I have been having fun writing some press releases and sending them out to the press. What do you think of them?" I liked them, and am sending a typical one for your scrapbook. It is from the *Detroit News,* dated Friday, October 12, 1934:

A sojourn on a tropical island on moderate income; a vacation under cloudless skies for the average man. The U.S. government through Harold L. Ickes, Secretary of the Interior, guarantees against piratical charges promising regulations covering rates and grades of service. This is no ordinary advertisement. This is a statement from one of the most practical and hard-headed members of President Roosevelt's cabinet, Secretary of the Interior Harold L. Ickes. When asked about government competition with private business, Ickes gave credit for the government going into the hotel business to former Republican President Herbert Hoover. "When we took over," said Ickes, "there was an appropriation on the books for $6,000 to remodel Bluebeard Castle. At first, not knowing much about it, I held it up, but after Governor Paul M. Pearson got through with me and got me hepped up, I raised the appropriation to $90,000 as a starter." So now the government is in the hotel business. An old and legendary pirate fortification has been reconditioned to provide a bath with every room, a dining terrace above St. Thomas harbor, and equipment for every outdoor sport. The climate is ideal all year round. Winter temperatures hover between 70 and 80 degrees; in summer, between 80 and 90—never above 91.[37]

On October 27, 1934, I received word that two members of the famous Figueroa musical family of Puerto Rico were due in St. Thomas October 31 on the French steamer *Macoris.* On their way to Paris, they had expressed a wish to see me. I was waiting for them when the ship docked on the appointed morning. It was not long before Jaime Figueroa and his brother José descended the gangway. We greeted each other like old friends. The father of the boys, Don Jesús Figueroa Iriarte, and I had known each other for years as a result of our respective musical activities. Don Jesús was a celebrated Puerto Rican composer and director of bands and orchestras.

The Figueroas were a most unusual family: father, mother, five sons, and three daughters—all musically inclined. José, born in 1905 and the oldest of the boys, had begun his musical studies under his father's direction. Observing the boy's remarkable aptitude for the violin, Don Jesús sent him to the Madrid Conservatory of Music, where his brilliance attracted special attention from his teachers. Upon graduation, José was granted the Sarasate Award, the highest honor conferred by the conservatory. Shortly after, José played in the Royal Theatre of Madrid. His performance was spectacular. Word of his brilliance spread throughout musical circles in Europe. Jaime followed in his older brother's footsteps, also winning the Sarasate Award. Having studied at the École Normale de Musique in Paris, Jaime was chosen to represent France in the World Music Festival to be held in Austria. He was to compete on the violin against the world's best. This was the reason for his trip on the SS *Marcoris*. After he left his home and family in Puerto Rico, St. Thomas was the first stop on his way to Paris. That evening, I invited a group of friends and music lovers to come to my home to hear Jaime. It was a musical feast. He played for over an hour and held his audience spellbound. One of a group of musical friends also traveling on the *Marcoris* was an accomplished pianist. He accompanied Jaime. The result was perfection.[38]

As a member of Governor Pearson's cultural committee, I had been asked to head a small group assigned to welcome Edna St. Vincent Millay, one of America's best-loved poets. The lady was due to arrive in St. Thomas from New York in a few days, aboard the SS *Scanpenn* of the American Caribbean Line. We were waiting at the foot of the gangway on January 2, 1935, when Miss Millay and her husband, Eugen Boissevain, descended the stairway.[39] Mr. Boissevain was a large man, and next to him Miss Millay seemed particularly small. She was dressed in white, and when presented with a bouquet of yellow roses, her green eyes twinkled and a smile lit up her delicate face. I judged her to be in her early forties. The government had provided transportation, and we took the Boissevains to the house they were to occupy during their stay, a house located at the top of the 99 Steps and owned by Mrs. Rosa Mallingholm.

I traveled in the car with the Boissevains and while en route chatted with them. Mr. Boissevain was a friendly, outgoing man who spoke with a foreign accent. He told me that he was a Dutchman and in the coffee-importing business in New York. "My business right now, however," he said with a smile, "is to take care of my talented and delicate wife." Miss Millay was a native of Rockland, Maine. She had been educated at Vassar and from her college days had attracted attention as a poet of great promise. In 1922 she won a Pulitzer prize. During the early 1920s, she lived a bohemian life in Greenwich Village, New York, and mingled with artists and writers. She married Eugen Boissevain in 1923 and moved to Steepletop, a farm away from the city. Here she worked on her poetry and developed a mastery of the sonnet form which earned her national recognition and acclaim.

Frail in health and suffering from a respiratory disorder, Millay had been advised by her physician to spend the winter in a warm climate. Friends suggested the beautiful and unspoiled island of St. Thomas. Her first impressions were very favorable. When we got to the house, the place was open and ready. Miss Millay ran inside like a young girl and out onto the porch overlooking the harbor. We met her standing there like one entranced: "It's beautiful," she said. "I love it. I am going to be happy here." A few days later, on January 8, Mrs. Millay came to the St. Thomas Public Library at the invitation of Governor Pearson, who was there to dedicate a beautiful new library desk, a masterpiece of cabinetry built by a local craftsman, E. D. Simmonds. After the ceremonies, librarian Miss Nellie Richardson sat behind the desk and served her first customer—Edna St. Vincent Millay.[40]

As official greeter, I found myself actually enjoying the opportunities to have close contact with some of the illustrious visitors to the island. I got into the habit of calling a friend in Government House to find out who was coming next. "Let me see," he would say, "this is the beginning of February 1935; well, the duke and duchess of Kent are due here on Wednesday, February 13, on a Pan American flight headed south. They will be here for a matter of hours while their plane refuels. However, I got a big one for you. On February 26, Douglas Fairbanks, Sr., the screen star, with party of four persons, will be arriving on the motor ship *Europa* from London. They will be staying here for a few days and then leave aboard a chartered yacht, the *Caroline*, which will take them to Martinique, Curaçao, and through the Panama Canal to Tahiti and other islands in the South Pacific. Mr. Fairbanks has had a rough time in London with newsmen and cameramen. Actually he got into fistfights with some of them. He has asked the governor to assist him with a few trusted people to protect his privacy while he is here. It is an assignment made to order for you, Bandmaster." I was excited. Of all people, Douglas Fairbanks, Sr., was one of my favorite movie stars. He was an island favorite as well. Islanders loved his swashbuckling, daredevil stunts on the screen. Every picture featuring him packed the local movie house. His *The Mark of Zorro* (1920) was brought back three times by popular demand.

While in Europe, Fairbanks's activities made headlines. He mingled with celebrities who included the prince of Wales. His wide-open romance with Lady Sylvia Ashley created waves. Lord Ashley sued his wife for divorce and named Fairbanks as the cause. From far-off Hollywood, Mary Pickford sued Fairbanks for a divorce, naming Lady Ashley. Douglas Fairbanks with his golden-haired companion and three others arrived here at approximately 6:00 P.M. the afternoon of February 26. Our committee met them at the foot of the gangway and took charge as their escort. Fairbanks was most friendly and very relaxed. He spoke freely with two local newsmen and accepted with his famous grin the hurrahs and cheers of the large crowd which had gathered at the wharf. Lady Ashley clung tightly to his arm. There was little need for the requested privacy, so at ease was Fairbanks and his party. They walked along the waterfront followed by throngs of cheering people. Before getting into the launch to take them to the *Caroline*, Fairbanks came over to our committee, shook hands with me and my two colleagues, and thanked us for meeting them and escorting them to the launch.[41]

A series of events in early 1935 brought the Washington–Virgin Islands political pot to a boil yet again and led to the ouster of Governor Pearson. My friend Drew Pearson started it with a serious political blunder. Under the title "A Mississippi Judge," Drew launched a savage attack on T. Webber Wilson, judge of the federal district court of the Virgin Islands. Someone had convinced Drew that Wilson was the man behind the scenes, the leader of the opposition to his father in the islands. Drew's article appeared in the *Nation*, a magazine with a large, important following, especially in the Washington area. The article cast Wilson in the role of a prejudiced southern opportunist unfit to hold court in a black community. Indirectly, the article reflected on the men responsible for the appointment of Wilson to the post. The article supported Governor Pearson and severely condemned Judge Wilson.

To make matters worse, the press section of the Interior Department circulated copies of the article widely. Then hell broke loose! The men responsible for Wilson's appointment—Senator Pat Harrison of Mississippi, Postmaster General James A. Farley, and Attorney General Homer Cummings—demanded a public apology from Interior Secretary Ickes for the vicious propaganda coming from his department. Ickes apologized and lamented the "slip-up." Harrison conferred with President Roosevelt, and both Harrison and Farley were reported to have urged the resignation of

Governor Pearson. On January 26, 1935, it was reported that Harrison was moving for a congressional investigation into the affairs of the government of the Virgin Islands. For several years, Drew Pearson had corresponded with me regularly. On more than one occasion, he had sought my advice. Had he once mentioned his intent to attack Judge Wilson, I would have urged him not to do so and told him that Wilson was no enemy of his father—that someone was feeding Drew absolutely erroneous information. The fact was that Judge Wilson had skillfully kept himself away from the political turmoil and had refused to become a part of the conflict, despite the efforts of the Pearson opposition to involve him.[42]

In the first week of May 1935, the town was besieged by an influx of unwelcome visitors. Swarms of mosquitoes were all over us, big ones, biting and stinging ones—that special kind that breeds in crab holes near swamps. They were being evicted from their usual haunts at Lindbergh Bay (formerly Mosquito Bay), as a result of the draining and filling work taking place. An unseasonal westerly wind blew clouds of the insects toward and over the town. The reclamation project at Lindbergh Bay was a result of Governor Pearson's efforts to make our island a better place in which to live. The swamps posed a potential health menace. They were known to harbor the Anopheles mosquito, responsible for malaria. Governor Pearson succeeded in having the project done with national WPA [Works Progress Administration] funds under the supervision of the U.S. Army Corps of Engineers. Aside from eliminating a health menace, the large area of flat land, when reclaimed, was a valuable and desirable piece of real estate. In 1935 people were already talking about its potential as a field on which to land airplanes.

Captain Peckham, of the dredge boat *Captain Huston,* recently commissioned in Philadelphia and sent to Puerto Rico and then temporarily to the Virgin Islands by the War Department, invited me to come out to view the project.[43] The boat, anchored offshore, pumped sand from the bay to fill the swamps at a cost of $1,000 per day, and it was estimated that the project would require ninety days. Captain Peckham, Lieutenant Truss, Messrs. Thigpin and Auld—all U.S. Navy men—were in charge. When I got there, I noticed that groups of curious townspeople were already on the spot, watching. About a dozen others, men and women wearing high rubber boots, were wading in the proximity of the pipe outlets where shells and other objects besides sand and clay were pouring out. From time to time I could hear the excited voices of collectors as uncommon shells of exquisite patterns came within their reach. Captain Peckham took me aboard the dredge and showed me around. Four large steam boilers, lathes, and drilling and sawing machines were housed on the first deck. The second deck was reserved for quarters of the crewmen and officers totaling thirty-five.[44]

One morning, June 25, 1935, to be exact, I was walking up the steps of the midtown post office when I heard my name called: "Bandmaster Adams." I looked around. The caller was no other than Paul Yates. There he was, cigarette in hand, slouched against a wire fence. "Did you call me?" I asked. "Yes," he said, "I want to talk with you." I never had liked the man. His widely known treacherous activities against the Pearson administration (of which he had been a part) had made me like him less. I had been happy when Interior Secretary Ickes fired him for disloyalty and insubordination.

Yates came up to me in a slow-motion manner and, with a cynical look on his face, said, "I want you to tell your friend Pearson that he has cooked his goose. Here," he said, "read these," and he handed me two cablegrams, one from Millard E. Tydings, senator from Maryland, addressed to Paul M. Pearson, governor of the Virgin Islands. It read: "If you will take back my appointee, Eli Baer, as your government attorney, I will vouch for his 100 percent loyalty. You won't regret it." The other cablegram was a reply from Governor Pearson to Tydings. It said: "I want no deals. I solidly endorse Secretary Ickes' removal of Baer."[45]

"Where did you get these cablegrams?" I asked. Yates pointed to a house halfway up the hill: "I am a houseguest of Eli Baer," he said. Birds of a feather stick together, I thought.

"For your information, our friend Millard Tydings is chairman of the Senate Territories Committee," said Yates, "and he has promised to authorize a congressional inquiry into the Pearson Administration. You have seen so much, Adams; let me show you some more. Here are a few of my remarks to the Senate Territories Committee":

> I, Paul C. Yates, state that in my opinion, Interior Secretary Ickes is drunk with political power and is using any medium of publicity to malign and cast into disrepute every public official and every influential citizen who opposes his arbitrary and ill-advised protection of the Pearson administration. This administration is hateful and odious to the residents of the territory. Interior Secretary Ickes has ignored myriad complaints, prayers, petitions, and specific charges against Pearson by the people of these islands.

Yates looked at me. "What do you think, Adams?" I replied quickly, "I think you're crazy!"[46]

On July 10, 1935, I received a letter dated July 4 from Drew Pearson:

Dear Bandmaster Adams: That congenital troublemaking fellow, Paul Yates, who has been giving my father such a hard time in the islands, has been here in Washington since last week, continuing his activities. He has been strutting the corridors of Congress like a gamecock, buttonholing anybody who will listen to him. He takes full credit for the congressional inquiry into the affairs of the Virgin Islands and the Pearson Administration, which began yesterday. By the time it is over, Yates chortles, the nation will be shocked by the revelations and Interior Secretary Ickes will be out of office, taking my father with him. Bandmaster, I think the man is sick in the head. He is obsessed with the idea that in a New Deal Democratic administration, there is no place for a Republican, especially a leftover Hoover Republican. Yates is fanatical about it. He says it is his mission to get Pearson, even if he has to pull him out by his "entrails."

My partner, Bob Allen, co-author of our column—"Washington Merry-Go-Round," hates Yates's guts. "Wait until I get hold of that S.O.B.," he tells everyone within earshot, "I will consider it a patriotic duty to sock it into him!" It turns out that Bob Allen knew Yates when they were newsmen in Washington, and he helped Yates get the job as administrative assistant to my father. Now the thought comes back to haunt him. Bob's squat, powerful frame shakes when he talks about "socking it into Yates." Well, it happened yesterday morning, outside the senate caucus room. The two men ran into each other. "Hello, you double crossing S.O.B.," snarled Allen. Yates muttered something back. Both men swung fists and missed. Bystanders stepped in to part them. Both men wrenched loose and tore into each other. Yates got the worst of it. He was no match for the burly Allen. Bob made a few fast swings and landed some blows on Yates's face, opening some cuts and bruising his nose and mouth. Yates's face was bleeding when he was assisted to a first-aid station. Capitol police escorted Allen, uninjured, to a detention area from which he was later released. Naturally, this skirmish in the halls of Congress made headlines.[47]

The Tydings committee investigating conditions in the U.S. Virgin Islands opened its hearings on July 2, 1935, in the U.S. Senate caucus room. Yates's charges were contained in a forty-eight-page communication to the committee. It was incredible to us that an insignificant, disgruntled nonentity such as Yates could have aroused top political interest and anger in Washington, culminating in a full-fledged congressional investigation. We who lived here in the islands knew that Yates's charges were a conglomeration of empty sensationalism and hearsay with no substance. Evidently firing off these salvos was an important part of Yates's troublemaking technique, which from all appearances was proving itself effective.

A close friend and longtime observer of the V.I.-Washington political scene said to me: "Adams, it is hard to believe that this man Yates came out of nowhere and has played such havoc. In his short time here, he has turned these islands into snarling, spitting, tumultuous cages of political tomcats." This local tumult seemed to spread to Washington, too, for the investigation was hardly days old when an angry Millard Tydings warned Interior Secretary Ickes to stop interfering with the workings of his committee—to keep his hands off. Ickes had been clamoring for an opportunity to cross-examine witnesses in the probe. As the investigation proceeded, embarrassment mounted. One by one, Yates's charges proved to be a hodgepodge of empty gossip. Editorials appeared in the Washington press commenting on the trivia and the apparent waste of taxpayer money. Several senators resigned from the investigating committee.

After a luncheon with President Roosevelt, Secretary Ickes, who was joined by Senator Tydings, discussed the V.I. probe with the president. All parties decided to drop the investigation. One day latter, the *Washington Herald* carried a story that retired navy admiral William Veazie Pratt, former U.S. naval chief of staff, had been offered the Virgin Islands governorship.[48] The large pro-navy group in St. Thomas was delighted with the news. Sources close to President Roosevelt indicated that in the event of the admiral's acceptance, the president would seriously consider returning the islands to the political peace and economic stability of naval administration. Hopes of pro-navy advocates soared, only to be dashed when Pratt turned down the offer. Speculation continued concerning the status of Governor Pearson. Some said that he planned to resign; others said that he already had done so. On July 24, 1935, a radiogram from Governor Pearson in Washington, D.C., to his wife in St. Thomas cleared the air. The radiogram said: "President Roosevelt and Interior Secretary Ickes today invited me to become assistant director of the Federal Housing Administration. It is a prestigious, important position. I have accepted. I assume duties next week."

On July 26, 1935, the director of the Division of Territories and Island Possessions advised the acting governor in St. Thomas by radiogram that upon the recommendation of Secretary Ickes, the president had nominated Lawrence W. Cramer, lieutenant governor of the Virgin Islands, to become governor, succeeding Paul Pearson.[49] On this same day another, equally important announcement was made. This time, President Roosevelt, upon the recommendation of Attorney General Homer Cummings, announced the promotion and transfer of the Honorable T. Webber Wilson from the judgeship of the U.S. District Court of the Virgin Islands to the Federal Board of Parole. That day, the U.S. Virgin Islands lost two very special and highly qualified individuals. Both were victims of vicious politics and venomous propaganda. Our territory was the big loser. Yates, the "congenital troublemaker," was the big winner. He had accomplished his purpose. By using the technique of the "big lie" and manipulating others to use it, Yates had persuaded important persons in high places to take him seriously. When the farce was exposed, irreparable damage already had been done.

In the case of Wilson, false charges were made that he was bringing American justice into disrepute in the Virgin Islands and that he was the behind-the-scenes leader of the opposition to Governor Pearson. Nothing could have been further from the truth. Time and again, Wilson spoke out in protest against any faction or group using his name in political controversy. Time and again, the island press spoke in favor of the judge's integrity, of his readiness at all times to dispense justice, and of his impartiality in dealing with all who came before him. In the short time that he had been with us, Judge Wilson had won the love and respect of the people.

After the announcements of July 26, 1935, and when the dust had settled, a few thoughtful and courageous people paid tribute to Paul Pearson. Here is one striking example:

> Paul M. Pearson came to our shores four years ago to be our first civilian governor after fourteen years of naval rule. As governor, Pearson, a visionary, dreamed and lived to see many of his dreams come true. He labored under handicaps and disadvantages that would have submerged a man less gifted with patience, love for humanity, and understanding of the ignorance and weakness of his fellow men. Calumny and avarice, linked with ingratitude, attacked his administration on every side. Subordinates plotted with rabble-rousing politicians to attack every creative thought and effort coming from him. Ignorant people were worked into a frenzy of disrespect. A good man, sincerely interested in the people's welfare, was maligned mercilessly from public platforms. Agitated crowds were manipulated and encouraged to riotous behavior. It was a disgraceful episode in V.I. political history.[50]

Just as Pearson left the governorship, his project to drain and till the swamps at Lindbergh Bay suddenly took on new significance. The governor's original intent had been to eliminate a health menace posed by the presence of malaria-carrying mosquitoes. The new significance of the stretch of flat land reclaimed from the swamps came with a totally unexpected announcement from Washington. Early in August 1935, President Roosevelt ordered the U.S. Navy to resume activities in the Virgin Islands. As islanders understood it, the civilian administration of the islands would stay in place. Naval activity was to take the form of a small U.S. Marine

Corps air squadron to be based on St. Thomas. Islanders were jubilant. For years many of them had been advocating civilian government for the islands with some form of naval base to bolster the economy. And here it was, all of a sudden. It was almost too good to be true.

The transport USS *Antares* was soon on its way, bringing the first batch of marines and equipment. Acting governor Robert Herrick served notice upon local school authorities to evacuate immediately the building occupied by the Charlotte Amalie High School (formerly the marine barracks). Lieutenant Colonel Moore, U.S. Marine Corps, commander of the small air squadron assigned to St. Thomas, flew in from Quantico, Virginia, to look around and to determine the most suitable sites for the airport and marine headquarters. When interviewed by the press, myself included, Moore informed us that the marines and equipment en route to St. Thomas were part of a unit from Quantico. Seventy marines, ten officers with seven cars and trucks, a portable machine shop, and six airplanes would be the nucleus for the base. He stated that the marine barracks would have to be repaired and remodeled and numerous improvements made before the men could comfortably settle down to routine duty. "It would probably take about six months to get set," he said. The affable colonel believed that the golf course together with nearby Lindbergh Bay and the filled swampland, when worked on, would make a usable flying field. Not many airports are so close to a seashore, he said, offering seaplane access as well as a place to land planes. He was agreeably surprised to find a level stretch of ground so well located in the trade and prevailing winds.[51]

The Virgin Islands political upheaval of 1933–35, which swept Governor Pearson, Judge Wilson, Government Attorney Baer, and Administrative Assistant Yates from office, had hardly quieted when it became known that Secretary Ickes was planning his first visit. The official reception committee was alerted that Secretary Ickes and party were scheduled to arrive in St. Thomas by plane on the afternoon of January 9, 1936, via Puerto Rico. Our committee was asked by Governor Cramer to prepare a program for the two-day visit and to meet and take charge of the visitors.

When Secretary Ickes stepped off the plane, he was accompanied by Dr. Ernest Gruening, director of territories and island possessions; Raymond Ickes, the secretary's son; and two high-level assistants from the Department of the Interior. Secretary Ickes was a heavy-set, bespectacled man. He wore a white suit and white shoes and a broad-brimmed straw hat. In response to my words of welcome, he shook my hand warmly and said that he had been looking forward to the visit. While waiting for the secretary's plane, Governor Cramer had come over to me and said: "Bandmaster Adams, there is a change in the program. I have just received a note from Chairman Viggo Christensen that because of Secretary Ickes's tight schedule, the Colonial Council is meeting in extraordinary session right now and would like us to bring the secretary directly to their meeting hall." Chairman Christensen officially welcomed the secretary and party on behalf of the people of St. Thomas–St. John. A clipping in my scrapbook quotes Mr. Ickes's response:

> Gentlemen, I think it would have been a kind act on Governor Cramer's part if he had given me warning that I was to come straight from the plane to meet you and to make a few remarks. The Governor did not give me time to wash up and I feel unkempt. However, I would not let anything like that interfere with the pleasure this opportunity affords me of greeting a Colonial Council of which I have heard so much during the last two-and-a-half years. When I went to Washington in the spring of 1933, I planned to visit all the National Parks and Reclamation projects in the western part of the country. I planned also to visit Hawaii, Alaska, Puerto Rico, and the Virgin Islands. Before I had warmed my chair in Interior, the President made me administrator of the huge billion-dollar Public Works program, an awesome and time consuming job.
>
> The Roosevelt Administration, as you know, came into power when the United States was going through the most desperate and the most critical depression in its history. Upon my shoulders was placed, and I repeat the word, "awesome" responsibility of allotting billions of dollars for Public Works projects "to prime the economic pump" and to help the nation get back on its economic feet. Do I have to tell you of the need for intense scrutiny to prevent waste and corruption in a program of this magnitude? I think your Governor, not only your present one, but his predecessor, will attest to the fact that at all times, in spite of my overwhelming duties, I lent a sympathetic ear to any plea from the Virgin Islands. At no time did I lose sight of the well-being and welfare of the people of the Virgin Islands.[52]
>
> It has been and continues to be the desire of the Franklin D. Roosevelt Administration to do everything in its power to bring about the social and economic rehabilitation of these islands. We want to clear your slums. We want to see to it that every man, woman, and child has enough to eat, sufficient clothing and shelter, an opportunity for schooling. We would like the Virgin Islands at the end of our New Deal administration to be happier, to be more firmly grounded on a social and economic basis than before. We are very hopeful of our economic approaches: of buying land and of homesteading it, of growing sugarcane and of making sugar and rum. We are doing everything in Washington to bring about the desirability of the Virgin Islands as a resort for tourists. We want to bring home to the people of the United States

the advantages of these islands, climate, scenery, beautiful beaches; all the natural magnificence that you have here.

Already our experiment with the Bluebeard Castle Hotel is proving itself to be a success. We are going to add to it, more rooms, more public facilities. We can foresee a time when, if tourism is properly handled here, that the maximum development we build on that Bluebeard site will not be adequate. There are a great many more sites here, beautiful places that can be developed for hotel purposes. You have magnificent beaches, beautiful scenery, and exceptional places to drive. When we add some more scenic roads the islands will be even more attractive. However, remember this: government cannot continue to develop the resort facilities here indefinitely. What we can do, what we are doing, is to make a start in the hope that private interests will take over once the great possibilities in the tourist trade have been demonstrated.

On another vital subject, we want you to have all the home rule that is possible. It will be a happy day for us in the United States when you can have as much home rule as any comparable constituency on the mainland. In closing, I want to assure you of my great interest in these islands. What we are doing here through the Public Works program will go a long way in achieving the goals that I have mentioned. As long as I remain administrator of the Federal Public Works program, I will give you every bit of help possible. Let me leave you with this comment. In proportion to your size, these islands have been receiving more attention and a larger per capita allotment of federal funds than any other section of the United States. I know because most of this federal funding passes through my hands.[53]

The original schedule called for Secretary Ickes to stay on St. Thomas that night and all of the next day (January 10), visit St. Croix the morning of January 11, and return in time to depart for the U.S. mainland that same afternoon—two days and two nights. Governor Cramer said to me: "Adams, I know this is a tight schedule, but see what your people can do with it." Bright and early next morning we took the secretary and party on a sight-seeing tour. Mr. Ickes was interested particularly in seeing projects started under the auspices of the New Deal: Bluebeard Castle Hotel, the V.I. Cooperatives, the agricultural experiments, the beginning of slum clearance, and low-cost housing. One of the highlights of the tour was a visit to hilltop Louisenhoj—the showplace castle, dwelling house, and gardens of Arthur Fairchild.[54] Looking down on Charlotte Amalie, with magnificent vistas in all directions, Mr. Ickes was visibly impressed. He said to me with a wry smile: "In such beautiful surroundings, how could the inhabitants become so politically violent?" Then as if to answer his own question, he said: "I realize that in one of his early speeches, Governor Pearson urged the people to develop 'divine discontent.' They developed 'discontent' all right, but there was nothing 'divine' about it," the secretary chuckled.

That night, January 10, 1936, there was a dinner at Government House in St. Thomas followed by a reception. The reception was well attended by government officials and townspeople. Plans called for an early-morning departure for St. Croix and a quick inspection of New Deal projects there.[55] We made our plans not expecting catastrophic events to change them; however, change them they did. The night of Mr. Ickes's arrival, the beautiful St. Croix Government House was destroyed by fire. Our St. Croix plans had centered on the gracious building and its antique mahogany furniture, its mirrored public rooms, its crystal chandeliers and candelabras—relics of a historic past. The secretary and party were to be entertained there. Now they would see the dismal remnants of a disaster: stark and blackened walls, charred wood.

We arrived in Christiansted, St. Croix, early on the 11th. Led by Governor Cramer, we headed for King's Street and the burnt-out remains of Government House. It was a solemn group that looked upon what was left of one of the most imposing structures on St. Croix. It did not take us long to get the details. At about 7:00 P.M. the evening of January 9, a siren in Christiansted had advised the people that Government House was on fire. Started in the pantry by an exploding kerosene Frigidaire, flames spread in many directions. Successful efforts were made to remove government records from the front section of the building used by federal and municipal offices. Firemen and volunteers worked into the wee hours before getting the blaze under control.

I was standing next to Mr. Ickes when Governor Cramer said to him: "What do we do now? Will we have to take money earmarked for rehabilitation projects to repair this building or erect another?" "Forget about erecting another one," Mr. Ickes replied. "I doubt if you have the skilled workers to put up a massive stone frame like this one. The problem as I see it is to restore this place to what it was and to make the interior fireproof. I do not know how much it will cost, nor do I know where the money will come from. However, as soon as I get back to Washington, I will find the funds somewhere."[56] Close contact with Secretary of the Interior Ickes revealed to us the quality of the man. Direct, sincere, and forceful, he dealt with problems head-on, whether in the Virgin Islands or on the U.S. mainland. In his early sixties, a graduate of the University of Chicago, Harold Ickes left a successful practice in the Midwest to take on the job at Interior. In a short time he became one of President Roosevelt's most energetic, dependable, and trusted cabinet members.

Just over a year later, I received a telephone call from a guest at Bluebeard Castle Hotel. He said that his name was Thornton Wilder.[57] He was an author, a professor of comparative literature at the University of Chicago, and a close friend of Edna St. Vincent Millay. She had been most enthusiastic about a vacation and rest-cure spent on St. Thomas in 1935 and had urged Wilder to visit. "If you go," Wilder reported she had said, "be sure to contact our friend Bandmaster Adams. He is on the governor's staff and will be most helpful to you. Besides, you should get to know him."

"So, Bandmaster Adams," Wilder said, "now that I have contacted you, would you care to have lunch with me here at Bluebeard's?" I accepted and we fixed a date. The name Thornton Wilder rang a bell. I went to my bookshelf and there it was, a book by Wilder, *The Bridge of San Luis Rey*. This literary work had attracted considerable attention in the late 1920s and in 1928 had been awarded the Pulitzer Prize. I remembered the story well. Somewhere in Peru, a crude bridge strung across a deep ravine had collapsed, sending to their deaths a number of people crossing the bridge at that precise moment. Wilder had researched the lives of those persons right up to the moment of the disaster. Skillfully and starkly, he had told the story.

We met for lunch on October 23, 1936. Wilder was waiting for me on the terrace overlooking the town. My impression of him was that he was a man of about forty, well built and of better than average height, slightly bald. He wore heavy turtle-shell glasses. After a few preliminary remarks, I came to the point quickly. "Mr. Wilder," I said, "I am happy to meet a man of your literary stature. I must tell you that besides being a musician, I am a reporter for a mainland newspaper as well as the local press. Do you mind if I consider this meeting not only a social one but an interview as well?" Mr. Wilder smiled, "Go right ahead, Bandmaster. From my short stay here, you can report me as being enthusiastic about the island, its scenery, and what I have seen of its people. Furthermore, one of my hobbies is mountain climbing and I plan to do some hiking among your hills." And he pointed to the mountain range easily visible from Bluebeard's terrace.[58]

Wilder was in a talkative mood and told me a good deal about himself. He had spent his early boyhood years in China and spoke the language fairly well. His father, a member of the U.S. consular service, had taken him there. On his return to the United States, he had specialized in education and taught in several American colleges. Then he turned to writing. During the luncheon, Wilder confided that two days before, he had started work on a play and that he found the environment at Bluebeard's very conducive to creative effort. The play that resulted, *Our Town*, won a Pulitzer Prize in 1938 and is considered a classic of the American theater.

I saw a good deal of Thornton Wilder during his stay. He visited my home, went through my library, listened to my records, and autographed my copy of *The Bridge of San Luis Rey*. He promised that on his return to the states, he would send me his latest novel, *Heaven's My Destination* (1935). He had brought a copy with him, but on a visit to the local library he had been so well received by librarian Enid Baa and her staff that he had given it to the library, autographed. I could hardly wait to read it. I went to the library and returned home with the book. Once started, it could not be put down. It was a hilarious satire on the times. Its central character, twenty-three-year-old George Brush, a naïve, innocent young man, was on his way to heaven and en route tried to save and take along with him as many souls as possible. Good and evil were starkly established in his mind, and his dogged pursuit of good created many ludicrous situations.

In one such situation in Kansas City, Brush was taken by friends to a Sunday dinner at an establishment run by a matronly person called Ma Crofurt. This lady had a sizeable number of daughters and nieces. Brush liked the atmosphere and became a frequent visitor to the place. He enjoyed the lively young women at the dining table. He also enjoyed the ritual of taking some of them to the movies at regular intervals. Eventually after many unique and humorous situations, the truth dawned on a very shocked and disillusioned young man—he was in the center of a house of prostitution. In discussing the book with Wilder, I mentioned this particular episode. He chuckled, "Bandmaster, that was taken from real life. As a naïve young man, it happened to me!"[59]

On March 27, 1938, I received a telegram from Drew Pearson relaying the sad news of his father's death. Hours later, radio reports informed the local public of the demise of the former governor. He had been ill for many weeks due to a paralytic stroke. The end had come suddenly in his sixty-seventh year. I was saddened by the news. Paul Pearson had been different from all other governors with whom I had served. There was nothing military about him. He was a humble man with intense feeling for his fellow men and an urgent desire to serve them. Dr. Pearson brought to the Virgin Islands job a solid background in education. A graduate of Baker College in the Midwest, he had done graduate work at Northwestern University and Harvard. For a time, he was professor of public speaking at Swarthmore College, Pennsylvania. While there, he edited a literary magazine. He was founder and president of the Swarthmore Chautauqua Association, whose purpose was to bring culture, musical and literary, to the masses. He delivered lectures and recitals before many Chautauqua clubs and colleges.

None of this extensive educational background prepared Dr. Pearson for what awaited him in the Virgin Islands. While later calling the islands a "veritable poorhouse," President Hoover had helped make them just that by taking impulsive step to remove the naval presence, the major economic prop to the islands. Dr. Pearson came into a territory that had gone bankrupt overnight. Many people had lost their jobs. Cash registers had stopped ringing. Many residents, as a result, were bitterly opposed to civil government and turned that hostility against the new governor as its representative. They clamored for the return of the navy. Though somewhat bewildered, Dr. Pearson kept his calm. There was a quality in his character of tolerance for those who piled unnecessary obstacles against him. He saw a bright lining in every dark cloud, and his sheer optimism helped to keep high the morale of those around him. "Just wait," he would say, "as soon as I get my social and economic rehabilitation programs in place, we will turn this thing around."[60]

Memorial services for the late governor were held in the islands' churches and schools. Flags were flown at half-mast for three days. Officials who had served with the deceased eulogized him. I kept newspaper accounts of some of those eulogies, particularly those of Morris de Castro, who had served on Governor Pearson's staff, and D. Victor Bornn, who continued to serve as manager of the V.I. Cooperatives—an outlet for local crafts started by Governor Pearson. In his remarks, D. Victor Bornn remembered:

> Paul M. Pearson fell in love with these islands almost from the moment of his arrival. His infatuation for them grew deeper, day by day, in the face of all manner of discouragement. The fact that he requested of his family that his remains be cremated and that his ashes be strewn in the Caribbean near these Virgin Islands, is eloquent proof of his abiding love for them. His love was not mere infatuation with beautiful scenery, delightful climate or other physical attractions. He was vitally interested in the betterment of the people and to this end he labored mightily.
>
> It is not difficult to find around us lasting monuments to his efforts. He improved our roads and created new ones. He drained our swamps and created land on which our airport has been built. He improved our hospitals. He created a homestead program. He created a V.I. Cooperative. He personally brought a Bluebeard Castle Hotel into being.
>
> We must acknowledge a deep debt of gratitude to this socially minded man and to his tenacious leadership.[61]

On November 21, 1938, Frederic D. Dorsch, second member for Frederiksted town, municipal council of St. Croix, proposed a resolution to the Legislative Assembly, meeting in St. Thomas, offering the U.S. Virgin Islands as a place of safety for refugee peoples. The resolution, though general, was prompted by the furious persecution of the Jews in Nazi Germany. That condition, having grown for several years, suddenly had reached unprecedented heights.

In revenge for the deportation from Germany and merciless beating of his father, an elderly Polish tailor named Grynszpan, his seventeen-year-old son, Herschel, acting impulsively and not thinking of the consequences, walked into the German Embassy in the rue de Lille, Paris, on November 7, 1938, and pumped five bullets into the German third secretary, Ernst vom Rath. The undersecretary's death was the signal for an unparalleled orgy of Nazi anti-Semitism. In every city and town of greater Germany, synagogues were burned, Jewish shops smashed and plundered, and thousands of Jews beaten and some even murdered. The destruction was wrought by groups of young men and boys who wore Nazi-party uniforms, arrived in Nazi-party automobiles, acted with military precision, and were not hindered by the police.

In response, the Dorsch Resolution read as follows:

Be it resolved by the Legislative Assembly of the Virgin Islands of the United States in session assembled: WHEREAS the world conditions have created large refugee groups and WHEREAS such groups will eventually migrate to places of safety and WHEREAS the Virgin Islands of the United States being a place of safety can offer surcease from misfortune.

Now therefore be it resolved by the Legislative Assembly of the Virgin Islands of the United States in session assembled, that it be made known to refugee peoples of the world that when and if existing barriers are removed that they shall find surcease from misfortune in the Virgin Islands of the United States, and be it further resolved that copies of this Resolution be forwarded to the President of the United States, the Secretary of State, the Secretary of Interior, the Secretary of Labor, and members of the press.

When the Dorsch Resolution was brought to the floor of the Legislative Assembly, the Honorable Joseph Alexander, veteran legislator from the Christiansted district, made an impassioned speech:

Members of this legislative body, we, representing but a small part of the civilized world, stand revolted by what we are seeing happening in Nazi Germany: a bloody program against a defenseless people. I think I speak for this body when I say that every instinct in us cries out in protest against these outrages. I think I speak for this body when I say that if we saw a group of ruthless ruffians set upon a helpless man or woman in a public street and proceed to beat that person or persons, we would not want to be silent. If we saw a fanatical mob burn and pillage property and possessions of innocent people, we would not want to stay silent. If we saw a brutal band of desperadoes drive helpless families from their homes and businesses, we would not want to stay silent. If the civilized world wants to pretend that these things are not happening; if they, particularly the nations of the Western world, want to stay aloof, then we, a very small part of that civilized world, must express our vehement protest against such barbarism. It is true that our puny efforts might get us nowhere, nevertheless the spirit that goes with our protest is commendable. What is happening in Nazi Germany is not a Jewish question, a Catholic question, or a Protestant question, but one that goes to the very roots, the foundation on which a moral and civilized world is built.

The resolution was passed unanimously.[62]

Copies of the Dorsch Resolution were sent to top officials in Washington, D.C. Responses from the U.S. president and the secretary of state were brief, mere acknowledgments. The secretary of labor expressed interest and sought more information. Interior Secretary Ickes was enthusiastic. "A great idea," he responded. "Why not offer the U.S. Virgin Islands as a temporary refuge, a breathing space for those waiting their turn to enter the United States legally; or to enter other Western countries, which, if given sufficient time and encouragement, might warm up to the idea of accepting some of the displaced people, particularly skilled craftsmen and technicians." Ickes suggested that "considering the limited Virgin Islands space, inadequate housing and general lack of accommodating facilities, a limit of not more than 2,000 refugees might be accommodated in the U.S. Virgin Islands in any one given year; and . . . federal assistance would have to be given to provide adequate facilities." "As numbers of refugees from the Virgin Islands sanctuary were permitted legal entry elsewhere," continued the secretary, "their places would be filled by others, never to exceed the 2,000 ceiling in any one given year."

Despite his reputation for being tough, quarrelsome, and stubborn, Secretary Ickes was a compassionate man. Human suffering in any form, large or small, affected him and offered him a challenge to do something about it. As he looked out on the world of 1938, what Ickes saw sickened his spirit. In Germany the Nazi government of Hitler had raised to an organized frenzy its brutal and bloody program against a defenseless people. In Spain the victorious forces of Generalissimo Francisco Franco had all but overwhelmed the leftists. Young men trying to hold out against the fascists were being slaughtered by the thousands. A flood of refugees was emerging with no place to go, with no country showing any willingness to accept them. Ickes tried to arouse the Roosevelt administration to protest against the outrages; to pay heed to the desperate plight of these hopeless people; to develop a program of asylum, of open borders to permit many to enter the United States. He pleaded also for the United States to urge other Western countries to do the same.

Ickes's pleadings were not heeded. Isolationists and biased officials in the State Department urged Roosevelt to stay aloof, and he followed their advice. Other Western countries also stayed aloof as if pretending that what was happening was not real. The wholesale indifference of the Western world to this mass slaughter was appalling and a stigma against worldwide morality in that nightmarish period of the twentieth century. A slight ray of light had appeared at that time, the Dorsch Resolution, improbably placed in the Virgin Islands of the United States.

Helping human beings in distress was nothing new for Ickes. Nor was he averse to ignoring and bypassing bureaucratic red tape to accomplish his ends. In April 1938 an executive order fashioned at his desk at Interior paved the way for Virgin Islands government secretary Robert Morss Lovett to allow a group of European refugees to enter the Virgin Islands via Tortola without visas. Ickes asked his staff to prepare his plan for presentation to the president and to his fellow cabinet members. His staff did so, but pointed out to the secretary that one main obstacle remained that could prevent implementation of his Virgin Islands plan. There was a stipulation in U.S. law preventing those who had already entered the country (however that entry occurred) from qualifying for regular entry into the United States under its quota system. This proviso, if enforced, would void the Virgin Islands plan. Ickes's response was typical: "Laws are made to be changed, and, if necessary, we will change or modify this one."[63]

Ickes and his legal staff entered into discussions in October 1939 with representatives of the U.S. Labor, State, and Justice departments in an effort to exempt the U.S. Virgin Islands from the objectionable stipulation. The Labor Department people went along 100 percent. However, the State Department representatives, acting under direct orders from Assistant Secretary of State Breckinridge Long, adamantly opposed granting exemptions from the immigration stipulation to anybody, including potential refugees in the U.S. Virgin Islands. Representatives of the Justice Department remained uncommitted. Ickes was not the kind of man to accept what he considered unreasonable opposition easily. He arranged for an appointment and went to see Long.

He told the assistant secretary: "I came here in person to stress to you the great human emergency that exists in Hitler's Europe. America cannot stand by with its eyes closed and its hands folded. Since Germany annexed Austria, scores and scores of men of great ability and culture have committed and are continuing to commit suicide from sheer desperation. These people, and others like them, could make a great contribution to our country and our culture. It seems terrible that our doors are closed to them. I came here in person to ask you why you are so adamant against opening even small areas of hope?"

"Ickes," Long responded with what amounted to a sneer, "the trouble with you bleeding-heart liberals is that you think with your hearts and not with your heads. Any so-called refugee havens that you open now will become zones from which undesirables will pour into this country. Let me make my position clear. I and my department will not be a party to this plan. I want you to know, Ickes, that I have and will continue to do all in my power to keep American doors closed to refugees."

Ickes recognized what he was dealing with. Long was one whose ingrained prejudices left little room for compassion for fellow human beings in distress. It went further than that. Keeping "undesirables" out of the United States became a passion with Long. His was one of the loudest and most effective voices raised against a plan to create "free port zones" for refugees. Various areas scattered throughout the United States would provide temporary shelter for European refugees until the war was over. This idea was fought and blocked effectively by the U.S. State Department. It was a tragedy that a so-called liberal like Franklin D. Roosevelt listened to people like Long and his associates in the State Department instead of a compassionate visionary like Ickes. This decision cost countless lives.[64]

10 The Power of the Press (the 1940s)

Editor's Note: *In February 1940 Adams took over as owner, publisher, editor, and roving reporter for one of St. Thomas's historic newspapers, the* Bulletin. *This venture, especially in its cultural coverage, recalled his* St. Thomas Times *(1921–23); however, unlike Adams's first paper, the new publication was not attached to the U.S. Navy and thus could be a more independent as well as political voice. The paper had one important advantage over its rivals: Adams's trusted position as welcoming coordinator for the islands' governor gave him valuable access to visiting politicians and celebrities as he was frequently able to combine his hosting duties with interviews. Thus the* Bulletin *could scoop its competitors and offer unique perspectives on local happenings. In this way, Adams interviewed such figures as the Dominican Generalissimo Trujillo and composer Irving Berlin. His interviews reveal a fascination with childhood background—a line of questioning consistent with his notions about the cultural and social environment's influence on the individual. Trujillo's grandmother, for example, dutifully instilled in him virtues of discipline, learning, and hard work; as a child, Berlin escaped a violent Russia to realize his dreams. Berlin's success further affirms not only the power of black music through his borrowings from ragtime and jazz but also the virtue of self-improvement. Both composers were largely self-taught talents, and Adams revels in the affirmation of Berlin's success.*

Adams's newspaper proprietorship came to a sudden end with the bombing of Pearl Harbor and his recall to active duty from the Naval Fleet Reserve. Sent back to Cuba, Adams created what appears to be the navy's first documented and official racially integrated band by combining eight of his former band members with an all-white unit already stationed at Guantánamo. Drawing on his connections in the Virgin Islands, Adams engineered his return to St. Thomas a year later along with his native bandsmen in order to form the second United States Navy Band of the Virgin Islands, an all-black unit that served the islands' newly commissioned submarine base. Adams writes little of his World War II experience; rather, the memoirs focus on federal high jinks in Washington, D.C. The popular government secretary, Robert Morss Lovett, for example, was called to testify before the House Un-American Activities Committee, then named after its chairman, Martin Dies. Lovett enjoyed strong support in the islands, and eventually his supporters circumnavigated the crisis, but not without bringing Congress and the president into conflict over the separation of powers. Adams's characterization of government as full of intrigue and interference disrupting sincere effort not only underscores the islands' precarious situation as a territorial dependent but also helps explain his own decision to support local officials while refraining from running for office himself.

On January 26, 1940, I found myself one of a capacity crowd that attended a session of the Virgin Islands district court to witness a new federal judge in action. Of particular interest to many of us was the fact that the newcomer, Herman E. Moore, forty-seven years old, of Chicago, Illinois, was the second Negro to be appointed district judge of the Virgin Islands by Franklin Delano Roosevelt. The first, Judge William H. Hastie, appointed in 1937, had resigned the position several months before to become dean of the Howard University Law School. It was obvious to me, watching Judge Moore in court, that he was a man of dignity, poise, and considerable legal experience. Several cases came before him that morning. In one instance, a defendant pleaded guilty to the charge of carrying a deadly weapon; in another, a confessed burglar pleaded guilty on two counts. Before pronouncing sentence, Judge Moore spoke kindly to the defendants. He urged them to do better and to walk the straight road after they had served their sentences. The judge showed firmness and compassion, and onlookers in the courtroom were impressed.

The appointment of Mr. Moore came as a surprise. No one in the islands had ever heard of him. For that matter, Negro congressmen and news hawks in Washington had never heard of him. Secretary Ickes, it was reported, was the one who swung the appointment. It did not take us long to get some background information on the new judge. He was born in Jackson, Mississippi. The son of a physician, the young man received his early education in Jackson schools. From there he went to Howard University, where he graduated magna cum laude. His name appeared often on the university's honor rolls. He was president of the Alpha Phi Alpha fraternity and associate editor of the Howard University journal, and firmly set his course toward becoming a lawyer. Accordingly, he studied law at the Boston University Law School, where he was awarded a bachelor's degree in 1918 and his master's in 1919. During his postgraduate days, he established a reputation as a writer of legal briefs for various Boston law firms. This helped him in becoming assistant attorney for the Boston elevated railway, the first Negro in that post. In 1921 Moore came to Chicago and practiced law there. For eighteen years he was a member of the Cook County Bar Association. Illinois governor Horner appointed him assistant commissioner of the Illinois Commerce Commission in 1934. He remained there until his appointment to the federal judgeship in the U.S. Virgin Islands with the solid and enthusiastic esteem of his former associates.[1]

On February 29, 1940, the following news item appeared in the local press:

> It is reported that as of two days ago, Bandmaster Alton A. Adams, U.S. Naval Fleet Reserve, took over the editorship and management of *The St. Thomas Bulletin,* the oldest daily newspaper in St. Thomas. Bandmaster Adams is no stranger to the newspaper field. During the days when the navy administered the U.S. Virgin Islands, Bandmaster Adams took time out from his musical work to edit *The St. Thomas Times,* a weekly paper of fine appearance and excellent subject matter.
>
> It is no secret that in recent years the historic newspaper, *The Bulletin,* has fallen far from its former stature and usefulness and has barely managed to survive. We believe that under the firm and creative management of Bandmaster Adams, *The Bulletin* will once again come alive and regain the public's confidence and respect. We welcome editor Adams into the field.

The press report was correct. I had been approached by a group of prominent persons who urged me to take over the management and editorship of the *Bulletin.* They selected me, they said, as the one person, in their opinion, who could take over the newspaper and build it back to the position of respect for which it had been known. They promised financial backing and a free hand. I accepted and assumed the post on February 27, 1940.

In a simple statement, I said:

> Today the task of carrying on the management and editorship of *The Bulletin* has fallen on me. I trust I may prove capable. Under my direction *The Bulletin* will be an independent newspaper in the sense that it will not be used for motives other than the public good. Its primary function will be to print the news. When the editor's views are deemed necessary, they will be given honestly and in clear unmistakable language.

The *Bulletin* is indeed historic. It was the first daily newspaper to come into existence in St. Thomas. It was started in the year 1874, as an all-English-language offshoot of the bilingual *St. Thomas Tidende*, a biweekly government-controlled newspaper. In those days the government supervised all aspects of journalistic expression. To get a special grant as editor and to operate a printing office, it was necessary to pass an examination before the police authorities. In every case a sworn statement was necessary that at no time would the editor permit the use of his columns for anti-government agitation. Controversial matters were referred to the government for approval and clearance. This press and censorship law, a relic of the mid-nineteenth century, was only abolished in 1917 with the transfer of the islands to U.S. sovereignty.[2]

My first move after taking over the management of the *Bulletin* was to plan for the transfer of the newspaper from its cramped and very unsatisfactory quarters downtown. We arranged to relocate at No. 6B Wimmelskaft Gade (Back Street), Queens Quarter, in the entire ground floor of a building known as the Eureka Hotel (later, The Gate). The rooms, four or five in number, were large and airy, with high ceilings. For my office, I selected the rooms at the southeastern corner, one block away from the center of Main Street (Dronningens Gade). With my desk in place and with some quick painting and carpeting contemplated, I knew that I could be comfortable there.

On that first day of my assuming management of the newspaper, February 27, 1940, I received my first communication from the local government addressed to me as editor. The communication was from the Honorable Dr. Robert Morss Lovett, government secretary, who had taken over as acting governor for Governor Cramer, who was in Washington. Dr. Lovett informed me, as he did other interested parties, that he had received word that morning that Generalissimo Rafael Leónidas Trujillo Molina, ex-president of the Dominican Republic, was on his way to St. Thomas for a visit. The generalissimo was due to arrive the following morning and planned to dock at the West Indian Company aboard his yacht, *Ramfis*. It was Trujillo's stated intention to exchange calls with the acting governor. In keeping with protocol, Dr. Lovett and staff planned to meet the *Ramfis* when it docked. Editors and key newsmen of the local press were invited to join the reception group. I was delighted to accept the invitation. What better way to start my editorship than with a front-page interview with Generalissimo Trujillo, the "strongman" of the Caribbean? He was at the peak of his achievements in his island domain and was enjoying great popularity with his people.

At 10:15 the next morning, acting governor Lovett, accompanied by staff and members of the press, Dominican consul Emile A. Berne, and Vice Consul J. Percy Souffront, as well as Lieutenant Colonel Francis P. Mulcahy (commanding officer of the marine air base in St. Thomas), boarded the *Ramfis* and paid their respects to the generalissimo, who stood with his staff on the foredeck. As if at a given signal from Colonel Mulcahy, planes of the local air base roared overhead, circled, and dipped their wings in military salute to the generalissimo. Trujillo was obviously pleased. He smiled continuously and waved his arms aloft in happy response.[3]

At the time of his visit to St. Thomas, Generalissimo Trujillo was acclaimed at home and abroad for the excellent job he had done in restoring order and prosperity to his country. Taking over the presidency of the Dominican Republic from the faltering leadership of Horacio Vasquez in 1930, with the country in a condition bordering on chaos, Trujillo's firm hand and sound economic policies had brought the country from confusion and near anarchy to a high standard of living. Ten years of strong leadership and skilled management earned for Trujillo the respect of outsiders and the idolatry of his own people. In light of this popular endorsement, it was not difficult for acting governor Lovett, an outstanding American liberal, to feel comfortable in greeting and entertaining Trujillo. At 7:30 P.M. on February 29, 1940, the second night of Trujillo's visit, acting governor and Mrs. Lovett entertained the generalissimo and his party at a dinner at Bluebeard Castle Hotel. Besides the acting governor and his wife, his staff, and members of the press, the generalissimo's daughter Flor de Oro and a lady companion were honored guests. The ladies had arrived at Bluebeard Castle several days before by steamer. Toasts and complimentary remarks were the order of the evening. The local press, too, was favorably inclined toward the generalissimo. Here is one press reaction of March 1, 1940:

> The courtesies being paid to his Excellency, Rafael Leonidas Trujillo Molina, are deserved and are our tribute to one of the outstanding administrators of present times. It is not often that we are privileged to meet a constructive statesman and patriot whose deeds are of social and economic significance to his country, and of considerable interest to the world in general. It is notable that President Trujillo, when he considered the time right, gave over the power he had built to the representative body of his country; that the National Democratic Congress had to be persuaded to accept his retirement. Dr. Juancito B. Reynardo, Trujillo's successor, was inaugurated two years ago on Aug. 16, 1938.[4]

As a member of the local press, I attended the dinner honoring Trujillo and his daughter. Wearing my naval uniform, I found myself seated next to the generalissimo's military aide General McLaughlin, an ex-marine and trusted confidant. Before the evening was over, we had swapped backgrounds and become good friends. At my request, McLaughlin promised that he would try to arrange a press interview for me with the generalissimo. McLaughlin was as good as his word. He called me next morning, early. The interview had been arranged. Generalissimo Trujillo had agreed to see me at eleven o'clock, March 1, 1940, aboard the *Ramfis*.

We met in the beautiful and spacious lounge of his yacht. Trujillo greeted me warmly. He was an impressive figure of medium height, slender and handsome in his admiral's uniform, an array of medals covering his chest. I was informed that while the generalissimo was conversant with the English language, he felt more at ease with his native Spanish. His daughter Flor de Oro, fluent in both languages, graciously offered to translate. Through her, I stressed that the readers of my newspaper were particularly interested in knowing something of the family's background. In a relaxed mood, the generalissimo complied. He was forty-nine years old, born October 24, 1891, in San Cristóbal, a small town in the province of Santo Domingo. He was the fourth child of Don José Trujillo Valdez and Doña Julia Molina Chevalier. On his father's side, he was of pure Spanish stock. The Trujillos had come to the New World during the early days of America's discovery and colonization. One of his forebears had been a prominent general in Cuba who had won important victories over insurgents seeking to break away from Spanish rule. This particular forebear had been decorated, time and again, by the Spanish Crown.

On his mother's side, the Chevaliers came from the France of Emperor Napoleon I. One of his forebears, the Marquis Joseph Chevalier, had come to Hispaniola in the early days of the nineteenth century as a member of the entourage of General Le Clerc, sent by Napoleon to put down widespread rebellion, to pacify Hispaniola, and to reestablish French rule. Le Clerc was married to Pauline Bonaparte, sister of the emperor. Trujillo was proud of his heritage. This was the background that brought him to the leadership of the military. He graduated from the Dominican military academy with the rank of second lieutenant. He gained promotion from one rank to another with remarkable speed until he attained the position of brigadier general, commander-in-chief of the Dominican Army. Under his command, the country's military installation gained prestige beyond the island's frontiers.[5]

Trujillo seemed to enjoy talking about his boyhood and his early upbringing in small-town San Cristóbal. With his brothers and sisters, he had attended the village school, but it was his grandmother, Doña Louisa Ercine Chevalier, who exerted influence on the children. His grandmother was a lady of quality who had absorbed the traditional culture of her aristocratic French family background and who felt it her duty to pass this culture on to her grandchildren. She devoted every moment of time away from household duties to work on their minds. She taught them to read and write. She stressed the importance of discipline and hard work. She detested idleness. She urged self-sufficiency. She held strongly to the belief that God helps those who help themselves.

Trujillo's first job, under the guidance of his uncle, Don Pina Chevalier, was as a telegraph operator. He was given an assistant position in the town's telegraph office. From there he was sent to the main office in the nation's capital. Trujillo was twenty-five years old when his country was occupied by U.S. marines in 1916. It was not the first U.S. intervention in the Dominican Republic. In 1905, when Trujillo was fourteen, U.S. president Theodore Roosevelt, brandishing a big stick and the Monroe Doctrine, had taken over the Dominican customhouses and arranged a receivership to pay off European creditors. The island republic, as a result of a series of internal revolutions, was hopelessly bankrupt. Foreign warships were poised to enter Dominican ports to take over the customs to try to collect money owed to their nationals.

The United States stayed in the Dominican Republic in a supervisory role backed up by its military form 1916 to 1924, when the marines were withdrawn. The fiscal condition of the island showed marked improvement. Meanwhile, the U.S. military took over the training of the Dominican army. Trujillo's relationship with the U.S. marines was a good one. As a sergeant in the Dominican army he struck up friendships with the Americans. One of these friendships which endured was with McLaughlin, who also was a sergeant and an up-and-comer in the marines. With Trujillo on his way to the top, McLaughlin retired from the marines and became Trujillo's confidant and military adviser. During a social and economic crisis in 1930, the then president of the republic, Horacio Vasquez, meekly turned over the government to the revolutionists. Not being able to fathom this weakness on the part of the executive, Trujillo resigned as commander-in-chief of the Dominican armed forces and retired to his home. Insurgents united under the banner of the revolution sought him there and got his permission to proclaim him a candidate for office of president of the republic. Trujillo won unopposed.[6]

When I took over as editor, roving reporter, and publisher of the *Bulletin,* I did not realize how much I would enjoy interviews. Hardly a month passed but some remarkable individual or situation presented itself calling for press attention. Often friends alerted me to these opportunities. On

June 15, 1940, I interviewed Daniel Henley, a native of St. Thomas who had left the island on November 16, 1939, as a sailor on the Greek ship *Eleni Stathatos*. The steam freighter arrived in England on December 12, leaking badly. The *Stathatos* went on drydock, was repaired, and left for Vera Cruz, Mexico. Let Daniel Henley tell the story:

> We had hardly left the British coast on January 28, 1940, when we were torpedoed by a German submarine. Two lifeboats were launched just before our ship sank. One of the lifeboats, badly damaged, capsized. Thirty-three of the ship's complement, officers and men, some of them pulled out of the water, crowded the one remaining lifeboat. There had been no time to secure food and water.
>
> What followed was a nightmare in a furious North Atlantic gale with the men in the tossing lifeboat holding on for dear life while the wind howled around us and icy temperatures went well below zero. We had no protection from the intense cold. Things had happened too fast for us to secure warm clothing, blankets, or covering for our bodies. On the afternoon of the second day, the second mate went mad and started eating the flesh from his hand. The rest of us were too immobilized by the cold to try to stop him. By eight o'clock in the evening, six of the occupants of the boat, including the crazed second mate, had frozen to death. With great difficulty, we threw them overboard. By morning, four more had suffered the same fate. By the time the strong tides carried us to the Irish coast, twenty-three men had frozen to death.
>
> Having to help, with partly frozen limbs, to throw my fellow seamen into the icy sea remains to me like a constant nightmare. Off the Irish coast, we encountered a motor launch that towed us into a nearby port. Ten of us that were left of the original thirty-three were rushed to a hospital where four more died. The remaining six of us, in various stages of frostbite, recovered slowly.
>
> When I could manage it, I left Ireland. I took passage on the SS Orbata of the Pacific Steamship Navigating Company and went to Cristobal, Panama, where I spent two months and twenty-seven days regaining my health with the kind help of Dr. J. D. Odon of the quarantine service there. From Cristobal, I went to Curaçao, then to St. Kitts, where I boarded a small fruit boat which brought me back to St. Thomas. The warmth of the tropical sun, which I had always taken for granted, took on new meaning for me. I hope never to leave this island again.[7]

The morning of October 10, 1940, I was alerted to the fact that the night before, three convicts from Devil's Island, the French penal colony off the coast of French Guiana, had arrived in St. Thomas in an open twenty-one-by-six-foot canoe. As editor–publisher–roving reporter for the St. Thomas *Bulletin*, I found this news of special interest. A few months before, I had been commissioned by a national press service to go to St. Croix to interview fourteen escaped convicts from the same notorious penal colony. Much had happened in those few months. The French government on the European continent had surrendered to Hitler. The Vichy government, headed by Marshal Philippe Pétain, had been set up. This government collaborated with the Nazis. I was most curious to find out what effect these drastic political changes in Europe had on the French penal system in the Caribbean. Perhaps the three escaped convicts in the canoe might give me the answer.

I met and talked with the ragged, weary, and hungry-looking men. Leaving Devil's Island on July 28, the convicts had gone to Tobago, St. Vincent, and St. Kitts, from which latter island they had come to St. Thomas. Henri Roulet, the thirty-eight-year-old spokesman for the group, told me that he had been sent from France to Devil's Island for stabbing an army officer. Charles Grouzet, the second man in the canoe, fifty-seven years old, had been imprisoned for burglary. Georges Girod, the third man, thirty-two years old, was sent to Devil's Island for being an accomplice to murder. Explaining the terrible hardships in the penal colony, the men said that since all prison discipline had ended with the Nazi takeover of continental France, hunger-maddened convicts were roaming all over the colony. Due to the collapse of France, most of the Devil's Island guards, who had received no pay in months, had abandoned the island. "Most of the convicts," said Henri Roulet, "were loyal to General de Gaulle's government in exile." Captain Chandon, de Gaulle's representative in Georgetown, Demarara, had left the area, taking with him 110 colonial infantry from the island and 200 convicts who expressed the desire to join and fight for the de Gaullists. The three convicts in the canoe admired de Gaulle so much that they named their canoe *General de Gaulle*. Henri Roulet estimated that there were more than two thousand prisoners left on the island. Most of them were desperate for food and without medical care or supervision of any kind. They could not get out through regular channels. They did not have money to buy passage on a boat no matter how cheap. The broken-down island government was run by Admiral Robert, head of the French colonial government in the Caribbean. Admiral Robert was a Pétain man and was intensely hated by the people. A handful of convicts, like Henri and his two companions, had stolen canoes and escaped.[8]

My job as editor of the St. Thomas *Bulletin* and as its "top" reporter (due to lack of funds and staff) fitted neatly into my volunteer efforts as chairman of the governor's reception committee. From the beginning, I enjoyed the reception committee work and the close contact with unusual

and renowned people who visited St. Thomas. Now I was in a unique position to scoop interviews with these celebrated people for my newspaper.
On November 11, 1940, I received a phone call from Government House.
Acting governor Lovett was on the line: "Bandmaster Adams, once again
we are calling on you for help. Word has just been received that the brand
new passenger liner SS *America* of the United States Lines has run into
bad weather on her way to Puerto Rico. Because of very high seas in San
Juan Harbor, the ship is skipping San Juan and is coming here ahead of
schedule. The *America* is due here tomorrow with four hundred passengers. According to my wife, who is a passenger aboard, there are many
celebrities who require special handling.

"As you may know, Bandmaster, Mrs. Lovett and I were on a vacation on
the U.S. mainland and were both scheduled to return on the *America* to St.
Thomas. My plans changed abruptly when I received orders to return to St.
Thomas by plane immediately to greet Treasury Secretary Henry Morgenthau, who is presently my guest at Government House and is requiring
my full attention. That is why I am calling on you and your committee to
meet the ship and to take over the welcoming duties in your usual skilled,
efficient manner.

"As a musician, it should excite you to know that the famous songwriter
Irving Berlin and his wife are being entrusted to your care. Also in the
group that my wife has selected to be taken to Government House are Gloria Swanson, the screen star; Mrs. Alice Duer, novelist and noted writer for
the *Saturday Evening Post;* George W. Armitage, head of the tourist board
in the Hawaiian Islands; and Congressman Sol Bloom, chairman of the
House Foreign Affairs Committee, with his wife and daughter."

The thought of taking care of Irving Berlin truly excited me. Here was
a musical genius who had produced hits such as "Alexander's Ragtime
Band," "This Is the Army," "As Thousands Cheer," "What'll I Do," "Reaching for the Moon," and a host of other numbers for the Ziegfeld Follies, the
Music Box Revue, and other shows. The man was at the height of his creative powers, and the musical world and the public were expectant of
greater works to come. I could hardly wait to meet him."[9]

At 8:00 A.M. the morning of November 12, 1940, the SS *America*
anchored at the entrance to St. Thomas Harbor. Launches were lowered, and
by 9:30 A.M. the first passengers began arriving at King's Wharf. A crowd of
locals waited at the landing. Word had gotten around that the Hollywood
screen star Gloria Swanson, a passenger aboard, was planning to spend the
day ashore. Swanson had been an idol of local moviegoers from the days of
the silent films, and here was a chance to see the celebrated lady in person.

Nor were they disappointed. As she stepped ashore, looking as glamorous as was expected, islanders swarmed around her, taking photographs and requesting autographs. The lady was friendly and accommodating. Meanwhile our reception committee was on hand with lists of those persons entrusted to its care. Plans called for a scenic tour highlighted by a visit to hilltop Louisenhoj and its magnificent vistas, then a luncheon at Bluebeard Castle Hotel Terrace, to be followed by a reception at Government House. I had arranged with my colleagues that Irving Berlin and his wife would be my special charges. It was a unique opportunity for me to interview this celebrated musical genius.

I recognized the Berlins as they stepped ashore from the ship's launch. Both looked exactly like the picture I had seen of them. He was a slender man of medium height, almost fragile looking next to his sturdy wife. He seemed to be in his early fifties, his wife somewhat younger. I led them to my waiting car. I had arranged for a chauffeur so that I could give them my undivided time and attention. When I introduced myself, Berlin's brown eyes flashed from behind horned-rimmed glasses: "Bandmaster Adams," he said, "I have heard of you. Didn't you and your band tour the United States during the 1920s? I recall I was in Philadelphia at the time working with a group of talented Negro musicians. We were pioneering in new fields of ragtime and jazz music, creating strongly syncopated melodies into a new dance craze that was sweeping the country. It was an exciting time. Some of these friends mentioned to me the uniqueness of an all Negro naval band that had come up from the West Indies and was on a goodwill tour. Several who attended your concert were impressed with the discipline of the group, the quality of the music, and the dignity and ability of its leader."[10]

At about 11:00 A.M. we left King's Wharf and the ever increasing number of passengers landing from the *America*. Our four-car convoy, carrying more than a dozen guests of acting governor and Mrs. Lovett, headed for the hills and a scenic tour. I was in the No. 4 car with the Irving Berlins. Directly ahead of me were Mrs. Lovett, Gloria Swanson, and two other guests. In cars No. 1 and No. 2 were Mrs. Alice Duer, George Armitage, Congressman Sol Bloom, his wife and daughter, and several members of our reception committee who served as drivers.

Finding myself in such close contact with a musical genius like Irving Berlin was like a dream come true. We talked music from the beginning and we enjoyed it. I told him that a quarter of a century before as a young bandmaster with a fledgling band, I had tramped the streets of Charlotte Amalie to the music of "Alexander's Ragtime Band," which popularized ragtime music in the Virgin Islands the way ragtime had been popularized on the U.S. mainland. "As you know, Adams," Berlin replied, "ragtime is of American Negro origin and from my beginning as a composer, its syncopated melodies attracted me. Moreover, I have a sentimental attachment to ragtime. 'Alexander's Ragtime Band' was my first big hit. It came out in 1911, and in those days it was a record breaker with more than one million copies of sheet music sold. It all began as a piano ragtime piece called 'Alexander and His Clarinet.' Its strong pulsating beats and rhythms attracted attention among some of my friends and they encouraged me to develop it. 'Alexander's Ragtime Band' was the result."

From time to time, Mrs. Berlin urged her husband to look out of the car's window at the magnificent views that were unfolding, but Berlin seemed more interested in continuing his musical discussion. "Don't worry, Mrs. Berlin," I said. "Where we are going you will see all this and more too."

"You know, Adams," continued Berlin, "most of my big hits came from scores I wrote for musical shows. Take 'God Bless America,' for instance. I wrote that song in 1918 for a World War I army musical show. It was set aside and forgotten. Twenty years later, on Armistice Day 1938, Kate Smith introduced it to the American public and it became a smash hit, one of America's favorite songs. Royalties are still rolling in to the tune of hundreds of thousands of dollars. My friends tell me that it threatens to dislodge the American anthem.[11]

"Adams, luck plays a part in songwriting. You try and you try, and then one time you strike it right; a simple and appealing melody, the opportunity to present it in the right place, and you have a hit. Back in 1919 I wrote a song for the Ziegfeld Follies of that year, 'A Pretty Girl Is Like a Melody.' The timing, the place, and the sentiment were just right and it went over big. It became a theme song for Ziegfeld extravaganzas that followed. In 1935, I wrote the score for the musical film *Top Hat*, in which Ginger Rogers and Fred Astaire introduced two of my songs, 'Isn't This a Lovely Day' and 'Cheek to Cheek.' Both went over big. These songs and songs such as 'Always,' 'All Alone,' and many others were simple and appealing melodies written for shows and films. Do you remember 'Oh, How I Hate to Get Up in the Morning'? I wrote that for that same army show way back in 1918. Where did it come from? My own experience. In those army days, I loved to sleep until noon, bugles or no bugles. Anyway, Adams, I seem to be doing all the talking. Let's hear from you. How did you get started in music?"

"Mr. Berlin," I said, "I grew up in a home in which music played an important part. My father was a guitar player. He had no formal musical education. He played by ear, not by note. He formed a local group of similar musically attuned friends, vocalists and instrument players who met regularly in our home. So from the time I was a child, I was surrounded by this musical atmosphere. At age nine, I received a small flute as a gift, and I began to teach myself to play. From that time on, music began to become a part of my life and thoughts, and I could not get enough of it. At age fourteen I joined a small band as a flutist. The band grew in size and later developed into the island's first native brass band. In 1909, at the age twenty, I organized the St. Thomas Juvenile Band. By 1917 this band had developed into a first-class organization.

"That year, our band was taken over by the U.S. Navy. I became the navy's first black bandmaster, and my musicians became the navy's first all-black band. I must admit, Mr. Berlin, the only formal musical training I ever received was a correspondence course that I took in harmony, counterpoint, and composition."

Berlin smiled. "Adams," he said, "to this day I am unable to read harmony. I arrange notes with one finger on a piano, and an arranger takes down what I play by ear. On occasions I have asked friends who are musically knowledgeable if I should take time off to study composition. Invariably, I have gotten the same answer: studying composition and theory might help you a little, but it could cramp your style, your freshness and originality."[12]

Our four-car convoy soon arrived at the entrance to Louisenhoj Castle. As the passengers disembarked, Mrs. Lovett approached me and said, "Bandmaster, my companion, Gloria Swanson, has been asking me about the history of this place. I am sure the rest of our guests are curious too. Would you oblige?" I said I would try.

"During the early part of the nineteenth century," I said to the group gathered around me, "a prominent Danish family, the Magens, lived at Estate Louisenhoj and controlled most of the land adjacent to the beautiful bay on the northern side and the harbor on the southern side. Upon the summit of the hill, commanding magnificent views on all sides, a modest villa, Louisenhoj, was built.

"Estate Louisenhoj remained in the hands of the Magens family for the duration of the nineteenth century. In the early twentieth century, members of the Magens family, before leaving the islands, sold their interest in Louisenhoj to Carl La Beet for $850. In 1918 La Beet sold the property and land around it, comprising thirty-six acres, to a wealthy American, Arthur Fairchild, for the sum of $3,500. Mr. Fairchild was a world traveler with a particular interest in Italy, Greece, and the rest of the Mediterranean. He was so struck by the beauty and uniqueness of the Louisenhoj site that he decided to build a dream house and castle on the stone foundations of the old house. A man of money and fine taste, he spent years directing local artisans to create a masterpiece in stone, embodying architectural ideas that he had gathered in his travels. So much for a very brief history. Folks, go in and see with your own eyes what he has created."

We were met at the Louisenhoj gate by Mr. Alphonse Nelthropp. "Mr. Fairchild," he said, "is now on the northern patio, entertaining Treasury Secretary Henry Morgenthau and friends. He has asked me to take you on a tour of the castle and grounds, and after that he would like you to join him." Mr. Nelthropp, a most gracious man, took us through the columned Roman gardens,[13] the outer and inner patios, and up and down stone stairways to the main rooms with their fine furnishings. Finally, we were taken to the base of the tower, where two persons at a time climbed the narrow wooden stairway to the top to witness a most spectacular 360-degree view. It was an unusual day. The ocean stretched in all directions like a flat blue carpet. The visibility was remarkable. We looked out on the Atlantic and its islands to the north and east—Hans Lollik, Jost Van Dyke, St. John, Tortola, Virgin Gorda, and several islets. We saw St. Croix to the south, standing clear on the horizon; Culebra, Vieques, and Puerto Rico to the west. Looking down from the tower's southern retaining wall, the entire city of Charlotte Amalie and its harbor unfolded. On descending the stairway, Irving Berlin said to me, "Adams, after all this spectacular natural beauty, I am ready to graduate from songwriting and try my hand at a symphony."

We joined Mr. Fairchild and his guests on the north patio. Secretary Morgenthau and Congressman Bloom were old friends. The secretary seemed intrigued with the idea of meeting Gloria Swanson and the Irving Berlins. Secretary Morgenthau recognized me. The evening before, as a member of the local press corps, I had attended an interview with him at Government House, where the secretary explained the reason for his visit and answered questions. He had come partly for pleasure as well. As the man responsible for raising the money for the huge defense buildup, the treasury secretary had been touring areas on the mainland and the territories to see what was happening. "In that way," he said, "I will be better able to explain to the various authorities what is being done with the money." He found the islands very beautiful, restful to the eye and soul. Next time, which he hoped would be soon, he would bring his family with him for a longer stay. When asked why the islands were being left out of the Selective Service System, Morgenthau said he did not know but would be glad to bring the matter to the attention of the president and the secretary of war on his return to the mainland.

We stayed on the northern patio for more than an hour. The visitors could not get over the overall beauty and commented on how well a gifted and talented aesthetic like Arthur Fairchild had planned his dream house to achieve maximum effect. Our guests were reluctant to leave. In the saying of goodbyes, I was within earshot and heard Secretary Morgenthau say to Irving Berlin, "I am honored to meet you. Your morale-building contribution to American patriotism through your songs and plays have made the workload easier for people like me."[14]

At midday November 12, 1940, our group of passengers from the SS *America* left Louisenhoj delighted with what they had seen and the hospitality they had received. The next scheduled stop was a visit to the terrace at Bluebeard Castle Hotel, where a special luncheon awaited. As we were getting into the cars, Mrs. Lovett came over to me and said, "Bandmaster Adams, there is a slight change in schedule. Gloria Swanson has promised to appear at the Robert Herrick School, which is not far from here. If the rest of you want to go ahead, we will meet you at Bluebeard. However, if you want to come along, I promise you that it will be a short stop." We agreed to go along. With Swanson's car leading and our three cars following, we stopped at the Robert Herrick School. It was a small stone building set in surroundings of beautiful tropical foliage. A gracious teacher, Lucille Roberts, and neatly dressed children were waiting in a state of excitement. Gloria Swanson went in, greeted one and all, made a short speech, asked questions of the children, then came outside and had a photograph taken. To a chorus of farewells, she left as suddenly as she had come.[15]

At 2:30 P.M. we arrived at Bluebeard Castle Hotel, where preparations had been made by the management to receive us. Spacious tables, each with a central display of island flowers, were arranged along the edges of the terrace so that the guests could enjoy the maximum view of the harbor, the city, and the hills behind it. And enjoy it they did—they moved from one vantage point to the other, excitedly pointing out to each other some particular area that caught their fancy. Finally, all parties were seated at their tables ready to enjoy. Irving Berlin, seated next to me, expressed his feelings: "Adams, this has been a most memorable day. It has been one beautiful experience after another. So much natural beauty everywhere. My wife and I are already planning to come back for a longer stay." Midway in the meal, Berlin pushed back his chair and said to me, "Adams, all along the way you have been taking notes. That is the newspaper man in you. But let me get back to speaking to you as a musician. You have told me about your humble beginnings and how you were drawn to music. So let me tell you something about my humble start.

"I was born in the old country, a small village in Russia. The date was May 11, 1888. My family name was Baline. We were very poor. My father was a Talmudic scholar and a cantor in the synagogue. Pogroms and their aimless killings were prevalent in those days, recreational outings for Cossacks. Even as a very young child I remember hiding in a dark corner of the house, listening to the passing hoofbeats of the horses and the screams of victims. We fled from the pogrom and came to America in 1893. I was five years old. We settled in the heart of New York's Lower East Side, abject poverty and pushcarts all around us. My father died when I was eight. Young as I was, I went out on the streets and tried to earn some money. When I got older, seventeen years to be exact, I became a singing waiter at bars. That is when I began to compose songs and sing them. The customers seemed to like them and that encouraged me. So that is how it all started. The rest is history."

When we finished our delicious luncheon, some members of our party went on a guided tour of the hotel and climbed to the top of Bluebeard's Tower. Berlin and Swanson did not join the group. They were too busy signing autographs for local and hotel groups alike. At 4:00 P.M. our convoy of cars took our guests back to King's Wharf, where after many fond farewells they boarded launches to return to the SS *America*.[16]

On January 7, 1941, Charles Harwood, a former U.S. district court judge in the Panama Canal Zone, was appointed governor of the Virgin Islands by President Roosevelt. Harwood succeeded Lawrence Cramer, who had resigned. A New Yorker by birth, Harwood was a graduate of Hamilton College and of New York University Law School. Admitted to the New York Bar in 1904, he practiced law in that state and was very active in New York Democratic politics until 1937, when Roosevelt appointed him to the district court judgeship in the Canal Zone. My relationship with Governor Cramer had been excellent, and I was sorry to see him leave. I did not meet the new governor until March 6, 1941, when I was called into his office. He was an impressive-looking man in his early sixties. He shook hands with me warmly. "Adams," he said, "I am happy to meet you personally. You have been highly recommended to me by acting Governor Lovett for the fine work are doing as chairman of the governor's Cultural Committee. Here is my first assignment for you. The artist Steven Dohanos of the Federal Works Agency's fine arts section is due to arrive here shortly on the cruise liner SS *Washington* to install murals in our post office. I want you to meet him, inspect his work, and report your impressions to me."

Just a few weeks later, on March 17, I met Dohanos at the post office. Workmen were busy installing his murals in the lobby. The artist, with his sleeves rolled up, was supervising the installation. I introduced myself. Dohanos was responsive in a gracious, friendly way. In a short time, I knew something about his background. He was thirty-four years old, a native of Lorain, Ohio. Already his watercolors, prints, and murals had gained permanent status in important museum collections in the United States. That year, 1941, he had won the competition to design the National Tuberculosis Christmas seal over many competitors. He was a member of the Society of Illustrators, and his present home was in Westport, Connecticut. The two murals for the Virgin Islands Post Office lobby were executed under the auspices of the Treasury Department's Section of Fine Arts and the Federal Works Agency's Public Building Administration, which decorated federal buildings with murals and sculptures. Dohanos received his commission to do the St. Thomas work as a result of designs submitted in an open competition.[17] After hearing the purpose of my visit, the young man said with a smile, "I will be happy to review the work with you.

"I suppose you want to know the reasons for my choice of subjects. First and basic is the desire to relate my mural subject to various aspects of the life of St. Thomas: to the island's history, past and present.

"Let us start with the mural on the western wall. Here is what I mean by relating subject matter loudly to the everyday life of the island. There before you are two heavy-set native women looking seaward. With their type of dress, calico predominating, and their wide-brimmed straw hats placed firmly on their heads, these women and others like them are common sights that we see around us and take for granted. In a powerful mural, you cannot take characters for granted. They project too strongly. Now look at what surrounds the two women. Directly behind them is a large coal pot with a heavy iron receptacle resting on it. Alongside is a large bag of charcoal. I do not have to tell you what an important part this type of cooking and cooking material played in the past—colorful, primitive, but effective. Heaped around these objects are large bundles of bright-green plantains, imports from neighboring islands, brought here by small trading sloops. And projecting into this collective picture are more than strong hints of the sailing craft themselves, a heavy suggestion of ropes and sails partly lowered. In midstream there is a less obstructed example of an island sloop about to take in sail. On a platform off to the right are two large fish, apparently tuna, waiting to be weighed, gutted, and cut. In all cases I have tried for a strong sunlit effect, emphasizing the objects portrayed.

"Now let us take a look at the mural on the eastern wall that the workmen are now fitting into place. Here is an example of what I mean when I talk about combining past and present. What do we see? An oversized sixteenth-century cannon occupying a large section of the mural. Nearby is a pyramid of cannon balls on a grass mound whose base is decorated with conch shells. Towering in one corner of that mural as symbols of the present are two radio towers. In the background with all of its red-walled antiquity is Fort Christian, the oldest fortification on the island. To balance that, I have placed a modern cruise ship on the horizon: the old and the new, the past and the present."[18]

Word had gotten around town that two famous movie actors, Robert Taylor and his wife, Barbara Stanwyck, were due to arrive in St. Thomas aboard the SS *America* the morning of April 30, 1941. In a search for a refuge from moviemaking and all the tumult that goes with it, they were to meet Johannes Rasmussen to preview the Caneel Bay Plantation resort on St. John. Knowing my experience with the governor's welcoming committee, Rasmussen had asked me to help take care of his guests. When the cruise liner docked, a crowd of moviegoers were on hand, eager to see two screen favorites in the flesh and possibly to get autographs. As our reception committee of two had planned, Rasmussen was to go aboard to fetch the couple while I waited on the dock below in the large car which was to take us to Red Hook, where we planned to transfer to a launch that would take us to St. John and Caneel Bay. When Rasmussen escorted the couple down the gangway, cheers broke out from the crowd, and there was a surge of people eager to get as close to their idols as possible. The couple responded to the crowd's friendliness. Taylor waved his arms enthusiastically and Stanwyck blew kisses, but there was no time for autographs. The couple was rushed into the waiting car and off we went!

On the way to Red Hook, I had a chance for a quick impression. Taylor was a trim, well-built man, a little over six feet tall, about 175 to 180 pounds in weight. His eyes were blue and set in a startlingly handsome face. I would have guessed his age to be in the early thirties. Stanwyck was as I had expected, a well-figured woman expressing strength and good looks and radiating confidence and self-reliance. I had been told that she was four years older than her husband. Stanwyck said to me, "Mr. Adams, I am surprised that we seem to be so well known here." "Well known?" I replied. "Had you picked anyone at random form that crowd, you really would have been surprised at what he knew about you, your films, who you played with, and when. Only yesterday, someone asked me if I had seen you and Mr. Taylor in the film *His Brother's Wife* [1936]. I said I had not, and he proceeded to give me the details."

"Funny you mentioned that one," said Stanwyck. "That was the picture that brought us together. It led to an 'on and off' courtship and in one of the 'on' moments, he proposed. We were married on May 14, 1939. Now we owe it to ourselves to take a good rest and a delayed honeymoon."

"What are you people doing? Talking shop?" said Taylor. "I heard part of it. Since you people know so much about my wife, what do you islanders know about me?"

I laughed, "I am an islander, and I will tell you what I know. I have seen many of your pictures. *Magnificent Obsession* [1935], in which you starred with Irene Dunne, is one of my favorite pictures of all time. Another one, your latest *Billy the Kid* [1941], I am looking forward to seeing. I hear that it is great."

"Thanks for saying that, Adams," said Taylor. "Of all the pictures I have made, that is the one I have enjoyed doing most."[19]

From Red Hook we transferred to a launch and headed for St. John. It was one of those rare days when Pillsbury Sound was as calm as a lake. Visibility in all directions was at its best. The string of islets—Thatch Cay, Grass, Mingo, and Congo—stood out above their waterline. There was Jost Van Dyke to the north and Tortola looming large and blue to the northeast. St. John lay directly ahead. "This is magnificent," Taylor said, "like a tropical Switzerland." "Breathtaking," Stanwyck said. Before tying up at the Caneel Bay pier, we instructed the captain to take us on a tour of the northside beaches, starting with those on the Caneel Bay side. We passed Durloo and Whistling cays and went into Trunk and Francis bays. At the request of our guests we got as close to the shore as possible in Trunk Bay. Taylor and Stanwyck insisted on stepping ashore. Taking their shoes off and with Taylor rolling up his trousers almost to his knees, the couple proceeded to disembark and to walk on the incredibly white sand. After pacing back and forth, they went into the water up to their knees.

Taylor exclaimed: "All this is incredible. I have never seen such white sand and such crystal-clear water. This is heaven itself!" At Mary's Point the launch turned back and headed for Caneel Bay. We tied up at the pier and went to the commissary. The Taylors wanted to inspect one of the cottages on a nearby hill. On the way there, we took them on a side trail to get a glimpse of Hawksnest Bay and the beaches on that side. Startling white stretches of sand carved into the dense green vegetation came down almost to the water. "I cannot believe what I am seeing," Taylor said, as Stanwyck nodded in agreement. The cottage that we visited was one of five on the plantation set up to receive guests.

"As you can observe," I said, "this cottage and the other four, all built alike, are constructed to withstand heavy winds and tropical conditions." Taylor and Stanwyck stood on the balcony and gazed in all directions.

"Who conceived of utilizing this magnificent place for visitors?" Taylor asked.

"Here is the man right here, Johannes Rasmussen," I said. "He saw the potential for developing tourist facilities here and urged the West Indian Company to acquire the acreage. He pointed out that the company was already in the building supply business and had architects and engineers on its payroll and a superb master carpenter, Nielsen, known for his ability to construct strong tropical-style buildings."

"God bless you, Mr. Rasmussen," Stanwyck said. "You have discovered heaven, and as a result, others will discover it. Put us on your reserve list for the entire month of August."[20]

Early in May 1941, the local press association, of which I was president, received an invitation from the Rebild Bakker National Park Committee in Jutland, Denmark. We were urged, as former Danish West Indian possessions, to send representatives to the annual Fourth of July celebration to be held in the hills outside the city of Alborg, Jutland. This year's celebration, stated the invitation, was of great significance, and the Rebild committee was hoping for a great ingathering of Danes. We contacted the local Danish consul here for more information, and he supplied it:

> You should consider this invitation strictly symbolic. I hardly think the Rebild committee in Jutland expects persons from the Virgin Islands to cross a submarine-infested Atlantic to come to Denmark with war raging all around. In Denmark, itself, the story is different. At the Lincoln birthday celebration at Rebild this year, February 12, 1941, thousands of Danes gathered to demonstrate their love of democracy and their spiritual affinity with all things democratic. As you know, Denmark was invaded and occupied by the Nazis last year, April 1940, and though the Germans declared that they would respect Danish neutrality and political independence, the Danish people do not trust them and are anxious to demonstrate Danish solidarity and determination to preserve not only their freedom and national independence, but their form of government.
>
> The Rebild Park in Jutland was a gift from Americans of Danish birth. It was dedicated in the year 1912. Danish Jutland was picked because it contains about one half the population of Denmark. In 1934, someone came up with the idea to build a Lincoln-type log cabin on a commanding Rebild site. The idea had tremendous appeal. Logs were marked and shipped from each of the forty-eight states of America, all contributing to the building of the cabin. This log cabin served as the core of a museum telling the story of Danish emigration to America from pioneering days. Early Americana occupy a prominent place.

During years of peace, quite a number of Virgin Islanders had visited Rebild Bakker and participated in the activities.[21]

The year 1942 opened to the sound of guns worldwide. The catastrophe of war seemed to be spreading everywhere: Europe, Africa, and the Far East. Here in the Virgin Islands, we sat restless and worried, reading startling newspaper headlines or listening to vivid radio reports, hoping all the while that the United States would not become involved. On June 22, 1941, Hitler's Germany, with easy victories on the continent and with overconfidence in its military prowess, attacked the Soviet Union. By December 1941 millions of Germans and Russians were locked in fierce battles. The nature of events told us that the United States was getting closer and closer to being drawn in. In March 1941 the U.S. Congress voted Lend-Lease aid to help a desperate Britain. President Roosevelt and Prime Minister Churchill met in the Atlantic to formulate a joint policy against ruthless German submarine warfare. To protect U.S. shipping from the increasing submarine attacks, the United States occupied Greenland and Iceland in April and July of 1941 and set up antisubmarine bases there. This seemed to make the Germans bolder. Attacks on U.S. Atlantic shipping continued with increased intensity. Submarine attacks in the Caribbean brought the war closer to us. Several times in 1941, the Red Cross called me (often at night) to help with boatloads of victims whose ships had been torpedoed nearby. It was a matter of feeding the hungry and finding dry clothes and shelter. In more severe cases of badly burned and injured people, we helped as stretcher bearers, moving victims to waiting ambulances.

When Japan, without warning, attacked Pearl Harbor on December 7, 1941, we knew that the die was cast. The United States was in the conflict on both the Atlantic and Pacific fronts. As a reservist in the U.S. Navy, I knew what to expect. On April 3, 1942, I received an official notice from Washington, D.C., calling me back to active duty. I was ordered to report to Guantánamo, Cuba, as quickly as possible. I got my affairs in order: I suspended operations as publisher and editor of the *Bulletin* as of April 9. To quote from the *Virgin Islands Daily News* edition of April 10: "The St. Thomas *Bulletin,* published here for 68 years, suspended publication yesterday. After lying dormant for several years, *The Bulletin* was revived a little more than a year ago by Alton A. Adams, Sr., who has been called to active duty in the U.S. Navy. During his period as publisher-editor, Mr. Adams, intelligently and objectively, did much to revive community respect for the newspaper."[22]

I had been at the Guantánamo naval station no more than four months when I received a letter from Governor Charles Harwood. It was a warm and friendly letter. The governor stressed how much I was missed in St. Thomas, particularly at Government House. He wanted to know what and how I was doing. In reply, I poured out my frustrations, my homesickness, and my unhappiness. The governor's quick reply brought me hope. He had gotten together with Captain A. H. Balsey, commandant of the Naval Operations Base at St. Thomas, and G. K. G. Reilly, commanding officer of the newly commissioned submarine facility there. Jointly they had petitioned the Navy Department in Washington, asking for the recall of Alton A. Adams to reorganize the Navy Band of the United States Virgin Islands. A strong case had been presented. A reactivated naval band in the U.S. Virgin Islands, as it had done before, would promote closer relations between the armed forces and the civilian population. Next, I received a cablegram from Governor Harwood telling me that the petition was well received in Washington and to get ready for transfer back to St. Thomas. In early 1943 the transfer order came through.[23]

Words could hardly describe my joy in returning to St. Thomas. Nor can words express my appreciation to Governor Harwood, Captain Balsey, and Commander Reilly. These gentlemen, led by Governor Harwood, had cut through mounds of red tape to effect the transfer. Also they had secured U.S. Navy permission for me to bring back to St. Thomas eight former Virgin Island bandsmen who had returned to active duty at Guantánamo. These men, I hoped, would serve as the core for the reactivation of the former United States Navy Band of the Virgin Islands. When the navy transport arrived at the West Indian Company dock early in February 1943, and we walked down the gangway, I understood the great urge that certain people returning from exile felt—the desire to kiss the home ground—for I was overwhelmed with such an urge. There was a crowd waiting at the dock to greet us, family, friends, and former bandsmen who had retired from active service. I passed the word to them to stand by because they would be, I hoped, essential parts of the newly reorganized band.

I could hardly wait to get to Government House to express to Governor Harwood my deep appreciation for his efforts on my behalf. Governor Harwood was very cordial. "Bandmaster Adams," he said with a smile, "as the saying goes, there was a method to my madness. When you left St. Thomas I realized what a tremendous job of public relations you were doing for all of us, particularly here in Government House. You left a gap that I could not fill. To put it mildly, your return is of great benefit to all of us. Call on me for whatever you need in reorganizing the Virgin Islands naval band." The reorganizing of the band was easier than I had expected. Within two months, twenty-one bandsmen were in training, many of them with years of experience. We gave our first concert on April 30, 1943, at the official opening of the submarine base. This initial concert was dedicated to Commander Reilly.[24]

I had hardly returned from Cuba and settled back into my routine in St. Thomas when a crisis arose. This time it affected our popular and most beloved government secretary, Dr. Robert Morss Lovett. Dr. Lovett was ordered to come to Washington, D.C., to appear before a congressional appropriations subcommittee, one dealing with un-American activities. Lovett was called to answer charges that he was a member of organizations of which communists were also members. Lovett was one of thirty-seven persons on the federal government payroll whom the un-American committee, headed by Representative Martin Dies, had recommended for dismissal. Dr. Lovett was a courageous man with an outstanding record in the field of liberal education at the University of Chicago and the New School of Social Research in New York. On the recommendation of Secretary of the Interior Harold Ickes, he had been appointed government secretary for the Virgin Islands. A man in his seventies, very liberal in his outlook, kind, considerate, and helpful to all who came in contact with him, Dr. Lovett had soon won over the hearts of the people of the Virgin Islands. An editorial in a local paper of April 29, 1943, expressed the mood:

> The charges against Dr. Robert Morss Lovett appear to be flimsy and unjustified. Because he has been a steadfast champion of the principles of democracy, liberty, and fair play, because he is a liberal, because he hates to see his fellow men live in misery and hunger, because he lives above political hypocrisy, he is branded a communist. Robert Morss Lovett is doing a splendid job here in the Virgin Islands and no one realizes it better than people who work with him.

Dr. Lovett was a good friend of mine. We had worked closely together on community matters. I went to his office and expressed my distress. "What are they trying to do to you?" I asked. Dr. Lovett was in good humor. His eyes twinkled. "Bandmaster," he said, "there is a big war going on and some people who call themselves 'patriots' are getting overly protective and anxious. They are worried about organizations I belong to, about the company I keep. What am I going to do about it? I guess I will go out and join a few more of those organizations."[25]

Like all other supporters of Dr. Lovett, I followed the newspaper and radio accounts of his ordeal with keen interest. Representative Dies, chairman of the committee, opened the proceedings: "Dr. Lovett, we call you here because your are an employee of the federal government. These are trying times. A global war is raging. Accordingly, I am not going to mince words. I think I speak for a majority of the committee when I tell you that we do not like the organizations of which you are a member, nor the company that you keep. How do you justify accepting federal funds and hanging around with a bunch of subversives—out and out communists bent on overthrowing this government? Before you reply to my question, let me say this—our committee does not have the power to hire you or to fire you. However, if we are not satisfied with your reply, we do have the power to delete from the territorial budget funds to pay your salary!"

Dr. Lovett was calm and dignified in his reply: "Chairman Dies, committee members, I am not aware of being part of any subversive activity. Nor am I aware of associating with any person or persons bent on overthrowing this government. I agree there is a war going on and human emotions in many areas are at high pitch, so much so that many persons are overreaching to rumor and propaganda. My associates in those so-called 'subversive organizations' are longtime friends from the field of education. I know them to be intellectuals, decent persons, and loyal Americans, as loyal as anyone sitting in this room. As for my answer, I see no reason to remove myself from these organizations or these friends. Nor do I wish to do so."

John H. Kerr, a member of the subcommittee, was next to question the government secretary. "Dr. Lovett, would you continue to serve in your present capacity if your salary was cut in half?" Dr. Lovett answered, "Yes!"

Mr. Kerr then asked, "Would you continue to serve if your salary was entirely eliminated?" Dr. Lovett replied, "As long as my services are not rejected by the people of the Virgin Islands, as long as the president of the United States and the Department of Interior retain me as government secretary, I will continue in office!"

At this point, Chairman Martin Dies said angrily, "I suppose you realize, Dr. Lovett, that your attitude will make it extremely difficult for us to keep in the budget, funds to cover your salary."[26]

On May 5, 1943, word spread throughout the community that political fireworks could be expected that evening in the Virgin Islands legislature. A fiery meeting was in the offing, with the full legislature from St. Thomas and St. John planning a heated protest to the congressional Committee on Un-American Activities in Washington D.C., objecting to any attempt to remove the government secretary of the Virgin Islands. It was circulated that the legislature would demand that all ridiculous charges against Dr. Lovett be dropped. Public feeling against the Dies committee was running high. A letter in a local newspaper the day before had caught the mood perfectly:

Someone should tell the Dies committee that we do not care if Dr. Lovett is a communist or a Turk. We are satisfied with him. Washington should be coaxed into sending us a few more registered or unregistered communists, or what not, so long as they possess Dr. Lovett's character, compassion, and capacity for human understanding. Who among us can forget that incident recently, when a group of European refugees, fleeing from Hitler's German and denied entry into Cuba and other havens, found refuge here. And why? Strictly because of Dr. Lovett. He opened his heart to them. He cut through all kinds of red tape. He made a deal with the government of Tortola to give them temporary refuge there until he could clear the way to get them into St. Thomas. He saved them.

The public had been invited to the meeting, and by 8:00 P.M. the legislative hall was packed. I had gotten there early and secured a front-row seat, reporter's pad and pencil in hand: "Rather than remove Dr. Lovett, we should get out a petition to make him governor of the Virgin Islands," Omar Brown, chairman of the legislature, declared that evening. "From my experience with him, Dr. Lovett represents the very essence of true Americanism. It is those persons who are branding our government secretary a communist who should be investigated for un-American activities," he added.

The Honorable Roy Gordon asserted, "If Dr. Lovett is a communist, then I will line up with him tomorrow. I'll sacrifice my life to see that justice is done in this case." Gordon warned that "if Mr. Lovett is removed, trouble would be stirred up in the Virgin Islands and I think that in these trying times, America has enough trouble on its hands to look to stir up a hornet's nest here." "In voting for this resolution tonight," Senator Oswald Harris declared, "I am doing what ninety-nine percent of the people of the Virgin Islands want me to do."[27]

Lovett had been tireless in his efforts to save a group of refugees fleeing Hitler's Germany. He contacted and diplomatically pressured every Washington official he knew to overcome the bureaucratic red tape that surrounded the entry of European refugees into the United States at that time. His greatest help came from Interior Secretary Ickes. As a Chicago newspaper reporter and later as a prominent Chicago lawyer, Ickes had become very active in trying to reform Chicago politics. It was during this period that Ickes met Lovett, who as a prominent and very liberal professor at the University of Chicago was also active in the political reform movement. Both men had reputations for honesty, integrity, and outspoken bluntness, and working together, they became very close friends. It was with Ickes's support that Lovett was authorized to approach the Tortola government and request that it provide a temporary stay for the refugees until they could gain entry to St. Thomas. As soon as an established family in St. Thomas offered to provide board and shelter and a guarantee that the refugees would not become public charges, the number guaranteed for would be admitted.[28]

By a voice vote on Tuesday, May 18, 1943, the U.S. House of Representatives, acting on the recommendation of the House Appropriations Committee, adopted a $134,000,000 deficiency appropriations bill. This bill included a rider stopping the pay of Robert Morss Lovett as government secretary of the Virgin Islands, along with that of two staff members of the Federal Communications Commission on grounds that these three individuals were unfit to continue in federal government employ. It was expected that strong opposition to the rider would develop in the Senate in view of the known opposition to the House action by both Secretary Ickes and President Roosevelt. On May 20, 1943, Ickes appeared before a closed session of the Senate Appropriations Committee to testify in opposition to the rider. Ickes said he had known Lovett for forty-five years and there was no question of Lovett's loyalty to the United States. "If Robert Morss Lovett is a Communist, then I am a Hottentot," Ickes told the closed session.

> The people of the Virgin Islands have known Dr. Morss Lovett continuously and intimately for the last four years. Their tribute to him is truly remarkable in its strength and unanimity. The two municipal councils of the islands, meeting in joint session, unanimously approved letters from their two chairmen to the U.S. Congress. The letters said the people of the Virgin Islands have found Dr. Lovett to be a gentleman, a scholar, a patriotic citizen, and a humane administrator. As professor of English literature at the University of Chicago for forty-five years, Dr. Lovett has been widely acclaimed for his teachings and his social concepts. He has written eleven books in his field and he was an associate editor of the New Republic for twenty years. His only son was killed in action in Belleau Wood, France, in the last war. Throughout his life, Dr. Lovett has been profoundly interested in civil liberties, the maintenance of peace, the rights of labor and an orderly and constitutional improvement of our economic and governmental procedures. This record obviously does not make Dr. Lovett unfit for government service.
>
> As government secretary for the Virgin Islands, Dr. Lovett is chairman of the boards of police, tax review, liquor control, harbor pollution, labor policies, lottery, and juvenile schools. His office acts as liaison between the municipal councils and executive departments. His work includes inspection of the three islands and giving advice on unemployment, relief, domestic, alien, and truancy problems. To say, as the Dies committee does, that the Virgin Islands can do without a government

secretary is absurd, especially with the present governor, Charles Harwood, spending so much time in Washington, D.C. Dr. Lovett's only
offense in the eyes of Representative Martin Dies and the House Un-
American Committee seems to be that Dr. Lovett has far too readily
joined or lent his name to almost any organization or cause that was
directed toward those ends that he has cherished.

In letters to President Roosevelt and Secretary Ickes dated May 21,
1943, Ashley L. Totten, president of the Virgin Islands Civic Association,
representing ten thousand or more native Virgin Islanders residing on the
U.S. mainland, branded as unfounded and utterly ridiculous charges of un-
American activities hurled against Lovett. "The native people of the Virgin
Islands," said Totten, "hail Robert Morss Lovett as the greatest humanitarian sent to the Virgin Islands since their transfer from Denmark to the
United States in 1917. As a matter of fact," continued Totten, "Robert M.
Lovett is without doubt, the one top official sent down from the U.S. mainland who earns the salary he receives. The Dies Committee has made many
glaring blunders in judgment. This is another glaring one. It will be a
financial and moral burden removed from the nation when this Dies Committee is disbanded."[29]

In an interview with the local press on the morning of June 26, 1943,
Lovett expressed deep gratitude and satisfaction over the many kind words
said about him by many friends and supporters in the Virgin Islands and
on the U.S. mainland. Commenting on the efforts of the Dies committee to
blacken his name, Lovett said it was unfortunate that the committee would
be pursuing a personal vendetta against him at a time when the country
was at war and when there were so many more important things to be
done. "The Dies Committee in its report," said Lovett, "has stated that if I
am to continue in office here in the Virgin Islands, I will be in a position to
propagate my subversive philosophies to you through control of government money spent in the Virgin Islands and that I could otherwise influence the native mind through my government position. You and I know
how ridiculous these charges are, but the Dies Committee continues to
maintain its stand in the face of overwhelming evidence against its position." Lovett hinted that he might file a case with the court of appeals,
which could eventually go to the Supreme Court, to clarify whether a committee of the Congress had the right to attach riders to bills that clearly
invaded the executive powers of the president. "The Interior Department,"
said Lovett, "is anxious for me to make a test case. I am considering it."[30]

The U.S. Senate by a voice vote on May 28, 1943, approved the $143 mil-
lion deficiency appropriations bill and rejected the rider declaring Lovett

unfit to hold government office. Rejection of the House rider was partly in response to heavy pressure from the Department of Interior and the White House and partly from senators themselves who considered the Dies committee's action, particularly against Dr. Lovett, nothing but a vindictive witch hunt. According to congressional rules, the bill then had to go to a House and Senate conference committee for discussion, stalemate, or compromise. Liberal newspapers in Washington and New York celebrated the Senate's action:

> An encouraging item in the flood of news from the nation's capital is the refusal of the U.S. Senate to go along with the House in a rider removing federal funds from the deficiency appropriations bill to pay the salaries of Virgin Islands Government Secretary Lovett and two other federal employees on grounds that they are subversive.
>
> The Dies Committee has been adamant, stubborn, and vindictive, particularly against Dr. Lovett, who they claim is the most dangerous and subversive of the lot. This in spite of a loud chorus of influential voices declaring Lovett as subversive as Abraham Lincoln; Lovett's patriotic services to his country far exceed that of all his congressional opponents combined.
>
> If the time has come when a man is to be repudiated by a group in Congress because he stands on his own feet and supports minority groups, then God help America! This bitter campaign against Dr. Lovett is by no means over, but so long as we have honest men in the U.S. Senate, we have nothing to fear.

This optimism of the liberal press proved unfounded. In a surprise and unexpected move, the small group of senators in the conference committee, evidently influenced by political favors offered them by their House colleagues, agreed to accept the House rider to the bill. This self-serving action of a few senators was a sudden reversal of the Senate's position. With only a few more days remaining before the fiscal year closed, this unexpected maneuver created a delicate and embarrassing situation for the U.S. Senate.[31]

When told of the conference committee's work at a hastily called local press conference on June 24, 1943, Dr. Lovett shrugged his shoulders. "Unexpected," he said, "but not surprising. Washington is full of political deals." In response to a question from a reporter, Dr. Lovett expressed the belief that the limited time left before the congressional adjournment, just a few days, would force an unwilling Senate to go along with the House and accept the conference committee report. Asked if he believed that the U.S. president, angry at the House for encroaching on the powers of the executive, would veto a bill removing from the federal payroll specific employees, Lovett said he felt that his matter was not important enough for the president to "lock horns" with the Congress. "Already," said Lovett, "because of delay in the passage of the Deficiency Appropriations Bill, hundreds of federal employees have not received their salary checks for the month of June. A factor that troubled me and continues to trouble me is that right here in the Virgin Islands, St. Thomas and St. Croix, sixty-five to seventy federal employees have fallen into this category of the unpaid. I will accept whatever happens." Lovett added, "I have made it clear on several occasions that if the Department of Interior and the people of the Virgin Islands wish me to remain in office here, I will do so. The shutting off of federal funds will not disturb me, as I am prepared to work without pay."

Lovett was wrong in his assessment of the Senate and the president's reaction. The Senate continued to back Lovett and, angry at being betrayed by a handful of its members, sent them back to conference with a strong message: "If the House refused to budge from its demands, the Senate was prepared to stay in session indefinitely and to stop the legislative clock if necessary." Also, word had leaked from the White House that an angry president was prepared to veto a bill clearly encroaching on executive power. Radio reports heard in St. Thomas on July 2 said that the U.S. House and Senate had finally reached a compromise whereby Lovett and two FCC employees under dispute, would remain in federal service until November 1943, when their appointments were due to come up for review.[32]

On July 12, 1943, President Roosevelt reluctantly signed the controversial deficiency appropriations bill into law. The next day, he addressed Congress on the issue. He accused the lawmakers, particularly the House of Representatives, of blatantly encroaching on the powers of the executive. "What started as a tempest in a teapot involving three federal employees," he said, "has grown into a major constitutional question that must be settled, in the courts if necessary." He said he approved virtually all of the bill except the House rider. "That rider," the president said, "is nothing more than a bill of attainder that provides punishment without trial and violates the separation of powers implicit in the U.S Constitution. This congressional action is not palatable, permissible, or acceptable under our American system, and the executive branch of this government will not be bound by it. The Deficiency Appropriations Bill, which I signed reluctantly," he added, "in so-called compromise form, provides that three federal employees would remain on the federal payroll until November 15, 1943, and would continue in office thereafter only if their appointments are submitted by the president and confirmed by the U.S. Senate. In signing this compromise bill, I have been placed in the same position as the U.S. Senate, having to accept it at the last minute as part of legislation to provide urgently needed funds for carrying on essential governmental functions. If I had been able to veto the objectionable rider, I would have done so, but that would have vetoed the bill in its entirety and would have severely delayed vital, indeed essential services."[33]

Not to be outdone, Secretary Ickes found a hole in the appropriations bill that skirted the whole mess. News dispatches from Washington, D.C., dated October 13, 1943, described his tactic:

> In a political maneuver that must have caught Congressman Dies and his "witch-hunting" colleagues with "their pants down," the Interior Department and its tough, crafty secretary, Harold L. Ickes, have come up with an astute decision that retains Dr. Robert Morss Lovett on the administrative staff of the Virgin Islands. Technically, Dr. Lovett no longer carries the title "government secretary" of the Virgin Islands. The Dies committee and its followers in Congress saw to that when they successfully and maliciously put through a rider to the 1943 Deficiency Appropriations Bill lopping off federal funds to pay for a government secretary in the Virgin Islands.
>
> Under his new appointment by the Interior Department, and his new title "special administrative assistant to the governor," Lovett will occupy the same office in the administration building. Also, the scope of his activities will remain substantially the same. What will the Dies committee and its congressional followers do about maneuvers on the part of Interior? If the Dies committee wants to go all out in a fight to oust Lovett from federal government services, there is nothing to prevent them from striving to eliminate federal funds in the next Deficiency Appropriations Bill to pay the salary for "special administrative assistant to the governor," which is also a federal position.
>
> It is doubtful that Martin Dies or his followers would want to carry political vindictiveness and irresponsibility so far. President Roosevelt's rebuke to the House and indirectly to Martin Dies, seemed to have sobered many. The important thing for the Virgin Islands is that Lovett is back with us in the same position, regardless of title, and in which he did such valuable work.
>
> In an interview with the local press shortly after his return from a month and a half vacation on the mainland, Lovett commented upon his new duties. "They remain essentially the same except for the title," and Lovett added jokingly, "I am no longer entitled to be called 'Honorable.'" "If I had my way," Lovett added, "I would have continued to test the constitutionality of the rider eliminating funds from the Deficiency Appropriations Bill to cut my salary. However, I am happy to be back in whatsoever position in which I can continue to serve the people of the Virgin Islands."[34]

11 Tourism and the Hotel Association (the 1950s)

Editor's Note: *Adams considered tourism the islands' economic lifeline, and history has certainly proven this basically true. (According to the* World Fact Book *of 2002, tourism accounted for 80 percent of the Virgin Islands' GDP.) Given Adams's economic determinist social philosophy, in which social progress is predicated on economic success, it is no surprise that he turned his social service efforts to the tourist industry after his final discharge from the U.S. Navy in 1945. As chairman of the Virgin Islands Power Authority from 1947 to 1953, Adams worked to secure reliable electric and telephone service. After converting the top floor of his large colonial-era home into a guesthouse in 1947, Adams began welcoming visitors with home cooking and tales of island history. Adams claims to have just broken even financially from his hotel venture, but to have gained enormously as a person. He tells of friendships formed with visitors such as cellist Bogumil Sykora, piano prodigy and activist Philippa Schuyler, African American intellectual W. E. B. DuBois, and West Indian statesman T. Albert Marryshow. In 1952 he again accepted a leadership post, this time as president of the Virgin Islands Hotel Association, a position he held for nineteen years. As had the navy band, the association bridged competing social interests: in this case, business and labor, islanders and continentals, large hotels and small guesthouses. Adams saw his presidency as educational. On one hand, he worked to help islanders understand the business dynamics of tourism, often taking unpopular positions against laws taxing visitors or raising the minimum wage. On the other, he taught the usually nonnative managers of larger corporate hotels that traditions in the Virgin Islands must temper business decisions. One vehicle for such community mentorship was his weekly addresses on WSTA radio. Adams's values remained consistent throughout his adult life. His work in the tourist industry followed the same philosophies of economic development and cultural preservation that he had brought to his musical career.*

The Virgin Islands' tourist affluence is no overnight miracle, no chance occurrence. As far back as the mid-1890s, St. Thomas was already gearing its development and the attitudes of its people to accommodate visitors. I recall that in my youth, at the West India Company landing dock, the first encounters with seaborne visitors were in small boats called bateaus. These boats, which could hold no more than two persons, were propelled with one oar by boys and sometimes young men who swarmed the rails of visiting ships to dive for coins thrown by passengers who would marvel with delight at the dexterity displayed by the swimmers to capture each prize. Similar feats were also performed whenever the ships anchored in the stream. The only unfortunate incident reported to have resulted occurred one day when an unruly shark deprived Jimmie Bo, the island's best diver, of one of his big toes. He limped the remainder of his days, but this did not in any way prevent him from carrying on his profession. Visitors on landing days would also throw coins among groups of boys who would chase them in the streets while evading the police.

Long before the swanky ocean liner and the jet, tourists sought the beauty of this tropical spot by means of the comparatively small passenger and cargo boats of yesteryear. It is not so very long ago that the Quebec Line's *Madiana, Fontabelle,* and *Guiana* were the only vehicles that linked St. Thomas with the world beyond its sister Virgins. In those days there were no travel agencies or travelers' guides to tell the tourist where to go and what to see, so tips passed by word of mouth. Tourists coming here used to flock to the western and eastern cemeteries, and many would amuse themselves reading epitaphs on tombstones of personalities from the past. And, of course, Bluebeard's Castle and Blackbeard's Castle would also be main points of attraction because of the gruesome stories—part historical truth and part entertaining legend—told about these two famous pirate landmarks.[1] When there were no travel agents or packet tours and no go-now-pay-after visitors, the chief Virgin Island attraction was the much-publicized pirate Bluebeard, who had murdered his wives in the tower, according to the version most frequently told. Visitors considered it a must to climb the spiral stairway leading to the top of Bluebeard's tower to view a panorama of unbelievable beauty and to etch their names on the inner surface of its thick, massive rounded wall.

Tourism was far from an organized industry then. Instead of the many souvenir and gift shops found today along the main avenues of St. Thomas, local wares were peddled by a small army of street vendors, mainly women and children. On such occasions as the arrival of the *Columbia*, a ten-thousand-ton vessel of the Hamburg-American line, the whole town would flock to King's Wharf on Main Street to welcome (and gaze at) the visitors. The tourists themselves were men and women of wealth and leisure who spent lavishly on such native articles as the dried pod of the flamboyant tree (royal poinciana), known locally as shack-shack, or the straw hats made by residents of Frenchtown. Cabs, the only means of vehicular transportation then, were decorated with the flaming-red blossoms of the flamboyant.

With the change of sovereignty, this tourism consciousness continued to grow. Realizing the economic importance of tourism to the islands, the Virgin Islands navy band was sent to the United States in 1924 to advertise the islands' tourist assets. The band also was lent to the municipality to play at the Emancipation Garden on tourist days and at evening balls held at the Grand Hotel. Places of interest around St. Thomas—John Brewer's Bay, Lindbergh Bay, Magens Bay, and K. C. (Kroth Canal) Bay, now Caneel Bay— began to be promoted. The owners of these pleasure spots were induced to develop them as attractions to visitors. The purchase of the Sachem Estate for a luxury hotel at the cost of $40,000 was urged, but the Municipal Council turned it down because it was considered an enormous amount of money for such a project. It was at this time (1931) that Pearson became the first non-naval American governor of the Virgin Islands. Pearson picked up the tourist trend and based the whole economic policy of his administration on it.

After World War II, the government organized a tourism committee, and it became obvious to its members that not enough was being done to accommodate the great influx of visitors. In response, owners of large homes were encouraged to renovate them and take in guests. I was one of the first to take advantage of this program, converting my home, a lovely old mansion, into the Adams 1799 Guest House in 1947. I maintained it as such until 1983, averaging about 120 room requests each year.[2] The building has nineteen rooms on three levels, and I used seven rooms at the top level to accommodate guests, which included three double bedrooms, one single bedroom, two baths, a dining room, and a grand parlor. Located at 1-B Kongens Gade (King Street), it was built in 1799 and was used by managers of the East Asiatic Steamship Company of Copenhagen, and government records show that the first private owner was the future governor Peter von Scholten.[3] It is a stone, brick, and marble structure on a rock foundation with walls four-feet thick that taper inwards. Its contrasting arches interest construction engineers, and the tray-shaped parlor ceiling trimmed with intertwining rings, all handmade, interested a team of architects from the Royal Danish Academy of Fine Arts. They spent a couple of days in the building and considered it a good example of Danish architecture.[4]

Frankly, I have never made money, nor lost any, in the hotel business. What I have acquired is considerable experience and knowledge through my contacts with the great variety of guests who have stayed under my roof.[5] My small guesthouse has brought me Cinderella-like benefits, for instead of going to a university for knowledge, I had the advantage of having professors, in many guises, come to me and actually pay me in both money and learning. I profited greatly from the quality of my guests over the years. Among those who made the profoundest impression on me were the great Russian cellist Bogumil Sykora, the lovely and talented Philippa Duke Schuyler, and the brilliant Dr. W. E. B. Dubois.

Bogumil Sykora, together with his wife, Julieta, and young child, Tanya, spent nineteen days with me, during which time I enjoyed his daily rehearsals and spent my evenings eagerly listening to him discourse on his world travels and relate his experiences with world-famous figures and musicians, many of whom, like Sergey Prokofiev, had sent him glowing testimonials. My most cherished moment came, however, when this internationally acclaimed virtuoso, the musical rival of Pablo Casals, honored me by asking me to orchestrate one of his compositions. The reason Sykora gave for his several visits to the Caribbean was the influence of the great Cuban violinist Brindis de Salas, whose brilliant playing in Russia had inspired Sykora to pursue his musical studies seriously. Sykora explained that he came to the Caribbean now and again to breathe the air that had produced such a master. Sykora was over six feet in height, massively built, but with a pleasing countenance and a warm, inviting smile. He had lost his entire family in the Second World War and then came to reside in New York City, teaching music at one of the universities, where he met his new wife, one of his pupils. She too was an accomplished cellist.

I was instrumental in arranging for Sykora to give a 1958 recital in the Charlotte Amalie auditorium—a concert that will ever live in the memories of those who were fortunate to be in the audience. He played the works of the great masters wonderfully; but the number that elicited the greatest applause was "Tears of Israel," a traditional klezmer melody which he rendered with such emotion that tears trickled down his cheeks to the fingerboard of his instrument, the rhythmic swaying of his body unconsciously inspiring similar movements by his enraptured audience. For several years thereafter we kept up a correspondence, until the arrival of a letter from his wife informing me of his death. I have recently received a letter from that talented lady, stating her wish to return to St. Thomas and perform the same concert numbers that her illustrious husband gave so many years ago. I have agreed to help her arrange this visit and am eagerly looking forward to the occasion.[6]

Philippa Duke Schuyler—musician, author, composer, lecturer, prodigy —was the kind of person that any race, community, or nation would have gladly sent forth as an ambassador of good will. She was the daughter of Josephine and George Schuyler, the distinguished writer and newspaperman. The first time I came across the name of George S. Schuyler was in an article he wrote in the *American Monthly*, a magazine published and edited by Henry L. Mencken. The article intrigued me, creating a desire to meet the author and to read more of his writings. This was in the late 1940s. It was not long after that I received a letter from Schuyler himself, then editor of the New York edition of the *Pittsburgh Courier*, asking me to write a weekly column on the Virgin Islands as well as a column on general topics and to review books for the newspaper—all of which I did for several years. This contact developed into a lifelong friendship with his family that lasted until their deaths. In my humble opinion, George Schuyler ranks among the greatest writers and journalists of my time.

I came to know Philippa when she was at a tender age, and grew to love her as one of my own daughters. It was from my home that she left, unchaperoned, in 1952 to enter the world of professional music with her great and dazzling genius.[7] Throughout her career we kept up a steady correspondence, she keeping me informed of her travels, experiences, and successes. Her last letter to me was written in 1967, just before she met her tragic death in Vietnam, where she was serving as a correspondent. This is how Philippa described our first encounter in St. Thomas in 1950:

> When I landed in St. Thomas, Virgin Islands, in March 1950, the strong winds whipped me vengefully, as they once lashed buccaneers' sailing vessels long ago. . . .
>
> After my recital, I stayed at the Alton Adams Guest House, an enormous old mansion that had seen pirates and slavers. Mr. Adams, the patriarch of the island, lived with his wife, and nineteen of his children and grandchildren in the proud, battered white house.
>
> Though nearly sixty, he would run up and down the steep, cruel, dizzying, overhanging steps that rose on the perpendicular hill that led to his historic home like an antelope—while I limped lamely behind. He is tall, dark, with keen blue eyes that miss nothing. Once a Navy band conductor, he is now a Patron of the Art.

One day, a lobster was prepared in my honor. . . . Some Virgin Islanders came to visit me after supper. As I had been covered with a painful mass of mosquito bites the night before, I was glad to be distracted by their tales of St. Thomas in the violent buccaneer era. This history was bloody, fantastic, and colorful.[8]

It was in the summer of 1922, on my first trip to the United States, that I met Dr. W. E. B. DuBois, then editor of *The Crisis* and the acknowledged spokesman of the Negro intelligentsia in the United States. The introduction was made by Harry Watt, a native Virgin Islander living in New York City. Our interview was, however, quite different from those of other outstanding Negroes I had met previously. He was cold and informal, his manner almost bordering the rude. I did not, however, feel hurt, but disappointment. I immediately sensed that this behavior resulted from the fact that I had brought with me, and presented publicly, a different attitude toward race relations—one which existed in the Virgin Islands under both Danish and American sovereignty.

Our second meeting, during the American tour of the Navy Band of the Virgin Islands two years later, witnessed quite a change in both the manner and attitude of DuBois. His reception was very warm and cordial. I believe that the band—its music and its positive reception—accounted for this change. Our music and bearing had spoken both eloquently and forcibly about our native sense of pride and self-esteem. No words were needed. The learned doctor was now most vociferous in his welcome, and he did much to make the band's tour a success. I was certainly happy about the change, for Dr. DuBois had been an early inspiration to me as well as other Virgin Islanders and West Indians. We had eagerly read and appreciated his writings, especially *The Souls of Black Folk* (1903).

Nearly thirty years later, in the summer of 1952, I was honored to have DuBois and his second wife, Shirley, as guests in my house. His visit strengthened and deepened our relationship. I did all I could to make my visitors comfortable and happy. I took pictures of them in their swimsuits while they swam at the beautiful beach at Smith's Bay, I introduced them to Governor Morris de Castro and other local dignitaries, and I arranged for him to give a lecture (in conjunction with Drew Pearson, another visitor) under the auspices of the Chamber of Commerce at the Grand Hall of the Hotel Italia (a building on Curaçao Gade, now extinct).

But the most stimulating moments we spent together during his all-too-short stay took place in the evenings at my home when the two of us discussed world affairs, particularly as they touched on racial matters. I spoke about my native islands and why I thought that because of our unique background and environment we held a different racial attitude than American Negroes. Indeed, as I explained, race had little meaning for most Virgin Islanders because we judged a person by his deeds and not his color, and we expected the same in return. DuBois tended to see everything and everyone in purely racial terms, but he admitted that he envied me for my indifference to racial considerations. He had a dry sense of humor, and his conversation revealed the deep love he had for his race. However, I found his broad genius and great intelligence somewhat disturbing and self-damaging because of his overriding preoccupation with race. And I often pondered, and still ponder, whether this great man was mentally still a slave—a slave to embittered passion and hatred for the white man. This concern so affected me that each night upon leaving his room after our discussion, I was possessed by an intensely sympathetic feeling for him. And I felt sorry for mankind because his great mind, which could be so useful to the world at large, had to be dedicated solely to the Negro problem.

What added much to the already lofty stature of DuBois in my eyes was his admission to me, during several of our talks, of the wisdom of Dr. Booker T. Washington's leadership over the recently emancipated Negroes, as that quiescent policy was essential for their survival in a still hostile society. As a consequence of this visit, a strong relationship developed between DuBois and me. We corresponded intermittently, and he sent me many autographed copies of his books. This lasted until his death in Ghana in 1963.[9] (It has always seem ironic to me that this great man, who joined others in persecuting the Jamaican Marcus Garvey for preaching his back-to-Africa idea, should have eventually made Africa his home and been buried there.)

There were others besides guests who came to the Adams 1799 Guest House, singly and in groups, to discuss matters of varying interests. Among them was T. Albert Marryshow, the well-known journalist, orator, and statesman of Grenada, British West Indies.[10] I first learned of Marryshow through a series of articles he wrote in his news journal, the *West Indian*, entitled "Fergueson Must Go." Fergueson was a leading British official stationed in the colony, and the articles were so forcible and forthright that the official in question did go—he was recalled by the British government. As a result of those articles I became a subscriber to the *West Indian*.

My first contact with Marryshow himself was through direct correspondence. I wrote an article for his newspaper supporting his plea to local authorities for the retention of the Grenada military band that was about to be disbanded. From his editorial reply I realized that he was acquainted with my activities in music and my leadership of the Navy Band of the Virgin Islands. The upshot was a steady correspondence between us lasting twenty-five years. We finally met in person during the Caribbean Commission meeting held in St. Thomas. Our encounter was dramatically covered by P. L. Prattis of the *Pittsburgh Courier,* who in his column reported on the conference:

> Folks, there's just so much to tell, I hardly know where to start. Maybe it was the first night I was here and I went out. T. Albert Marryshow of Grenada says to me "come on, kid" and I went. We all piled into an automobile. Along with us came Garnet Gordon of St. Vincent, H. Simmonds of Jamaica, Owen Brisbane of the Windward Islands, and Betty Phillips. It was just after dinner. A five mile drive brought us to our destination—the home of Alton A. Adams, first and only Negro bandmaster in the United States Navy. It was, of course a treat to meet Bandmaster Adams. You will doubtless recall that he visited the United States with his band some years ago and created a sensation. He and Marryshow had been steady correspondents for the past twenty five years, but had never seen each other. This was a great evening for the two men, a time when they were to meet in person after mental and spiritual communion for a quarter of the century. Throughout the evening Marryshow continued to mutter: "Just to think, after twenty-five years." This man Marryshow is well known in some circles of the United States. An excellent conversationalist, he held you entranced as he recited challenging passages from the works of the late Countee Cullen and from Claude Mackay. Never had I heard Mackay's "If We Must Die" spoken with greater stirring emotion.
>
> Of course we are meeting an unusually high type of West Indian at this conference, but it ought not to do any harm to some of the folks back home who think sort of big of themselves to let them know that these West Indians themselves are first rate men, well educated, cultured, experienced with broad outlook. Men like Gordon and Marryshow of the Windward Islands, [Grantley] Adams of Barbados, Anderson and Courtenay of British Honduras, Woolford of British Guyana, Simmonds of Jamaica, Wainsoota of Guadaloupe, Winford of Martinique and Christian of the Leeward Islands, hold their own anywhere and in any group. It would do your heart good to see them in action.[11]

The above-mentioned remarks in respect to the intellectual and educational stature of those West Indian leaders are no exaggeration. This was demonstrated in their conference deliberations and in a public lecture they gave one evening in Emancipation Garden before a large audience of cheering listeners. Marryshow, the principal speaker, was slender, well built, and personally attractive. His voice was so well poised as to reach the entire audience. He spoke for nearly an hour, interrupted often by lusty shouts of bravos. He explained the reason for the organization of the Caribbean

Commission and its broad objectives, concluding with warm words of appreciation and gratitude from the commission to the people of St. Thomas for their courteous hospitality which made it very difficult for them to leave our beautiful paradise.

I stood with Owen Brisbane in the vast motley crowd cheering this man's silver-tongued oratory and listening to what my forebears termed the king's English. I was, however, amused by the several elbow nudges from Brisbane, who during Marryshow's speech would remind me that all I was hearing was done on Seven-Up. He explained that besides reciting and composing verses for the several beautiful damsels who made up the visitors, all Marryshow drank was Seven-Up.[12] Marryshow spent the next day at home with me and my family. I then took a snapshot of him which I have in one of my scrapbooks as a memento. The last time I saw him was on his return from England, when he stopped here to see me for a few hours.

The gallery of stimulating or learned persons who have at one time or another stayed at my guesthouse is much too extensive to bear detailing here. Among the notables I would just like to mention the following: Mr. and Mrs. Philip Hemingway (brother of Ernest); E. Franklin Frazier, the noted [African American] sociologist; Allen Weinstein, a fine young historian; and Ushigmia, editor of the *Federal Bulldozer*. Three guests who made a profound impression upon me were Miss Nadia Madan, a nuclear physicist from India; Dr. William Kearney, a professor of journalism at Hampton Institute; and Dr. Amon Nekoi, a professor at the University of Ghana. They were all brought to St. Thomas by Dr. Alonzo Moron, then president of Hampton Institute, to give special courses at the local high school. During their residencies, we spent many enlightening evenings discussing a wide variety of subjects: Miss Madan on the underdevelopment, vastness, and richness of her country and the deplorable poverty and desperation of its people; Dr. Kearney on the race question in the United States; and Dr. Nekoi on Ghana's struggle for independence and present battle for economic survival.

Other interesting guests were Cornell Franklin and Stephen Kuzma, professional painters from the United States who came to capture on canvas the beautiful island that they had heard so much about. Like so many guests, they taught me much about their art and about my own island as seen through the eyes of others. And like many other guests, they were truly appreciative of the amenities offered by the small guesthouse as opposed to a large hotel. In a letter of appreciation they wrote: "It meant very much to us to have been allowed to see St. Thomas through the vantage point of your house [rather] than from some large, impersonal hotel.

As a result, we have the fondest memories of our stay there, and feel that we have a better understanding of the islands than many visitors do."

It is not amiss to make an observation concerning the role which small hotels played and are still playing within the general context of island tourism. While they cannot and do not attempt to imitate the activities of larger establishments, they nonetheless have the opportunity as well as the responsibility of offering a special sort of intimacy—personal contact between guest and proprietor—that larger establishments by the very nature of their size cannot provide. As new facilities developed—such as the conversion of two military buildings into the Trade Winds and Carib Beach hotels—the tourism movement grew and managed to keep ahead of the demand for accommodations.

Impressive and useful as were these efforts, they proved to be mere drops of water in the streambed of a meaningful tourist trade. Large and improved hostelries with know-how management were needed to house, entertain, and feed the steadily increasing number of visitors. The Municipal Council then followed the example of Puerto Rico in establishing a tax exemption law which encouraged the building of the first modern tourist facility in 1950—the Virgin Isle Hotel. I recall as a young man reading a story by the famous writer Frank Harris of how great and able men in times of national crises would come to the fore and take the reins of leadership. Harris relates that one day he followed a cart drawn by oxen rumbling through the streets with a heavy load of potatoes. He observed that when the cart traveled on smooth roads, the little potatoes were all happily perched on the top, but when the cart reached the rough and rugged cobblestones, the large potatoes would forcibly come to the top and the little potatoes would settle at the bottom. It was at such a moment, when the economic prospects of the island seemed dark, dreary, and foreboding and local efforts were paralyzed, that two men, Sidney Kessler and Benjamin Baynes, arrived on the scene. With incredible, abiding faith in the future of the island, they invested over $3 million to build the Virgin Isle Hotel and, by so doing, gave to the Virgin Islands a much-needed economic entrée to the elite tourist market. Two other essential ingredients for a thriving tourist industry were electrical power and a modern telephone system.

As the two factors which plagued community life, there still exist today those of electric power and communication. It is necessary, if only for historic interest, to relate something concerning the creation of the St. Thomas Power Authority. The purpose of the authority was to sanction a municipal electric plant and distribution system for the municipality of St. Thomas and St. John. By executive order of the governor the telephone system was placed under the management of the Power Authority in 1947. The Power Authority Board consisted of three persons—a chairman, a secretary, and a member whose term was approved by the Secretary of the Interior. In 1948 I was appointed to the board and elected by my colleagues as its chairman. The other members were R. C. Spenceley, secretary-treasurer, and Albert Maduro, member. Gerald Berne filled the place of Maduro after the latter's death. I served on the board for six years, and I take pride in the fact that we brought about many necessary reforms.

The telephone system was initiated in St. Thomas in 1906 as a private venture under concession from the Danish government. It was purchased several years after the acquisition of the islands by the United States and placed under the supervision of a naval public works officer assigned to local government. It operated in this way until the change of administration in 1931, when it became a budgeted activity of the municipal government under the superintendent of public works. Management was later placed under the supervision of a telephone board. This removed the system from budgetary control and permitted surpluses accrued to be used for improvement and extension. In 1947 Governor William Hastie transferred the system to the St. Thomas Power Authority. This system was of a local battery (magneto) type. The plant had a negligible value.

The telephone system, as well as its employees, seemed to have been neglected for many years before the Power Authority took over. It was not, however, until the impact of increased business and tourism was felt that the inadequacy of the long-outmoded system could no longer be tolerated in a steadily increasing and growing community. The blame for this apparent lack of foresight was laid almost entirely on the overworked operators at the switchboard. No one took the time to get to the bottom of the real trouble. The operators took both blame and abuse and accepted them with a commendable magnificence of spirit and patience. It was this situation that brought out my first broadcast over station WSTA to the general public. Fortunately, except for the low wages paid the employees, no problems of such a nature existed in the electrical system. Those which were found were caused by the change of the system from DC to AC. Another challenge was determining rate structures for commercial, industrial, and private users of electricity.

The first task of the Power Authority Board when I joined was to effect the required reorganization of the system. This was found imperative not only for the efficient working of the establishment but also for engendering a desirable spirit of good relationship between the public and the functionaries of the power system. This was done by the enactment of rules and regulations covering the rights, duties, and obligations of the general manager and his office staff, and by having the general manager in his technical capacity direct and control the activities of the system's field workers, such as electricians and lineman. The task of reorganization also carried with it recommendations of improvement, covering not only the duties of telephone operators but also the rights of these functionaries to decent and courteous treatment from seemingly irate users of the telephone, adequate salaries, adjustment of working hours, and arrangements for improved working and rest conditions for telephone operators and other workers. The governor was also requested to grant time and a half in cash payment to electricians and linemen for overtime work, instead of the former practice of granting time off. The important innovation in the new system was the complete ownership and control by the authority of all poles and lines including extensions. Also all telephones and meters in private homes were owned by the authority.[13]

Common interests banded the individual hotels into one group, and following a preliminary meeting on June 9 the Hotel Association of the Virgin Islands was officially formed on July 7, 1952. The first meeting is described in the association's own minutes:

> On June 9th, five hotels met to form an Association. Present were: Bluebeard Castle Hotel, Grand Hotel, Flamboyant Hotel, Trade Winds Hotel and the Virgin Isle Hotel. Caneel Bay Plantation, St. John, was unable to attend because of transportation difficulties, and Water Isle Hotel found it impossible to attend that day, although both establishments expressed regret and extended best wishes for the first organizational meeting. When the election of officers took place, it was proposed that Mr. Alton A. Adams, who was not present, should become the President; consequently a telephone call was made to him and he was offered the appointment. At the time Mr. Adams felt unable to serve as President, although he agreed to accept the First Vice Presidency.
>
> The officers elected were Mr. Ernest Gordon of the Flamboyant Hotel as President, Mr. Alton Adams, First Vice President, Mr. Reuben Barnet and Mr. Henry Kimmelman as Second Vice Presidents, Mr. Hein Christensen and Mr. Thomas Dell as Secretaries.[14]

Included in the amalgamation was a keen desire to preserve the beauty of the islands, to maintain their culture and local manner of living, and to protect their history. To destroy these qualities and attributes would destroy the attraction which brought visitors to the islands and to association establishments. In its bylaws the association dedicated itself to respect the people of the islands and their established community life. The principles and aims of the association were as follows:

1. To unite the hotels and guesthouses of these islands as an organized and harmonious body for the protection and promotion of the mutual interests of its members

2. To lend mutual assistance to one another to the best of each member's ability

3. To adhere to the basic principles of good and proper ethics in the hotel business among the member hotels of the association and with other hotels of other associations

4. To maintain ethical standards and principles common to all associations and hotels in their relations with travel agencies, transportation agencies, and agencies engaged in fostering tourism

5. To inspire confidence and respect for the communities and their people in these Virgin Islands

6. To stimulate and encourage tourism to the Virgin Islands in every ethical manner possible and to cooperate with all individuals and bodies likewise engaged in this objective

7. To offer at all times the services of its highly experienced and technical personnel in promoting tourism and the economic development of these islands

8. To cooperate with local and federal government insofar as possible and practicable in all matters in which hotels have concern and can be of assistance

9. To cooperate in the preservation of the tradition and culture of the local life of the Virgin Islands.[15]

It may be of interest to know why and how the Adams 1799 Guest House became a member of the Hotel Association, and how I came to serve as president for nineteen consecutive years.[16] One day in June 1952 a telephone call from Hein Christensen informed me that a group of hotel people were at that moment meeting in the Flamboyant Hotel to organize an association of hotels and had requested the membership of my guesthouse and that I be the president. To say that I was flabbergasted would be to put it mildly, and were it not for the seriousness of Hein, I would have considered the matter a huge joke. I asked myself what good my guesthouse of seven rooms could be to the association, and what help I could give to it as its president—since I had no experience whatever in large hotel operation. The only thing to do, therefore, was to graciously refuse. But Hein was insistent that I accept the offer. In the end, my guesthouse became a member, and I agreed to serve as first vice president. I changed my reply when I recalled the help I had received from Hein years before when I was chairman of the St. Thomas Power Authority. One good turn, I concluded, deserved another. It was a decision I never regretted. On September 15, 1952, I replaced Mr. Gordon, who had returned to the United States, as president of the association.

To celebrate its first anniversary in the summer of 1953, the Hotel Association sponsored a charity ball to benefit the newly opened Knud-Hansen Memorial Hospital. I delivered the following address over the invaluable radio station WSTA for the occasion:

> On Sunday afternoon, August 2, a vast concourse of people, comprising all walks of life in the community, attended the opening ceremonies of the newly-built Knud-Hansen Memorial Hospital. The event to me was one of the most touching and inspiring scenes I have witnessed for quite a long time in this island or for that matter any other place. The scene was indeed touching and especially so as the institution was named by a grateful and appreciative people for a worthy man—a man the memory of whose worth, humanity, and altruistic work may perhaps outlive the massive structure we now dedicate to him for the exemplary service he so unselfishly rendered during a lifetime of sacrificial devotion to suffering humanity.
>
> The editor of the St. Thomas *Daily News,* in commenting on the economic factor involved in the maintenance of this institution, calls it a "Challenge." He is right. It is truly a challenge to this municipality with its economic assets reduced to zero. The fact is, the institution is here. It is ours. It has to be maintained. It has to move along with the rapid strides daily made in medicine and surgery.
>
> The Hotel Association of the Virgin Islands, of which I have the privilege and honor of being president, has, along with other organizations, accepted the challenge mentioned by Editor Melchior of the *Daily News,* and is endeavoring to contribute its bit toward the maintenance and growth of this magnificent institution. Its primary contribution takes the form of a colorful dinner-dance at the luxurious Virgin Isle Hotel on the night of August 19. The proceeds of this undertaking will be donated to the hospital. For this dinner-dance no complimentary tickets will be issued. Every member of the Association is purchasing his ticket. Besides, the management of the Virgin Isle Hotel is giving the free use of its establishment. The $7.50 per ticket covers $2.50 to the purchase of the dinner. This figure represents the actual cost of the material for the dinner. All other things, music, waiting service, etc., have been gratuitously donated. Every cent of the remaining $5.00 per person goes to the hospital fund. The expenses involved in the distribution of prizes will be covered by donations from various business establishments in the island. Among these prizes is included a 3-day trip to

San Juan, Puerto Rico, with accommodation at the luxurious Caribe Hilton.[17]

The Hotel Association is keenly aware of its civic duties and responsibilities. It cannot be denied that each member hotel is an integral part of the very fibre of our community life and interest. It simply asks for mutual understanding, cooperation, and good fellowship. In this instance the Association requests your attendance on the night of its worthwhile endeavor. Your acceptance will go a long way toward proving your deep concern for the successful maintenance of the Knud-Hansen Memorial Hospital.

Let me say this here and now. It is my deep conviction that in the heart of nearly every native of this island is the desire to do the right thing and to feel the right way. And I sincerely believe this to be also true of those citizens from the mainland who come here to be among us and of us. As I watched many of the eager and happy faces from among the tremendous gathering at the opening of the hospital on Sunday, August 2, there was to me something profoundly impressive and stirring, due no doubt to the vitalizing magnetic current which emanated from the beautiful memory of the life and work of Dr. Knud-Hansen.

Let me cite an incident by no means rare, which might paint a striking picture characteristic of the man himself in the minds of those who were not privileged to know him. It was during an epidemic of fever in the community several decades ago. The physicians were all kept busy day and night, with hardly any rest or sleep, administering to the many patients.

Dr. Knud-Hansen had just reached home, tired after many sleepless days and nights, hoping now to catch at least a few winks undisturbed, when his doorbell rang and an anxious mother, insisting on seeing him, protruded herself in the hallway. "My child is very ill, Doctor. He is delirious and I'm worried over him. Please come and have a look at him," she anxiously pleaded. "If you do so, I know my child will get better."

"Nah!" gruffly replied the doctor. "I can't come. I'm tired and hungry. Go and get another doctor. I'm sorry."

Not to be so easily dismissed, the woman countered thus: "But I don't want any other doctor. I want you because I know my child would live if you come."

"Do you understand vat I say, voman? I'm tired, get another doctor. So now please go avay," he blurted out as he turned slowly away from the woman.

Crestfallen, the woman departed. She, however, did not get very far when a car stopped by her and a deep voice from within said to her, "Get in, my good voman. How do you know your child is going to die? Are you a physician?" Too happy to hold any argument with the doctor, she just turned on him grateful eyes and smiled through her tears.

In relating this incident, the mother remarked that from the moment Dr. Knud-Hansen entered her home, she felt that the life of her child was saved. The life of the child was saved, and he was seen among the throng at the opening ceremonies of the hospital on August 2.

It is said by a well-known writer that "to appreciate anything is to be deeply or keenly sensitive of or sensitive to its qualities or influence, to see its full import, be alive to its values, importance and worth." The tribute paid to the qualities of Dr. Knud-Hansen, and the value and importance of the hospital itself, is a most profound and beautiful expression of a people's appreciation and gratitude. The spontaneous activities of the two groups of softball players in the ballgame played for the benefit of the hospital are evidence of the spirit of helpfulness and civic pride which permeates throughout the length and breadth of this community.

Every human being must accept the responsibility of being a fellow citizen—a contributing member of the social group which vouchsafes him safety and protection. The hospital—any hospital—brings vividly to mind the thought that we are all victims or beneficiaries of accident. Whatever our station, be it rich or poor, we find ourselves involved when the economic structure collapses. That security for which we all strive is a delusion, for the result depends upon an infinite variety of incalculable circumstances.

Fellow citizens, my appeal to you this evening over this invaluable radio station WSTA is to urge your cooperation to the fullest with us and others in an endeavor to help maintain our hospital. Join us in our effort on the night of August 19. By so doing, you will be contributing something substantial—something worthwhile financially to this worthy institution. If for some reason or other you cannot attend the dinner-dance, send in a contribution anyhow, however humble, to our secretary, Mr. Thomas Dell, at the Virgin Isle Hotel. Remember that, to use the words of the poet Goethe, "the tiniest hair throws its shadow."

The members of the Hotel Association have gone all out in their efforts to help this cause. These efforts will be successful only to the extent to which you make it—by your cooperation, by your attendance, by thinking in terms of human service rather than in terms of mere dollars and cents. Let us keep in mind the fact that the real and enduring values of life come not from material possessions. Let us keep in mind the fact that the vicissitudes of life are various and the way of life fortuitous.[18]

By the 1950s the hotel industry in the Virgin Islands was a vast and highly developed one, offering opportunities to men and women comparable to any other great industry. It therefore required the necessary employer and employee qualifications. From the humble task of waiter or busboy, opportunity spirals upward in advancement for the ambitious to that of management. The required skills are a matter of training and education. The several attempts the Hotel Association made to have a training school for hotel workers established on the island are evidence of the knowledge and understanding of the vital role skilled employees play in the industry's success. Much stress is often placed on wages, and justly so, to protect the laborer, but mention is seldom made of the important factor of increased production to enable the employer to meet the constantly increasing demands of labor. The association believed that one way to correct this disadvantage was to train future employees, which is the obligation not simply of the hotels but also of the entire community.

Beginning during the administration of Governor Archie A. Alexander (1954–55), a program of such a kind was carried on for several years with a great measure of success.[19] Let me tell you about the Hotel Training School, its sponsors, and the names of those who attended classes and were graduated, thus disproving the assertion that Virgin Islanders consider hotel work beneath them. The school's letterhead gives the structural details of its administration:

HOTEL AND RESTAURANT TRAINING
SPONSORED BY THE DEPARTMENT OF EDUCATION
INSULAR BOARD FOR VOCATIONAL EDUCATION AND
THE HOTEL ASSOCIATION OF ST. THOMAS

[Personnel:] *Administrative Staff:* Mr. C. F. Dixon, Mrs. Lenora P. Williams, and Mr. E. Leonard Brewer, Coordinator. *Advisory Board:* Mr. Harry Goeggel, Mrs. Louise Scott, and Mr. Thomas Dell. *Instructors:* Mr. J. Antonio Jarvis, Mrs. Louise Scott, Mr. Harry Goeggel, Mr. Thomas Dell, Mr. Henry Wazney, Mr. Russ Eddy, Mrs. Kramser, Mr. Rudolph Galiber, and Mr. E. Leonard Brewer.

The graduation exercise of the hotel training program at the high school auditorium on Monday, February 28, 1955, offered the following program:

Introductory Remarks	Mr. E. Leonard Brewer, Coordinator
Address	Dr. G. Robert Cotton, Commissioner of Education and Executive Director—Voc. Ed.
Discussion: The Hotel Training Program	Mr. Thomas Dell, Secretary of the Hotel Association and Graduates
Presentation of Certificates	Hon. Archie A. Alexander, Governor of the Virgin Islands
Remarks	Mr. Alton A. Adams, President, Hotel Association

Graduates

Rita Bastian	Gerald James
Leale Battiste	Evelyn Jones
Florence Charles	Archibald Larcheveaux
Mavis Chinnery	Donald Marcelli
Gloster Dublin	Lema McBean
Olive Esannason	Eleanor McFarlane
Elaine Faulkner	Helario Melchior
Franklin Ferdinand	Margarita Melchior
Clarzissa Gabriel	Marion Nicholson
Gloria Gibbs	Aubrey Ottley
Eleanor Harrigan	Sonia Ottley
Elroy Harrigan	Rudolph Penn
Inger Parke Harrigan	Warren Petersen
Clothilda Hodge	Roy Raymo

In all there were over one hundred registered trainees from the high school, all of them Virgin Islanders.[20]

A booklet published by the American Hotel Association was the result of a survey of more than one hundred newspapermen and an almost equal number of hotel executives.[21] Newsmen were asked for suggestions as to how cooperation with hotels might be improved and for frank statements as to the faults and virtues of hotel executives in dealing with newspapers. As a result of this survey it was found that hotels get many millions of dollars worth of publicity, but they boot away opportunities for much more. The association also learned that hotels are especially vulnerable to some types of bad news over which they have no control, and that responsible newsmen know that and want to protect them. It was brought out in the open that the greatest difficulty which beset newsmen is the obtaining of bad news—for the simple reason that to attempt to hide bad news is a normal reaction, if an unwise one. Experienced hotelmen or other businessmen know that bad news cannot be hidden. Hotelmen were advised not to obstruct newsmen in getting the news, for in doing so, they lay themselves open to much more damaging publicity than if they helped. Hence the value of a good press relationship. The result of the discussion might well be extended, with profit to the general public, to include what might rightly be termed the community-press relationship.

It is necessary to have a clear definition or understanding of what journalism implies in influence, in responsibility, and in objective. Its influence may be truly gauged by what Thomas Jefferson once said of it—that he would rather live in a country with newspapers and no laws than in a country with laws and no newspapers. Journalism is a profession which deals primarily with news of public interest—events, conditions, processes in the development of public opinion or of public action. In short, it deals with anything that might have touched or may likely touch the public consciousness. In so doing, in its news and its views, it assumes a sacred definite responsibility in these two important functions of public service; or since these twin brothers, news and views, brook no conceivable boundaries or limitations in their infinite variety, they encompass us all. The functions of public service they embody carry a definite responsibility for the truth of that which they present.

Whether we choose to ignore it or not, the fact remains that the editorial page of a newspaper exercises a constant influence upon the opinion of its readers and in consequence entails upon its editor a serious obligation and a delicate care, to be fulfilled only when its responsibility is fully realized in every effort to use it for the public good. It is because of the seriousness of this obligation, which the free press of today assumes, that the Associated Press demands of its reporters and correspondents strict adherence to the creed of a factual, nonpartisan, nonpolitical news report. The byword of this leading wire service is "impartiality," and its guiding principle is "accuracy and responsibility." "Straightforward news," it points out, "is the only news acceptable to a press representing every conceivable political, economic, and social point of view in a free society." Not only the Associated Press but any responsible, fair-minded press, journal, or newspaper for that matter does, or should do, its best to supply this kind of news in fulfillment of the implied constitutional guarantee of the public's right to know. Another Associated Press staffer states that, while it would be a disservice to emphasize bad news out of proportion, it would be unthinkable to attempt to suppress news of any kind. "Nothing," he claims, "could be better calculated to destroy public confidence, quickly and completely." A totalitarian government, he further pointed out, may release only the good news and hide its failures. In a free country it is the duty of the government, press, radio, and television to report the facts, good or bad, for the strength of democracy lies in an informed people. In the exercise of its power, there are three ways by which we may judge the quality of a newspaper: its conception of right, the character of its service, and the realization of its responsibilities and obligations in a profound devotion to the public interest. Its performance in a community is of general concern.

It seems to me that the general community, especially governmental agencies, federal and municipal—like the hotels—need an awakening to a clearer and better understanding of the role that the free press plays in the daily lives of each and every member of the community through its power—its influence for good or bad in every aspect of community activity. These Virgin Islands are steadily growing economically, politically, and, I may say, in terms of press service. The major press services are represented here, as well as leading newspapers and magazines. It is my belief, however, that our press services, local and foreign, especially the latter, are often derelict in their bounden duty in giving the news, good or bad. Too often we either ignore or soft-pedal certain types of news important enough to affect adversely the community. Perhaps this attitude is because of a fear of possible reprisals of an economic nature against us. As an example, the press is often voiceless on many an injustice perpetrated on our people when men are sent here from Washington to fill high administrative positions in our local government in payment for some part they might have played in party warfare, a part in which these islands were in no way involved.

It was Alexander Hamilton who said that the liberty of the press consists in publishing the truth from good motives and for justifiable ends, though it reflects upon the government, on magistrates, on individuals. The freedom of the press has the guarantee of the Constitution of the United States. It is a freedom to be exercised for the protection of the people in order to preserve that hard-won liberty and for the security and progress of our public as well as private institutions. The press is the most powerful agency in maintaining that liberty which is considered the most precious possession of humanity. The press is to no little extent the guardian of public morals through its constant revelation of wrong. It is said that with most people the fear of publicity is a more potent influence in behalf of uprightness than fear of the law. Let those of us then who represent the Fourth Estate—the press, the newspaper, the radio—give serious thought to the ethical responsibility we have assumed and use our every effort as purveyors of news and interpreters of events to fulfill that responsibility wisely and sincerely for the public welfare. Striking evidence of the growing nature of these Virgin Islands is that leading press agencies, newspapers, and magazines are today alert to our happenings and often seek news concerning people and events connected with them. We should be thankful that through our press and newspapers we have a voice powerful and influential enough to reach the mind and heart of the great American public in respect to matters of communal concern.

After my resignation as president of the Virgin Islands Hotel Association, Mr. Thomas Dell, our former secretary and then manager of the Isabella Home Housing Company, sent me a letter which reads:

My Dear Alton,

I have just read in the Travel Weekly of your resignation as President of the Hotel Association after 19 years in office. I can only say that Mr. Bressler has a job ahead of him in trying to fill your shoes.

Alton, I doubt if any in St. Thomas realize more than I all that you did for the hotels of the Association and of the role you played so very admirably in fostering tourism to the Islands. I wonder just what tourism would have been like in the Virgin Islands without the guidance which you gave. I presume many would never recognize nor credit the progress to you, but then there are so many who never can even see the noses on their faces.

I am sure neither of us really knew the extent that tourism would flourish in the Islands—at least the manner in which it did. I am sure you also know that our efforts greatly assisted in taking out the bumps and straightening the path of the tourism course in the long road traveled to the present time. We must not dismiss the work that Henry Kimmelman did nor that of many others, likely no longer in St. Thomas, in the laying of the tourist foundation there.

I do hope, Alton, that you are very well, that life now is being kind to you and that you are enjoying the days remaining in your life of long service to the people and islands where you live. The islands should remember you for a long time after you have gone.

As for myself, I remember you as warmly now as I did when I enjoyed the friendship of our years of Association as well as the inspiration of your leadership and personality. It was a great pleasure to me to work with you, and I hope that every succeeding day will be most kind to you.

The letter brings to mind the many midnights for years spent over telephones discussing and planning association activities: presenting Christmas Day radio programs each year from the Virgin Isle Hotel, with script and songs rendered by the workers there, and times spent together in bringing to an often indifferent community, one sometimes hostile to tourism, the indisputable fact that tourism was the answer—the panacea to the islands' economic woes, if not guarantor of its survival—and the richness of the peoples' background and environment was a vital factor in the process and progress. All of these efforts and contributions were made possible by the help of

Thomas Dell. What Hein Christensen was to me in the case of the St. Thomas Power Authority, Dell was to me in the case of the Hotel Association.

The Hotel Association accomplished much over the years, acting with sincere faith in concerted efforts for a common purpose. I believe this effort has been made with the satisfying conviction that its work is not only for a special group interest but also, of more importance, for a community interest. The members of the association committed to their job with the vigor, enthusiasm, and determination of enlightened American citizens willing to live up to the tradition of the best service for the fairest price. Among my list of the Hotel Association's accomplishments, I would include the following:

1. Winning the repeal of the 2 percent tax levied by the local administration on tourists and other visiting guests in 1952. It was an uphill struggle that was successfully brought to a close in the U.S. District Court of the Virgin Islands[22]

2. Operating a training program for hotel employees, described above

3. Establishing a special fund for the pharmaceutical branch of the Knud-Hansen Memorial Hospital with a contribution of over $30,000, and contributing to the Damon Runyan Cancer Fund[23]

4. Contributing expenses connected in the review by the Supreme Court of the United States of the divorce test case *Alton v. Alton*[24]

5. Awakening the people of the islands to the significance of the hotel as a factor in the life of the community by means of special weekly broadcasts and newspaper articles (beginning in 1953), featuring not only the hotel industry but also the historical life of the Virgin Islands and their people; and, not the least important, the entertaining of visiting travel agents to the island

6. Becoming a member of the American Hotel & Motel Association

7. Extending the runway of the Harry Truman Airport, through the influence of Lawrence Rockefeller

8. Bringing to the attention of the federal government through Congressman Chudoff the pressing problem of water shortages

9. Calling vigorous attention of the federal government to the need for a modern telephone system in the islands

10. Sponsoring appearances of musical artists on the concert stage of the islands and helping to restore Carnival[25]

11. Organizing, sponsoring, and paying the expenses connected with a Miss Virgin Islands in the person of Miss Edna Golden of St. Croix to compete in a United States pageant in New York City on June 7, 1956

12. Organizing, sponsoring, and paying the expenses of a full four-year undergraduate scholarship given to a student pursuing a degree in hotel administration. This scholarship began with a fund-raising ball in 1975 and was named the Alton A. Adams Scholarship. The first award was given in 1976 to Ray Fonseca, who attended Florida State University.

These achievements have come from a combination of that basic faith in the purpose of a group and the vigorous promotion of that faith.[26]

A quick glance at the material side of the islands' rapid growth after tourism entered into the picture indicates how well these principles were carried out. In 1952 the total revenues at the end of the fiscal year were $1,533,000. In 1959 the figures presented were $5,224,159.95, with a possible increase at the end of the year to $7,000,000. In 1952 there was a budget of $2,250,000. In 1959 this totaled $8,000,000. The amount spent in 1952 for public education was $458,000, compared with $1,853,000 seven years later. The Health Department in 1952 was allotted $550,000 as compared to $1,000,000 in 1960. In social welfare spending, we find in 1952 the sum of $63,000 and in 1959 the revealing sum of $5,000,000. In tourism and trade 1952's total of $52,000 grew by 1959 to $221,000, an increase made possible by Governor John Merwin. These statistical figures were reflected in change of dress and manners, in the character of purchases made in the stores, in increased comfort and refinement of the physical surroundings. All reveal a rapid economic advancement. And if motorcars are an index of prosperity, we find further significance in the fact that the island of St. Thomas alone has a car for every three inhabitants.

These figures show the material side of the islands' prosperity, which in no way reflects its interior life—the real life—that is, the ideas, the passions, and the dreams of the people in the community. When taking into consideration the human factor in the economic scale of the islands' progress, we also find heartwarming improvements. Note the positions held by natives in government and private business today as compared to those held before. Look at the personnel in our Senate, courts (municipal and federal), hospitals, and schools, as well as the many modern houses built and owned by natives. This is evidence of the intellectual and economic advancement of the whole and demonstrates a sound, healthy, steadily growing progress toward those political rights and powers we desire, including the rights given us by the United States president to elect our own governor (since 1969) and to make our own constitution. Admittedly, not all of these advances can be directly attributable to the astonishing growth of tourism after the Second World War. Nevertheless, it is clear that without the motor of economic progress powered by the tourist industry, political and social progress would not have been as rapid as it has been in these islands.

Within the framework of tourism, the hotel industry plays a special and distinctive role in contributing to the economy. Thus the thousands of cruise ship tourists who spend a few hours in port actually spend but a limited amount in our shops, since they are going to other ports where they will also be looking for bargains. A hotel guest, on the other hand, spends more than a day or two here, and practically all his tourist dollars remain here. Tourism as an industry is accepted and is eagerly sought after by the entire world. To us, in these Virgin Islands, it is basic to our economy. Because of this, it must be zealously guarded and intelligently guided by means of an overall community planning superboard so that it would actually be of real benefit to the people whom it was originally intended to serve—a benefit, I repeat, not only in terms of dollars and cents but also, and more so, in maintaining values of character, integrity, and human dignity in the Virgin Islands.[27]

Editorial Methods

Mark Clague

The first notice of Adams's memoirs project is found in the *Weekly Journal* of St. Thomas in June 1973.[1] Alton Augustus Adams, Sr., worked on these memoirs over approximately fourteen years. The complete resultant manuscript, which is published here for the first time, seems to be the product of two periods of work: chapters 1 through 6, 8, and 11 were written throughout the 1970s and intended for publication as a whole, and chapters 7, 9, and 10 were added in the early 1980s. Over time, pages from the manuscript were separated and some lost, while unique copies of the three later chapters, along with a scrapbook and other manuscript materials, were given by Adams to Virgin Islands historian Isidor Paiewonsky and thus separated from the whole. Despite over a decade of labors, multiple revisions, and the assistance of two collaborating scholars, George Tyson and Samuel Floyd, the manuscript remained unfinished at the author's death in 1987.

The process of reconstructing the full text from among Adams's many manuscripts revealed the memoirs to be a collage of previous writings combined with new text, drawing upon a lifetime of writing and observation. The goal of my editing was to produce a coherent, clear, and accurate version of Adams's book while preserving his literary voice. I have chosen to produce not a critical edition but a scholarly realization informed by historical sources and archival research. It is hoped that this method presents Adams's thought in as compelling, accurate, and complete a form as possible and thus serves both general readers and scholars. Structurally, the body text and footnotes of the memoirs are Adams's own, and my editor's introduction and the notes at the back offer my own editorial and scholarly commentary.

All known manuscript sources for the memoirs are held in the Alton Augustus Adams Collection (AAC) at the Center for Black Music Research (CBMR), Columbia College Chicago, and the Adams Music

Research Institute in Charlotte Amalie, St. Thomas, U.S. Virgin Islands (AMRI). The sources used are detailed below. Although the materials given to Paiewonsky have yet to be located, they were published serially in his "History Corner" column for the *St. Thomas Daily News* between 1987 and 1992. Over two hundred articles containing Adams's writings appeared on an almost weekly basis over this period.

CATALOG OF MAIN SOURCES FOR MEMOIRS HELD
IN THE ADAMS COLLECTION

Note: The primary source that served as the starting point and authority for each section is marked by an asterisk.

	Sources (held at CBMR in Chicago unless otherwise noted)
Chapter 1	• First page of document with corrections, titled "The Memoirs of Alton Adams, Sr., 1889–1973"
	• Complete seven-page clean typescript, titled "Preface"
	• Complete thirteen-page typescript, titled "I Introduction"*
Chapter 2	• Seven-page typescript with light corrections and some insect damage
	• Twelve-page, hand-numbered typescript with light editing
	• Incomplete twenty-three-page typescript with light corrections and minor insect damage, titled "Chapter I"*
Chapter 3	• Complete nine-page typescript with light editing, titled "II"
	• Complete seventeen-page typescript with corrections, titled "Chapter II"
	• Clean eighteen-page typescript, titled "Chapter II"*
	• Five-page, heavily edited typescript about Adolph Sixto
Chapter 4	• Clean thirty-five-page typescript, titled "Chapter III"*
Chapter 5	• Complete eight-page typescript with heavy corrections, titled "The Navy Band of the Virgin Islands 1917–1931"

- Eight surviving pages of various revisions and expansions of previous draft
- Incomplete forty-seven-page typescript with light corrections, titled "IV"*
- Three-page clean typescript, titled "Public Library"

Chapter 6
- Incomplete twenty-six-page typescript with light corrections, titled "Chapter"
- Incomplete twenty-five-page typescript with light corrections, titled "V" (the label "IV" also appears)*

Chapter 7
- "History Corner" excerpts; see end-of-book notes; microfilm held at the Enid Baa Library (St. Thomas)*

Chapter 8
- Incomplete fourteen-page typescript with light corrections, titled "The Naval Administration: An Evaluation"*

Chapter 9
- "History Corner" excerpts; see end-of-book notes; microfilm held at the Enid Baa Library*

Chapter 10
- "History Corner" excerpts; see end-of-book notes; microfilm held at the Enid Baa Library*

Chapter 11
- Complete twelve-page typescript with light corrections, titled "Tourism and the Hotel Association" and "Chapter VIII"
- Incomplete twelve-page typescript with no corrections, titled "Tourism and the Hotel Association" and "Chapter VIII," with the "VIII" crossed out and "VII" inserted*
- Complete twelve-page edited typescript, titled "Adams 1799 Guesthouse, Its Compensation"
- Complete twelve-page typescript, titled "Adams 1799 Guesthouse—Its Compensation" and "IX"*

An appreciation of Adams's working method clarifies the nature of the memoirs. The deepest roots of the text are found in approximately twenty hours of audiotapes—recorded oral-history interviews done with the author on St. Thomas by St. Croix historian George Tyson in the early 1970s. These tapes were transcribed for Adams by paid assistants, so that chapter drafts seem to have been available by 1973. Comments from Adams attached to a grant proposal to the Virgin Islands Council on the Arts dated June 1979 state that Adams, a longtime professional writer, was disappointed with the recording and transcription process: "Personally, I do not consider taping to be an adequate substitute for the written, considered word."[2]

Examination of the manuscript drafts suggests that as his work continued, Adams became increasingly focused on the text, revising and adding material from his earlier essays, speeches, radio scripts, letters, newspaper articles, and other archival documents held in his extensive scrapbooks. While he identifies longer excerpts from his own previous writings that are woven into the memoirs, he adapts smaller selections freely and without comment. Many extended passages parallel earlier writings or seem based on such sources and contain verbatim quotations. When source documents for these quotes survive in the AAC or at AMRI, they are identified in my notes at the back. Thus the memoirs can be described as a collage—an artistic assembly of usually journalistic sources brought together in an aesthetic whole with new contributions to crystallize and express the thoughts and ideas of the author.

When possible, I have extended Adams's collage approach to fill gaps in the narrative with other writings by the author. My editorial insertions are detailed in the editorial backnotes to each chapter. Good examples are found in chapter 11, where the discussion of journalism is from a separate article unassociated with the memoirs but concerning tourism and the press, while the section on "Electrical Power and Telephone Communication" and the conclusion concerning the "Adams 1799 Guesthouse" appear to belong with the memoirs material but are not explicitly attached to any extant chapter.

Whenever possible, I checked dates and names in the original manuscript and corrected them tacitly if needed. Such a fact-checking process is typical of any nonfiction editing, but seems especially important here, as Adams's spoken interview and transcription process invited variants in the spelling of proper nouns. When a consensus arose from the sources, that common approach was used, but variants still exist on the islands today. AMRI librarian Shirley Lincoln on St. Thomas helped me check proper names and conferred with island elders on typical spellings. Standard editorial practice has been followed, and in most cases, minor editorial interventions, when not thought to change the meaning of the text, have been made without comment—for example, grammatical, typographical, and punctuation errors have been corrected or regularized silently. When I felt changes were significant or there was danger of misrepresenting Adams's meaning, my editorial adjustments to the text have been described in the backnotes. However, detailing each and every change, no matter how tiny, would have unnecessarily cluttered the text and detracted from the reader's experience. Further, manuscript errors were of uncertain genesis.

They could be attributed to Adams, to the typists he employed, or to his scholarly collaborators, including myself (however unintentionally). In summary, the creation of a perfect text that captured the exact result Adams would have produced had he been able to see his book through to publication was impossible, and to have documented every editorial change with unrealistic precision would only have misrepresented the result. Although this book cannot be identical, I hope it is close to what Adams would have published. Given the sometimes unfinished and incomplete state of the surviving source text, I have done my best as editor to respect Adams's work while using my historical training and research insights to offer an informed and useful version. The interested reader is referred to the archival documents that served as the basis for this volume for further clarification. Any errors remaining are entirely my responsibility.

It has been both my pleasure and honor to help bring these memoirs to publication.

Editorial Notes

Mark Clague

As editor, I have written the comments given here as backnotes. Notes written by the author, Alton Augustus Adams, Sr., are presented as footnotes on the pages of the memoir itself. My notes are of two types. Some describe the content of Adams's original typescript whenever I as editor have deemed changes I made to be significant enough to warrant fuller description and explanation. In contrast, minor adjustments to grammar, typography, or punctuation are often made without comment to avoid unnecessarily disrupting the text. (See Editorial Methods for further explanation.) These notes may also identify source documents, usually written by Adams himself, used as the basis for the memoir, if such documents survive in the Alton Adams Collection (AAC) of the Center for Black Music Research (Chicago) and the Adams Music Research Institute (St. Thomas). Items cataloged in the AAC are identified by series, box, and item number using the following abbreviation to save space: AAC§Series.Box.Item. Thus the code "AAC§V.2.10" indicates that a document labeled item 10 is stored in box 2 of series 5 and held in the Alton Adams Collection. A second type of editorial backnote offers scholarly commentary, additional historical information, or source information used for fact-checking, further reading, and research. These editorial comments help minimize changes to Adams's text while enhancing the historical breadth and precision of the project as a whole. For example, Adams's memoirs contain little detail about his second assignment to Guantánamo Bay, Cuba, in 1942, whereas I found information in Virgin Islands newspapers that affirms and expands the narrative presented in the memoirs. Backnotes 23 and 26 for chapter 10 contain this additional information.

INTRODUCTION

Epigraph from remarks given at the Adams Music Research Institute/Center for Black Music Research (AMRI/CBMR) "More Than a Bandmaster" symposium, May 10, 2006, Bertha C. Beschulte Middle School, St. Thomas.

1. W. E. B. DuBois, *The Souls of Black Folk* (Chicago: A. C. McClurg, 1903; repr., New York: Dover, 1994), 3.

2. Quotations from chs. 1 and 5 of the present volume.

3. According to the 2002 U.S. Census report for the Virgin Islands, 76.2 percent of the population self-identified as black or African American (see www.census.gov). In 1917, census data put the black population at 87 percent (Albert A. Campbell, "St. Thomas Negroes—A Study of Personality and Culture," *Psychological Monographs* 55:5 [1943], 5).

4. Adams, "Electing Our Governor," undated press clipping likely from the early to mid-1960s, when the Virgin Islands Constitutional Convention was occurring (1964–65), AMRI.

5. Isaac Dookhan, *A History of the Virgin Islands of the United States* (Kingston, Jamaica: Canoe Press, 1974, repr., 1994), 194–95.

6. Ibid., 144–47; social equality and respect, however, could not be created by royal decree; von Scholten went so far as to invite whites and blacks to the same government social events, but with limited effect.

7. See Neville A. T. Hall, *Slave Society in the Danish West Indies: St. Thomas, St. John, and St. Croix* (Mona, Jamaica: University of the West Indies Press, 1994), especially "Attitudes to the Future: Race and Class," 220–24. Eddie Donoghue's *Black Women: White Men: The Sexual Exploitation of Female Slaves in the Danish West Indies* (Trenton, NJ: Africa World Press, 2002) offers harrowing accounts of slavery's moral disorientation.

8. Campbell, 82.

9. An envelope from DuBois to Adams postmarked February 15, 1952, survives in the AMRI collection.

10. The shift in Adams's relationship with DuBois was likely facilitated by pianist and author Maud Cuney-Hare, who as an important contact and friend of DuBois first met Adams in 1924.

11. While information is scanty, Adams reports meeting with members of the militant civil rights organization the Black Panthers in the late 1960s, primarily to discourage their activities in the Virgin Islands on the grounds that aggressive tactics would create a problem that did not exist.

12. See Sylvia Stipe, "Alton Adams, Sr., Plans Memoirs to Help," *Weekly Journal* (June 7, 1973), 14, which quotes Adams as saying his "whole aim has been to give service in my life."

13. Tanya Schlesing, "Alton Adams: A Point of View," *All-Ah-Wee* (St. Thomas) 1:3 (1977), 30.

14. Ifeoma Kiddoe Nwanko, *Black Cosmopolitanism: Racial Consciousness and Transnational Identity in the Nineteenth-Century Americas* (Philadelphia: University of Pennsylvania Press, 2005), 5–21.

15. Von Luckner was known during World War I as the honorable raider "Sea Devil." He later established a training school for wealthy European and American boys aboard a four-mast ship that sailed annually between Europe and the Americas. According to Adams's son, this ship spent several days in St. Thomas each year during the 1920s and '30s, when the navy band would entertain on board. As a result, a friendship developed between Adams and Von Luckner. Several autographed portraits of Luckner are held in the AMRI collection.

16. The list of white role models here is from Adams's article "Passing the Dead Line," which draws heavily on the ideas of Thomas Tapper (AAC§VI.1.4).

17. Harold Cruse, *The Crisis of the Negro Intellectual* (New York: Morrow, 1967), especially section II, "1920's–1930's—West Indian Influence," 115–46.

18. In a Nov. 30, 2000, article, "Emancipation Garden Has Changed Constantly through the Years," Edith deJongh Woods states that the original Victorian bandstand was erected in 1879; *Daily News* (*DN*), 28 and 29. Repairs made in 1907 may well have been inspired by the founding of the Native Brass Band. The current bandstand, built in the late 1960s to replace the original, was renovated in 1997.

19. Adams mentions this date in these memoirs, and his son, Alton Adams, Jr., states that the article appeared in a local paper (personal communication, March 2006); the article has yet to be located.

20. Adams's navy service (service number 100 11 96) is confirmed by the National Personnel Records Center in St. Louis, Missouri, a division of the United States National Archives and Records Administration. Prior to 1825 all navy musicians were classified first as "seamen" and served in music roles only as secondary duty (Patrick Jones, "A History of the Armed Forces School of Music" [Ph.D. dissertation, Pennsylvania State University, 2002], 68). Pioneering black music historian Eileen Southern identifies Nimrod Perkins, a navy drummer aboard the *Diligence*, as the only black navy musician whose name has been preserved from the American Revolution. She identifies three black navy musicians as serving during the War of 1812: George Brown, bugler on the *Chesapeake*; Cyrus Tiffany, fifer on the *Alliance*; and Jessie Wall, fifer on the *Niagara* (*The Music of Black Americans: A History*, 3rd ed. [New York: W. W. Norton, 1997], 65–66). In the nineteenth century, as segregation and discrimination increasingly became the rule in the U.S. Navy, a musician's service classification was no longer readily available to blacks. In 1942 the NAACP petitioned the government for greater opportunity, and soon all-black navy bands were formed from the graduates of the navy's black music school at Great Lakes NTS. (See Samuel A. Floyd, Jr., *The Great Lakes Experience, 1942–1945* [Carbondale: Black American Studies Program, Southern Illinois University, 1974]; a revised version of the same title is found in *The Black Perspective in Music* 3:5 [Spring 1975], 17–24, and an additional article by Floyd, "An Oral History: The Great Lakes Experience," is found in *The Black Perspective in Music* (*BPIM*) 11:1 [Spring 1983], 41–61.) It is certain that more early black navy musicians have yet to be identified. Samuel Floyd has copies of photographs of black musicians playing aboard navy ships prior to World War I,

usually in racially integrated groupings, but these musicians' talents were not recognized as such. They worked officially as shipboard regulars in the kitchens or as officers' servants. Adams and his bandsmen, on the other hand, were classified as musicians and paid at regular navy rates for musicians. Jones has identified apparently black musicians among the students in navy music school photos prior to and just after World War I (106–9). Further, Adams's band was not the first band of color in the U.S. Navy. On tour in the Philippines in 1908, the flagship *Georgia* enlisted the services of twenty-five Filipino musicians who became the "Filipino Band of the U.S.S. Georgia." The band was active until at least 1911, but was directed by a series of noncolored navy bandmasters, including Frank Zangari (an Italian). The players were multi-instrumentalists who performed in three guises—as band, orchestra, or mandolin club. (See Gustav Saenger, "A Representative Filipino Band," *The Metronome* 27:6 [June 1911], 15.) It is not certain how these musicians were classified in navy records or paid. African American newspapers such as the *New York Age* did cover Filipino news in 1924 and treated Filipinos as among the "colored" races (see "Filipinos at Annapolis," *New York Age* [May 20, 1922], 4). This ensemble is distinguished from Adams's unit in that it did not have a director of color and was attached to an American ship. Rather, its musicians were cultural ambassadors. It seems likely that the training of these musicians might have been affiliated, if only indirectly, with the activities of the African American band director Col. Walter H. Loving, who directed the U.S. Army's Philippine Constabulary Band (and orchestra) from 1902 to 1916 (see Claiborne T. Richardson, "The Filipino-American Phenomenon: The Loving Touch," *The Black Perspective in Music* 10:1 [Spring 1982], 2–28).

21. A typical period of service with any one navy band remains two to three years; other than Adams's band, the only musical exception to this practice is the United States Navy Band in Washington, D.C., which was founded later than Adams's unit, in 1925. The ability of these bands to keep personnel together for longer periods of time no doubt contributed to their superior quality. The excellence of Adams's own band was further motivated by the political import of its position; knowing they represented their race, Adams and his band worked hard to honor this responsibility.

22. The rank of chief petty officer topped the enlisted (noncommissioned officer) hierarchy during World War I and carried with it considerable honor and responsibility for leadership. It was typical up through World War II for noncommissioned officers to lead navy bands. In fact, it took the popularity and prestige of John Philip Sousa to first place a bandleader in the ranks of commissioned officers. Sousa received the rank of lieutenant when he enlisted at age sixty-two in 1917 (Paul E. Bierly, *John Philip Sousa: American Phenomenon* [Englewood Cliffs, NJ: Prentice-Hall, 1973], 77–78). Further prestige was given to navy bands in 1925 with the founding of the United States Navy Band (previously the Washington Navy Yard Band) and the subsequent elevation of leader Charles Benter to the rank of lieutenant. Through World War II the only bands to have commissioned officers as leaders were the U.S. Navy Band in

Washington and the Naval Academy Band. All unit bands had enlisted band-leaders (Jones, 72–73). As of 2006, bandleaders are typically commissioned officers ranging from O1-Ensign through O6-Captain.

23. This publication may be a unique effort in the history of the U.S. Navy, in particular because its weekly issues were not given away, but sold for eight cents each (see April 22, 1922, issue—AAC§VII.1.4).

24. A brief item in the New York *Amsterdam News* of October 24, 1928, states that Adams was in New York, staying with Romeo L. Dougherty, theater and drama writer for the same newspaper. Adams returned to the islands on the steamship *Lorenzo* of the New York and Porto Rico Line (AMRI).

25. Samuel Coleridge-Taylor (1875–1912), a black British composer and conductor, directed the U.S. Marine Band in Washington, D.C., in 1901 and conducted white orchestras in New York during a 1910 U.S. visit. Born in the Danish West Indies, Adams possessed the same European pedigree as Coleridge-Taylor, which may have helped him ascend the podium as well—with the critical difference that the Virgin Islands were by then part of the United States.

26. Racially integrated bands were not otherwise sanctioned in the navy until after 1948. Musician 1st Class James B. Parsons was the first black navy bandmaster of World War II; he led the all-black Navy Band B-1, which began training in May 1942 and was stationed in Chapel Hill that July (Jones, 112–14).

27. Adams's letter of release from the U.S. Fleet Reserve is dated May 11, 1945 (AMRI).

28. See Mark Clague, "Alton Augustus Adams, Sr.," in *International Dictionary of Black Composers*, vol. 1, edited by Samuel Floyd (Chicago: Fitzroy Dearborn, 1999). While many histories prominent in band scholarship fail to mention Adams, this is not indicative of racism per se. The nineteenth-century black bandmaster Frank Johnson lived in Philadelphia, and much of his music was published in piano arrangements during his lifetime. His name appears regularly in these same histories because information on him has been readily available.

29. New World Records LP 266, 1976; released as CD 80266; Samuel Floyd, "Alton Augustus Adams: The First Black Bandmaster in the United States Navy," *The Black Perspective in Music* 5:2 (Fall 1977), 173–87; Raoul F. Camus, ed., *American Wind and Percussion Music*, Three Centuries of American Music, vol. 12 ([Boston]: G. K. Hall, 1992); brief biography on page xl based on Floyd 1977; full score on 323–36.

30. Exceptions here are the various editions of *Who's Who in Colored America* that mention Adams (see, for example, 1st ed. [1927], 1; 3rd ed. [1932], 1–2; and 7th ed. [1950], 58), as well as D. Antoinette Handy's *Black Conductors* (Metuchen, NJ: Scarecrow Press, 1995), 483, which is based on Floyd 1977.

31. Three of these scrapbooks are held in the CBMR Archives. At least one was given to St. Thomas historian Isidor Paiewonsky and has yet to be located.

32. Draft of introduction held in AAC; one black narrative that Adams fails to mention is *The History of Mary Prince: A West Indian Slave, Related by Herself . . .* , first published in 1831 by F. Westley and A. H. Davis in London (repr., New York: Dover, 2004).

33. AAC: from early typescript to ch. 2. According to the "Introduction" to the finding aid for Record Group 55 at the National Archives, materials were shipped from the islands to the Federal Records Center in Alexandria, Virginia, in two accessions, the first in April and the second in June 1954. The first shipment was from St. Thomas and is presumably the project with which Adams was involved.

34. Grant proposal to Virgin Islands Council on the Arts, June 1979 (AAC§V.1.10).

35. Personal communication with Gwendolyn Adams, June 23, 1998.

36. See Adams, "Dedicated to the Memory of JPS, Leading Bandmaster of His Time," *Focus* (April 4, 1971), 6 and 14 (AAC§VI.1.19–20).

37. Letter from Goldman to Adams, Feb. 2, 1937 (AAC§II.2.22).

38. Adams's brief letter of application is found in the AAC (§II.2.24), as is Goldman's letter of March 9 (§II.2.26). In his essays on both Sousa and Goldman held in the AAC, Adams notes that he never received a letter of acceptance from the ABA. A subsequent letter from Goldman dated Feb. 22, 1938 (AAC§II.2.28), makes no mention of the ABA situation.

39. "Candidates Proposed and Elected," Minutes of 1937, p. 3; "Secretary's Report" in Official Convention Minutes, 1939, p. 1, series II.5.1, American Bandmasters Association Archives, University of Maryland.

40. On March 3, 2006, the ABA granted Adams its first posthumous membership; he was formally inducted on May 10 and 12, 2006, in the Virgin Islands at two events held in his honor: a scholarly symposium and a concert by the Navy Ceremonial Band (see "Bandmaster Alton Adams Honored Posthumously," *St. Thomas Source* [March 25, 2006]; and Ananta Pachem, "American Bandmasters Membership Finally Extended to Alton Adams at Colloquium Celebrating His Life," *St. Thomas Source* [May 10, 2006]).

41. Stuart Hall, "Negotiating Caribbean Identities," in *New Caribbean Thought: A Reader*, ed. Brian Meeks and Folke Lindahl (Mona, Jamaica: University of West Indies Press, 2001), 24–39 (quote on 26).

42. From an early draft of his opening chapter (untitled six-page edited typescript in AAC, ca. 1972). Similar verbiage is also used in a memoirs-related grant proposal (see AAC§V.1.10).

43. Sandra Pouchet Paquet, *Caribbean Autobiography: Cultural Identity and Self-Representation* (Madison: University of Wisconsin Press, 2002).

44. Ruth Moolenaar, *Profiles of Outstanding Virgin Islanders*, 3rd ed. (St. Thomas, VI: Department of Education, 1992); Ruth M. Moolenaar, *Legacies of Upstreet: The Transformation of a Virgin Islands Neighborhood* (St. Thomas, VI: We From Upstreet, Inc., 2005).

45. Ogese T. McKay, *Now It Can Be Told: An Autobiography* (St. Croix, US VI: Caribbean Printing, 1991); Karen C. Thurland, *Peter G. Thurland, Sr.: Master Cabinetmaker and Bandleader* (St. Croix, US VI: Antilles Graphic Arts, 1994).

46. Using financial support from the GI Bill, Adams also studied writing via correspondence from 1952 to 1954 with the Palmer Institute of Authorship in Hollywood, California, taking courses in both article and fiction writing. His assignments and correspondence are preserved in AAC§VI.2.1–67.

47. Dookhan, 274–77.

CHAPTER 1. A HISTORICAL MEMOIR

1. Hardanger is a form of geometric white-work lace with roots in Norway.

2. Adams cites Arnold's definition of culture, "a knowledge of the best that has been said and done in the world." The text quoted here comes from the preface to Arnold's 1873 book, *Literature and Dogma.*

3. Burnham was premier (prime minister) of Guyana from 1964 to 1980 and president from 1980 to 1985. British Guiana became independent Guyana in 1966.

4. In an earlier version of this section, Adams lists the following authors: Emily and Charlotte Brontë, Robert Browning, Edward Bulwer-Lytton, John Bunyan, Lord Byron, Anton Chekhov, Alexander Dumas, Gustave Flaubert, Oliver Goldsmith, William Hazlitt, Victor Hugo, Blasco Ibanez, John Keats, Henry Wadsworth Longfellow, Pierre Lotti, Thomas Babington Macaulay, Guy de Maupassant, Edgar Allan Poe, François Rabelais, Jean-Jacques Rousseau, John Ruskin, Percy Bysshe Shelley, Alfred Lord Tennyson, Ivan Turgenev, and Walt Whitman (AAC§VI.1.5).

5. One might surmise that the "charmingly elderly gentleman" as well as one of the islanders who opened their homes to the author was likely Adams himself. Known as the dean of the Virgin Islands press corps, Adams had long been valued by journalists for his knowledge of local history.

6. Adams indicates no source; probably a local press clipping. Olympio was born in 1902 and died in a 1963 coup. He served as prime minister of Togo from 1958 to 1961 and president from 1961 to 1963.

CHAPTER 2. THE ST. THOMAS CRAFTSMEN
OF THE NINETEENTH CENTURY

1. The record of Adams's baptism at Frederick Lutheran Church confirms this date. He was baptized on March 23, 1890 (p. 221).

2. Savan is a neighborhood east of Bluebeard's Hill and north of Market Square in Charlotte Amalie, St. Thomas.

3. The 1916 date for the stroke is provided by Jacob Adams's death notice in *DN* (Feb. 17, 1919) and *St. Croix Avis* (Feb. 21, 1919, 1), which states that his stroke occurred three years before his death. These articles also place him as a member of Old Unity Lodge No. 356 and list his employer as the St. Thomas Dock, Coaling, and Engineering Company.

4. Adams's manuscript reads "Odd Fellows Lodge" at this point; corrected to match obituary (see previous note).

5. Middle name provided by Enid Adams Questel, personal communication, May 30, 2005.

6. The term *governess* implies superior manners and education; a more usual term would have been *house maid*, although an almost familial relationship among domestics and their employers was expected in St. Thomas.

7. Birth records for Adams's parents have yet to be located. Adams's manuscript gives a birth date of 1872, yet the census of 1900 states that Adams's mother was older than his father. Adams gives his father's birth date as 1860 but states that he died in 1919 at the age of fifty-seven—an error of two years. Although it is an educated guess, it seems possible that Adams would be more likely to mix up birth years than he would ages. Thus, the editor has chosen to assign the 2 from the date given to his mother to his father, thus changing 1860 to 1862, which is consistent with his death at the age of fifty-seven in 1919. Then the birth year originally assigned to Adams's father is given to his mother. The only possible flag of a problem is that she would have then been twenty-nine when she gave birth to Alton in 1889—rather old at the time for a first child. Yet her age is confirmed by the baptismal records at the Frederick Evangelical Lutheran Church on St. Thomas. The age of his mother is listed as twenty-nine years and his father's as twenty-eight (p. 221). His godparents are listed as Archibald Dinzey, John Sebastian, R. Iteines, Susanne Cooper, and Caroline Delhon. The memoirs manuscript reports his mother's middle name as "Evangeline"; it appears as "Elizabeth" in Alton's baptismal record, "Evangeline" in his sister Edna's record, and "Evangelina" in his brother Julien's. (Spelling variants are common in these documents, probably because of differing spelling practices among the Danish and English speakers who filled them out.) Consistent with local custom at the time, Adams's parents were not officially married at the time of his birth. Her religion is listed as "D.R." or Dutch Reformed; his father's as "M" or Moravian. Jacob Adams's profession is listed as "tomrer," which is Danish for carpenter.

8. The name *Althea Peterson* is not included in the memoirs draft but is identified in Linda Benjamin's biography for young readers, *Alton A. Adams* (St. Croix, US VI: CRIC Productions, 1987). This source also indicates that Adams's mother died when he was thirteen years old, that is, circa 1902–3, although in chapter 4 Adams states that she was forty-six when she died, circa 1906, which is the date used here. An obituary has yet to be located.

9. Baptismal records at Frederick Evangelical Lutheran Church confirm Edna's birth date as Jan. 18, 1894, and report that her parents had been married in the church since Alton's birth. She was baptized on May 6 (p. 252). Julien Zeitzemar Adams's birthday is given as Dec. 30, 1895, and date of baptism as March 1, 1896 (p. 262).

10. Baptismal records at Frederick Lutheran identify one of these sisters as Anita Henriette Wilhelmine Adams, born Nov. 19, 1899, and baptized Dec. 24 of the same year (p. 280). The other sister seems not to have lived long enough to have been baptized.

11. According to an unidentified clipping held at the AAC, Julien Adams was sixty-five when he died, and left a wife, Clare, and three children, Elmo,

Herbert, and Mrs. Rita Adams Benjamin. He had fourteen grandchildren. His first wife was named Eudocia (Enid Adams Questel, personal communication, May 30, 2005).

12. Edna Augusta "Auntie" Adams was Adams's last surviving sibling. The editor interviewed her in the company of Gwendolyn Adams (one of Alton, Sr.'s children) in 1997, when she was 103 years old. She died on February 25, 1999, at the age of 105 and is buried in Western Cemetery on St. Thomas (funeral program held at the University of the Virgin Islands).

13. Complicating the religious mixture further, Ella Adams was raised Catholic within a largely Jewish environment. Her paternal grandfather, Joseph Robles, was a prominent Jewish merchant, and her sister was married to the St. Thomas rabbi (Alton Adams, Jr., personal communication, January 2006).

14. Adams's uncle's children included Archibald A. Dinzey, Jr. (b. 1888, d. March 31, 1910), who played baritone horn in the St. Thomas Native Brass Band, and Eldred E. Dinzey (also b. 1888), who played alto and baritone horn.

15. The program reproduced here comes from an early draft of the chapter. Adams likely cut this example because, as originally printed in the *Times*, errors undercut his overall argument that the islands were unusually sophisticated. In the original, the title of Rossini's opera is given as "Barbara of Civile" and Malibran is uncapitalized and spelled "malobran." Such typographical errors are typical of press notices in the nineteenth century for touring ensembles throughout the United States.

16. Adams also lists a bass singer named Bosley who took up residence after a tour stop with the Fisk Jubilee Singers and sang with the Lutheran choir. Unable to confirm either a stop by the Jubilee Singers at St. Thomas or a singer named Bosley in the group or on the islands, the editor has removed this section.

17. Giglioli wrote the first biography of Adams, published in the *Jacobs' Band Monthly* (hereafter *JBM*) 1916 (see p. 339).

18. The definition of *parrotine* as well as the story of Adams listening at his father's feet was added from the first draft of the memoirs (AMRI).

19. Monsanto worked for Santi Hestres as his valet (AAC, early ch. 2 draft). *Gade* is the Danish word for "street"; "Vester Gade" means "West Street."

20. An early draft mentions that Evelyn's voice ranked "in range and beauty . . . with the mezzo soprano Maude Glanvil, now Maude Essannason, who is still alive and in her nineties and attending worship in the Lutheran Church." Adams also notes that "the organist of the church was Miss Anna Callwood, a remarkable pianist and organist. She was the sister of Clifford Callwood, Manager of the Hamburg American Line shipping and coaling station."

CHAPTER 3. THE VALUE OF EDUCATION

1. This section on discipline and the curfew has been added from a fragment of typescript, possibly intended for a speech (AMRI).

2. Details of the school day and location of the Moravian Town School adapted from Benjamin.

3. Adams adopts this text from an article, "Miss Mary Meyers: School-teacher and Friend of Humanity," written on the occasion of Meyers's retirement and preserved in the Adams Scrapbooks, *DN*, Nov. 9, 1933 (AAC§II.4.134). These articles report her birth date as June or July 10, 1869, the date of her retirement from teaching due to poor health as June 30, 1933, and her death as occurring on February 7, 1939.

4. Originally an Anglican, Manning (b. July 15, 1808; d. January 14, 1892) was the English cardinal priest of Sts. Andrew and Gregory on the Coelian Hill and the second archbishop of Westminster. He was influential in social justice teaching (Catholic Encyclopedia Online).

5. Quotation restored from earlier chapter draft (AAC§VI.1.43).

6. Schomburg was born in Puerto Rico but came to the islands as a boy—probably to St. Croix. Adams and Schomburg corresponded in 1927. See Schomburg to Adams, Jan. 27, 1927 (AAC§II.1.61), and Adams to Schomburg, Feb. 1, 1927 (Schomburg Papers, New York Public Library). The letters discuss black musicians and composers including Brindis de Salas and the Chevalier de Saint Georges, as well as life on St. Thomas.

7. Ding's Alley (or Ding Alley) is a side street near the Memorial Moravian Church that divides the Federal Court Building from the police station, more typically known as Kanal Gade (Moolenaar 2005, 11).

8. Adolph Sixto, *Time and I; or, Looking Forward* (San Juan News, 1899; repr., St. Thomas: Enez Ione Harvey Trust, 2006); see www.timeandibook.com.

9. An enormous multipart article titled "The Virgin Islands, U.S.A." by Sixto runs in at least twenty-one separate issues of the *Bulletin* from June 28 through August 20, 1925. The article protests against "negativisms" in a number of news reports that disparage the potential of the islands—in a way similar to the argument described here. Sixto also argues that race relations on the islands are of a distinctly different character than in the U.S. mainland—an argument that Adams makes in these memoirs—although Sixto admits only that "color prejudice was somewhat unknown in these islands" before the U.S. purchase. Class—what Sixto labels the "masses versus the classes"—is clearly the primary social marker and division in Sixto's essay. He addresses a broad range of social and political issues. Similar to Adams's argument, his balanced assessment of the naval administration both criticizes the initial "fear and hatred" the navy created and remarks on the new opportunities and courtesy extended to islanders working for the government. Sixto identifies prohibition and taxation as two policies injuring the islands' trade and economy and advocates the return of agriculture to St. Thomas in hopes of economic improvement. Copies of the *Bulletin* containing this series can be found in Record Group 55, Records of the Government of the Virgin Islands, National Archives, Washington, D.C.

10. Some of this personal enmity toward Sixto can be found in a letter of response from "H. L." in the *Bulletin* of July 31, 1925, headlined "Sixto Ridicules the Dead," which addresses Sixto's critique of the islands' Colonial Council, the island government that operated in cooperation with the naval

governor. Sixto accuses the council of inactivity, particularly concerning urgent social needs, because its members supposedly are concerned with only their upper-class interests. Although Sixto names no one explicitly, his correspondent takes bitter personal affront and accuses him of speaking "irreverently of dead heroes because they are not here to defend themselves." This response adds some background to Adams's defense of Sixto, particularly in terms of Sixto's class concerns. Clearly, Sixto's lack of business success was mocked by some to dismiss his ideas altogether.

11. Adams himself completed at least four courses of correspondence study in both music and writing. See ch. 4.

12. This tale warns against advice from advisers personally invested in the outcome. It is the story of a fox that loses its tail in a trap and, rather than admit its embarrassment, proposes that all foxes should give up their tails.

13. This quote is typically credited to Thomas Alva Edison.

14. This was true of Adams's father, who apprenticed at Royal Mail to learn carpentry. Tradesmen who learned their skills at Royal Mail gained unusual expertise and earned higher wages.

CHAPTER 4. MUSIC IN THE VIRGIN ISLANDS AND THE FOUNDING OF THE ADAMS JUVENILE BAND (1910)

1. Adams's folk music manuscript was destroyed in a 1932 fire (see ch. 9).

2. Johan Peter Nissen, *Reminiscences of a 46 Years' Residence in the Island of St. Thomas in the West Indies* (n.p.: Senseman & Co., 1838). Bamboula performances survived for tourists in the later nineteenth century.

3. The stems Adams refers to are likely the one- to two-foot-long stems of an individual papaya leaf, which have a hollow bore like a flute's.

4. Adams's affection for this obsolete instrument is clear in his article "The Flageolet—History and Technic," *JBM* 3:5 (May 1918), 80–83. In an aside Adams writes: "In the beginning of my career while studying the flute, my parents sent to my grandmother . . . for a flute for me, but whether it was her fault or the fault of the translation, instead of sending a flute proper to my regret, she sent a flageolet with which I just fooled for some time until it finally disappeared. Then I began to play around with another of its family, the ocarina, and developed into an expert performer" (82). The memoirs manuscript at this point states that the flageolet "was said to be invented in 1881," which is false, at least in terms of the instrument generally. Adams may be referring to a keyed model, but the phrase has been removed here to avoid confusion.

5. Information added from Adams interview with Sam Floyd reported in "Islands' Rich Musical Heritage Nurtures Protege," *DN*, Jan. 25, 1988.

6. An earlier draft of the memoirs suggests that Adams's conflicts with Francis's son Rothschild may date from this period. Rather than leaving Francis's shop immediately after the master's death, Adams appears to have worked there under his several sons and other students, now master shoemakers themselves. Centrose, a friend of Francis, oversaw the business, and Adams made

shoes for sale. According to the original draft: "He [Adams?] quit one day in disgust. He was annoyed by some of Rothschild's dealings within the business" (AMRI).

7. The thinkers on the relationship of music to society that seem to have influenced Adams include John Ruskin, Walter Jacobs, Emil Medicus, Thomas Tapper, and, later, Cyril Scott.

8. Advertisements for "Lessons by Mail in Harmony, Counterpoint, and Composition" from a "Hugh A. Clarke, Mus. Doc. 223 South 38th Street, Philadelphia" ran regularly in the *Etude* at this time. See, for example, 22:10 (October 1904), 428. Diploma held at AMRI.

9. Adams completed the Regular Course of Study in the Advanced Composition Department of the University Extension Conservatory of Chicago, Illinois, on September 3, 1930, and received a bachelor of music degree from the same institution on July 21, 1931.

10. Adams seems to intentionally avoid mentioning the name of the violinist, Ulderique Donastorg. Jean Delphin Alard (1815–88) was professor of violin at the Paris conservatoire from 1843 to 1875.

11. Information in this paragraph is taken from Sebastien's obituary in the November 20, 1940, issue of the *Bulletin*, written by Adams.

12. An undated reminiscence of Lafranque written by Adams is preserved at AMRI. Adams praises the guitar as a "miniature orchestra in itself" and describes Lafranque's self-taught virtuosity as "a gift from above." In the musician's repertory were operatic arias including "the dreamy melodies of *Freischütz, Oberon, Euryanthe,* and others." Adams celebrates Lafranque's ear, especially his ability to imitate complex harmonies despite a "very scant knowledge of music from the standpoint of musical symbols [notation]." He describes Lafranque as a "fine conversationalist, neatly and spotlessly attired," whose "jolly presence was always a welcome one among his friends." A closing anecdote, apparently frequently retold by Lafranque, sheds light on the musical culture of the islands:

> A friend of his who played the flute (not [Adams]) was enamored of a young lady and desired to give vent to his pent up emotions of contemplated bliss in the form of a serenade during an early moonlight morning under the window of his heart's ideal. The combination consisted of flute, violin, and guitar, a most romantic one indeed. The father of his lady love seemed not to have cherished the choice of his daughter's affection, and obviously did not look with favor on the little flute as a means of giving his daughter the economic security he desired nor the bliss she anticipated. Cautiously and apprehensively the trio approached and took position under the window. In a few minutes beautiful dreamy harmonies filled the air. Instead of the young lady appearing at the window as was the custom, the father appeared and enquired the number of performers. The young man felt more at ease, remarking that the query was

meant to make preparations for them. He was quite right, but it was not in the way he conjectured. "Take that and divide among you, you idle loafers!" he bellowed from on high and did not remain even long enough to see the hasty departure of the trio while brushing off the shower of what was evidently not pure, unadulterated water, nor rain, from their instruments and persons.

13. In his manuscript, Adams gives the date of 1906 for the formation of the Native Brass Band, but *Lightbourn's Mail Notes* of July 16, 1909, indicates that the band paraded in celebration of its "second anniversary." Documentary evidence has been preferred to memory and thus the 1907 founding date has been used. The 1906 date may reflect the formation of Sebastien's own amateur group, which preceded the band's.

14. Adams's qualifications of this band as the first "local" and only "native" band are significant. Regular band concerts had been held in the Emancipation Garden bandstand since 1888, when a Dr. Charles Taylor mentions that "a military band plays in Emancipation Garden twice a week" (Thursday and Sunday afternoons). Presumably the only military band on the islands at that time would have been a Danish contingent, and thus that band was neither local nor native. While it is clear that St. Thomas had enjoyed regular band performances prior to the founding of the Native Brass Band, it is uncertain for how long the military band had performed in the bandstand or whether it had performed in other locations. In a heavily corrected typescript intended for a talk (AAC§VI.1.45), Adams offers additional details on the development of the Emancipation Garden bandstand and the activities of the Danish band. Apparently a Danish band of five or six musicians performed at a much smaller gazebo in Adams's youth. When a forty-piece Brazilian Band en route to the 1904 Louisiana Purchase Exposition (World's Fair) in St. Louis stopped in St. Thomas and offered a concert, it needed an appropriate place to perform. Finding the bandstand too small, the group set up against the north wall of Fort Frederick. This incident raised awareness of the need for an enlarged bandstand, yet the island's treasury could not support a new musical building. Adams reports that a "summer house" on the site (located where the bust of the king of Denmark was later installed) from which soft drinks and candy were sold during the Danish band performances was being torn down. Its oversize cone-shaped roof, which provided shade, was adapted as the roof of a new, larger bandstand—completed in time for the return visit of the Brazilian band. Adams's father oversaw construction (see figure 5). What prompted Adams's talk was the rebuilding of the bandstand. He argued for more than simple rebuilding, for the original had been assembled without acoustical considerations. He preferred a flat ceiling within the cone-shaped roof to help propel sound out to the audience. See also Edith deJongh Woods, "Emancipation Garden Has Changed Constantly through the Years," *DN* (Nov. 30, 2000), 28–29.

15. Lionel Valdemar Roberts, Sr., was born in St. Thomas January 13, 1879, and died February 11, 1946. He is remembered as a politician through his work

reconciling competing drafts of what would become the 1936 Organic Act to provide for greater self-governance by the people of the Virgin Islands. Known in his youth as a star cricket player (the largest ballpark on St. Thomas is named in his honor), Roberts had a career that in many areas overlapped with Adams's. Both were bandmasters and composers, both were passionate about local politics, and both published in newspapers. Roberts wrote the satirical column "Hait Boobie" for the *Emancipator*. (See Moolenaar 1992, 191.) Much like Adams, Roberts undertook correspondence study in music and claimed to have received a diploma from the Wilcox School of Music in New York (1910) and the Seigle Meyers Conservatory of Music in Chicago (*DN* [October 6, 1934], 3).

16. Adams and Roberts later became rivals, and thus the representation of events here reflects Adams's bias. In many ways the pair's leadership styles and ambitions were very similar. Adams would later be accused of domineering leadership as well (see ch. 5).

17. Programs of the Native Brass Band printed in *Lightbourn's Mail Notes* show that Roberts was not always unsupportive of his assistant director. On June 2, 1909, Roberts's band performed a program including the "Polka (Concert) Piccolo Solo 'Thro' the Air'" by Damm as arranged by Adams and presumably performed by him as well. On April 30, 1909, the band performed one march by Roberts titled "St. Thomas Militia March" and closed the concert with one of Adams's compositions—"Moving Day." As the final slot on a program is considered a location of honor for one of the strongest compositions, the program order here offered Adams an implicit compliment. Given that Adams broke with Roberts by June 1910, it is possible that Roberts simply did not wish to play another of his assistant's works again so soon. He also may have preferred to balance each Adams work with one of his own. That there was a rivalry between the two men even from within the Native Brass Band seems implicit in Adams's account.

18. A rapid-fire series of articles and responses in the *DN* of Oct. 2–12, 1934, testifies to the continuing feud between Adams and Roberts. In the "Unwritten Music History," appearing in the paper on Oct. 2 and 5, Roberts claims Adams as his pupil and blames Adams's breakaway on class tension:

> The progress of The Municipal Band was not altogether accepted by those in the upper strata, the performers apparently having come from too low down, so an attempt was made in 1909 to split the harmony when young Rothschild Francis was encouraged to leave and help in the formation of another band in competition. After its failure Mr. Francis was honest enough to make this confession. This gave rise to another attempt that should be considered partially successful when Mr. Alton Adams in 1910–11 was called for the same purpose as Mr. Rothschild Francis and a band was organized under the name of Adams Juvenile Band. This band was recommended through a petition sent to President Woodrow Wilson at the transfer of the islands in 1917 clandestinely signed by the enemies of the Municipal Band

comprised in the upper strata. That succeeded in giving Adams Juvenile Band preference as a Navy band upon the arrival of Capt. William Wallace [sic] White of the U.S.S. Vixen who traded with Mr. Adams individually. Thus was the first native institution of merit sacrificed at the altar of hate, envy and malice—an irretrievable loss.

Adams responds in the Oct. 9 and 10 issues, denying that he was a student of Roberts, claiming to have helped instruct the bandsmen after its reformation following the departure of Sebastien, and denying any plot by leading people in the community to kill the Municipal Band. He also denies that any petition was sent to President Wilson on behalf of the band, saying, "The [Adams Juvenile] band was selected [to become the U.S. Navy Band of the Virgin Islands] for the simple reason that it was superior." Further articles include ad hominem attacks by both men and their supporters. This spat must be understood in the context of larger political developments on the islands; it represents a battle between two political strategies. Roberts was among those who fought for the navy administration's removal, and thus his success was Adams's loss. In 1934, when this newspaper exchange occurred, Roberts and Adams remained political rivals, and their musical disagreements serve in proxy for political differences. Likewise the pair of opposed personalities are emblematic of broader trends. Neither Adams nor Roberts stood alone in his position. The public display of this private controversy must also have been a good way for the *Daily News* to sell papers.

19. The age range of the Juvenile Band members is given variously from eight years to thirteen or eighteen years.

20. This traditional nineteenth-century method of instruction by beginning away from an instrument with solfege is still in use in the twenty-first century. See Katherine Brucher's Ph.D. dissertation, "A Banda Da Terra: Bandas Filarmónicas and the Performance of Place in Portugal," University of Michigan, Ann Arbor, 2005.

21. Congregational minister John Curwen (1816–80) codified the Tonic Sol-Fa method of teaching vocal music, drawing on a number of English and European methods of musical instruction. His method consisted of a simplified music notation meant as a first step toward reading staff notation. Pitches were indicated within a key by using the first letter of the corresponding solfege syllable (do, ray, mi, fa, sol, la, ti). Rhythm was indicated by separating the syllables with barlines, half barlines, and colons to indicate strong, medium, and weak subdivisions of the meter. Later Curwen added hand signs, still familiar to music educators in modified form through the Kodály method. Curwen first published his method in 1858 in a book titled *The Standard Course of Lessons on the Tonic Sol-fa Method of Teaching to Sing*. Here, Adams appears to adopt the solfege component while modifying the rhythmic syllables. Adams also shares Curwen's belief in the moralizing influence of music.

22. In gratitude for Sebastien's assistance in founding the band, and beginning during Oliver's initial governorship (1917–19), Adams's navy band played a serenade concert for Sebastien each New Year's Day (AAC§VII.1.4).

23. This is the opening of Ralph Waldo Emerson's "Friendship," Essay VI in *Essays* (1841), retitled *Essays: First Series* in 1847.

24. A postcard in the AMRI collection dated January 5, 1914, offers thanks to Adams for an evening of shared music making and is sent from Hror Hystrom, a Swedish sailor from a warship that visited St. Thomas.

25. The first draft of the memoirs tells a story of Adams's father's reaction:

> One evening while Bandmaster Adams was getting ready for the
> Juvenile Band's first concert in the Emancipation Garden, he asked
> his father, "Are you coming to hear the concert?" "Who me?" he
> responded. "I have my work to do. Hard work! I have no time for
> such nonsense!" When Bandmaster Adams returned home from the
> concert that night, his father was in bed, and appeared fast asleep.
> However, a friend later told him [Alton] that he'd never seen a man
> so proud. His father was right there at the concert telling everyone
> near him, "That's my boy! That's my boy!" Jacob Adams smiled
> with pride during his son's entire concert.

26. Adams's MS credits *Lightbourn's Mail Notes* with this review and gives the concert date as June 9, 1910. However, the original article is found in the *St. Thomas Tidende* of March 1, 1911, and provides the correct date. Sebastien was president of the Revived Mutual Improvement Society (a men's group of the local Anglican Church), which sponsored the band and provided the performance venue. Early accounts of the band's activities are rare, but a fourth-anniversary concert was scheduled for June 9, 1914, and delayed one day by weather ("News of the Day," *Lightbourn's Mail Notes* [June 11, 1914, 2). June 9, 1910, may be the date of the band's first meeting or rehearsal.

27. This paragraph on Carnival was added from a corrected typescript in AAC, not originally part of the memoirs draft (§VI.1.42).

28. Adams offered a "Biography of Mr. Fred Lax" in *JBM* 1:8 (August 1916), 83–84. He reports that Lax was born in Hull, England, in 1856, but that he came to the United States in 1881 following a promising European career that included ensembles in Durham, Scarborough, Leeds, and Manchester under conductors such as Ed de John, Charles Halle, Sir Arthur Sullivan, Richard Strauss, Hans von Bülow, Camille Saint-Saens, and Charles Gounod. In the United States Lax began playing with Patrick S. Gilmore's band and then joined the Boston Symphony in 1889. He claims that Lax composed and arranged over six hundred pieces for instruments and voice. Adams praises him as the "premier flutist" in the United States. That Lax was self-taught may be another reason why Adams felt a connection.

29. The Emerson quotation above and the hurricane anecdote are taken from an article by Adams titled "Mr. Elphege Sebastien: An Appreciation," *St. Thomas Times* (hereafter *STT*) 1:29 (April 22, 1922), 1 (AAC§VII.1.4).

30. According to the website of the Royal Danish Naval Museum, the *Ingolf* was an armored schooner built in Copenhagen and commissioned for

the Royal Danish Navy in 1878. From August 1896 it was used as a training schooner until its decommissioning in 1926.

31. Adams writes in an earlier draft: "I never went to Denmark, but some forty years later Prince Axel returned to the Virgin Islands as Chairman of the East Asiatic Company. I met him at a reception, showed him his worn, but cherished card, and introduced myself. He looked at the card and then at me, and said, 'I remember the occasion quite well, but that has to be your father.' 'No, it was me,' I replied, and we both laughed and fell to sharing our recollections" (AAC).

32. Daniel became the French consul. His commission of Adams, likely in 1911, falls within the social rhetoric of the serenade tradition.

33. The sheet music publishing house operated by Walter Jacobs began distributing a magazine from Boston called the *Cadenza* in 1894 for players of banjo, mandolin, and guitar. In 1910 Jacobs began the *Jacobs' Orchestra Monthly* and six years later the *Band Monthly* Adams refers to here. Adams's belief that it was time to recognize the band as distinct from the orchestra seems to parallel Jacobs's decision to offer the new band-specific magazine. Rather than the leading publication, in 1916 *Jacobs' Band Monthly* was brand new. Adams's position as band columnist is remarkable. The choice affirms the excellence of Adams's writing, the compelling nature of his musical philosophies, and the commonalities his philosophy had with Jacobs's own. It also speaks to Adams's ambition.

It is likely that the editors of the magazine were unaware of Adams's race, or at least allowed his race to remain ambiguous. All of the magazine's columnists had photos that accompanied their bylines except for Adams. A profile of Adams appearing in 1916 did not mention his race, and it was not even implied in the pages of the magazine until Frank Seltzer's profile article on Adams's navy band appeared in July 1920. This piece includes photos of Adams conducting (albeit from a distance) but still does not mention his racial identity. By this time, Adams had not written his regular monthly column for almost two years. He continued to contribute sporadically after his race became public, confirming that the magazine still supported him. None of this necessarily implies that Adams withheld his racial identity intentionally, although he did do so with Thomas Tapper (see ch. 5). His race may also have been obscured by the editors of the magazine. It seems likely that readers would have assumed that an educated, soon-to-be naval bandleader writing "The Band" column for a prominent national magazine would have been white. Thus, reader prejudice might well have kept hints of Adams's black identity unappreciated by most. One article by Adams that might have revealed his race to some readers was a Feb. 1918 profile of the black West Indian singer Philip Gomez that was accompanied by a prominent photo that made a clear correlation between black racial identity and the native Virgin Islander.

34. Sousa also performed Adams's music. Adams's navy band scrapbooks held in the AAC contain programs from Sousa's 1921 Willow Park Season

outside Philadelphia (§VII.3.2). On August 15, 1921, Sousa ended the final concert of the day (beginning 9:45 P.M.) with Adams's "Virgin Islands March." On the 7:45 P.M. performance for August 8, 1922, Sousa programmed Adams's "The Governor's Own" between a scene from Puccini's *La Bohème* and Johann Strauss's waltz *Artist's Life (Kunstlerleben)*.

35. In a published essay and accompanying typescript held in the AAC titled "John Philip Sousa as Man and Musician 1854–1932," Adams describes Sousa's accepting attitude concerning race, citing first his embrace of Adams's music and Adams's candidacy for the American Bandmaster's Association. Then Adams discusses the point on aesthetics made here, quoting an interview with Sousa by Marie Davenport-Euberg apparently published in the *Bellingham Register*. He quotes Sousa telling of watching "Negro boys and girls— yes, and men and women too" dancing alongside regimental bands during the U.S. Civil War "with that abandon which characterized the Negro and his sense of rhythm." Sousa continues: "Hypnotized by the music and wild excitement, they would execute their steps along the line of march, gesticulating, and prancing, but always in rhythm to which they gave the soul of animation and lightheartedness and enthusiasm." Sousa concludes that "when I came to write my marches these things were in my subconscious mind though I wasn't aware of it until later." This explanation leads to Adams's claim here that Sousa's marches were influenced by Afro-American musical traditions. See publication from *Focus* (Sunday, April 4, 1971), 6 & 14 (incomplete copy in AAC§VI.1.19); complete typescript AAC§VI.1.20.

36. Names added from Adams's "Address on Edwin Franko Goldman" (AAC).

CHAPTER 5. THE UNITED STATES NAVY BAND
OF THE VIRGIN ISLANDS (1917–1923)

1. For a full account of the transfer, see "The Sale and Purchase," in Dookhan, 243–64.

2. In an earlier draft, Adams identifies the organizers of the union as Jackson with "Gustave Lange, Ralph de Chabert, Elskoe, Ralph Bough, Joseph Alexander, Amphlett Leader, C. T. Brow and others." He also states that Jackson spoke (at least some) Danish (AAC§VI.1.11).

3. Figures used here are confirmed by Dookhan, 240.

4. These lost benefits included living quarters, a plot of ground for growing vegetables and grass, and in some instances, the keeping of a cow or horse (AAC§VI.1.11).

5. Local historian Harold Willocks states that Jackson was dismissed from his teaching position in the Danish public schools because of his pro-labor views (Harold W. L. Willocks, *The Umbilical Cord: The History of the United States Virgin Islands from Pre-Columbian Era to the Present* [Christiansted, St. Croix: Harold Willocks, 1995], 227).

6. Willocks notes that the first issue of the *Herald,* distributed on November 1, 1915, listed Jackson as founder, president, and editor (228). A free preview issue was available on October 29. Readers were sent to the plantations to recite the news to those who were illiterate or could not afford to buy the papers. The *Herald* was published until 1922, but only the 1915 issues survive in the collection of the Enid Baa Library in St. Thomas.

7. Alton Adams, Jr., had a remembrance of Judge David Hamilton Jackson written by his father published in October 2002 and distributed to the Department of Education, St. Croix, and local broadcast media. It represents a slightly earlier version of the text here.

8. See Adams, "The Virgin Islands: The Danish West Indies Now Included in the United States of America," *JBM* 2:5 (May 1917), 65–69, for more information on the transfer ceremony and Adams's hopes for American sovereignty. An analysis of this essay is found in Mark Clague, "Instruments of Identity: Alton Augustus Adams Sr., the Navy Band of the Virgin Islands, and the Sounds of Social Change," *Black Music Research Journal* 18:1–2 (Spring–Fall 1988): 21–65.

9. What is now known as Emancipation Garden is in the shadow of Denmark's colonial Fort Christian (built in 1672) and adjacent to the Charlotte Amalie town square, which served as one of the eighteenth century's most active slave markets. It is so named to commemorate Governor Peter von Scholten's emancipation of the slaves on July 3, 1848. See "Slave Protest and Emancipation," in Dookhan, 160–80.

10. Ogese McKay, a navy bandsman from St. Croix and a sometime critic of Adams, claims that the idea for the local navy bands originated with Captain White, who "noticed that the young boys in the street would whistle a tune as perfect as if they were musicians" (see McKay, 10).

11. The primary competitor would have been the Municipal Band under the direction of Lionel Roberts. Much was at stake as a job as a navy bandsman was among the best available on the islands at the time. See ch. 4 for an account of the feud between Roberts and Adams. While Adams claimed that his ensemble was the only professional band on the island, Roberts felt his band's loss resulted from intrigue. Whatever the reason, it is true that the Municipal Band had been associated with the Danish government and had received financial subsidies through the Colonial Councils of St. Thomas and St. Croix in return for public concerts. As late as 1916, the Danish governor L. C. Helweg-Larsen reportedly had plans to take the Municipal Band to Europe to perform (*DN* [October 6, 1934], 3). Adams was a published writer on music and a composer with a reputation that reached to the U.S. mainland; he had long experience as a music teacher. The younger Juvenile Band may also have had an easier time passing the navy's fitness requirements. In his *Brief History of the Virgin Islands* (St. Thomas, VI: The Art Shop, c. 1938), José Antonio Jarvis mentions the conflict: "For the few days when the choice between the Municipal Band under Leader Roberts, and the Juvenile Band under Adams was undecided,

speculation was constant. The advantage went to the Juvenile Band, which thereafter became an important economic unit in the community. The members were permitted a special uniform, and they lived at home under quasi-military rules" (132). Adams's claims that his band was artistically superior are supported by an article in *Lightbourn's Mail Notes* of June 5, 1913 (2), which states that the activities of Roberts's band went beyond music: the group organized a champion cricket team and a football team as well. In addition to their apprenticeship duties, then, the young members of the Municipal Band practiced athletics in the afternoons, thus limiting time for music rehearsal and individual music practice. Adams's band, in contrast, seems to have been focused entirely on music making.

12. Adams was reportedly the navy's youngest bandmaster at the time (age twenty-seven). See Julio Francis Edwards, "Bandmaster Adams Wins Fame," *Home Journal* (St. Thomas) (Dec. 14, 1960), 2.

13. Adams's original list did not contain instrument designations and included Alton Hall instead of Louis Taylor. The list here is taken from an article that seems more reliable because, among other clues, the instrument designations suggest it is taken from a program. The article also claims that all twenty-two members of the original navy band had been members of the Juvenile Band and that two members of the Juveniles, Arnold Potter and Lambert George, remained too young in 1917 to enlist. According to the article, Adams "kept [them] in the unit . . . until they were of age." See Julio Frances Edwards, "They Gave Prestige to the Virgin Islands," *Home Journal* (St. Thomas) (Nov. 30, 1960). Additional support for the preference of Taylor to Hall is that Taylor served on the staff of the band's paper, the *St. Thomas Times (STT)* and thus can be confirmed a member of the St. Thomas contingent, at least in 1921–23. Contemporary confirmation is offered by an account of the band's formation carried in *Lightbourne's Mail Notes* (two of its employees, Alphonse Domingo and Erle Williams became band members). This story was subsequently recast in *JBM* in July 1917 (quoted below), and this version in turn was reprinted in *DN* (AAC§VII.1.3).

14. Adams listed the pay as "approximately sixty" dollars a month. However, the *Bulletin* of June, 4, 1917 (1), states that "each musician [is] receiving $50 monthly, the Conductor $75, besides instruments, music and uniform free." The band's schedule was for "music daily at the barracks, morning and afternoon, from 8 to 9 and 5 to 6, and whenever otherwise required." Their debut concert as the navy band on Saturday, June 2, 1917, included an afternoon concert at Emancipation Garden followed by a march through town.

15. *JBM*, July 1917.

16. A sense of Adams's disciplinary focus comes from a *JBM* article titled "A Talk to Amateur Bandsmen on Preparedness," published in October 1917, just a few months after the induction of the navy band: "The only injustice that I ever did to my bandsmen (that I know of) was to give them everything free. Yes, free music lessons, free bandroom—*free everything*. The result was that they got to a certain degree in music, yet minus that strength and disci-

pline of mind that comes from battling with those forces which make the strong famous and the weak infamous" (59).

17. This paragraph restored from a manuscript fragment held in the private collection of Alton Adams, Jr.

18. Excerpt above taken from a single article (only Adams's second for the *JBM*) titled "The Band" (April 1916), 67–68. Sources for the following excerpt have yet to be identified.

19. The anecdote about the Emancipation Garden performance is taken from "Adams Sr. Shares Talent with Schools," *DN* (Feb. 8, 1988).

20. In the *Daily News* article cited in note 19, Adams credits Oliver with the idea for the two additional bands. The identification of one of these bands as being for St. John is incorrect. Both bands were on St. Croix.

21. Final three sentences in this paragraph taken from *DN*, ibid.

22. It is not clear what Adams means by "jazz" here. Typical would have been something closer to ragtime dance numbers, not the musical traditions developed in New Orleans by Louis Armstrong and others. Adams's World War II Virgin Islands band did have a jazz combo, made up of a contingent trained at Great Lakes.

23. AAC§II.1.19; also reprinted in *DN* (Feb. 22, 1988), 16.

24. The band influenced the community as well. Following Adams's example, Paluden Nicholson founded the St. Thomas Community Band. Its first performance was June 5, 1925, at the Apollo Theatre. It was inspired by the lack of music on the islands while the navy band was on tour in 1924. The Tortolo Band, a youth organization run by Pickering, was also an offshoot of the naval organization ("U.S. Navy Band in Review," *DN* [February 14, 1934], 3; "Community Band Will Be 18 Yrs. Old Tomorrow," *DN* [June 4, 1943], 1).

25. On August 1, 1917 (just over three months after he had taken office), Governor Oliver submitted an extremely negative report to President Wilson on conditions in the islands. He found the Virgin Islands' "community to be backward, even disgraceful, and the death rate to be very high with infant mortality being particularly disgraceful in a civilized community." Oliver protested that there was no family life, as 60 percent of the births were illegitimate. Thus, the governor's admonitions that the bandsmen serve as community models by, for example, getting married, directly addressed the problems identified in this report (Willocks, 261).

26. Although Adams does not mention it in his memoirs, he was Lutheran, according to *Who's Who in Colored America*, 1927. This same publication lists the Adamses' wedding date as June 6, but this is incorrect. The Oct. 6 date is confirmed by the marriage records of the Frederick Evangelical Lutheran Church in St. Thomas (p. 170). These records indicate that a marriage license was secured on May 10, 1917—before Adams entered the navy, but potentially in response to the opportunity. His bride, Ella, a devout Catholic, was divorced from A. Hansen in Aug. 1915, and thus her second marriage could not take place in the Catholic Church. The couple was married at the Lutheran parsonage by Rev. P. Kastrup; witnesses included Elphege Sebastian and H. Gomez.

Ella was born on Jan. 11, 1892, according to the baptismal accounts in the Roman Catholic Church Register of St. Thomas and the marriage certificate held by Alton Adams, Jr. Her parents were Ernestine (neé Daniel) and Julius Joseph. Catholic records indicate that after the death of Ella's first husband in 1955, her marriage to Adams was officially recognized by the church on March 4, 1965.

27. The eight children are Gwendolen (later "Gwendolyn") Marie (b. April 12, 1918; d. July 3, 2003), Merle Augustina (b. May 5, 1919; d. May 11, 1932), Hazel Augusta (b. June 11, 1920; d. Dec. 27, 1932), Enid Augusta Adams Questel (b. Jan. 19, 1922; married Bernard Questel), Olyve ("Olive" in baptismal records) Valentine Adams Finch (b. Feb. 14, 1925; married Earl Finch; d. 2001), Althea Augusta (b. Aug. 20, 1926), Eleanor Evangeline Adams Martin (b. March 20, 1931; died age twenty-eight), and Alton Augustus, Jr. (b. Nov. 8, 1928). Names of children taken from *Who's Who in Colored America*, 3rd edition, 1933, and adjusted with baptismal records where helpful. The middle names *Augustus* and *August(in)a* are family names that refer not only to their father but also to the middle name of their paternal great grandmother. Likewise, *Evangeline* is the middle name of their paternal grandmother. *Valentine* seems to refer to the coincidence of Olive's birth with the holiday. The funeral program for Ella Adams is held at University of the Virgin Islands library.

28. Marriage records held at the Enid Baa Library, St. Thomas, indicate that bandsmen who followed their director's lead included Paluden Nicholson (married to Clara Evelyn Monsanto April 3, 1918, at All Saints), Alton Hall (married to Verona Baady June 13, 1918, at the Moravian Church [*DN* (June 14, 1918), 2]), Raphael Bonelli (married Dec. 19, 1918, at Frederick Lutheran), Albert Pickering (married in 1921 at All Saints), and Arnold Martin (married Aug. 9, 1922, at All Saints). For each entry, the groom's profession as "Musician [or Bandsman] U.S.N." is listed prominently, confirming the elevated social standing that a job in the band provided. Cyril Michael (1898–1978) was admitted to the Virgin Islands Bar as an attorney in 1947 and became judge of the Police Court in 1954. In 1957 Michael became a judge in the Municipal Court of St. Thomas and was appointed presiding judge in 1965. He earned his law degree from La Salle Extension University of Chicago. Michael joined the Adams Juvenile Band at fourteen as a trombonist and was a featured soloist on the Navy Band's 1924 tour. He was promoted to first musician and served as acting bandmaster. He took correspondence courses in music while in the navy (Moolenaar 1992, 157). In his own memoirs, bandsman Ogese McKay represents the injunction to marry as a requirement when a bandsman had gotten a woman pregnant (McKay, 10–11).

29. More on Gomez can be found in Adams, "A Noted West Indian Singer," *JBM* 3:2 (Feb. 1918), 50–51.

30. The description of the library dedication and initial statistics were taken from a typescript article for the *Bulletin* dated August 6, 1940 (AAC§VI.1.37). See also http://www.library.gov.vi/baa/baahistory.htm. Three grants from the Carnegie Foundation, beginning with $10,000 in 1929, helped expand the

library. It moved to its current home in 1940 and was renamed in 1978 for Enid
M. Baa, who served as director of libraries, museums, and archives beginning
in 1933, when she became the first woman to hold a cabinet-level position in
the Virgin Islands. Additional information about Red Cross activities on the
islands may be found in a 1940 editorial by Adams (AAC§VI.1.55).

31. Adams gives a composition date of 1919 here, but gave Floyd (1977) the
date of 1917. As no evidence has been found placing the composition prior to
1919, the later date is accepted here.

32. Thus, Adams's second-ever music publication was distributed throughout the United States in October 1919, exposing a wide range of bandmasters
to his music and in turn introducing audiences to the Virgin Islands. A royalty
receipt shows that a second edition of the "Virgin Islands March," with the
new choral text, sold 467 copies between January 1, 1965, and June 30, 1968.
Adams received 25 cents per copy or $116.75 (AAC§VII.1.27).

33. Adams's music was often featured during the Goldman Band Free Concerts, under the direction of Edwin Franko Goldman (1878–1956), the band's
founder, and the Guggenheim Memorial Concerts, free summer concerts
offered by the Goldman Band, later under the direction of the founder's son
Richard Franko Goldman (1910–80). Programs preserved in the AAC document performances of both the "Virgin Islands March" and the "The Governor's Own" in the years 1922–24, 1963–68, 1970, and 1974–76 (§VII.1.28–37).
Adams's works were usually performed at the end of a concert as part of a closing set of two or three marches. Typically, Adams's piece was the penultimate
number and the concert ended with a march by Sousa. No record exists here of
the Goldman Band playing "The Spirit of the U.S.N." Adams's "The Governor's Own" was also played at R. F. Goldman's memorial following his death in
1980 (see AAC§VII.1.29).

34. Bill 1890 of the Fifth Legislature of the Virgin Islands (regular session)
accepts the new dedication and states that it "may be played on all significant
state occasions throughout the Virgin Islands" (AAC§VII.1.23–24). The bill
recognizes that the march "has come to be regarded over the years as the unof-
ficial anthem of the Virgin Islands." Following the rededication, then-governor
Paiewonsky appointed Adams as chairman of a committee of seven government
and community leaders to create words for this now official song. Enacting
Adams's vision of a tolerant and democratic society, the committee solicited
verses from the islands' inhabitants regardless of race, religion, gender, or class.
Arranged from the contributions of twenty-four residents, the final version of
the text includes four verses set to the tune of the trio strain. While praising the
natural beauty of the islands and noting the loyalty of Virgin Islanders to the
United States, the text was primarily a "song in praise of brotherhood." Its patriotic sentiments reflect idealized notions of freedom, democracy, liberty, truth,
love, and peace. With this new text and legal mandate, the march also critiqued
attitudes of racial intolerance stemming from the U.S. mainland in the 1960s and
actively distanced itself from this influence. As an anthem, the march confronted
and displaced "The Star-Spangled Banner" and thus reminded a new generation

of islanders that their heritage of racial tolerance was unique and historically distinct from that of the United States as a whole. Press releases and lyrics are found in AAC§VII.1.25–26.

35. Additional details here taken from "Adams' Most Famous Marches Inspired by Locals," *DN* (Feb. 15, 1989), 15.

36. The dedication concert is described more fully in AAC§VII.1.12. Bill 1890 of 1963 also accepts the rededication of "The Governor's Own" to the people of the Virgin Islands and states that "over the years" it had "come to be regarded as the particular march of the Governors of the Virgin Islands" (AAC§VII.1.23). "The Governor's Own" refers both to the march and also to the band, which was known by that same epithet.

37. Adams reassumed this leadership position not long after his return to St. Thomas from Cuba in 1933.

38. "Music [Curriculum]," in *Course of Study for the Elementary Schools of the Virgin Islands of the U.S.A. (Grades I to VI, inclusive)*, Educational Bulletin No. 2 (US VI: Department of Education, 1922).

39. "Bandmaster from Virgin Islands Visits Marine Band," *Leatherneck* 5:29 (May 20, 1922), 1. The article clearly identifies Adams as black and notes that the Marine Band had played "The Governor's March" *(sic)* at its "last public concert" prior to Adams's visit.

40. Biographical corrections made in this paragraph are based on *African-American Odyssey: The Stewarts, 1853–1963* by Albert S. Broussard (Laurence: University Press of Kansas, 1998), as well as *American National Biography* (www.anb.org). Angelina Weld Grimké should not be confused with her great aunt Angelina Emily Grimké.

41. The Lincoln Memorial dedication took place on Memorial Day (May 30), 1922; speakers included President Warren Harding, former President William Howard Taft, and Dr. Robert Moton, principal of the Tuskegee Institute, who gave the keynote address.

42. No article by Adams is found in the *Journal of Negro History*.

43. Adams may mean Liberty Bond Commission here.

44. An earlier draft states that this photo had been "sent [to] me by another Virgin Islander living still in Washington—Paul Christopher."

45. Adams refers here to "Modern Helps to Music Students," *JBM* (Dec. 1916).

46. The full title of the book is *Youth and Opportunity: Being Chapters on the Factors of Success*. It was published by two New York houses in 1912. *The Music Life* (1891) was published in Philadelphia by Theodore Presser.

47. Much of Adams's text concerning Tapper is self-quoted verbatim or paraphrased from a September 29, 1923, article in *STT*, 1, 6.

48. Quotation restored from ibid. Carlyle's precise words are "Cast forth thy Act, thy Word, into the ever-living, ever-working Universe: it is a seed-grain that cannot die; unnoticed to-day (says one), it will be found flourishing as a Banyan-grove (perhaps, alas, as a Hemlock-forest!) after a thousand years" (Carlyle, *Sartor Resartus* V, 1833–34).

49. In 1933 a high school band was founded by Miss Alicia Geib, but was soon directed by Alton and Julien Adams. Aimee Estornell conducted the orchestra in 1934, having been its director "for many years" ("High School Band Gives Concert," *DN* [Dec. 7, 1934], 1).

50. Quoted in full from Adams, "Music—An Appreciation," *JBM* 1:9 (Sept. 1916), 68–71.

CHAPTER 6. THE NAVY BAND'S 1924
UNITED STATES TOUR

1. The entire story of the 1924 trip is told by Adams in a long series of newspaper articles published in the Virgin Islands (tour scrapbooks, AAC). For further analysis of this tour, see Mark Clague, "Instruments of Identity: Alton Augustus Adams, Sr., the Navy Band of the Virgin Islands, and the Sounds of Social Change," *Black Music Research Journal* 18: 1–2 (Spring–Fall 1988), 21–65.

2. The V.I. Commission included George H. Woodson (Iowa), Cornelius R. Richardson (Indiana), Charles E. Mitchell (West Virginia), Jefferson S. Coage (Delaware), and W. H. C. Brown (Virginia). The commission's visit was a result of a growing rift between local government and the navy. In 1922 the Colonial Council of St. Thomas (which was still active, since the navy had chosen to continue the islands' operation under Danish law) sent Rothschild Francis—a bandleader, journalist, and union organizer—to Washington, D.C., to solicit relief for economic and political stagnation on the islands (Willocks, 262). (A good example of the stagnation felt by the islanders concerns U.S. citizenship; although most natives expected citizenship in 1918, this right was not granted to most islanders until 1927.) In response, the 1924 commission was sent to investigate. The native navy band was one of the few bright spots in the commission's ensuing report.

3. Original letter found in AAC§II.1.39.

4. The *New York Age* was a national African American weekly newspaper published from 1905 to 1959.

5. Goldman wrote similar articles for publications such as the *Dominant*.

6. Adams had written Goldman a letter in preparation for the tour, to which Goldman responded on June 13, 1924, after some delay. Adams had clearly identified himself as "colored," for Goldman writes: "I was glad to hear from you, and you may rest assured that the fact that you are a colored man does not change my regard for you. Prejudice of race or creed do [*sic*] not exist in my make-up." In this same letter, Goldman asks Adams to bring the score and parts to his "Virgin Islands March" (AAC§II.1.44).

7. This account, included in the 1924 tour scrapbook held in the AAC, was likely written by Dougherty for the *Amsterdam News*, but the source has yet to be identified. The article suggests that Adams conducted the Goldman Band on Wednesday, July 2, 1924; this date is confirmed in an unidentified St. Croix clipping (AAC§VII.3.11 & 19). Goldman's claim that this was Adams's first visit to New York is incorrect.

8. Letter from Goldman to Adams, Feb. 2, 1937 (AAC§II.2.22).

9. Adams's language here minimizes the racial discrimination behind the rejection of his two applications to join the ABA (see editor's introduction). He did not receive a letter granting him eligibility for membership.

10. Only thirty-eight are pictured in the tour photograph (see photographs in this volume). All records located so far indicate that the touring ensemble included all active bandsmen from both St. Thomas and St. Croix. Other reports that sixty-six musicians took part in the tour are incorrect. Adams may have had sixty-six musicians under his direction at the height of the islands' ensembles (three twenty-two-piece ensembles), but also may never have reached this maximum. Forty-six musicians are shown in a pretour publicity photo taken in the Virgin Islands (see "Virgin Islands Naval Band to Tour U.S.," *Chicago Defender* [May 31, 1924], 3).

11. Calvin Coolidge, Jr., died on July 7, 1924, from blood poisoning. His death transfixed the nation and profoundly depressed the president. See *The Autobiography of Calvin Coolidge* (New York: Cosmopolitan Book Corporation, 1929), 190.

12. The "morris chair" mentioned here seems to refer to a style first devised by the firm of the English designer William Morris. The more common types are wooden with a reclining back and high armrests that would not be appropriate for musical performance. Adams's manuscript states that "morris chairs" were provided, but this seems unlikely and has been corrected here.

13. One who was there was the "father of the blues," W. C. Handy, whose home at 442 St. Nicholas Avenue was near the park. Handy wrote Adams a letter on Sept. 18, 1924, to congratulate him for his "splendid organization" (AAC§II.1.51).

14. *Monkey chasers* is a derogatory phrase once used by some African Americans to refer to West Indian blacks. It encapsulates the tension between these two African diasporic groups. Marcus Garvey, in particular, was labeled such publicly by African American leaders. See "1920's–1930's—West Indian Influence," in Cruse, 115–46; and Lloyd W. Brown, "The West Indian as an Ethnic Stereotype in Black American Literature," *Negro American Literature Forum* 5:1 (Spring 1971): 8–14.

15. Unidentified clippings in Adams scrapbooks (AAC) likely from the *Amsterdam News,* which through Dougherty offered unusually rich coverage of the band's visit.

16. Adams uses this patriotic anecdote in a number of speech and radio address drafts held in the AAC.

17. Other last-minute requests for performances could not be fulfilled, including an invitation from the black community of Chicago (1924 tour scrapbooks, AAC§VII.3.18).

18. According to www.theshiplist.com, the *Praesident,* at 1,849 tons, entered service in 1905 for the line's West Indies Service. It was seized by the United States in 1917. The Hamburg-American Packet Company was formed in 1847 to service a Hamburg-to–New York route. The journey took forty

days. Gradually growing in size and coverage, service to the West Indies began in 1870 and continued through 1939. Passenger service ceased during both world wars.

 19. Original letter is preserved in AAC§II.1.48.

 20. Clipping from *Boston Chronicle* preserved in AAC§VII.3.27.

 21. All but the first nineteen words of this quotation are missing from all extant versions of this chapter. The full article is found in book 3 of the Adams Scrapbooks (AAC).

 22. From the song "Home, Sweet Home," by the "English Mozart," Sir Henry Rowley Bishop (1786–1855), with words by John Howard Payne, composed for the English opera *Clari, or the Maid of Milan* (1823). See Nicholas Temperley, "Bishop, Sir Henry R.," in *New Grove Dictionary of Music and Musicians* (New York: Macmillan, 2000).

CHAPTER 7. THE CLOSE OF THE NAVAL YEARS (1925–1931)

 1. *The Daily News (DN)*, May 3, 1988. Paul E. Joseph, a St. Croix naval bandsmen, wrote similar music appreciation articles for the *St. Croix Avis* (see "Music Notes" [Feb. 12, 1919], 2). For more on White, see Victoria von Arx, "Clarence Cameron White," *International Dictionary of Black Composers*, vol. 2 (Chicago: Fitzroy Dearborn, 1999), 1199–1206.

 2. Following sporadic celebrations and a 1923 national observance, a coordinated National Music Week was first celebrated throughout the United States in May 1924. See Charles M. Tremaine, *History of National Music Week* (New York: National Bureau for the Advancement of Music, ca. 1925).

 3. Due to the short lead time, Adams planned most Music Week events himself. Details of program added from last section of AAC§VII.1.16. Adams's Music Week activities are confirmed in "U.S. Navy Band in Review," *DN* (Feb. 14, 1931), 3, and contemporary accounts such as "Music Week Program," *Bulletin* (May 8, 1925), 3, and "Music Week Events," *Bulletin* (May 9, 1925), 3.

 4. *DN* (May 9, 1988). The U.S. Centennial of Flight Commission website, www.centennialofflight.gov, confirms the outlines of Adams's description, as does "Airship at Virgin Islands," *New York Times* (May 7, 1925), 20.

 5. *DN* (May 16, 1988), 15.

 6. *DN* (May 23, 1988).

 7. *DN* (May 30, 1988).

 8. It is possible that Adams means Felix *Dreyschock* here, yet Dreyschock taught primarily in Leipzig, so the original "Dryschock" is retained.

 9. *DN* (June 6, 1988), 19.

 10. *DN* (July 11, 1988), 22.

 11. *DN* (June 20, 1988).

 12. *DN* (June 17, 1988). Grigg was of Danish and English ancestry and worked in the Health Department on St. Croix beginning in 1921 (see Moolenaar 1992, 88).

13. *DN* (July 5, 1988), 20. For more on Cuney-Hare, see Douglas Hales, *A Southern Family in White and Black* (College Station: Texas A & M University Press, 2003). Cuney-Hare's 1936 book, *Negro Musicians and Their Music* (Washington, DC: Associated Publishers), includes a chapter on music in the Virgin Islands based in part on information she received from Adams.

14. The film of which Meier writes is likely *The Black Pirate*, which is the only feature film released in 1926 in which Fairbanks had a starring role.

15. *DN* (June 13, 1988), 18.

16. *DN* (July 18, 1988), 20.

17. *DN* (July 25, 1988).

18. *DN* (Aug. 2, 1988), 15.

19. *DN* (Aug. 8, 1988), 17. See also "Governor Trench Dies Suddenly," *New York Times* (Jan. 7, 1927), 19.

20. *DN* (Aug. 15, 1988), 20.

21. *DN* (Aug. 22, 1988), 20; "Evans Made Governor of Virgin Islands," *New York Times* (Jan. 19, 1927), 17. See also letter to the editor by Adolph Gereau describing ceremony and excitement at news of citizenship: "Virgin Islanders' Joy at Citizenship," *New York Times* (March 20, 1927), XX16.

22. *DN* (Aug. 29, 1988), 24.

23. James Reese Europe was killed on May 9, 1919. Possibly Adams was considered to replace him in 1919, although this is unlikely as the ragtime and jazz dance music Europe's band made famous was not in Adams's repertory. More likely, in 1926 Adams was offered the job of conducting Europe's former unit—the 369th black infantry army band. According to Reid Badger's *A Life in Ragtime: A Biography of James Reese Europe* (New York: Oxford University Press, 1995), Europe and his band were mustered out of the army in February 1919 to perform as the civilian ensemble the Hellfighters Band, capitalizing on their wartime fame. Playing only sporadically after their leader's death, this band ceased to exist not long after a memorial concert in May 1920 (223).

24. *DN* (Sept. 5, 1988), 16.

25. *DN* (Sept. 12, 1988), 22.

26. *DN* (Sept. 19, 1988), 18.

27. *DN* (Sept. 26, 1988), 20.

28. *DN* (Oct. 3, 1988), 16.

29. *DN* (Oct. 10, 1988), 16.

30. *DN* (Oct. 19, 1988), 17.

31. *DN* (Oct. 24, 1988), 21.

32. *DN* (Oct. 31, 1988), 28. This column and the one that follows reprint letters by readers recounting their personal memories of Lindbergh's visit. The event is covered by the *New York Times* in three articles: "Lindbergh 1,051 miles over Sea to Virgin Islands" (Feb. 1, 1928), 1; "St. Thomas Makes Lindbergh Freeman; San Juan Hop Today" (Feb. 2, 1928), 1; and "Circles St. Thomas and HOP" (Feb. 3, 1928), 5.

33. *DN* (Nov. 21, 1988), 36. Romer and his canoe are pictured in "The Lone Oarsman of the Atlantic: Franz Romer," *New York Times* (Aug. 19, 1928), 91.

34. *DN* (Nov. 28, 1988), 20.

35. *DN* (Dec. 5, 1988), 21. Romer's departure is described in "St. Thomas to New York in Canoe," *New York Times* (Sept. 9, 1928), 2.

36. Text recovered from an early manuscript draft (AAC§VII.1.16) and details added from contemporary newspaper accounts in the Navy Band Scrapbooks (AAC§VII.3.18). Date provided by "Virgin Islands Governor on Tour," *New York Times* (March 12, 1930), 60.

37. *DN* (Dec. 12, 1988), 27.

38. *DN* (Dec. 19, 1988), 21. Brown's assignment to the islands is covered in "Expert Goes to Aid of Virgin Islands," *New York Times* (June 22, 1930), N1.

39. *DN* (Dec. 27, 1988), 20.

40. *DN* (Jan. 3, 1989), 14.

41. Harriet Connor Brown, *Grandmother Brown's Hundred Years, 1827–1927* (Toronto: McClelland and Stewart, 1929).

42. *DN* (Jan. 9, 1989), 16.

43. *DN* (Jan. 17, 1989).

44. *DN* (Jan. 23, 1989), 17.

45. *DN* (Jan. 30, 1989), 15.

46. *DN* (Feb. 6, 1989), 18.

CHAPTER 8. THE NAVAL ADMINISTRATION (1917–1931)

1. Laye originally published this novel as *Dramouss* in Paris. It appeared in an English translation of the original French two years later under the title *A Dream of Africa* (London: Collins, 1968).

2. Evans's book was originally published in 1945 by J. W. Edwards of Ann Arbor, Michigan.

3. Jarvis, *Brief History of the Virgin Islands.* The following quotations are taken from ch. 15, "Fourteen Years of the Navy," 131–42.

4. Jarvis discusses "Cha-chas" on pages 201–3 of his *Brief History.* They are Roman Catholic immigrants of French descent from St. Bartholomew or St. Barths. Jarvis describes them as "clannish" and "intensely emotional and patriotic." The term *Cha-cha* is derogatory.

5. An additional outspoken critic of the naval administration was Rothschild Francis, another of Adams's rivals. Francis edited a biweekly newspaper, the *Emancipator,* that served primarily the lower classes of the Virgin Islands. In an article of January 4, 1922, titled "Then and Now," Francis notes a shift in the behavior of naval personnel from racist to "strong advocates" (1). During World War I, when the naval administration first came to the islands, a large contingent of servicemen were assigned to the islands in combat roles. This seems to have put increased pressure on race relations. With the war over, combat soldiers were transferred off island and much of this tension receded. Francis

further accuses the islands' "propertied class" of supporting the navy in order to further its own interests. Laborers preferred a "civil form" of government, according to his article. Yet Francis closes with a surprisingly positive endorsement of the navy administration that Adams would have appreciated: "The present officials [in 1922] loaned to us by the Navy serve gratuitously. They are select men possessing much tact and reliability, democratic in make-up and strong advocates of a higher civic life for the plain people." Of the years immediately after 1917, he writes, in contrast: "Several of the officials that came here after the transfer were exceedingly autocratic and first rate Negro haters. They wanted to govern the people in the same manner as they did battleships and regiments."

6. By "free," Adams refers to the absence of taxes on goods moving through the port.

7. The oil extracted from Chalmugra (also Chaulmoogra) seeds was used to treat leprosy.

8. John Boynton Priestley (1894–1984) was a British journalist, novelist, playwright, and essayist.

9. The manuscript version of this chapter in the AAC is incomplete, as if the final pages are lost. Since the draft itself draws heavily on portions of an essay Adams wrote titled "The Navy's Contribution to the Virgin Islands," dating from after World War II (AAC, unnumbered), closing material to complete the present chapter has been adapted from this work. Other sources are found in a 1960 "Address" published in the *Home Journal* (April 12, 1960) and preserved in AAC§VI.1.1.

CHAPTER 9. CIVILIAN GOVERNMENT AND POLITICS (THE 1930S)

1. *DN* (Feb. 20, 1989), 18.

2. *DN* (Feb. 13, 1989). Gift was an ardent navy supporter and critic of the Pearson administration. The *New York Times* described her as "president of the Suffragist League." She presented a mahogany walking stick to President Franklin D. Roosevelt during his 1934 visit, as well as "a letter setting forth complaints against the Pearson administration." The letter was necessary since a protest parade planned by the league against Pearson was banned by police. See "St. Thomas Crowds Hail Roosevelt," *New York Times* (July 8, 1934), 1.

3. *DN* (Feb. 27, 1989).

4. According to Richard V. Oulahan's article for the *New York Times*, Hoover was on St. Thomas for only five hours and heard pleas for the economic health of the islands, including the benefits of the naval presence and the damage done by Prohibition to the market for sugar and thus to the agricultural and manufacturing health of St. Croix. Hoover participated in a "colorful parade which brought forcibly to his mind the fact that the population of the islands is overwhelmingly Negro." Both Herbert D. Brown and Captain Evans were present for Hoover's visit, the latter still overseeing the naval withdrawal.

The population of the islands is given as 22,000. See "Virgin Island Wets Put Plea to Hoover during 5-Hour Call," *New York Times* (March 26, 1931), 1.

5. *DN* (April 3, 1989), 20.

6. *DN* (April 24, 1989), 22.

7. Summary of Pearson's cultural program, taken from Adams's typescript "Governor Paul M. Pearson—First Civilian Governor" (AAC§VI.1.14).

8. Date confirmed by telegram from Adams to his wife (AAC§II.1.108); Merle died on the evening of May 9 from an unexpected, sudden illness, possibly meningitis ("Local," *Bulletin* [May 10, 1932], 2). Adams's bitterness about the navy's departure may have been exacerbated by this death and the question of whether the navy's superior medical resources could have made a difference.

9. Adams reports a figure of 1,500 deaths, but 3,500 is the official Cuban count. See www.tierramerica.net/2001/1111/iacentos.shtml.

10. Wife of Ellis Stone, the lieutenant commander of the St. Thomas Naval Base in 1924, who was directly in charge of the band during its tour.

11. Henry Edward Krehbiel, *Afro-American Folksongs: A Study in Racial and National Music* (New York: G. Schirmer, 1914). Some indications of Adams's own research can be found in his influence on Maude Cuney-Hare's writings and Adams's own article "Whence Came the Calypso" (AAC).

12. Text crossed out in the manuscript reads, "after which all that remained for burial was her spine that was found among the ashes of the rubble." The details told here are poignantly confirmed by a set of telegrams (AAC§II.1.112–14).

13. The ineffectiveness of the local firefighting arrangement and its inability to save his daughter may provide an additional reason that Adams was so angry about the dismissal of the navy. When the navy left, so did its firefighting equipment and expertise. See letter from Proctor to Adams, September 6, 1932, in Adams scrapbook (reprinted *DN* [May 29, 1989]).

14. The story of the 1932 fire is based on an untitled manuscript in the AAC, along with two *DN* articles with memoir excerpts, June 19, 1989, and June 16, 1989 (18).

15. *DN* (July 3, 1989), 17; more information on the house can be found in Edith deJongh Woods, "House on Kongens Gade Was Home to Alton Adams," *DN* (July 25, 2003), 26–27. During the naval years, the building served as the administrative headquarters of the naval hospital located next door. The hospital was later destroyed in a hurricane.

16. This section is taken from an unfinished draft in the Adams memoirs materials; band, orchestral, and solo piano versions of "Childhood Merriment" survive (AAC§VIII.1.5–13).

17. *DN* (July 10, 1989), 18. While correspondence in the AAC confirms this characterization of Adams's relationship with Governor Pearson, Adams's account here seems to compress time a bit. A memo affirming Adams's verbal appointment as chair of the St. Thomas Music Committee is dated March 8, 1934—eight months after his return to St. Thomas (§I.2.2)—but no mention is made of a position in the schools. However, in a letter to Pearson six days

later, Adams makes it clear that he is seeking a job to support his family. Pearson was clearly devoted to improving the cultural education of the islands, but Adams found his initial proposal (engaging a harmonica instructor) disappointing (§I.2.5). This letter also suggests Adams was again associated with the islands' Music Week celebrations.

18. *DN* (July 17, 1989), 18. Drew Pearson, with Robert S. Allen (Washington bureau chief for the *Christian Science Monitor*), first published *Washington Merry-Go-Round* anonymously as a book (New York: H. Liveright, 1931). Following the sequel and the subsequent revelation of their authorship, the two journalists resigned their positions and began publishing the weekly column. At its height, the column was read by sixty million readers in over six hundred papers. See Jim Heintze, "Biography of Drew Pearson," American University Archives, 2006, www.library.american.edu/pearson/biography.html.

19. *DN* (July 24, 1989), 18.

20. *DN* (July 31, 1989), 17.

21. *DN* (Aug. 7, 1989), 18.

22. The holograph score in Adams's hand has survived (AAC§VIII.1.30).

23. *DN* (Aug. 15, 1989), 15.

24. *DN* (Aug. 21, 1989), 16. Details of Eleanor Roosevelt's visit are preserved in "Studies Virgin Islands," *New York Times* (March 9, 1934), 24. She spent the morning of March 8 swimming and visiting the Bluebeard Hotel project, and "inspected farm projects around Lindbergh Bay and watched the building of roads, draining of swamps and repairing of schools." She visited St. Croix and returned to St. Thomas in the afternoon, departing immediately for San Juan, Puerto Rico.

25. *DN* (Aug. 28, 1989). The *New York Times*, in covering the president's visit, noted the performance of Adams's song: "The President stopped in Emancipation Garden . . . to listen to a song of welcome composed by Alton Adams, Negro bandmaster of the Naval Reserve, and sung by a thousand high school pupils, clad in bright ginghams and white starched suits which contrasted with their black faces and sparkling eyes." See "St. Thomas Crowds Hail Roosevelt," *New York Times* (July 8, 1934), 1.

26. *DN* (Feb. 19, 1990), 16.

27. *DN* (Feb. 28, 1990).

28. *DN* (March 5, 1990). The author's mention of labor leader Morris Davis hints at a prevailing conflict underlying Virgin Islands politics of the period, one that Adams does not address directly in these memoirs—namely, the competing needs of the islands of St. Thomas and St. John versus the largest Virgin Island, St. Croix. While naval bases and tourism benefited St. Thomas and its close neighbor St. John, the economy of St. Croix was distinct and primarily agricultural. St. Thomas had long dominated the Virgin Islands politically, and Adams's views reveal his deeply St. Thomian perspective. Generally speaking, the politicians of St. Croix had pushed for a civilian rule that would better recognize the needs of their own island. At least some opinions concerning the

Virgin Islands that Adams dismisses as misinformation or intrigue reflect the genuine needs of St. Croix and the preferences of certain politicians there.

29. *DN* (March 12, 1990).

30. *DN* (March 19, 1990), 15.

31. *DN* (Oct. 2, 1989), 18.

32. *DN* (Oct. 9, 1989), 25.

33. *DN* (Oct. 16, 1989), 16, 19.

34. Charles Edwin Taylor, *An Island of the Sea: Descriptive of the Past and Present of St. Thomas, Danish West Indies, with a Few Short Stories about Bluebeard's Castles* (St. Thomas, DWI: the author, 1896).

35. The section about the Bluebeard pageant comes from an AMRI typescript, with details added and confirmed by two *DN* articles, "Governor Paul Pearson's Dream Come True!" (Dec. 24, 1934), 1; and "Christmas Day Was Gala" (Dec. 27, 1934), 1. Bluebeard's Castle in St. Thomas is considered by local legend as the setting of the tale used by such composers as Jacques Offenbach for the 1866 operetta *Barbe-bleue* (Bluebeard) and Béla Bartók for his 1911 one-act opera *Bluebeard's Castle*. Although the tale, which warns women of disobedience and curiosity, was codified by Charles Perrault in his 1697 *Histories ou contes du temps passé* (Stories or tales of past times), the legend travels in many different versions, including the variant told here.

36. The version of the Bluebeard legend told here is taken from two of Adams's pieces republished in *DN*, Oct. 23, 1989 (19), and Oct. 30, 1989 (16).

37. *DN* (Nov. 20, 1989), 18.

38. *DN* (Nov. 27, 1989), 16. Details in Adams's account do not match recent scholarship, notably Frank M. Figueroa's "The Figueroas: Puerto Rico's First Family of Music," *Latin Beat Magazine* (May 2004). Adams's account here has been corrected, but it is not precisely clear whether it was Jaime or José who performed for Adams. José appears to have been the more experienced and accomplished musician (he played first violin in the Figueroa Brothers Quintet), but it was Jaime who had studied in Paris more recently, so he is identified here as the likely performer and competitor.

39. The details of Millay's arrival are confirmed by "News of the Day," *St. Thomas Mail Notes* (Jan. 3, 1935), 4. Millay and her husband left New York on Dec. 28, 1934.

40. *DN* (Dec. 4, 1989), 24.

41. *DN* (Dec. 11, 1989), 21.

42. *DN* (April 9, 1990), 20. Only one letter from Drew Pearson to Adams is to be found in the AAC (§II.2.39) and is dated April 3, 1941. It suggests a more formal and distant professional relationship than the close friendship described in the memoirs. A letter of March 31 from Adams to Drew Pearson does state that clippings from Adams's *Bulletin* editorials were included (§II.2.38).

43. The dredge boat *Huston* was built by the Bethlehem Steel Corporation, Barrows Point, Maryland, and delivered in 1910. See hull no. 113 at www.colton company.com/shipbldg/ussbldrs/prewwii/shipyards/bethsparrowspoint.htm.

44. *DN* (Dec. 18, 1989), 25.

45. The Tydings investigation of the administration of the Virgin Islands received extensive national press coverage that confirms the details of Adams's account. Articles in the *New York Times*, however, offer a broader view. Judge Wilson, for example, is seen by the *Times* as the primary opposition to Governor Pearson. The *Times* also describes the Tydings investigation as "adjourned" but not abandoned, and represents the resignation and reassignment of both Pearson and Wilson as a face-saving gesture in which "President Roosevelt put an end to the Virgin Islands fight . . . by ousting both fighters." See "A New Governor," *New York Times* (July 28, 1935), E1. The political ordeal can be traced in the *New York Times* during 1935 in often front-page articles such as "Island Inquiry Expected" (Jan. 26), 11; "President Confers on Virgin Islands" (Feb. 17), 20; "Senate Group Asks Inquiry on Islands" (March 1), 1; "Ickes Asks to Be Heard" (April 5), 6; "Rule of Pearson Series of Storms" (April 7), 33; "Majority Opposes Pearson's Regime" (April 9), 22; "Virgin Isles Form Pivot in Struggle" (April 5), 6; "Pearson Defends Record in Office" (April 10), 18; "Discord Is Shown in Virgin Isle Rule" (July 9), 9; "Ousting of Judge Demanded by Ickes" (July 10), 1; "Shake-up Imminent in Virgin Islands" (July 12), 1; "Navy May Receive Virgin Isles' Rule" (July 16), 7; "Pearson Resigns Virgin Isles Post" (July 24), 1; and "Tydings to Press Virgin Isles Study" (July 25), 1.

46. *DN* (March 26, 1990), 19.

47. *DN* (April 2, 1990), 19. The fight described here is detailed in "Fist Fight Marks Virgin Isle Inquiry," *New York Times* (July 3, 1935), 8.

48. *DN* (April 17, 1990), 19.

49. *DN* (April 23, 1990).

50. *DN* (April 30, 1990), 23; Paul Pearson's personal papers are held by the Friends Historical Library at Swarthmore College (RG 5/121).

51. *DN* (Dec. 28, 1989). In addition to the Marine Corps planes, the navy maintained the USS *Antares*, a training ship, in St. Thomas harbor. See "St. Thomas Hails Advent of Cramer," *New York Times* (Sept. 15, 1935), E12.

52. *DN* (May 22, 1990), 17.

53. *DN* (May 28, 1990).

54. "Louisenhoj" is pronounced locally as "Lou-eez-un-hoy."

55. *DN* (May 7, 1990).

56. *DN* (May 14, 1990).

57. Wilder's visit and his stay at Bluebeard's are confirmed by "Thornton N. Wilder Here," *DN* (Oct. 16, 1935), 1, and "Novelist Visits Library," *DN* (Oct. 16, 1936). *Our Town* was written in multiple locations.

58. *DN* (Jan. 22, 1990), 18.

59. *DN* (Jan. 29, 1990), 21.

60. *DN* (Feb. 5, 1990), 15.

61. *DN* (Feb 12, 1990), 19.

62. *DN*, July 15, 1991 (20), and July 22, 1991 (22). See also Ron Roizen, "Herschel Grynszpan: The Fate of a Forgotten Assassin," *Holocaust and Genocide Studies* 1:2 (1986): 217–28. The pogroms subsequent to Grynszpan's act of

resistance include *die Kristallnacht* (the Night of Broken Glass) of November 9, 1938, which is considered by many to mark the beginning of the Holocaust.

63. *DN* (July 29, 1991), 16.

64. *DN* (Aug. 7, 1991), 24. The article "Delays War Haven on Virgin Islands," *New York Times* (Dec. 13, 1940), 11, corroborates Adams's account here. Ickes argued that a refugee program would be an "economic benefit" to the islands and that only "a few hundred refugees could be received."

CHAPTER 10. THE POWER OF THE PRESS (THE 1940S)

1. *DN* (Aug. 13, 1990), 22. According to the Just the Beginning Foundation website (www.jtbf.org), which tracks the history of black judges in the United States, Hastie and Moore were not just the first black judges appointed to the District Court of the Virgin Islands but also the first at that level of the judiciary in the United States as a whole. Adams here describes Moore as "president" of the Cook County Bar Association, but no evidence has been found to support this claim, and "member" has been substituted. Moore's nomination is covered in "Moore Awaits Confirmation; Lauds Friends," *Chicago Defender* (Aug. 5, 1939), 3. The article confirms Secretary Ickes's role but credits Illinois senator James M. Slattery with the initial nomination. Moore's wife, Marie Johnson Moore, moved a few months after her husband, who left Chicago for the islands via Washington, D.C., in August 1939 ("Mrs. Herman E. Moore Views Life in Virgin Islands," *Chicago Defender* [Aug. 26, 1935], 18). See also Gilbert Ware, *William Hastie: Grace under Pressure* (New York: Oxford University Press, 1984); and Herman E. Moore, "The Virgin Islands and Its Judicial System," *National Bar Journal* (Dec. 1945).

2. *DN* (Aug. 20, 1990), 16.

3. *DN* (Aug. 27, 1990), 25.

4. *DN* (Sept. 4, 1990), 17.

5. *DN* (Sept. 10, 1990), 24.

6. *DN* (Sept. 17, 1990), 19. Historians today generally view Trujillo as a dictator. See Richard Lee Turits, *Foundations of Despotism: Peasants, the Trujillo Regime, and Modernity* (Stanford, CA: Stanford University Press, 2003).

7. *DN* (Aug. 23, 1991), 18. The website http://ubootwaffe.net confirms the sinking of the *Eleni Stathatos* two hundred miles west of Scilly Island (off the coast of England) by U-boat 34 at 4:21 A.M. on Jan. 28, 1940.

8. *DN* (Sept. 5, 1991), 25.

9. *DN* (Oct. 22, 1990), 19.

10. *DN* (Oct. 29, 1990).

11. *DN* (Nov. 5, 1990), 29.

12. *DN* (Nov. 12, 1990), 19.

13. *DN* (Nov. 19, 1990), 16.

14. *DN* (Nov. 26, 1990), 16.

15. *DN* (Dec. 3, 1990), which also contains reminiscences by Victor Bryan, a student at the Herrick School who met Swanson.

16. *DN* (Dec. 10, 1990), 21.

17. *DN* (Dec. 17, 1990), 25. Adams's discussion avoids the common mistake of crediting the Works Progress Administration with post office murals, and thus testifies to the strength of his reporting methods. When the first New Deal art project, the Public Works of Art Project (1933–34), ended, the Section of Painting and Sculpture was created in 1934 under the Treasury Department. It continued to be responsible for post office projects after the creation of the WPA Federal Art Project in 1935. The Federal Works Agency was a banner organization that encompassed all federal art programs. In 1979, responsibility for FWA projects was transferred to the General Services Administration. See Marlene Park and Gerald E. Markowitz, *Democratic Vistas: Post Offices and Public Art in the New Deal* (Philadelphia: Temple University Press, 1984); and Patricia Raynor, "Off the Wall: New Deal Post Office Murals," *EnRoute* 6:4 (Oct.–Dec. 1997). Biographical details here confirmed by Air Force Art Collection data files (see www.afapo.hq.af.mil). In addition to his murals throughout the United States, the social realist artist Steven Dohanos (1907–94) is best remembered for hundreds of cover illustrations he created for the *Saturday Evening Post*. Curiously, Adams does not report the titles of the murals, which Park and Markowitz give as *The Virgin Islands, U.S.—The Leisurely Native Tempo* and *The Virgin Islands, U.S.—The Outer World Significance*. This may be a simple oversight or may cast doubt on the titles; they may refer to designs other than the final ones executed or may have been assigned by someone other than Dohanos.

18. *DN* (Dec. 24, 1990), 27.

19. *DN*, Dec. 4, 1991 (26), and Dec. 9, 1991 (22).

20. *DN* (Dec. 16, 1991), 24.

21. *DN* (Nov. 25, 1991), 24.

22. *DN* (March 18, 1991), 20.

23. "Alton Adams Tries to Reorganize 'Rag Tag' Band" *DN* (March 25, 1991), 19. Adams rejoined the service officially on June 5, 1942, presumably in Cuba. The appointment of a black bandmaster to head the twenty-six-member all-white Guantánamo contingent made Adams the first known black person to direct white navy musicians. Adams's race was not received well, and several white musicians reportedly wrote to their congressmen requesting transfer (personal communication, Alton Adams, Jr., May 2006). Such transfer requests were reportedly denied, although the simple fact that the photo of Adams's second band has only eighteen players, including the eight recalled black musicians, suggests that sixteen of the original twenty-six white members had either missed the photo or somehow left the band. Adams found "distraught, demoralized, 'rum-drinking'" musicians who had deteriorated musically without a director and who were required to do "menial enlisted men's jobs" in addition to playing. He requested that his musicians be relieved of these other duties to focus on music (Floyd 1977, 179). Adams established the same six-hour daily rehearsal and regular performance routine he had used to create his first navy band. Within a year, the band improved dramatically, but was then split up when Adams returned to St. Thomas.

24. *DN* (April 5, 1991), 17.
25. *DN* (April 9, 1991), 16.
26. *DN* (April 15, 1991), 21. Even before leaving St. Thomas for Cuba, Adams had begun advocating for the renaissance of the Virgin Islands band, which would allow him to stay near family and provide music for his community. While initial requests were denied, a letter of Sept. 1942 from Harwood announces the approval of such a plan by the navy (AAC§II.2.45). Adams and the eight Virgin Islanders in the Cuba band were to be transferred as the seeds of a twenty-three-piece all-black unit at the St. Thomas Submarine Base. By March 25, 1943, instruments had arrived in St. Thomas, and Adams was set to recruit additional players to fill out the band ("Instruments for Navy Band Received," *DN* [March 25, 1943], 2). Four new native musicians, including two who had been serving as cooks for the navy, played successful auditions: Lincoln Powell and Oliver Best of St. Thomas, plus J. O. Breedy and A. A. Libert of St. Croix ("Four Virgin Islands Musicians Join U.S. Navy," *DN* [April 8, 1943], 1). Adams had hoped to reinstate most of his original bandsmen, but many (including his brother, Julien) were unable to pass a required physical. Other bandsmen were recruited from off island to fill out the ensemble. At least four of these new bandsmen were black musicians from the Great Lakes Naval Training Center sent as a combo to provide jazz and dance music as a secondary ensemble that would also play with Adams's band. The four musicians were Arnold "Scrippy" Bolling (drums), Henry "Little Red" Hunt (trumpet), Benny Freeman (tenor saxophone), and Henry B. Richardson (clarinet). The quartet helped train some of Adams's musicians in their style, subsequently expanding the dance unit. They reportedly returned to the Great Lakes in late 1944 (Floyd 1977, 179, 182).

The renewed Virgin Islands band played its first concert on April 30, 1943, as a serenade to Commander G. K. G. Reilly, who had helped form the band ("U.S. Navy Band in Premiere Concert at Submarine Base," *DN* [April 30, 1943], 1, 4). The band's stated function recalls the motivation behind the founding of the original ensemble in 1917. Balsey is reported as having been "interested in promoting closer relations between the armed forces and the civilian population, and he believes that the band can do much toward this end." The band played for sporting events and "I Am an American Day" and gave Sunday-evening concerts in Emancipation Garden. These weekly concerts continued until May 28, 1944. Shortly thereafter the band was transferred again, this time to Puerto Rico. Again Brown and Adams played solos for a farewell concert crowd reported to number more than a thousand people ("Navy Band Thrills Large Audience in Closing Concert," *DN* [May 31, 1944], 1, 4). In his opening remarks at the concert, Adams named several members of the band who had been with him for thirty-four years, since the first concert of his Juvenile Band in 1911: Oliverre Sebastien, Herbert Brown, Conrad Gomez, Arnold Martin, and Lambert George ("Acting Governor Gives Public Recognition of Navy's Service to Community; Adams Makes Speech," *DN* [June 1, 1944]).

The *San Juan Breeze* of June 11, 1944, welcomed Adams's band to Puerto Rico with a photo and a caption: "Welcome Aboard—to Chief Musician Alton

A. Adams and his twenty-two men forming the new Band. Many of the boys were in there pitching when 'jive' and 'swing' were infants. From this military outfit is lifted a group of ten who break out the brass under the baton of Music Joseph Maduro for the Dance Orchestra—and brother, they're solid" (*San Juan Breeze* 5:33 [Puerto Rico: U.S. Naval Air Station, June 11, 1944], 3). After the end of the war, Adams soon left active duty (May 11, 1945) and returned to St. Thomas. Adams stayed on in the Fleet Reserve until 1947, retiring with letters of commendation for his thirty-year tenure. On February 22, 1987, he was awarded an honorary appointment in the Virgin Islands National Guard as "Command Sergeant Major" (certificate held at AMRI).

27. *DN* (April 23, 1991), 20 (paper is dated incorrectly on this page, reading "April 20").

28. *DN* (May 1, 1991), 28. The Paiwonsky family took in seven refugees, three men and a family of four. Additional editorials concerning the Lovett situation are reprinted in *DN* (May 22, 1991), 27.

29. *DN*, May 28, 1991 (19), and June 5, 1991 (27).

30. *DN* (June 12, 1991), 28.

31. *DN* (June 17, 1991), 26.

32. *DN* (June 25, 1991), 20.

33. *DN* (July 3, 1991), 24.

34. *DN* (July 8, 1991), 23. *All Our Years: The Autobiography of Robert Morss Lovett*, written by Lovett and published by Viking Press in 1948, contains an account of his service for the Virgin Islands as well as a transcript of his testimony before the Dies committee. The Lovett saga is told in a series of 1943 articles by the *New York Times*, including "Ickes Denounces Lovett Removal" (May 16), 8; "Bill of Attainder" (May 20), 20; "Ban on Salaries Upheld" (June 24), 23; "Senate Rejects Bill Ending Salaries of 3" (June 25), 5; "Compromise on FCC Men" (June 27), 12; "Congress Snarls Put Off Recess" (July 4), 1; and "Roosevelt Signs Six Big Fund Bills and Criticizes One" (July 13), 1. Lovett eventually resigned in March 1944 at the request of Ickes to avoid a continuing budget war in the next round of appropriations ("Lovett Quits as Virgin Island Official; Was Target in Congress over Subversion," *New York Times* [March 14, 1944], 36). Lovett challenged Congress through the courts, arguing that its actions created an unconstitutional bill of attainder. He won a 1946 decision from the U.S. Supreme Court (*United States v. Lovett*, 328 U.S. 303) and received back pay ("Court Invalidates Lovett Discharge," *New York Times* [June 4, 1946], 6). He died in Chicago in 1956 ("Robert M. Lovett, Educator, Is Dead," *New York Times*, Feb. 9, 1956).

CHAPTER 11. TOURISM AND THE HOTEL ASSOCIATION (THE 1950S)

1. Atop what is known as "Bluebeard's Hill" and, coincidentally, just above the Adams homestead, the Bluebeard Castle survives as of 2007 as part of an active tourist resort with 170 rooms called Bluebeard's Castle Hotel.

2. The Adams Guest House was profiled in the travel section of the *Boston Globe*, Sunday, January 11, 1970, in a first-page feature titled "St. Thomas, Half Price," by Anne Wyman: "Personality can make the place and one place that deserves special mention is the Adams Guest House with only six rooms and rates of $12 double, with breakfast. Alton A. Adams, an octogenarian now, was the leader of the U.S. Navy's first and only all-Negro band, formed in 1917. (Adams stresses the fact that the black band was later integrated.)" According to the article, prevailing rates on the island at the time for standard hotels were $50 to $70 a day.

3. See ch. 9.

4. Details on the home added from an unidentified five-page typescript dating from 1970 titled "Answers" (AMRI). The data here are taken from answers 4–7. The yellow bricks in the structure were brought to St. Thomas as ballast on Danish ships, while coral can be found among the rocks in the masonry walls (Alton Adams, Jr., personal communication, Aug. 2005).

5. One guest who stayed at the house on Feb. 8, 1951, but refused to give a name, prowled the manager's quarters at night. When confronted by Adams, he leaped out a window. Having stolen $80, he was later captured and identified (see "Guest Turns Prowler Escapes with $80," *DN* [Feb. 9, 1951], 1).

6. Correspondence in the AAC suggests that this concert was to take place in the spring of 1979 (AAC§I.4.61).

7. Adams organized concerts for Schuyler on March 14, 1950, and April 15, 1952, at the Center Theatre (see "Wonder Pianist-Composer at Center Tonight," *DN* [March 14, 1950], 1, and "Philippa Schuyler in Concert Tonight," *DN* [April 15, 1952], 1). Schuyler's mother accompanied her on the first trip.

8. Philippa Schuyler, *Adventures in Black and White* (New York: Robert Speller and Sons, 1960), 20–21. See also Kathryn Talalay, *Composition in Black and White: The Life of Philippa Schuyler* (New York: Oxford University Press, 1995).

9. DuBois died on August 27, 1963, in Ghana on the eve of the March on Washington, when Martin Luther King delivered his famous "I Have a Dream" oration.

10. Theophilus "Teddy" Albert Marryshow (1887–1958) is known as the "Father of West Indies Federation."

11. This description indicates continuing ethnic tension between West Indian blacks and certain other blacks on the U.S. mainland.

12. Seven-Up, or 7UP, is a clear lemon-lime soft drink produced in the United States from 1920.

13. Power Authority section added to the memoirs from a working draft (AAC§VI.1.13).

14. AAC§IV contains records of the Hotel Association.

15. The principles outlined here parallel those listed in the Revised By-Laws of the Hotel Association of the Virgin Islands of May 27, 1957 (AAC§IV.1.1). The association met annually, rotating the place of the meeting

among its members and convening more often in the first years or when legal business was pending. Association minutes preserved in the AAC make clear that participation in the association was unreliable. When critical issues faced the industry, participation increased; at other times, interest waned. The association spent considerable energy collecting late dues from members and raising funds to pay for its advertising initiatives.

16. The Adams 1799 Guest House was a small player in the local hotel economy, and relations were often strained between large corporate hotels and smaller guesthouses. Adams's selection as president of the association was a wise tactical move, as it not only brought a knowledgeable and well-connected individuals to the service of the association but also bridged the gap between hotels and guesthouses and between so-called continentals, native islanders, and labor unions. Dues and voting strength in the association were proportional to the number of rooms maintained by each establishment. In an undated set of minutes, details of these figures are given. Adams Guest House had 4 votes, for example, and the Virgin Isles Hotel had 125 (AAC§IV.1.9). Adams had four guest rooms at this time.

17. The first dance raised $3,500 for the hospital fund (AAC§IV.2.18). A raffle of goods, including dinners and stays at member hotels, raised money in addition to the sale of entrance tickets (raffle tickets held by AMRI). The association's donations were targeted to purchase medicines for indigent patients. In a radio address promoting the ball in its fourth or so year, Adams claimed that this money reduced the length of hospital stays, thus saving the government money, and improved physician morale and quality of care while addressing the growing cost of health care for the islands (AAC§IV.3.23).

18. Adams's WSTA radio script is held in AAC (§IV.3.16). The same anecdote about mother and child and additional details of Knud-Hansen's service to the island are contained in an article by Adams, "Knud Knud-Hansen, M.D., F.A.C.S.—A Friend to Humanity," *Bulletin* (Sept. 23, 1940), 2.

19. The training program was first proposed by the Vocational Division of the Department of Education and seems to have been based on a similar initiative in Puerto Rico. The program is first mentioned in the minutes of the association in 1953 (AAC§IV.1.9). Correspondence in the AAC confirms the program's operation in collaboration with the public school vocational program, the governor's office, and the Hotel Association. It appears that the program was underfunded and that materials and instructional time were donated by the association. With the resignation of the program's coordinator E. Leonard Brewer in February 1956, the program appears to have evaporated. Thirty-two students graduated on February 27, 1956, representing a slight increase over the twenty-eight who graduated in 1955 (AAC§IV.2.53–54).

20. An undated flyer (AAC§V.1.11) advertises a later associate-degree program at the College of the Virgin Islands in "Hotel and Resort Management and Operation." Adams is depicted on the cover with the college in the background. An accompanying endorsement of the enterprise reads: "A DEGREE PROGRAM in hotel and resort management ought to upgrade the quality of pub-

lic hospitality services throughout the Caribbean, as well as open doors to a profitable future for many an ambitions young man and woman—Alton A. Adams, President of the Hotel Association of the Virgin Islands." The flyer is undated, but likely from the 1960s.

21. This section on the press has been inserted from an undated address by Adams, likely a radio script or a talk given to journalists (AAC§IV.3.31).

22. The tax is mentioned in the minutes of the association's first meeting. In fact, fighting the tax seems to be one of the inspirations for its creation. The "Ordinance to Provide Additional Revenues by Levying Certain Trade Taxes and Fees" was signed by Governor de Castro on July 5, 1952, and the association's first official meeting took place two days later. At that meeting the association drafted the following press release:

> Bill No. 136 of the Eighth Municipal Council of St. Thomas and St. John, which became law by the governor's signature on July 5, 1952, imposes a tax on all visitors to St. Thomas and St. John who stop in licensed hotels; [resolved:] that this law is vague, indefinite and impossible for hotels to conform to; that it is impossible to determine what is taxable and who shall pay the tax, as well as what right the hotel has to enforce the payment of the tax upon its guests. More important, the Association believes that this is a serious blow to the growing tourist industry of the islands and that the amount that could possibly be collected by the Council would be $10,000 and that much greater loss and danger to the well-being of the people of the Virgin Islands will result than the loss resulting from the worst hurricane disaster that ever hit or might hit the West Indies. Furthermore, that the law is discriminatory and that the yield of the tax is so small that it would be more economical and practical for hotels to pay the tax than for the Association to engage Counsel to combat this law were it not for the fact that this issue is so vital and so paramount to every aspect of the economy and well-being of the people of the islands that it is the duty of the Association, and as citizens, to fight this law to the bitter end so that the humble people of these islands may not be cheated by what looks like an easy tax to collect from visitors and tourists. [AAC§IV.1.2]

A copy of the tax bill and correspondence between the association and its lawyer are preserved in AAC§IV.1.44. The association was involved in several other legal issues concerning the Wage Hour Act and the minimum wage (arguing for relief in cases of employees who received tips), as well as the creation of an Innkeepers Law that would limit liability in cases in which a guest died.

23. Beginning in 1953, the association held an annual benefit costume ball to celebrate the anniversary of its founding. The first ball was held August 19 at the Virgin Isle Hotel. The idea for the benefit appears to have been Adams's, and he served as chairman of the first organizing committee ("Minutes," July 13, 1953, AAC§IV.1.3).

24. Divorce provided significant business to the hoteliers on the Virgin Islands, as the Virgin Islands (along with Indiana, Nevada, and South Dakota) offered so-called divorce havens, where couples living in most areas of the United States in which divorce was illegal or difficult to obtain, could visit, qualify for residency, and legally divorce. Typically the woman of the couple took up residency. In the Virgin Islands the residency requirement was six weeks, and valid grounds for divorce included simple "incompatibility" ("Unvexed Caribbean," *New York Times* [April 6, 1947], X14). While *Alton v. Alton* was dismissed in 1954 as moot, Virgin Islands divorce law was voided by the Supreme Court in 1955. See "Court Voids 'Quickie' Law on Virgin Islands Divorces," *New York Times* (April 12, 1955), 1; and Hendrik Hartog, *Man and Wife in America: A History* (Cambridge, MA: Harvard University Press, 2000).

25. A program for the 1953 Carnival that is held at AMRI suggests that the revival began in 1952 and was indeed sponsored by the tourist industry.

26. An earlier version of this list appears in a 1970 speech given by Adams upon his retirement as president of the Hotel Association. A yet earlier version presented to the Rotary Club of St. Thomas on June 4, 1970, included among the contributions the revival of the Virgin Islands Carnival, the creation of a Miss Virgin Islands pageant to select a contestant for Miss America, and the association's radio programs. These have been inserted into the comprehensive list presented here (AAC§IV.3.22).

27. This concluding paragraph was adapted from a speech given by Adams over WBNB-TV on April 1, 1970 (AMRI).

EDITORIAL METHODS

1. Sylvia Stipe, "Alton Adams, Sr., Plans Memoirs to Help," *(St. Thomas) Weekly Journal* (June 7, 1973), 14.

2. This grant application survives only in part (AAC§V.1.10).

Selected Bibliography

The editor offers these citations of works by and about Alton Augustus Adams, Sr., as guidance for further reading and research. The list reflects the state of knowledge about Adams's activities as of the publication of these memoirs and should not be considered definitive.

WRITINGS BY ALTON AUGUSTUS ADAMS, SR.

November 1, 1915. "Mendelssohn's Oratorio 'St. Paul' and the Rev. J. E. Weiss." *The Herald* (St. Croix) 1:1, p. 1.

November 8, 1915. "Is Music Strong beyond Its Power to Please? What Is There of Absolute Use in Music? I. Music a Human Necessity, or a Needless Accomplishment?" *The Herald* (St. Croix) 1:7, p. 3.

November 13, 1915. "Origin of the Banjo." Music in *The Herald* (St. Croix) 1:12, p. 3.

November 20, 1915. "The Negro and Music: Harry T. Burleigh, Renowned Negro Baritonist." *The Herald* (St. Croix) 1:18, p. 3.

November 24, 1915. "Negro Folk-Songs." *The Herald* (St. Croix) 1:20, p. 3.

December 4, 1915. "The Value of Music Theory to the Music Student." *The Herald* (St. Croix) 1:30, p. 3.

December 23, 1915. "Samuel Coleridge-Taylor—An Appreciation." *The Herald* (St. Croix) 1:6, pp. 2–3 (reprint of article from *The Dominant*).

March 1916. "The Band." *Jacobs' Band Monthly* 1:3, pp. 68–69.

March 1916. "The Flute." *Metronome*, p. 47.

April 1916. "The Band." *Jacobs' Band Monthly* 1:4, pp. 67–68, 70–71.

May 1916. [Untitled columnist's introduction.] The Band, *Jacobs' Band Monthly* 1:5, pp. 56, 58–60.

June 1916. "On Organizing a Band/Studies in Rhythm." The Band, *Jacobs' Band Monthly* 1:6, pp. 70–77.

July 1916. "Tune and Tone Practice/Studies in Rhythm." The Band, *Jacobs' Band Monthly* 1:7, pp. 79–82.

August 1916. "The Selection/Biography of Mr. Fred Lax." The Band, *Jacobs' Band Monthly* 1:8, pp. 78–84.

September 1916. "Music—An Appreciation." *Jacobs' Band Monthly* 1:10, pp. 68–71.

September 1916. "A Talk on the History and Technic of Band Instruments, The Clarinet/Harmonics/The Crescendo." The Band, *Jacobs' Band Monthly* 1:9, pp. 78–84.

October 1916. "A Remark/Band Instruments—History and Technic, No. 2: The Flute or Piccolo/Flute Romances." The Band, *Jacobs' Band Monthly* 1:10, pp. 79–84.

November 1916. "Band Instruments—History and Technic, No. 3: The Oboe Family/The Value of Music Theory to the Music Student." The Band, *Jacobs' Band Monthly* 1:11, pp. 75–80.

November 1916. "Behind the Scenes in Music Life." *Jacobs' Band Monthly* 1:11, pp. 82–83.

December 1916. "Historical Music Gleanings." *Jacobs' Band Monthly* 1:12, pp. 28–30.

December 1916. "Modern Helps to Music Students: The Music Magazine, the Correspondence System of Musical Instruction, the Talking Machine and Pianola or Piano Player/Band Instruments—History and Technic, No. 4: The Sax Family and the Saxophone." The Band, *Jacobs' Band Monthly* 1:12, pp. 70–73, 84–87.

January 1917. "A New Year's Talk to Band Leaders and Bandsmen/Band Instruments—History and Technic, No. 5: The Basset Horn, the Tenor and the Pedal Clarinet." The Band, *Jacobs' Band Monthly* 2:1, pp. 69–73, 80.

February 1917. "Band Instruments—History and Technic, No. 6: The Trumpet, the Cornet/As Regards the Metronome." The Band, *Jacobs' Band Monthly* 1:2, pp. 70–73.

February 1917. "The Educational Value of Music." *Jacobs' Band Monthly* 1:2, pp. 84–86.

March 1917. "Band Instruments—History and Technic No. 7—The French Horn/The Band on Parade." The Band, *Jacobs' Band Monthly* 2:3, pp. 70–75.

March 1917. "Historical Music Gleanings: The Music of the Greeks (continued from December issue)." *Jacobs' Band Monthly* 2:3, pp. 25–26, 86–87.

April 1917. "Band Instruments—History and Technic: No. 8—The Saxhorn Family." The Band, *Jacobs' Band Monthly* 2:4, pp. 68–72.

April 1917. "Historical Gleanings of Music: Greek Music (continued from March issue)." *Jacobs' Band Monthly* 2:4, pp. 29–31.

May 1917. "Something about the Flute: The Wood versus Silver and the Open versus Closed G Sharp/Teaching by Mail/Mr. Gustave Langenus and the Langenus Clarinet School/Band Instruments—History and Technic No. 9—The Trombone." The Band, *Jacobs' Band Monthly* 2:5, pp. 78–86.

May 1917. "The Virgin Islands: The Danish West Indies Now Included in the United States of America." *Jacobs' Band Monthly* 2:5, pp. 65–69.

July 1917. "A Word about Conducting/Teaching by Mail: Mr. H. A. Vander Cook and His System of Band and Orchestra Directing by Mail." The Band, *Jacobs' Band Monthly* 2:7, pp. 58–62.

August 1917. "Teaching by Mail: Mr. Eby and the Virtuoso Cornet School." The Band, *Jacobs' Band Monthly* 2:8, pp. 58–62.

September 1917. "Historical Music Gleanings: Greek Music (continued from the April issue)." *Jacobs' Band Monthly* 2:9, pp. 10–11, 66–68.

September 1917. "Queries." The Band, *Jacobs' Band Monthly* 2:9, pp. 58–60.

October 1917. "A Talk to Amateur Bandsmen on Preparedness." The Band, *Jacobs' Band Monthly* 2:10, pp. 58–62.

November 1917. "Historical Music Gleanings." The Band, *Jacobs' Band Monthly* 2:11, p. 66.

December 1917. "A Word about Jacobs' Monthlies." The Band, *Jacobs' Band Monthly* 2:12, pp. 60–62.

January 1918. "Historical Music Gleanings." *Jacobs' Band Monthly* 3:1, pp. 4, 6, 8.

January 1918. "A Talk to Amateur Bandsmen on Duty and Discipline." The Band, *Jacobs' Band Monthly* 3:1, pp. 64–66.

February 1918. "An Appeal for Higher Musicianship amongst Bandsmen/A Noted West Indian Singer [Philip Gomez]." The Band, *Jacobs' Band Monthly* 3:2, pp. 50–51.

March 1918. "In the Class Room: Lesson No. 1—Intervals." *Jacobs' Band Monthly* 3:3, pp. 50–53.

April 1918. "In the Class Room: Lesson II—The Scale." The Band, *Jacobs' Band Monthly* 3:4, pp. 74–77.

June 1918. "In the Class Room: Lesson No. 3 (continued from April issue)." The Band, *Jacobs' Band Monthly* 3:6, pp. 80–81.

July 1918. "Are You Thorough?" *Jacobs' Band Monthly* 3:7, pp. 54–56.

September 1918. "In the Class Room: Lesson No. 4 (continued from June issue)." The Band, *Jacobs' Band Monthly* 3:9, pp. 8, 10, 12.

November 1919. "A Musical Meandering." *Jacobs' Band Monthly* 4:11, pp. 16, 24, 30.

February 1920. "Whither Are We Drifting?" *Jacobs' Band Monthly* 5:2, pp. 16, 20, 22, 24, 26.

April 1921. "Concerning Music Literature." *Jacobs' Band Monthly* 6:4, pp. 86–87.

May 1921. "Band of the Palace: Port-au-Prince, Hayti." *Jacobs' Band Monthly* 6:4, pp. 73–74.

1922. "Music [Curriculum]." In *Course of Study for the Elementary Schools of the Virgin Islands of the U.S.A. (Grades I to VI, Inclusive).* Educational Bulletin No. 2. US VI: Department of Education.

April 1924. "Self Help in Playing the Flute." *Metronome*, p. 77.

September 18, 1924. "En Route with the Navy Band of the Virgin Islands." Clipping from *The Bulletin* (St. Thomas). AAC Scrapbooks.

September 1925. "Playing and Caring for Your Flute." *Metronome*, p. 22.

September 1926. "A Talk on the Sociologic and Aesthetic." *Metronome*, p. 45.

March 1927. "The Making of a Conductor." *Metronome*, p. 26.

October 1929. "Music Appreciation—An Appeal for Its Study." *Music Bulletin*, pp. 8–15, 17.

1934. "Corrections and Omission in Mr. Roberts [*sic*] 'Unwritten Music History.'" *Daily News* (St. Thomas), October 9, p. 3, and October 10, p. 3.

1934. "Letter to the Editor." *Daily News* (St. Thomas), October 12, p. 5.

1953. "Whence Came Calypso." *Virgin Islands Magazine* 8, pp. 35, 52, 57, 63, and 72.

April 12, 1960. "Address Delivered in the Emancipation Garden by Alton Adams on the Occasion of the Observance of the 43rd Year since the Transfer of the Virgin Islands." *Home Journal*, pp. 2, 4–5.

April 4, 1971. "Dedicated to the Memory of JPS, Leading Bandmaster of His Time." *Focus* [Sunday newspaper magazine from unidentified paper], pp. 6, 14.

n.d. "The Contribution of the Negro to Music." *Pittsburgh Courier* (undated copy held in AAC).

n.d. "Noted Bandmaster Asked Why Should We Segregate Ourselves Musically." *Pittsburgh Courier* (undated copy held in AAC).

MUSICAL COMPOSITIONS BY ADAMS

1909 or earlier. "Moving Day." Location unknown; may have been destroyed in 1932 fire.

1910. "H.M.S. *Ingolf* March." Location unknown; may have been destroyed in 1932 fire.

1912. "Doux rêve d'amour valse pour piano" (Sweet dream of love waltz for piano). Columbus, OH: Burt M. Cutler.

1914 or earlier. "A. J. B. March." Location unknown; may have been destroyed in 1932 fire.

1919. "Virgin Islands March." *Jacobs' Band Monthly* 3:10 and *Jacobs' Orchestral Monthly*, October.

1921. "The Governor's Own" (march). New York: Carl Fischer; reprint, 1964.

1924. "The Spirit of the U.S.N." (march). Boston: Cundy-Bettoney, 1925.

1925–26? "Sweet Virgin Isles" (for voice and piano).

n.d. "Bull Passin'" (band arrangement of a West Indian bamboula).

n.d. "Caribbean Echoes" (waltz serenade for band).

n.d. "Childhood Merriment." (waltz for band).

n.d. "Warbling in the Moonlight" (for solo piccolo and band).

RECORDINGS OF ADAMS'S COMPOSITIONS

"The Governor's Own." Recorded by Columbia Band for the Columbia Graphophone Co. 1923. (A series #7579), Mx. 90627.

"The Governor's Own Ceremonial March" (side A) and "The Official Virgin Islands March" (side B). Recorded by the Goldman Band under the direction of Richard Franko Goldman and distributed as a noncommercial "Semicentennial Souvenir." 1967. 45 RPM, #VI 82567.

"The Governor's Own." *The Pride of America: The Golden Age of the American March*. New York: New World Records, 1976. LP NW266; CD 80266.

"Spirit of the U.S.N." Recorded by the Black Music Repertory Ensemble. In *Black Music: The Written Tradition*. Chicago: Center for Black Music

Research, Columbia College, 1990. Distributed by College Music Society. LP CBMR001.

WRITINGS ABOUT ADAMS

"Bandmaster Adams from Virgin Islands." *Metronome* (July 1922) 57.
"Bandmaster Alton Adams Honored Posthumously." *St. Thomas Source,* March 25, 2006.
"A Band's Birthday." *Jacobs' Band Monthly* 2:7 (July 1917).
Benjamin, Linda White. *Alton A. Adams.* St. Croix, US VI: CRIC Productions, 1987. Children's book based on interviews with Adams.
Clague, Mark. "Alton Augustus Adams, Sr." *International Dictionary of Black Composers,* vol. 1. Chicago: Fitzroy Dearborn, 1999. Pp. 9–16.
———. "Instruments of Identity: Alton Augustus Adams, Sr., the Navy Band of the Virgin Islands, and the Sounds of Social Change." *Black Music Research Journal* 18:1–2 (Spring–Fall 1998): 21–65.
Cuthbertson, Clarence R. "The First Black U.S. Bandmaster." *Virgin Islander* (December 1979): 43–45.
Floyd, Samuel. "Alton Augustus Adams: The First Black Bandmaster in the United States Navy." *Black Perspective in Music* 5:2 (Fall 1977): 173–87.
Giglioli, Arturo. "Alton A. Adams." *Jacobs' Band Monthly* 1:6 (June 1916): 29–30.
Jones, Patrick M. "A History of the Armed Forces School of Music." Ph.D. diss., Music Education Department, Pennsylvania State University, 2002.
Lewin, Aldeth. "American Bandmasters Association Recognizes VI Composer Posthumously." *The Avis* (St. Croix), May 11, 2006. P. 5.
McKay, Ogese T. *Now It Can Be Told: An Autobiography.* St. Croix: Ogese T. McKay, 1991. Contains critical comments on Adams and unique reports of life in the navy's St. Croix bands.
Moolenaar, Ruth M. "Adams, Alton Augustus, Sr.: Musician, Composer, Educator, Entrepreneur, St. Thomas, 1889–1987." In *Profiles of Outstanding Virgin Islanders,* 2nd edition. St. Thomas, VI: Department of Education, Government of the U.S. Virgin Islands, 1992. Pp. 1–2.
Morris, Ayesha. "Legacy of V.I. Bandmaster Thrives despite Facing Racism." *Daily News,* May 11, 2006. P. 4.
Schlesing, Tanyaa. "Alton Adams: A Point of View" *All-Ah-Wee* 1:3 (1977): 28–32. Article based on interviews with Adams.
Seltzer, Frank R. "Famous Bandmasters in Brief: Alton A. Adams." *Jacobs' Band Monthly* 5:7 (July 1920): 18, 20–22.
"Success of Alton Adams, USN." *Metronome* (October 1921): 63.
Thomas, Dale. "Alton Augustus Adams: One of the Best-Known Musicians of the U.S. Virgin Islands." *Journal of Band Research* 41:1 (Fall 2005): 30–41.
"US Navy Band of Virgin Islands Is on Tour." *Metronome* (September 1924): 75.
"Virgin Islands Band Visits US and Has Success." *Metronome* (October 1924): 67.

"Virgin Islands Navy Band—Program." *Metronome* (January 1926): 37.
White, Lucien H. "In the Realm of Music: Alton Adams Is Only Race Band-master in U.S. Navy." *New York Age* 35:36 (May 27, 1922): 5.
Woods, Edith deJongh. "House on Kongens Gade Was Home to Alton Adams." *Daily News*, July 25, 2003. Pp. 26–27.

FILMS

Title unknown. Credited to government of the Virgin Islands by ESC (Educational Service Corporation), with Robert Pierce Films, Inc. (Washington, DC), n.d. Copy held in AAC. This brief film contains footage of Adams discussing the history of his band.

Index

Text: 10/13 Aldus
Display: Aldus
Compositor: BookComp, Inc.
Printer and Binder: Thomson-Shore, Inc.